EUROPEAN ENCOUNTERS

DAMES

Dansk Center for Migration
og Etniske Studier

CENTRE FOR RESEARCH IN ETHNIC RELATIONS

ERCOMER

EUROPEAN RESEARCH CENTRE
ON MIGRATION & ETHNIC RELATIONS

European Encounters

Migrants, migration and European societies since 1945

Edited by

RAINER OHLIGER
Humboldt University, Berlin

KAREN SCHÖNWÄLDER
Justus-Liebig University, Gießen

TRIADAFILOS TRIADAFILOPOULOS
New School for Social Research, New York

ASHGATE

Published by
Ashgate Publishing Limited
Gower House
Croft Road
Aldershot
Hants GU11 3HR
England

Ashgate Publishing Company
Suite 420
101 Cherry Street
Burlington, VT 05401-4405
USA

Ashgate website: http://www.ashgate.com

British Library Cataloguing in Publication Data
European encounters : migrants, migration and European societies since 1945. - (Research in migration and ethnic relations series)
1. Europe - Emigration and immigration - History - 20th century 2. Europe - Ethnic relations - History - 20th century
I. Ohliger, Rainer II. Schönwälder, Karen, 1959-
III. Triadafilopoulos, Triadafilos
303.8'094'09045

Library of Congress Cataloging-in-Publication Data
European encounters : migrants, migration, and European societies since 1945 / edited by Rainer Ohliger, Karen Schönwälder, and Triadafilos Triadafilopoulos.
p. cm. -- (Research in migration and ethnic relations series)
"Originated in a workshop organized by the Network Migration in Europe"--Ack.
Includes bibliographical references and index.
ISBN 0-7546-3086-2
1. Europe--Emigration and immigration--History--20th century. I. Ohliger, Rainer, 1967- II. Schönwälder, Karen, 1959- III. Triadafilopoulos, Triadafilos. IV. Series.

JV7590 .E943 2002
304.8'4--dc21

2002034480

ISBN 0 7546 3086 2

Printed and bound in Great Britain by MPG Books Ltd, Bodmin, Cornwall

Contents

List of Contributors

Pertti Ahonen is a lecturer in Modern European History at the University of Sheffield. (p.ahonen@sheffield.ac.uk or ptahonen@yahoo.co.uk)

Isa Blumi is a PhD candidate in the Department of History, New York University. (ngapeja@rocket-mail.com)

Esra Erdem is a PhD candidate in the Department of Economics at the University of Massachusetts, Amherst. (esrae@econs.umass.edu)

Umut Erel has a PhD in Cultural Studies from Nottingham Trent University. (umuterel@hotmail.com)

Andrea Klimt is a member of the Department of Sociology/Anthropology and Centre for Portuguese Studies and Culture, University of Massachusetts, Dartmouth. (aklimt@umassd.edu)

Eleonore Kofman is Professor of Human Geography in the Department of International Studies, Nottingham Trent University. (kofman@onetel.net.uk)

Hill Kulu is Senior Researcher at the Institute of Geography, University of Tartu, Estonia. (hill@math.ut.ee)

Volodymyr Kulyk is a Senior Research Fellow at the Institute of Political and Ethnic Studies, National Academy of Sciences of Ukraine, Kyiv. (kulyk@uct.kiev.ua or v_kulyk@hotmail.com)

Monika Mattes is a PhD candidate at the Technical University, Berlin and a board member of the Network Migration in Europe. (mmatimag@calvados.zrz.tu-berlin.de)

Rainer Ohliger is a researcher in the Department of Social Science, Humboldt University, Berlin and board member of the Network Migration in Europe. (rohliger@rz.hu-berlin.de)

Anne von Oswald received a PhD from the Freie Universität, Berlin. She is a freelance historian and works on migration and modern Italian history. She is also a board member of the Network Migration in Europe. (a.v.oswald@t-online.de)

Karen Schönwälder is a social scientist and a *Privatdozentin* at Justus-Liebig-Universität, Gießen. She is also a member of the Network Migration in Europe. (kschoenwaelder@t-online.de)

Damir Skenderovic is a visiting scholar at the Center for European Studies, New York University and Research Fellow at the Institute of Contemporary History, University of Fribourg, Switzerland. (damir.skenderovic@unifr.ch)

Barbara Sonnenberger is a historian in Marburg. She received a PhD from Philipps-Universität Marburg and now works as a school teacher. (sonnen.berger@freenet.de)

Laure Teulières is a historian and member of the Laboratoire DIASPORAS, Université de Toulouse. (laure.teulieres@free.fr)

Hallvard Tjelmeland is a professor of contemporary history at the University of Tromsø, Norway. (hallvard@sv.uit.no)

Triadafilos Triadafilopoulos is a PhD candidate in the Department of Political Science, New School for Social Research, New York. (441361@newschool.edu or triadafilos@yahoo.com)

Cătălin Turliuc is Senior Researcher at the Romanian Academy, A.D. Xenopol Institute of History, Iaşi, and Associate Professor at Petre Andrei University, Iaşi, where he is also Chairman of the International Relations Department. (xeno@mail.dntis.ro)

Wim Willems is affiliated with the Center for the History of Migration at the University of Amsterdam. (willems@pscw.uva.nl)

Acknowledgements

This volume originated in a workshop organized by the Network Migration in Europe (http://www.network-migration.org). The Network is a framework for the co-operation of scholars, practitioners and others interested in exchanging and distributing knowledge about the importance of migration in Europe's history and present. It is working toward the acknowledgement of the plural past and present of European societies, as well as their multiple links.

The publication of this book and the preceding conference was made possible by a generous grant from the *Gemeinnützige Hertie-Stiftung*. We would also like to express our sincere thanks to the *Bundeszentrale für politische Bildung* and the *Forschergruppe Gesellschaftsvergleich* at Humboldt University Berlin (funded by the *Deutsche Forschungsgemeinschaft*) for providing additional financial support for the original conference from which the contributions to this book were drawn. Without their help this international endeavour would not have been possible. We also thank James Ingram and Susanne Jordan for assisting in copy-editing as well as Dr. Ihor Stebelsky for permission to reprint the map on page 216.

The Editors

Berlin/New York, summer 2002

NETZWERK **MIGRATION** IN EUROPA

http://www.network-migration.org

Gemeinnützige
Hertie-Stiftung

PART I
INTRODUCTION

Chapter 1

European Encounters: Europe's Migratory Experiences

Karen Schönwälder, Rainer Ohliger and Triadafilos Triadafilopoulos

In the second half of the twentieth century, migration constituted one of the major challenges to European states and societies and one of the major forces shaping them. No consideration of Europe's development since the end of the Second World War could be adequate without giving due attention to the demographic changes, cultural transformations, political and social challenges and economic developments linked to forced and voluntary migrations.

Of course, migration was not a new phenomenon. While the long-term predominance of the nation-state paradigm tended to suppress proper attention to migration and ethnic plurality, it is now widely acknowledged that migration has been a feature of European history for some time.[1] In the nineteenth century, industrialization and the lure of emigration to the 'New World' prompted huge population movements. Indeed, between 1900 and 1920 alone, some twenty million Europeans emigrated overseas. Within Europe, hundreds of thousands of Irish moved to work in English factories, Poles were recruited to work in Belgian, German and French mines, and Italian construction workers migrated to the North to ply their trade. Political refugees fled after the failed revolutions of 1848 (and on other occasions), seeking refuge in Britain or North America.

Features of Post-war Migration

And yet, several specific features mark the period since the Second World War. First of all, the global conflagration ignited by the Nazi regime and its plans for a new world order prompted the displacement and resettlement of millions. 1 September 1939 marked the beginning of an unprecedented period of resettlement, emigration and expulsions. At the end of the war, the Allies counted 10.5 to 11.7 million displaced persons,[2] consisting of former forced labourers, prisoners of war or inmates of concentration camps. The redrawing of boundaries and compulsory population transfers that occurred at the end of the war affected several million more Europeans. Many Germans could not return to or were forced to flee homes in what were now (or again) Poland and Czechoslovakia; Yugoslavia and Hungary also expelled their ethnic German minorities. By October 1946, the authorities counted 9.5 million German refugees and expellees in the four zones of occupation.[3] In the following decades many more ethnic Germans left their homes to move westward (about 4.1 million between 1950 and 2000). Population transfers also involved Poles, and at the close of the war people were moved between Czechoslovakia, Hungary and the USSR, and Yugoslavia and Italy. Of the Jews who had managed to survive the Holocaust, some settled in Western Europe, while the overwhelming majority abandoned Europe for Israel or North America. Morawska estimates that

> [a]s the result of international and bilateral agreements concerning the redrawing of state boundaries and unmixing of peoples concluded in 1944-45 and under pressure of individual nation-states, about 17 million people – Polish, Lithuanian, Byelorussian, Hungarian, Romanian, Jewish, Czech and Slovak old or newly designated minorities, and, the largest group of all, Germans – [were] coercively relocated between territories. To this figure should be added well over one million minority refugees from popular hostilities that erupted across the region after the war ended.[4]

The second major group of post-war migrants was composed of people seeking work. Labour migration had a long tradition and recruiting agreements were commonplace in the 1920s. After 1945, however, migration by Europeans and non-Europeans seeking work in booming industries developed on a new scale. As Ambrosius and Hubbard point out: '[i]n the decade and a half after 1960 the dimensions of intra-European migration changed profoundly – quantitatively, geographically, and qualitatively'.[5] The post-war economic boom, the development of welfare states and, more generally, the expansion of states' material and social infrastructure created a vast demand for additional labour in Western and Northern European countries. The establishment of associations such as the Common Nordic Labour Market in 1954 and the European Economic Community in 1958 helped facilitate the movement of workers across borders. Bilateral agreements on recruitment signed during this period proved to be even more important in this regard. While estimates vary, approximately 20 to 30 million European and non-European labour migrants entered into the industrial centres of Europe during the 1960s and 1970s.[6] Additionally, colonial ties guaranteed, among others, Algerians and migrants from the Caribbean free movement to France and Britain, respectively. More recently, Southern Europe has also become a destination for foreigners seeking work or refuge. Since the late 1990s, several European governments have taken tentative steps to facilitate new labour migration, intended to fill demographic and skills gaps. It remains to be seen whether the enlargement of the European Union will lead to major movements of employment-seeking East Europeans.

Migratory movements in the decades following the Second World War were often closely related to the process of decolonization. While the continued existence of colonial or post-colonial bonds and structures initially gave some non-Europeans the opportunity to enter European 'mother countries' and their labour markets, the dissolution of European empires led to the 'remigration' of European settlers (such as the *retornados* to Portugal from Angola, Mozambique and Guinea-Bissau in the mid-1970s, or the *pieds noirs* from Algeria to France after the end of the French-Algerian war in 1962). Moreover, the transformations and conflicts that accompanied decolonization prompted many Algerians, Indonesians, Surinamese and African Asians to seek out new homes in France, the Netherlands and the United Kingdom. Thus, although African and Asian communities had been established in earlier decades, the increased scale of postcolonial migrations made subsequent encounters between 'natives' and 'strangers' all the more palpable. As Zolberg has noted: 'the domain of international migration expanded to encompass the entire world, so that the resulting encounters [were] more varied than ever'.[7]

Other non-Europeans came to Europe as refugees. While labour migration was halted in the mid-1970s, the arrival of refugees displaced by civil wars, putsches and individual or collective persecution became a mass phenomenon. And, like the labour migrants from the former colonies, the arrival of refugees from African or Asian countries came unexpectedly. For the most part, European politicians had anticipated political refugees fleeing Communist dictatorships. And, indeed, Soviet interventions in Hungary (1956) and Czechoslovakia (1968) led to the flight of thousands to the West. Similarly, many Poles fled their country as repression mounted in the 1970s and martial law was imposed in 1981. Waves of hostility and discrimination also drove hundreds of thousands of Jews out of East European countries, beginning with Holocaust survivors in the immediate post-war period and extending to the Bulgarian, Polish and Romanian Jewry in the 1960s and 1970s. This movement culminated in the mass flight of Russian Jews from the Soviet Union to Israel in the 1970s, a movement that continued, albeit under different conditions, into the 1990s and beyond. Since the 1970s in particular, the geographic origins of asylum seekers in Western Europe have broadened significantly with more and more people arriving from countries like Chile, Iran, Sri Lanka, Somalia, Sudan and Afghanistan, among others. Improvements in communication and transportation technologies have certainly played a part in this process. However, it is important to realize that in the 1980s and 1990s, major refugee movements have also originated in Mediterranean states such as Turkey and the former Yugoslavia. In short, refugee movements have expanded significantly. While in 1972 some 13,000 individuals sought asylum in Europe, the figure rose to 708,000 in 1992. In 2000, 453,000 people applied for asylum in a European country.[8]

While the scope, scale and character of migratory movements since 1945 account for their specificity vis-à-vis those of earlier eras, the framework in which these movements have occurred also differs significantly from those of the past. With the 1951 Geneva Convention, a new framework for the protection of refugees had been created which, when combined with political and economic interests, initially guaranteed refugees from Eastern Europe a relatively smooth acceptance into Western states. In the last two decades, however, the reception of refugees and asylum seekers has become a more contentious issue, and several European states as well as the European Union have helped build a 'Fortress Europe' which strives to limit access to its territory and to make living conditions for refugees unattractive.[9] Thus, though some have referred to the twentieth century as an age of human rights, it should also be characterized as a century of tight regulation and control of migratory movements by nation-states.[10] That said, the codification and widespread acceptance of human rights norms has ensured that refugees now enjoy a certain degree of protection and that their treatment is subject to scrutiny by institutions such as the UNHCR and a burgeoning human rights lobby. Rights of labour migrants and foreign residents in general have also been extended and codified – although it remains controversial whether these changes amount to the dawning of a 'post-national citizenship'.[11]

A Force of Change

The migratory movements summarized above have played an important part in shaping contemporary European societies, creating new opportunities and challenges in the process. As Federico Romero points out, 'the issue of migration and, more broadly, of the interconnection among various national labour markets and polities, deeply influenced the entire political and institutional configuration of Western Europe'.[12] And although it is important to realize that the majority of Europeans still spend their lives in the countries where they are born, Fassmann and Münz emphasize the 'growing internationalization of West European populations, labour markets and societies'.[13] As a consequence of migration, demographic and social structures have been altered. Labour and colonial migration has added a distinctive 'ethnic' feature to class relations. Recruited to do the less skilled, unhealthy, and burdensome work, labour migrants and their descendents are generally still disadvantaged as regards living standards, educational opportunities and positions in the occupational hierarchy. Most visible is the transformation of (Western) Europe's cityscapes by migrants. Not only have residential areas been transformed with the emergence of ethnic neighbourhoods; lifestyles and consumption patterns within the receiving societies have also been transformed as a result of cultural enrichment and variation. This two-way process has penetrated many areas of social and cultural life, bringing about new hybrid forms in areas such as cuisine, music, fashion and language. The growing influence of Islam as an expanding European religion and political force is closely linked to colonial and labour immigration.

Thus, migration has produced a series of complex transformations that have affected sending and receiving countries alike. These changes have produced both costs and benefits, be they social, economic, demographic and/or cultural. For example, labour migration to industrial centres in Northern and Western Europe allowed for the export of rural surplus labour in the European periphery while simultaneously providing much needed cheap labour for industry and services in the developed centre. This, in turn, led to profound changes in the rural structure of emigration countries, as whole regions were stripped of young able-bodied men and women. In the North, these very same men and women constituted a 'central plank for the prosperity of the richer countries'.[14] Networks spanning areas of origin and areas of destination altered the social and cultural life of those who stayed behind in other ways as well. 'Returnees' and visiting emigrants epitomized forces of cultural change, and their remittances were an important economic factor. The developmental impact of labour migration for the Mediterranean sending countries was, however, not as crucial as expected. In Eastern Europe, migrations meant mainly emigration and a loss of cultural and economic potential.

Post-war migration compelled European societies to face up to what has been referred to as the 'multicultural challenge'.[15] Given the ongoing pluralization of Europe as a consequence of immigration, this challenge is likely to persist well into the future. Pluralization presents both political and intellectual challenges. Political challenges include arriving at effective and just policies concerning immigrant incorporation and establishing criteria for regulating the movement of people across borders. The intellectual and political challenge also entails defining strategies that allow for the acceptance and recognition of plurality and plural identities within the same polity. Those called upon to take up these challenges have had to contend with established national paradigms of self and identity, which are often hostile to change and the incorporation of others. In extreme cases, purveyors of established national paradigms have deepened the challenge by rallying around xenophobic issues and politicizing them with the aid of extreme-right-wing and populist parties, such as the *Lega Nord* and the *Alleanza Nazionale* in Italy, the *Vlaams Blok* in Belgium, the *Front National* in France, the *Deutsche Volksunion* in Germany, the *Dansk Folkeparti* in Denmark and the *Schweizerische Volkspartei* in Switzerland. The headlong collision of radical exclusionist demands with calls for greater recognition and representation for newcomers is also likely to remain a volatile political issue well into the future.

Reclaiming Heterogeneity: The Diversity of the Migratory Experience

The integration of the migratory experience into European history is to some extent also a political project. Thus this volume opts for a perspective interested in tracing a European experience and in providing points of reference for the historical consciousness of Europeans. One guiding motive of this volume is the belief that there is room for a reconsideration of the post-war experience in the light of recent research.

Given the diversity of post-war developments, there is no easy way of organizing Europe's migratory movements and experiences into a simple narrative. The fourteen essays in this volume emphasize the multifaceted history of expulsions, flight and labour migration and the extent to which European history since 1945 is a history of migrations. The goal of improving our understanding of this European experience has compelled us to incorporate East and West in our intellectual purview. At the same time, an effort was made to resist the trend to identify 'Europe' with the narrow borderlines of the European Union.

Chapters by Phil Triadafilopoulos on post-war expulsions and Volodymyr Kulyk on Ukrainian Displaced Persons in Germany and Austria highlight aspects of the population movements and displacements that emerged as a direct consequence of the Second World War. The labour migration of the 1960s and 1970s is at the centre of contributions by Anne von Oswald, Karen Schönwälder and Barbara Sonnenberger and by Esra Erdem and Monika Mattes. Wim Willems deals with political responses to postcolonial migrations to the Netherlands, while chapters by Hill Kulu and by Rainer Ohliger and Cătălin Turliuc direct our attention to processes of labour migration and ethnic unmixing in Eastern Europe, taking Estonia and Romania as illustrative examples.

To a considerable extent, recent academic debates have focused on isolating common denominators of European developments. While this is of course a very important line of investigation, this volume seeks to reclaim heterogeneity. Thus Kofman and Erel forcefully argue for a more adequate recognition of a specific female migration history, which considers the experiences of female unskilled labourers, of skilled nurses and teachers and of women immigrating as family members or as refugees. Similarly, Mattes and Erdem argue that feminist perspectives can open up ways to a better understanding of the female migratory experience. As Kofman and Erel point out, mainstream European literature on migration is 'gender blind' and migrants are often treated as 'asexual categories'. Their contribution points to the deficiencies inherent in such approaches and possible ways forward. Isa Blumi's chapter focuses our attention on the ways in which classificatory schemes used to categorize immigrants can render some groups invisible and, on the other hand, on the importance of public recognition for a minority on its own terms.

While we have endeavoured to bring together the work of migration specialists from different countries and disciplines, we have also sought to highlight the advantages derived by reintegrating migration research more closely with interpretations of national and European societies and histories.[16] The benefits derived through such a strategy are substantial. For example, by pointing out the long-term influence of campaigns against 'overforeignization' and clarifying the 'ethnic grounds of Swiss nationhood', Damir Skenderovic's contribution helps us understand why opposition to immigration has been so widespread in Switzerland – a state usually held up as a model of multinational and polyglot coexistence. Similarly, Hallvard Tjelmeland explains how the arrival of tiny numbers of Pakistanis in Norway became such an important issue. He demonstrates that context-specific factors ensured that the arrival of a relatively small number of migrants would challenge national ideas of the community and the welfare state. Both of these chapters demonstrate that we need to consider aspects of societies' unique circumstances in order to make sense of their encounters with immigration and ethnic plurality. Migration policy cannot be understood without consideration of the ways in which it is linked to wider political aims, foreign policy considerations and economic developments and strategies.

Furthermore, we believe that the quality of recent academic debates in the field of immigration studies demonstrates the need for more detailed reconsiderations of historical developments. Quite often generalizations and theories stand on shaky empirical foundations; social scientists' 'short memories' often lead them to substitute the experiences of the last two decades for the whole of post-war history. Commenting upon publications in the field of immigration studies, Portes has noted that more detailed research into the inner workings of states' legislative and administrative bureaucracies is needed if theories are to advance beyond the most basic generalities.[17] As archival material for the period up to the early 1970s becomes available, longstanding interpretations of migration policies can and will be scrutinized and challenged. In this volume, the chapter by von Oswald, Schönwälder and Sonnenberger points to some directions that such reconsideration of established truths might take. Drawing on the example of the Netherlands and extensive archival research, Wim Willems presents 'five assumptions about government policy' to help explain why political responses to immigration often seem to be inadequate and why previous experiences are rarely taken into account.

Migration as a European Experience

The historian Hartmut Kaelble once described the labour migration of the 1960s and 1970s as 'the European network of the ordinary people'.[18] Millions of Europeans share the experience of long-term stays in foreign countries as workers, employees or students. It has been estimated that in 1970-71, 15 million foreign citizens lived in the Western half of Europe. In 1992-93 their number had risen to 19 million.[19] Between 1955 and 1973, about 14 million non-Germans migrated to West Germany. And between 1950 and 1984, approximately 1.15 million Portuguese shared the experience of emigration from mainland Portugal, a country of approximately 10 million inhabitants.[20] While Eastern and Western Europe were separated from each other, Czechs, Poles, Hungarians and other emigrants established networks among themselves and constituted bridgeheads of contact between East and West. Currently, much attention is given to transnational networks established through migration and driven by migrants' wishes to keep in touch with cohorts in other countries as well as friends and family 'at home'.[21]

As Kaelble suggests, migration may have been one of the processes that contributed to the development of positive attitudes toward European integration and helped call into question the necessity and naturalized understanding of borders and national bonds.[22] Similarly, René Girault considers the migrants' milieus as the fertile breeding ground [*Brutstätte*] of a European consciousness.[23] Migration may have helped constitute an '*Erfahrungsraum Europa*' – a European space of common experiences, or a 'lived Europe'.[24] In this volume, Andrea Klimt provides a contribution to the much-needed empirical exploration of changing identities in and attitudes to Europe by way of migration.

We should, however, be careful not to idealize the migratory experience. While in the 1960s, labour migration was celebrated in West Germany as a means of improving the understanding of different peoples, labour migrants experienced stark hierarchies and often unacceptable living conditions. While Europeans increasingly enjoy the common experience of freedom of movement, Europe was and continues to be a continent where many – not least Europe's non-European Union citizens – cannot move about freely and where the experience of barriers and hostility is all too common. As of late, 'a definition of immigration as a security threat and a problem' has prevailed and, as Theodora Kostakopoulou further notes, the restrictive approach to migration has had a 'negative impact on the formation of a European identity and the principles underpinning the European project'.[25] This trend has only intensified in the wake of the September 11 tragedy in New York City and subsequent 'war against terrorism'.

We should therefore not lose sight of the 'actual relations of unequal exchange and uneven development through which a common European identity was forged'.[26] As Stuart Hall reminds us, 'Europe's external relations with its Others has been central to the European story since its inception, and remains so'. But Hall also emphasizes that 'identity is always an open, complex and unfinished game. [...] It always moves into the future by a symbolic detour through the past'. If this is the case, it is important to influence this process to help ensure that outcomes are acceptable on moral and political grounds.

Claiming a Place in the European Consciousness

Within European nation-states, the plurality of the migrant past and present is often neglected. National paradigms and modes of interpretation still largely determine the prevalent images of the European Self. This leaves little room for the representation of border transcending phenomena such as migration. Often migrants are written into national memories as Others. In some cases, expelled minorities were even eradicated completely from public collective memory,[27] though there are also examples to the contrary. Pertti Ahonen's contribution to this volume takes the case of German forced migrants and demonstrates how these groups crucially influenced a state's narrative of the nation's history. Volodymyr Kulyk shows how post-war camps for Displaced Persons (DPs) provided an environment in which a national-as-migrant identity replete with a supporting historical narrative could be, if not created, then consolidated and disseminated.

Despite increasing Europeanization, institutions shaping the European historical consciousness and memory such as historiography are usually conceptualized along national borderlines. Border-transcending and border-destroying pan-European or transnational developments and processes do not find adequate room in these concepts. This is particularly true in the historical and media representation of migration and migrants. Within the emerging European space, plurality needs adequate space for representation, visualization and permanent commemoration. As Laure Teulières illustrates in her contribution to this volume, migration history offers a decisive opportunity to recognize this plurality. Moreover, the representation of the European migratory experience within a pan-European context provides an opportunity to intellectually challenge images of the past created by nation-states. Migration history can help de-centre European historical memory and strengthen a common European identity. Because it transcends politically and historiographically imagined and implemented borders, migration history provides an opportunity to create an image of the past that breaks through national concepts and limitations. It can also provide a point of reference and identification for those of immigrant origin. Isa Blumi's contribution to this volume highlights the need for such an approach.

Writing European migration history can provide an opportunity for broadening our understanding in another way, as well. European history could be narrated and represented 'from the margins', rather than from the hegemonic centres of the state and nation. Such a view and interpretation matches the historical and contemporary European reality, which is shaped by worlds and spaces of 'in-between'. In an age of globalization it could help to broaden and transcend a still-Eurocentric picture of the past which is not appropriate for the present or future. Historical representations of migration in and to Europe necessarily have a strong extra- or trans-European element. The history of colonialism and decolonization and the migrations caused by it are the best, though not the only example for this argument. This reminds us that the European migratory experience is not solely an experience of Europeans but involves people from many other backgrounds. Thus, in selecting a European framework, one should take care not to distort (twentieth-century) migration history in Europe by neglecting its global setting and the wider social, cultural and political context.

Notes

1 See for instance Lucassen and Lucassen, *Migration, Migration History, History*; Hoerder and Moch, *European Migrants*; Bade, *Europa in Bewegung*.

2 Jacobmeyer, 'Ortlos am Ende des Grauens', p. 368; see also his *Vom Zwangsarbeiter zum heimatlosen Ausländer*.

3 See Benz, *Die Vertreibung der Deutschen aus dem Osten*, p. 10. By 1949, this figure had risen to 12 million.

4 Morawska, 'Intended and Unintended Consequences of Forced Migrations', p. 1056.

5 Ambrosius and Hubbard, *A Social and Economic History of Twentieth-Century Europe*, p. 35.

6 Fassmann and Münz mention a figure of far beyond 20 million ('Europäische Migration – ein Überblick', p. 23).

7 Zolberg, 'Immigration and Multiculturalism in the Industrial Democracies', p. 51.

8 Joly, *Refugees*, p. 23; UNHCR, *Asylum Applications*; UNHCR, *Trends in Asylum Applications*.

9 See for instance the essays in Bloch and Levy, *Refugees, Citizenship and Social Policy in Europe*, and special issues of the *Journal of Ethnic and Migration Studies* and of the *Journal of Refugee Studies*.

10 Brubaker, 'Are Immigration Control Efforts Really Failing? p. 230.

11 For different viewpoints see Soysal, *Limits of Citizenship*; Joppke, *Challenge to the Nation-State*; and Bosniak, 'Citizenship Denationalized'.

12 Romero, 'Migration as an Issue in European Interdependence', p. 33.

13 Fassmann and Münz, 'Europäische Migration – ein Überblick', p. 16.

14 King, 'European International Migration 1945-90', p. 22.

15 Bade, *Europa in Bewegung*.

16 This is emphasized by Lucassen and Lucassen in their 'Introduction' (pp. 10, 33) to their volume *Migration, Migration History, History*.

17 Portes, 'Immigration Theory', p. 817.

18 Kaelble, 'Europabewußtsein, Gesellschaft und Geschichte', p. 19.

[19] Fassmann and Münz, 'Europäische Migration – ein Überblick', p. 24.
[20] Cavaco, 'A Place in the Sun', p. 175.
[21] See for instance the work of the British Transnational Communities Programme, www.transcomm.ox.ac.uk.
[22] Kaelble, 'Europabewußtsein, Gesellschaft und Geschichte', p. 2.
[23] Girault, 'Das Europa der Historiker', p. 86.
[24] See also Schmidt-Gernig, 'Gibt es eine "europäische Identität"?'.
[25] Kostakopoulou, 'The "Protective Union"', p. 509.
[26] Hall, 'Europe's Other Self', pp. 18-19.
[27] Referring to former citizens like Jews or other minorities, Morawska has attacked the 'deliberate obliviousness and distortion in the representations of history by East European nation-state cultural policies' ('Intended and Unintended Consequences', p. 1063).

References

Ambrosius, Gerold and William H. Hubbard, *A Social and Economic History of Twentieth-Century Europe*, Cambridge Mass., 1989.

Bade, Klaus J., *Europa in Bewegung. Migration vom späten 18. Jahrhundert bis zur Gegenwart*, Munich, 2000.

Benz, Wolfgang (ed.), *Die Vertreibung der Deutschen aus dem Osten. Ursachen, Ereignisse, Folgen*, Frankfurt a. M., 1995.

Bloch, Alice and Carl Levy (eds), *Refugees, Citizenship and Social Policy in Europe*, London, 1999.

Bosniak, Linda, 'Citizenship Denationalized', *Indiana Journal of Global Legal Studies* 7 (2000): pp. 447-508.

Brubaker, Rogers, 'Are Immigration Control Efforts Really Failing?' in: Wayne A. Cornelius, Philip L. Martin, and James F. Hollifield (eds), *Controlling Immigration: A Global Perspective*, Stanford, 1994, pp. 227-231.

Castles, Stephen, *Here for Good. Western Europe's New Ethnic Minorities*, London, 1984.

Cavaco, Carminda, 'A Place in the Sun: Return Migration and Rural Change in Portugal', in: Russell King (ed.), *Mass Migrations in Europe: The Legacy and the Future*, London, 1993, pp. 174-191.

Fassmann, Heinz and Rainer Münz, 'Europäische Migration – ein Überblick', in: Heinz Fassmann and Rainer Münz (eds), *Migration in Europa. Historische Entwicklung, aktuelle Trends, politische Reaktionen*, Frankfurt and New York, 1996, pp. 13-52 (also as *European Migration in the Late Twentieth Century: Historical Patterns, Actual Trends, and Social Implications*, Aldershot and Brookfield Vt., 1994).

Freeman, Gary P., 'Modes of Immigration Politics in Liberal Democratic States', *International Migration Review* 29 (1995): pp. 881-902.

Girault, René, 'Das Europa der Historiker', in: Rainer Hudemann (ed.), *Europa im Blick der Historiker. Europäische Integration im 20. Jahrhundert: Bewußtsein und Institutionen*, München, 1995, pp. 55-90.

Hall, Stuart, 'Europe's Other Self', *Marxism Today* 35 (1991): pp. 18-19.

Hoerder, Dirk and Leslie P. Moch (eds), *European Migrants: Global and Local Perspectives*, Boston, 1996.

Hollifield, James F., 'Immigration and Integration in Western Europe: A Comparative Analysis', in: Emek M. Uçarer and Donald J. Puchala (eds), *Immigration into Western Societies: Problems and Policies*, London, 1997, pp. 28-69.

Jacobmeyer, Wolfgang, *Vom Zwangsarbeiter zum heimatlosen Ausländer. Die Displaced Persons in Westdeutschland 1945-1951*, Göttingen, 1985.

Jacobmeyer, Wolfgang, 'The "Displaced Persons" in West Germany, 1945-1951', in: Göran Rystad (ed.), *The Uprooted. Forced Migration as an International Problem in the Postwar-Era*, Lund, 1990, pp. 271-288.

Jacobmeyer, Wolfgang, 'Ortlos am Ende des Grauens: "Displaced Persons" in der Nachkriegszeit', in: Klaus J. Bade (ed.), *Deutsche im Ausland - Fremde in Deutschland*, Munich, 1992, pp. 367-373.

Joly, Daniéle, *Refugees. Asylum in Europe?* London, 1992.

Joppke, Christian (ed.), *Challenge to the Nation-State. Immigration in Western Europe and the United States*, Oxford, 1998.

Journal of Ethnic and Migration Studies 24, 4 (1998): special issue 'The European Union: Immigration, Asylum and Citizenship'.

Journal of Refugee Studies 13, 1 (2000): special issue 'Changing Asylum Policies in Europe'.

Kaelble, Hartmut, ‚Europabewußtsein, Gesellschaft und Geschichte. Forschungsstand und Forschungschancen', in: Rainer Hudemann (ed.), *Europa im Blick der Historiker. Europäische Integration im 20. Jahrhundert: Bewußtsein und Institutionen*, Munich, 1995, pp. 1-29.

King, Russell, 'European International Migration 1945-90: A Statistical and Geographical Overview', in: Russell King (ed.), *Mass Migrations in Europe: The Legacy and the Future*, London, 1993, pp. 19-39.

Kostakopoulou, Theodora, 'The "Protective Union": Change and Continuity in Migration Law and Policy in Post-Amsterdam Europe', *Journal of Common Market Studies* 38 (2000): pp. 497-518.

Lucassen, Jan and Leo Lucassen (eds), *Migration, Migration History, History. Old Paradigms and New Perspectives*, Bern, 1999.

Morawska, Ewa, 'Intended and Unintended Consequences of Forced Migrations: A Neglected Aspect of East Europe's Twentieth Century History', *International Migration Review* 34 (2000): pp. 1049-1087.

Nikolinakos, Marios, 'Notes towards a General Theory of Migration in Late Capitalism', *Race and Class* 17 (1975), pp. 5-17.

Portes, Alejandro, 'Immigration Theory for a New Century: Some Problems and Opportunities', *International Migration Review* 31 (1997): pp. 799-825.

Romero, Federico, 'Migration as an Issue in European Interdependence and Integration: The Case of Italy', in: Alan S. Milward et al. (eds), *The Frontier of National Sovereignty. History and Theory 1945-1992*, London and New York, 1993, pp. 33-58.

Schmidt-Gernig, Alexander, 'Gibt es eine "europäische Identität"? Konzeptionelle Überlegungen zum Zusammenhang transnationaler Erfahrungsräume, kollektiver Identitäten und öffentlicher Diskurse in Westeuropa seit dem Zweiten Weltkrieg', in: Hartmut Kaelble and Jürgen Schriewer (eds), *Diskurse und Entwicklungspfade. Der Gesellschaftsvergleich in den Geschichts- und Sozialwissenschaften*, Frankfurt and New York, 1999, pp. 163-216.

Soysal, Yasemin N., *Limits of Citizenship. Migrants and Postnational Membership in Europe*, Chicago and London, 1994.

Thränhardt, Dietrich, 'Europe – A New Immigration Continent. Policies and Politics since 1945 in Comparative Perspective', in: Dietrich Thränhardt (ed.), *Europe: A New Immigration Continent. Policies and Politics in Comparative Perspective*, Münster, 1992.

Torpey, John, *The Invention of the Passport: Surveillance, Citizenship, and the State*, New York, 2000.

UNHCR, *Trends in Asylum Applications Lodged in Europe, North America, Australia and New Zealand, 2001*, Geneva, 31 January 2002.

UNHCR, *Asylum Applications in Industrialized Countries: 1980-1999*, Geneva, November 2001.

Zolberg, Aristide, 'International Migration in a Changing World System', in: William McNeill and Ruth Adams (eds), *Human Migrations: Patterns and Policies*, Bloomington/IN, 1978, pp. 241-286.

Zolberg, Aristide, 'Immigration and Multiculturalism in the Industrial Democracies', in: Rainer Bauböck et al. (eds), *The Challenge of Diversity. Integration and Pluralism in Societies of Immigration*, Aldershot, 1996, pp. 43-65.

PART II
THE PLURALITY OF THE MIGRATORY EXPERIENCE

Chapter 2

Einwanderungsland Deutschland: A New Look at its Post-war History

Anne von Oswald, Karen Schönwälder and Barbara Sonnenberger

Germany is a country of immigration, an '*Einwanderungsland*'. Although this seems an all too obvious fact, it was only recently acknowledged by the German government and all the major political parties. This move was encouraged by discussions about a need for new immigrants to help balance the demographic structure and close a skills gap. But as Germany may be entering a new phase of labour immigration, how much do we know about its previous experiences with this phenomenon?

Most accounts of foreign labour migration and West German migration policy up to the recruitment stop of 1973 rely on a number of similar assumptions: West Germany (like Switzerland) represents the typical model of a 'guestworker' policy. Between 1955 and 1973,[1] German employers, with the help of the manpower service and the state, recruited millions of foreigners to work on building-sites, in factories, mines and hospitals, but failed to consider the long-term consequences of this policy for German society. According to Stephen Castles, 'the state followed a short-term labour market policy in response to employers' demands, taking no account of possible long-term consequences for society'.[2] And Ulrich Herbert states that government policy was wavering, inconsistent and lacked a clear concept: it was 'blind to the future'.[3] As a period of a fairly single-minded labour market policy, the time from 1955 to 1973 appears rather uneventful. It was not before the early 1970s that the German government and public realized that 'they had called workers and human beings had come' (Max Frisch) and began to consider the questions of integration, return and immigration. And indeed, according to the dominant view, significant immigration did not occur before 1973. The 'typical 1960s migrant' of many accounts is a young, male, single worker; it is only in the 1970s that families enter into the picture. (Women, apart from wives and mothers, are generally not awarded much attention.)

This chapter will argue that this picture is not only in many ways incomplete, but that it has to be revised with respect to a number of points. The most obvious deficit stems from our very limited knowledge of the period. Partly because the developments of the 1960s and early 1970s seemed so obvious and mundane, and partly because archival material was not available until recently, the number of detailed studies on this period is very limited. Having said this, there are nonetheless a huge number of publications on various aspects of the post-war migration process to Germany. Contemporary studies have examined aspects of the aliens law and the economic pros and cons of labour migration. Furthermore, due to the tight controls exercized by the German state and labour administration, rich statistical information is available on the number of foreigners, the regional structure of settlement, their employment, etc.[4] However, very little has been published on, for instance, the trade unions, interethnic relations, the politics of local authorities or government policy before the mid-1970s. Research on migrants or ethnic minorities rarely takes a historical approach. Recently this situation has begun to change.[5] This text highlights a number of points in recent research which suggest the need for a revision of predominant views.[6]

Points of Revision

The following text identifies five 'revisionist' themes (this is by no means a complete list):

First, we believe that it is misleading to treat the years between 1955 and 1973 as one fairly uniform period. The narrow focus on the recruitment treaties obscures the fact that foreign migration to West Germany started before 1955 and did not accelerate before 1959. With regard to labour migration and government policy, it was the time around 1960 when more important decisions were taken. While 1973 remains a crucial turning point in government policy, it is questionable whether it was also the crucial turning point for the migrants' decision to stay or return, as it is often assumed to have been. For the employers' labour market strategies, the business cycle was at least as important as government policy, and in some branches of industry a slump in sales did not occur before 1974-75. Additionally, we would like to stress the importance of the 1966-67 recession, during which the number of migrants was radically reduced, the further development of the migration and immigration processes was called into question and public as well as internal political debates about the migration process and its consequences for German society subsided.

Second, it is wrong to assume that government policy and public perceptions were more or less exclusively focussed on foreigners as workers and labour market issues in general. In the mid-1960s and early 1970s lively and wide-ranging debates took place which addressed questions of integration and assimilation as well as permanent immigration and naturalization. Germany did not stumble into an immigration situation with its eyes closed.

Third, West Germany practised neither a rotation policy nor even a 'guestworker' policy – if we assume this to mean the existence and implementation of a coherent strategy aiming at short-term employment and the prevention of permanent settlement and family reunion. Although demands for a rigidly enforced limitation on the foreigners' stay were repeatedly put forward, a policy of forced rotation (*Zwangsrotation*) was rejected for various reasons which included foreign policy, economic and humanitarian considerations.

Fourth, migration patterns were more varied than is generally assumed. While it is often asserted that we can distinguish a 'guestworker' migration period from a subsequent immigration period, in fact many different patterns coexisted, ranging from single or repeated short-term stays in Germany to permanent immigration. Immigration began with migration (well before the 1970s) and the short-term (migrant) sojourner did not disappear in 1973. Furthermore, foreign migrants were not the timid and acquiescent 'guestworkers' (*die verschämten Gastarbeiter*)[7] of many accounts. While some migrants were prepared to accept living and working conditions and willing to adjust, from the 1950s onward we also find cases of self-confident foreign workers who refused to conform. By breaking their contracts (which happened frequently) or changing jobs, migrants could escape bad working conditions and use the power the labour shortages gave them to their advantage. Incidences of wildcat strikes staged during the 1960s also reveal hitherto neglected elements of migrant agency.

Fifth, the roles of migrants and other players have to be taken more seriously as active forces in the migration process. Migration policy and the migration and integration processes were influenced and shaped by a number of actors. For example, the policy of the federal government was not uniform but the result of different strategies pursued by different government departments. State governments, local authorities and employers could influence migration patterns and the conditions of settlement. The trade unions influenced policy as well as relations in the workplace. In order to fully understand this complex situation, additional and extensive research needs to be undertaken. Though not exhaustive, the comments presented in this chapter present a selective examination of several key questions, as well as some hypotheses and possible directions for further research.

Migration Control and Family Migration: Political Debates in the 1960s

In a number of ways, the time around 1960, rather than 1955, constituted a decisive period. Between July 1959 and September 1961, the number of foreign workers[8] in West Germany increased from 167,000 to 549,000. Labour shortages now occurred in all branches and regions, and in summer 1960 unemployment fell below one per cent. While only 85,000 foreign workers had entered the Federal Republic in 1959, more than 259,000 came in 1961. Increasingly, the metalworks and engineering industries needed additional workers, which meant that people were no longer mainly recruited as seasonal workers. Employers' organizations and the Federal Ministry for the Economy demanded that as many foreign workers as possible be recruited and that conditions to encourage foreigners to come for long-term employment be instituted.

In 1955, the conclusion of the first recruitment treaty with Italy was not viewed as a fundamental decision in favour of foreign employment on a significant scale. It is therefore not surprising that a strategic debate about long-term perspectives, historical experiences, trends toward permanent settlement or the implications of labour migration for German society did not take place. Rather than being a result of strategic planning, the conclusion of the treaty was a concession by the German government to the Italians, who were one of the key partners in the process of European integration.[9] However, in 1960 three things became clear: foreign employment would increase dramatically; Germany's economic development – at least in the medium term – would depend on the availability of a large foreign workforce; and foreigners were increasingly being recruited as part of the permanent workforce. As a consequence, the issues concerning the employment of foreigners and political responses to it became more important, with serious deliberations and conflicts taking place within and among federal ministries. The debates centred on two questions: First, the conflict surrounding the degree of liberalization and openness as opposed to an emphasis on security concerns, control and limited migration. Second, in response to the growing desire for family reunion and the resulting demand for accommodation, the question of permanent immigration was pushed onto the agenda.

In the first half of the sixties, a number of federal ministries and some *Länder* governments fought more or less continuously over the scale and the conditions of admission of foreigners. The Ministries for the Interior (responsible for the police, as well as admission and registration of foreigners) demanded that if the trends toward the liberalization of movement and the rapid expansion of foreign employment could not be stopped, they should at least be balanced by imposing tight controls and strict conditions of stay on foreigners. In particular, they wanted to introduce effective mechanisms in order to prevent the foreign workers from settling permanently in Germany. The issue of immigration was a constant subject of internal debate, as German officials were very conscious of the link between labour migration and immigration and not at all complacent in this regard. In spite of this, demands for effective anti-immigration measures failed.

The recruitment treaty with Turkey provides one example of a number of conflicts relating to the control of migratory movements. The initial 1961 version included a clause stating that residence permits would not be issued for a period extending two years; in addition, there were no provisions regarding family reunification.[10] In contrast to Greeks, Spaniards or Italians, whose stays were not restricted to a specific period, Turks had clearly been discriminated against. Rather than a negative or racist view of the Turks, the motive behind this act of discrimination was the intensified attempt to erect barriers against immigration at a time when the extension of migration seemed to be unstoppable.[11] Even though instruments designed to control and limit the stay of foreigners existed in the shape of residence and work permits, the explicit rotation mechanism of the agreement with Turkey was a new element in West Germany's recruitment policy. However, it did not last long. While the Ministry for the Interior had been successful in its insistence on a rotation and no-immigration policy in 1961, only about a year later these mechanisms were called into question. In the revised version of 30 September 1964, the German-Turkish agreement contained neither a clause limiting Turks' stays in Germany nor clauses ruling out family reunification, as the Interior Ministry had suggested. The interests of employers who wanted to keep experienced workers, supported by the Ministry for the Economy as well as the Foreign Ministry, which was prepared to give in to Turkish protests against discrimination and – to some extent – humanitarian concerns, had gained the upper hand. Although it was argued that the immigration of families could still be blocked (permits depended on the availability of adequate housing), foreign policy and economic considerations were ultimately given preference over fears about immigration.

Apart from the general regulation and control of migratory movements, internal political debates centred around a second group of problems linked to the immigration of families, their need for accommodation and the question of permanent settlement. Increasingly workers were joined by their families and the German authorities had to decide whether they should issue residence permits or try to obstruct a trend which signalled long-term settlement.[12] Different groups within German society demanded that the reunion of families be facilitated: Employers believed that workers would only be prepared to stay if they could live together with their families. Catholic circles thought that it was irresponsible to split up and possibly destroy Italian families, and to leave Italian children without fatherly care while Italian men fathered illegitimate children in Germany. At the *Katholikentag* of 1962, its president, cabinet minister Paul Lücke, stated that Catholics had to protect the 'guestworkers' from 'moral and spiritual' degeneration.[13] Workers who were separated from their families were thought to lack motivation at work and be more likely to drink excessively and commit crimes. The Italian government demanded that the living conditions of its nationals be improved, whereas the German Foreign Ministry feared that Germany's image abroad might suffer if the country appeared to act in an inhumane fashion. The migrants circumvented legal restrictions as family members entered the country as tourists, and German authorities shied away from removing them.

In the end, German authorities did little to facilitate family reunion (and still often refused permission), and housing programmes for immigrant families remained negligible. Nevertheless, officials and politicians began to accept that irreversible immigration processes had started – albeit in a contradictory and inconsequent way. As the president of the *Bundesanstalt für Arbeitsvermittlung und Arbeitslosenversicherung* (Federal Institute for Job Placement and Unemployment Insurance) suggested in 1964, 10 per cent of the foreign workers would stay permanently in West Germany. Furthermore, he maintained that it was time to realize that the employment of foreigners was not merely an economic question and that the separation of families was unacceptable.[14] In fact, the authorities often no longer discussed whether and on what scale Germany wanted immigration, but rather tried to estimate how many foreigners intended to stay. Repeatedly it was emphasized that the majority of migrant workers would return home – which in fact they did. At the same time, it was increasingly accepted that ten or maybe fifteen per cent of the migrant workers would stay, and in autumn 1964 this amounted to 100,000 workers plus families. Immigration was underestimated but not ignored.

Only in the case of non-European foreigners (then often called 'Afro-Asians') were political and social, sometimes openly racist, objections to their recruitment and immigration given priority. With regards to Europeans and Turks (the latter did not count as non-Europeans), the government refrained from introducing a consequent and effective 'guestworker' policy. Although permanent immigration was not intended and generally not welcomed, it was not effectively prevented, and a certain amount of permanent immigration, particularly from other member-states of the European Economic Community, was in fact tolerated.

Contrary to the dominant view of the 1960s as an uneventful time with complacent, narrow-minded governments and a more or less disinterested public, our research findings strikingly point to how lively and wide-ranging the political and public debates of the mid-1960s were. The arrival of the one-millionth 'guestworker' (in 1964) and the realization that the employment of foreigners and their presence in Germany had become a permanent phenomenon, provided the background to a multifaceted debate in newspapers and magazines about the implications of these developments and resulting political consequences. Assimilation, integration and even naturalization were already being discussed in the 1960s. Even more astonishing than the presence of some hostile (rarely openly racist) points of view is the fact that there were also early demands to acknowledge that 'guestworkers' were in fact immigrants and to ease naturalization.[15]

While the period between 1964 and the summer of 1966 was a time of fairly lively debate in government circles and the wider public, it subsided with the onset of the economic crisis in 1966-67. The crisis did not – as one might assume – instigate a reconsideration of recruitment policy. As thousands of foreign migrants quickly and more or less voluntarily left, competition for jobs was hardly an issue. It appeared that the 'guestworkers' fulfilled the intended buffer function. Political pressure on the government decreased. As the future extent of labour migration was unclear, it no longer seemed quite as urgent to develop a strategy for its management and the integration of foreigners. In an environment of important political and social challenges (a Grand Coalition was formed in December 1966, the student movement erupted, highly controversial laws on a state of emergency were being debated, the extreme right gained seats in regional parliaments), questions of labour migration and immigration were temporarily pushed into the background.

Integration versus Rotation: The 1970s

In 1972-73, the debate about rotation or immigration resurfaced in an intensified form. By this time, about 2.3 million foreigners were employed in the Federal Republic of Germany and the overall number of foreigners in the country amounted to more than three million. Conflicts about the future of labour migration and immigration came to a head when a number of local and regional authorities in Bavaria and Schleswig-Holstein told foreign residents that they would have to leave the country after five years, as permanent settlement was not welcomed. A few years before, a consensus had existed among federal and regional interior ministries that legal instruments should be used in order to prevent long-term settlement. However, by the early 1970s the situation had changed. Public debates about foreigners in Germany now focussed on their miserable living conditions, which seemed incompatible with the overall improvement of life and the idea West German society had of itself. Social reforms and humanitarian concerns ranked high on the agenda of the government of Social Democrats and Liberals (elected in 1969 and led by Willy Brandt). In January 1972, the government promised that no legal instruments would be used to enforce a limitation on the foreigners' stay.[16] The policy of forced rotation (*Zwangsrotation*) was widely condemned and increasingly regarded as the counter-image to a socially responsible and humanitarian-minded policy. This zeitgeist was one reason why politicians, who in 1972-73 came to the conclusion that the number of foreigners in West Germany should be reduced and that immigration posed unwelcome problems, felt unable to develop an effective strategy in response to these perceived problems.

In spite of the well-known restrictive citizenship law and insecure legal status assigned to the foreigners, West Germany never developed an effective 'guestworker' or rotation strategy which the government was willing to implement. This of course is not an entirely new discovery[17] – although the assumption that West Germany practised a rotation policy lives on in the academic literature. Given this situation, we would like to stress two points which, to date, have been insufficiently acknowledged: First, it is worth noting the extent to which internal debates and struggles about the regulation of migration processes took place. In these debates many aspects of immigration were addressed, and attention was not solely directed at labour market and economic issues. Second, it was not blindness or complacency which led Germany along the path toward becoming a country of immigration, but a complex interaction of different factors. These included economic and labour market issues, foreign policy considerations, the influence of the 'sending countries', EEC regulations, as well as humanitarian and social standards. Also included was the fact that there were more important aims than not being a country of immigration. Joining a number of recent publications, we would like to emphasize the limitations a restrictive migration policy faced. However, we do not agree that they can be sufficiently explained by pointing either to the 'corset' of international agreements (Soysal, Jacobson) or, alternatively, the relative autonomy of the nation-state (Joppke, Freeman). Rather, the complex interaction of different factors such as international obligations and foreign policy considerations more generally, as well as internal factors and forces, needs to be analyzed as it evolved over time – and this is where the need for a historical perspective comes in.

Employers' Strategies

In order to better understand the complex web of migration policy, we also need to know more about the main actors in this field. These include the employers who were certainly a significant force in West Germany and actively influenced migration policy as well as the development of the migration process. The strategies pursued by employers were not uniform, as different companies assigned different roles to the foreign workers. While migrants were sometimes recruited as part of the permanent workforce (usually at the bottom of the ladder), in other cases it was clear that the intention was to use them as a buffer in order to be able to respond to a rise or slump in sales. The latter was true, for instance, for the Volkswagen (VW) plant in Wolfsburg (and also for Opel in Rüsselsheim). VW frequently offered only six-month contracts for the busy summer period, which were not renewed. This, together with the tendency of the Italians to fluctuate between Italy and Germany, enabled VW to reduce their workforce in times of crisis without major conflicts.[18] VW decided not to employ foreign women and (in spite of a shortage of skilled workers) refused to offer training to their migrant labourers. The company pursued a policy based on the short-term employment of changing male workers which avoided any investment in measures aiming at the integration and settlement of foreign families.

However, smaller and medium-range companies, or those who paid less, were not in an equally strong position, and, as labour was scarce, it was one of their prior interests to tie workers to the company. Furthermore, there were also big companies in flourishing branches, like the chemical firm Merck in Darmstadt, which encouraged long-term stays by offering employment to couples and making family accommodation available. Employers circumvented government policy by recruiting workers without the necessary permits. Local and regional authorities were faced with demands to legalize this practice or to grant family members permission to live in Germany. Economic strength, the degree to which particular branches could hope for stable levels of production, as well as management strategies, influenced employers' attitudes to the employment of foreign labour. So far, our knowledge is limited to a few case studies, and it is difficult to gain access to company archives.[19]

We also know very little about the ways in which the policy of organizations like the *Bundesvereinigung der Deutschen Arbeitgeberverbände* (the Federation of German Employers' Associations) was shaped. To some extent, it seems to have reflected contradictory interests: In the early and mid-1960s, pressure was exerted to encourage long-term stays of foreign migrants, to ease family reunion and to provide government funding for housing programmes.[20] Controls and restrictions were resented as they complicated the recruitment of workers. But, from 1965 onwards, one leading official in particular made himself a key protagonist of a rotation policy.[21] To some extent this reflected the fact that even the attitude of employers was not narrowly economic. They were also concerned about the wider social consequences of immigration, and became increasingly worried that the employers would be held responsible for the foreign presence in German society. If a rotation policy was demanded, the government could be blamed for not enforcing it and thus tolerating permanent immigration.

Migrants and Migration Patterns: A Diverse Picture

How much is known about the migrants themselves? Earlier on, we questioned a stereotypical picture of the 'guestworker' which we would now like to challenge and discuss further. First, the socio-demographic structure of the foreign population was less uniform than is sometimes assumed. An examination of the age structure of Italian employees at the VW plant in Wolfsburg shows that already during the early recruitment period (before the 1966-67 crisis), 16.4 per cent were more than forty years old while 35.6 per cent were between the ages of 30 and 40. Less than half fit the picture of the young, male 'guestworker'. A significant share of the Italians were married (44.4 per cent), and many of them also had children (38 per cent of all Italians). In September 1966, two-thirds of all male foreigners working in Germany were married.[22] Compared with the overall age structure of the foreign workforce in West Germany, it is true that they were on average much younger than German workers. Before 1967, more than 90 per cent of those from the recruitment countries were below the age of forty-five. But the picture was slightly different for the Italians and it changed over time.

While car manufacturers like VW or Opel recruited men exclusively,[23] other branches of industry were more or specifically interested in employing women. For instance, at Merck in Darmstadt about one-third of the foreign workforce (end of 1966) were female, and in many cases whole families were employed. In 1966, the proportion of women among the foreign employees in West Germany was 25.8 per cent, rising to 30 per cent in 1973.[24] These figures illustrate that women often immigrated as workers and not only as wives. Employment offered an important avenue for family reunion as it was often easier to gain access to Germany as a worker than as a family member. At the same time, this process undermined attempts to prevent permanent immigration by restricting the arrival of families in Germany. In Darmstadt, an unexceptional town near Frankfurt, as early as November 1964 about one-third of those from the recruitment countries lived together as families; by June 1969 this was true for more than half of the migrants. There were differences between the nationalities however, with Greek migrants, from early on, often living in Germany as families or couples. Fewer Italians did the same, although many Italian men married German women.

As statistical information is scarce for the years up to 1967, researchers have been led to assume that family immigration was insignificant before the late 1960s or early 1970s.[25] However, the evidence for southern Hesse suggests that this is misleading and that in fact family immigration accompanied the recruitment process of the 1960s. As family reunion is regarded as one of the major indicators for long-term settlement, this observation also dispels the idea of the migration process as a sequence of an initial 'guestworker' period followed by a period of long-term immigration. Rather than being viewed as consecutive processes, we should consider migration to West Germany as having happened in a number of different forms at the same time. Different migration patterns coexisted. They include, at one extreme, the short-term sojourner and, at the other end of the spectrum, the permanent immigrant. The first group in particular is often neglected because they are outside the scope of several statistics. However, as our case studies suggest, numbers were relevant. Records for Darmstadt (a town with 120,000 inhabitants) show that almost one-third of those migrants who arrived in Germany between 1955 and 1967 stayed only for one period of less than eleven months with most actually leaving after a stay of less than six months. Of the Italians employed by VW, about 20 per cent left the company and the town after less than three months – and this was not a phenomenon of the early 1960s. Maybe we have to pay more attention to the new opportunities migration offered under conditions of organized recruitment, paid travel and company accommodation. These conditions, in addition to the proximity of Italy and the new freedom of movement within the EEC, probably made the decision to migrate to a foreign country easier and less final. Many people may have just checked out what it was like to work in Germany, and often found conditions unsatisfactory, missed their families or returned for other reasons. The Volkswagen study also suggests that there was a significant number of commuters – but other figures do not support this view.

In contrast, in Darmstadt the group of the potential permanent immigrants – defined as everyone who lived in West Germany for more than five years – comprised 17 per cent of those foreigners who entered Germany between 1955 and 1967.[26] According to survey studies for the *Bundesanstalt für Arbeit*, in autumn 1968 about 50 per cent of the male foreign workers and 39 per cent of the female migrants had entered West Germany at least four years ago (26 per cent had arrived more than seven years ago).[27] In 1972, during a time when the enormous expansion of foreign employment saw many newcomers joining the migrant workforce, a similar study concluded that 21 per cent of all foreign workers had lived in Germany (without longer interruptions) for more than seven years. Another 12 per cent had come before 1967, i.e., had lived in Germany for more than five years.[28] If we take the 1976 sample census (*Mikrozensus*) as an additional indicator, of 1.447 million heads of households, 28 per cent had entered Germany at least ten years earlier. Or, to put it differently, more than 400,000 heads of households had already lived in West Germany in 1966.[29] In 1966, the number of foreign workers ranged between 1.1 and 1.3 million. If we compare the two figures (this is of course not entirely satisfactory as not every worker was the head of a household and some 1976 heads of households may still have been children in 1966), we may conclude that, as a very rough estimate, one-third of the 1966 migrants became settled. In order to obtain an adequate picture of the migrant population we have to take into account how heterogeneous it was. Migration patterns were varied and coexisted in different forms rather than undergoing a transformation from a 'guestworker' to an immigration pattern.

Although there is a significant body of research on migrant and ethnic groups in German society, a major limitation is that macro- and micro-level analyses have not been sufficiently linked.[30] Sociologists and anthropologists have often been primarily interested in the change of norms and values and the relevance of the migration experience to the individual, while those interested in legal norms and policy developments sometimes underestimate the role of the subjects and the variety of their experiences. More attention should be given to the relationship between social and political structures and the everyday experiences and activities of migrants.

Adjustment and Protest

The common portrayal of migrants in the Federal Republic has largely painted them as the victims of an inhumane 'guestworker' scheme and a hostile state and society, and paid too little attention to the men and women who actively shaped their destiny. As stated above, we believe that the image of the '*verschämte Gastarbeiter*' is misleading and unfair. It was already mentioned how families circumvented the intentions of German authorities and managed to live together in Germany. In times when labour was scarce, workers had significant power and could escape (or resist?) bad working conditions or low wages by simply looking for another job. Although there were many different reasons why migrants broke their work contracts,[31] the frequency with which this occurred indicates that many of them did not acquiesce but actively shaped their lives. Furthermore, it is not true that migrants only became engaged in strikes from 1973 and that they were acquiescent in the 1960s. The 1973 strikes in the metalworks and engineering industries (the prime example is Ford in Cologne) were unprecedented in scale. But we have also found many examples of smaller wildcat strikes in the 1960s. Protests seem to have emerged spontaneously, with often only those of one nationality going on strike. They were caused by a variety of reasons, such as the sacking of a co-national (e.g., 1961 at Philipp Holzmann in Frankfurt), bad canteen food (1961, Buderus in Wetzlar), insufficient medical support (1962, VW) or discontent about the difference between the promised wages (before tax) and the amount of money actually paid out. In May 1961, 300 Spanish workers went on strike as their employer, BBC in Großauheim, announced a reduction in pay. In March 1962, 125 Greek miners in Herne went on strike about the time of their lunch break and because they wanted to prepare their own food. The conflict escalated, and eventually thirteen Greeks were deported by the police. In 1967 at Bahlsen in Hannover, female Spanish employees went on strike because a number of them had been transferred to other jobs. There are many other similar examples, but to date the conflicts of the 1960s have not been studied systematically.[32] Migrants' protests escalated quickly and took the form of strikes most probably because other opportunities to express discontent and exert pressure were not open to them. In several cases the *Betriebsrat* (workers' council) sided with the employers. That strikes occurred is all the more significant as employers frequently called the police and 'ring leaders' were expelled from the country – in particular if they were suspected of being Communists.

Of course, not every foreign migrant was a revolutionary, and certainly not everyone was ready to go on strike when they felt mistreated. At Volkswagen, many seem to have left if they found conditions unsatisfactory. And during the 1966-67 crisis, the German authorities and public were astonished by how readily many foreign workers accepted their dismissal and returned home. Once again, it is this variety of circumstances which has to be addressed and rediscovered behind ideas of the timid and acquiescent 'guestworkers' of the 1960s.

In conclusion, many questions remain unanswered and present new and exciting challenges for historians and social scientists. This article aimed to demonstrate that there is the need for a new look at established truths. We hope to have shown that it is worthwhile to study the specific constellations of the 1960s and the 1970s and – while nowadays it seems more common to make general observations on the experiences of liberal democracies – to expand our knowledge of specific regional and national developments.

Notes

1 In 1955 the first recruitment treaty with Italy was signed, and in 1973 the government announced a recruitment stop. Periodization usually follows Meier-Braun's suggestions, see his *Integration und Rückkehr?* Esser and Korte suggest distinguishing three phases within the 1955 to 1973 period (*Federal Republic of Germany)*. A different version of this text was published in *Studi emigrazione* 38 (2001): pp. 115-129.

2 Castles, *Migrants and Minorities in Post-Keynesian Capitalism: The German Case*, p. 42.

3 Herbert, *Geschichte der Ausländerbeschäftigung in Deutschland 1880 bis 1980*, pp. 232, 234. Influential accounts of migration policy and the migration process include Dohse, *Ausländische Arbeiter und bürgerlicher Staat;* Bethlehem, *Heimatvertreibung, DDR-Flucht, Gastarbeiterzuwanderung*; Lohrmann and Manfrass, *Ausländerbeschäftigung und internationale Politik*; Bade, *Vom Auswanderungsland zum Einwanderungsland?*

4 Statistical information can be found in the periodical *Wirtschaft und Statistik* and the regular *Erfahrungsberichte* of the *Bundesanstalt für Arbeit* as well as the *Repräsentativuntersuchungen* of the same institution.

5 See for more recent research: Motte, Ohliger and von Oswald, *50 Jahre Bundesrepublik – 50 Jahre Einwanderung*; Eryilmaz and Jamin, *Fremde Heimat*; Steinert, *Migration und Politik*; Hunn and Herbert, 'Gastarbeiter und Gastarbeiterpolitik in der Bundesrepublik'; Rieker, 'Südländer, Ostagenten oder Westeuropäer?'; Herbert, 'Geschichte der

Ausländerpolitik' (a revised and extended version of his *Geschichte der Ausländerbeschäftigung*).

6 The main basis are our own studies which also provide extensive evidence for the theses put forward in this text: Anne von Oswald carried out two case studies investigating employers' strategies and the migration patterns of Italian and Tunesian migrants at the Volkswagen plant and a supplier both in Wolfsburg ('Venite a lavorare alla Volkswagen!'). Barbara Sonnenberger studied the early years of labour migration to southern Hesse, the region south of Frankfurt, and immigration policy (*Die Anfänge der Arbeitsmigration in die Bundesrepublik*). Karen Schönwälder recently completed a wide-ranging comparative study of British and German responses to immigration and ethnic plurality, c. 1958 to 1973 (*Einwanderung und ethnische Pluralität*).

7 Bade, *Vom Auswanderungsland zum Einwanderungsland?*, p. 93.

8 We use the term 'foreign workers' in the sense of the German *Arbeitnehmer* or *abhängig Beschäftigte* which refers to those in dependent employment.

9 The agreement was signed on 20 December 1955. On its preconditions and motives see Steinert, *Migration und Politik*, pp. 220-238; Novi, *Die italienisch-deutsche Anwerbevereinbarung von 1955*.

10 The 'Deutsch-türkische Vereinbarung über die Vermittlung von türkischen Arbeitnehmern' was signed on 30 October 1961 and came into force from 1 September. For detailed examinations of the pre-history see Schönwälder, *Einwanderung und ethnische Pluralität*, pp. 210-215; Sonnenberger, *Die Anfänge der Arbeitsmigration in die Bundesrepublik*, pp. 79-81. In 1960, West Germany had signed recruitment treaties with Spain and Greece.

11 For a different view on this aspect see Jamin, 'Fremde Heimat', p. 155. The fact that the Interior Ministry tried to introduce similar discriminatory provisions in the recruitment treaty with Portugal (1964) supports our view, see Sonnenberger, *Die Anfänge der Arbeitsmigration in die Bundesrepublik*, p. 82.

12 For more detailed accounts and archival references see Schönwälder, *Einwanderung und ethnische Pluralität*, pp. 241-250; Sonnenberger, *Die Anfänge der Arbeitsmigration in die Bundesrepublik*, pp. 90-98.

13 Zentralkomitee der Deutschen Katholiken, *Glauben, Danken, Dienen*, p. 72.

14 See Anton Sabel, '"300 Mill. DM für Ausländerheime"', *Neue Rhein Zeitung*, 20 June 1964. In 1966, he raised his estimate of the share of immigrants among the foreign workers to 15 per cent.

15 See for instance 'Gastarbeiter oder Einwanderer?' *Kirchenzeitung für das Erzbistum Köln*, 12 April 1964, and the *dpa-report* of 11 April 1964: 'Kirchenzeitung: Gastarbeiter als Einwanderer ansehen'. Peter Tyroller in 1965 published a paperback in which he predicted that the government would have to realise that a significant part of the 'guest-workers' had become immigrants (*Der Kollege, der aus der Wärme kommt).* Gustav Stein, who sat on the board of the Federation of German Industries (BDI) and was a member of the *Bundestag* for the Christian Democrats, suggested that Germany should actively integrate and naturalize at least those foreigners who were prepared to become part of the German people (see his 'Den Arbeitsmarkt entlasten' on the front page of the *Industriekurier* of 10 February 1966). A detailed examination of public debates is in Schönwälder, *Einwanderung und ethnische Pluralität*.

16 'Mit ausländerrechtlichen Maßnahmen wird nicht auf eine zeitliche Begrenzung des Aufenthaltes ausländischer Arbeitnehmer hingewirkt', reply to a parliamentary question by Hussing et al., 'Politik der Bundesregierung gegenüber den ausländischen Arbeitnehmern in der Bundesrepublik Deutschland', Deutscher Bundestag, *Drucksache* 6/3085, 31 January 1972, p. 4.

17 Tomas Hammar, for instance, acknowledges the fact ('Comparative Analysis', p. 251), but see Treibel, *Migration in modernen Gesellschaften*, with an emphasis on rotation.

18 All references to Volkswagen and Wolfsburg are based on von Oswald's research, while references to Opel, Merck and Darmstadt are based on Sonnenberger's study.

19 There are a number of 1980s and 1990s studies, see e.g. Gillmeister, Kurthen and Fijalkowski, *Ausländerbeschäftigung in der Krise?*, but much less is known about the 1960s and 1970s.

20 See the *Jahresberichte der Bundesvereinigung der deutschen Arbeitgeberverbände* for 1965 and 1966. The BDA magazine *Der Arbeitgeber* in 1964 published an article 'Wann Familienwohnungsheime für Ausländer?' which reflects the demand for housing programmes as well as the awareness that family reunion was a step toward immigration, or – in this case – 'assimilation'.

21 Weber, 'Isolation oder Assimilation?'.

22 'Die beschäftigten ausländischen Arbeitnehmer', pp. 568-569. Figures refer to those from the recruitment countries.

23 In 1966, Opel employed about 5,000 foreigners of which 103 were women.

24 See Mattes, 'Zum Verhältnis von Migration und Geschlecht'.

25 Münz, Seifert and Ulrich, *Zuwanderung nach Deutschland,* pp. 63-64; von Breitenbach, *Italiener und Spanier als Arbeitnehmer in der Bundesrepublik Deutschland*, p. 48; Thränhardt, 'Aus Gastarbeitern werden europäische Bürger', p. 77.

26 Unfortunately the available statistics include only those foreigners who remigrated in the years up to 1979.

27 Bundesanstalt für Arbeit, *Ausländische Arbeitnehmer. Beschäftigung, Anwerbung, Vermittlung – Erfahrungsbericht 1969*, pp. 48-51. Data for the Federal Republic and for Darmstadt are not exactly comparable because the national surveys ignored shorter interruptions of the migrants' stay in Germany.

28 *Repräsentativuntersuchung '72 über die Beschäftigung ausländischer Arbeitnehmer im Bundesgebiet und ihre Familien- und Wohnverhältnisse*, pp. 32-33. At the time of the survey, the number of foreign workers was 2.215 million.

29 'Haushalte von Ausländern in der Bundesrepublik Deutschland.'

30 One study pointing in this direction is Pagenstecher's book, which analyzed interviews but relied on secondary literature for the political and social context (*Ausländerpolitik und Immigrantenidentität*). For recent studies exploring the relevance of the ethnic colony for the everyday life of migrants in the immigration country and the relevance of networks for the decision to migrate, see contributions by Behrendt and Yalçin-Heckmann in Waldhoff, Tan and Kürsat-Ahlers, *Brücken zwischen Zivilizationen.* See also Thomas Faist's contribution in: Pries, *Transnationale Migration*, various publications by Schiffauer, and Philipper, *Biographische Dimensionen der Migration.*

31 As this was perceived as a major problem, companies like *Volkswagen* as well as the *Bundesanstalt für Arbeit* tried to find out why foreign workers broke their contracts. Often they had found a better-paid job, but reasons also included homesickness or Germany's cold climate.

32 Mark J. Miller for instance lists examples of strikes in particular from 1969 onwards but relies on limited secondary sources. He did, however, in 1981 attack the 'thesis of political quiescence of migrant workers' (*Foreign Workers in Western Europe*, p. 6).

References

Bade, Klaus J., *Vom Auswanderungsland zum Einwanderungsland? Deutschland 1880-1980*, Berlin, 1983.

Behrendt, Günter M., 'Die türkischen "communities" von Hannover', in: Hans-Peter Waldhoff, Dursan Tan, Elçin Kürsat-Ahlers (eds), *Brücken zwischen Zivilisationen. Zur Zivilisierung ethnisch-kultureller Differenzen und Machtungleichheiten. Das deutsch-türkische Beispiel*, Frankfurt a. M., 1997, pp. 213-234.

'Die beschäftigten ausländischen Arbeitnehmer nach Wirtschaftsbereichen Ende Juni 1967 und nach bestimmten gesellschaftlichen Verhältnissen im September 1966 im Bundesgebiet einschließlich Berlin (West)', *Arbeit, Beruf und Arbeitslosenhilfe* 15 (1967): pp. 565-571.

Bethlehem, Siegfried, *Heimatvertreibung, DDR-Flucht, Gastarbeiterzuwanderung. Wanderungsströme und Wanderungspolitik in der Bundesrepublik Deutschland*, Stuttgart, 1982.

Breitenbach, Barbara von, *Italiener und Spanier als Arbeitnehmer in der Bundesrepublik Deutschland. Eine vergleichende Untersuchung zur europäischen Arbeitsmigration*, München, 1982.

Bundesanstalt für Arbeit (ed.), *Ausländische Arbeitnehmer. Beschäftigung, Anwerbung, Vermittlung – Erfahrungsbericht 1969*, Nürnberg, 1970 (Beilage zu Nr. 8 der Amtlichen Nachrichten der Bundesanstalt, 1970).

Castles, Stephen, 'Migrants and Minorities in Post-Keynesian Capitalism: The German Case', in: Malcolm Cross (ed.), *Ethnic Minorities and Industrial Change in Europe and North America*, Cambridge, 1992, pp. 36-54.

Deutscher Bundestag, *Drucksachen, 6. Wahlperiode.*

Dohse, Knuth, *Ausländische Arbeiter und bürgerlicher Staat. Genese und Funktion von staatlicher Ausländerpolitik und Ausländerrecht. Vom Kaiserreich bis zur Bundesrepublik Deutschland*, Königstein/Ts., 1981.

Eryilmaz, Aytaç and Mathilde Jamin (eds), *Fremde Heimat. Eine Geschichte der Einwanderung aus der Türkei*, Essen, 1998.

Esser, Hartmut and Hermann Korte, 'Federal Republic of Germany', in: Tomas Hammar (ed.), *European Immigration Policy*, Cambridge, 1985, pp. 165-205.

Faist, Thomas, 'Migration und der Transfer sozialen Kapitals oder: Warum gibt es relativ wenige internationale Migranten?', in: Ludger Pries (ed.), *Transnationale Migration* (Soziale Welt, Sonderband 12), Baden-Baden, 1997, pp. 63-84.

Freeman, Gary P., 'Modes of Immigration Politics in Liberal Democratic States', *International Migration Review* 29 (1995): pp. 881-902.

Gillmeister, Helmut, Hermann Kurthen and Jürgen Fijalkowski, *Ausländerbeschäftigung in der Krise? Die Beschäftigungschancen und -risiken ausländischer Arbeitnehmer am Beispiel der West-Berliner Industrie*, Berlin, 1989.

Hammar, Tomas, 'Comparative Analysis', in: Tomas Hammar (ed.), *European Immigration Policy: A Comparative Study*, Cambridge, 1985, pp. 237-304.

'Haushalte von Ausländern in der Bundesrepublik Deutschland', *Wirtschaft und Statistik* 1 (1979): pp. 45-47.

Herbert, Ulrich, *Geschichte der Ausländerbeschäftigung in Deutschland 1880 bis 1980. Saisonarbeiter, Zwangsarbeiter, Gastarbeiter*, Bonn, 1986 (translated as: *A History of Foreign Labor in Germany, 1880-1990. Seasonal Workers, Forced Laborers, Guest Workers*, Ann Arbor, 1990).

Herbert, Ulrich, Geschichte der Ausländerpolitik in *Deutschland. Saisonarbeiter, Zwangsarbeiter, Gastarbeiter, Flüchtlinge*, Munich, 2001.

Huber, Bertold and Klaus Unger, 'Politische und rechtliche Determinanten der Ausländerbeschäftigung in der Bundesrepublik Deutschland', in: Hans-Joachim Hoffmann-Nowotny and Karl-Otto Hondrich (eds), *Ausländer in der Bundesrepublik Deutschland und in der Schweiz. Segregation und Integration: eine vergleichende Untersuchung*, Frankfurt and New York, 1982, pp. 124-194.

Hunn, Karin and Ulrich Herbert, 'Gastarbeiter und Gastarbeiterpolitik in der Bundesrepublik. Vom Beginn der offiziellen Anwerbung bis zum Anwerbestopp (1955-1973)', in: Axel Schildt, Detlef Siegfried and Karl Christian Lammers (eds), *Dynamische Zeiten. Die 60er Jahre in den beiden deutschen Gesellschaften*, Hamburg, 2000, pp. 273-310.

Jacobson, David, *Rights across Borders. Immigration and the Decline of Citizenship*, Baltimore and London, 1997.

Jahresbericht der Bundesvereinigung der Deutschen Arbeitgeberverbände, 1. Dezember 1964 - 30. November 1965, vorgelegt der Mitgliederversammlung in Bad Godesberg am 1. Dezember 1965.

Jahresbericht der Bundesvereinigung der Deutschen Arbeitgeberverbände, 1. Dezember 1965 - 30. November 1966, vorgelegt der Mitgliederversammlung am 30. November 1966.

Jamin, Mathilde, 'Fremde Heimat', in: Jan Motte, Rainer Ohliger and Anne von Oswald (eds), *50 Jahre Bundesrepublik – 50 Jahre Einwanderung*, pp. 145-164.

Joppke, Christian (ed.), *Challenge to the Nation-State. Immigration in Western Europe and the United States*, Oxford, 1998.

Lohrmann, Manfred and Klaus Manfrass (eds), *Ausländerbeschäftigung und internationale Politik. Zur Analyse transnationaler Sozialprozesse*, Munich and Vienna, 1974.

Mattes, Monika, 'Zum Verhältnis von Migration und Geschlecht. Anwerbung und Beschäftigung von "Gastarbeiterinnen" in der Bundesrepublik 1960 bis 1973', in: Jan Motte, Rainer Ohliger and Anne von Oswald (eds), *50 Jahre Bundesrepublik – 50 Jahre Einwanderung*, pp. 285-309.

Meier-Braun, Karl-Heinz, *Integration und Rückkehr? Zur Ausländerpolitik des Bundes und der Länder, insbesondere Baden-Württembergs*, Mainz and Munich, 1988.

Miller, Mark J., *Foreign Workers in Western Europe*, New York, 1981.

Motte, Jan, Rainer Ohliger and Anne von Oswald (eds), *50 Jahre Bundesrepublik – 50 Jahre Einwanderung. Nachkriegsgeschichte als Migrationsgeschichte*, Frankfurt and New York, 1999.

Münz, Rainer, Wolfgang Seifert and Ralf Ulrich, *Zuwanderung nach Deutschland. Strukturen, Wirkungen, Perspektiven*, Frankfurt and New York, 1997 (new edition 1999).

Novi, Livia, *Die italienisch-deutsche Anwerbevereinbarung von 1955 im Rahmen der italienischen Wanderungspolitik der fünfziger Jahre*, MA-Dissertation, Universität Osnabrück, 1994.

von Oswald, Anne, 'Arbeitseinsatz der "Gastarbeiter" im Volkswagenwerk (1962-1974/75)', in: Katja Dominik, Marc Jünemann, Jan Motte and Astrid Reineke (eds), *Angeworben – eingewandert – abgeschoben. Ein anderer Blick auf die Einwanderungsgesellschaft*. Münster, 1999, pp. 83-100.

von Oswald, Anne, '"Venite a lavorare alla Volkswagen!" Strategie aziendali e reazioni degli emigrati italiani a Wolfsburg 1962-1975', in: Szzefano Musso (ed.), *Tra fabbrica e societá. Mondi operai nell'Italia del Novecento*, Annali della Fondazione G. Feltrinelli, Vol. 33, Milano, 1997, pp. 695-740.

Pagenstecher, Cord, *Ausländerpolitik und Immigrantenidentität. Zur Geschichte der 'Gastarbeit' in der Bundesrepublik*, Berlin, 1994.

Philipper, Ingeborg, *Biographische Dimensionen der Migration. Zur Lebensgeschichte von Italienerinnen der ersten Generation*, Weinheim, 1997.

Repräsentativuntersuchung '72 über die Beschäftigung ausländischer Arbeitnehmer im Bundesgebiet und ihre Familien- und Wohnverhältnisse. Beilage zu den Amtlichen Nachrichten der Bundesanstalt für Arbeit, no. 11, Nürnberg, 1973.

Rieker, Yvonne, 'Südländer, Ostagenten oder Westeuropäer? Die Politik der Bundesregierung und das Bild der italienischen Gastarbeiter 1955-1970', *Archiv für Sozialgeschichte* 40 (2000): pp. 231-258.

Schiffauer, Werner, *Die Migranten aus Subay. Türken in Deutschland. Eine Ethnographie*, Stuttgart, 1991.

Schönwälder, Karen, *Einwanderung und ethnische Pluralität: Politische Entscheidungen und öffentliche Debatten in Großbritannien und der Bundesrepublik Deutschland von den 1950er bis zu den 1970er Jahren*, Essen, 2001.

Sonnenberger, Barbara, *Die Anfänge der Arbeitsmigration in die Bundesrepublik. Nationale Politik und regionale Erfahrung in Südhessen (1955-1967)*, unpublished PhD-Dissertation, Marburg, 2000.

Soysal, Yasemin N., *Limits of Citizenship. Migrants and Postnational Membership in Europe*, Chicago and London 1994.

Steinert, Johannes-Dieter, *Migration und Politik. Westdeutschland – Europa – Übersee 1945-1961*, Osnabrück, 1995.

Thränhardt, Dietrich, 'Aus Gastarbeitern werden europäische Bürger – deutsche Erfahrungen mit der Arbeitsmigration', in: Christoph Butterwegge, Siegfried Jäger (eds), *Europa gegen den Rest der Welt? Flüchtlingsbewegungen, Einwanderung, Asylpolitik*, Cologne, 1993, pp. 68-84.

Treibel, Annette, *Migration in modernen Gesellschaften. Soziale Folgen von Einwanderung und Gastarbeit*, Weinheim and Munich, 1980 (rev. ed.: *Migration in modernen Gesellschaften. Soziale Folgen von Einwanderung, Gastarbeit und Flucht*, Weinheim, 1999).

Tyroller, Peter, *Der Kollege, der aus der Wärme kommt. Ist er Gast, Arbeiter oder Einwanderer?* Bremen, 1965.

'Wann Familienwohnungsheime für Ausländer?' *Der Arbeitgeber* 16 (1964): pp. 162-3.

Weber, Rolf, 'Isolation oder Assimilation?' *Der Arbeitgeber* 17 (1965): pp. 292-296.

Wirtschaft und Statistik.

Yalçin-Heckmann, Lale, 'Zum kollektiven Gedächtnis türkischer Migranten', in: Hans-Peter Waldhoff, Dursan Tan and Elçin Kürsat-Ahlers (eds), *Brücken zwischen Zivilisationen. Zur Zivilisierung ethnisch-kultureller Differenzen und Machtungleichheiten. Das deutsch-türkische Beispiel*, Frankfurt a. M., 1997, pp. 183-195.

Zentralkomitee der Deutschen Katholiken (ed.), *Glauben, Danken, Dienen. Der 79. Deutsche Katholikentag vom 22. August bis 26. August 1962 in Hannover*, Paderborn, 1962.

Chapter 3

Post-war Immigration to Estonia: A Comparative Perspective

Hill Kulu

Research on South-North migration in post-war Europe has a long tradition. For the most part, past studies have concentrated on migration and its determinants.[1] More recently, greater attention has been paid to the settlement and adaptation of immigrants and 'new' ethnic minorities[2] and the return of migrants to their former homelands.[3] Post-war East-West migration has received considerably less scholarly attention for a number of reasons. First, the migration streams were relatively modest and consisted of mainly short-term emigration from Eastern Europe.[4] Second, the poor quality of available data hindered research. In addition, East European scholars faced restrictions in treating 'politically sensitive' issues such as international migration.

Migrations between Eastern European countries and internal movements corresponding to the criteria of international migration have garnered even less attention. Yet such migrations were no less important. Inter-republican migration in the Soviet Union, and the case of post-war Estonia in particular, are significant cases in point. Protestant Estonia had been a part of the Russian Empire since the beginning of the eighteenth century. It gained independence during the course of the Russian Revolution in 1917 and the subsequent civil war. However, independence was short-lived. Estonia was occupied and annexed by the Soviet Union in 1940. During the post-war period, Estonia experienced large-scale immigration from other parts of the Soviet Union. As a result, the relatively homogeneous pre-war state became a multiethnic republic where immigrants of mostly Slavic origin and their descendants made up approximately two-fifths of the population.[5]

most common immigrants in the 1940s (Figure 3.2).[21] Many migrants also came from elsewhere in Russia. Later the proportion of immigrants from Northwest Russia decreased while those from the non-Russian republics increased. In addition to Russia, immigrants from Belarus, Ukraine, Moldova, and later from the Trans-Caucasus and Central-Asia, arrived. Thus, the migration hinterland of Estonia widened and the geographical background of the population diversified. Data pertaining to the ethnic origin of immigrants support this contention. A major portion of the immigrants were ethnically Russian. There were also many Estonians and (Ingrian) Finns, mostly from Northwest Russia, among those who immigrated in the 1940s. Later the proportion of other ethnic groups increased. Decreasing population growth in Russia and its increase in the areas of non-Russian population are generally seen as responsible for the widening of Estonia's migration hinterland.[22]

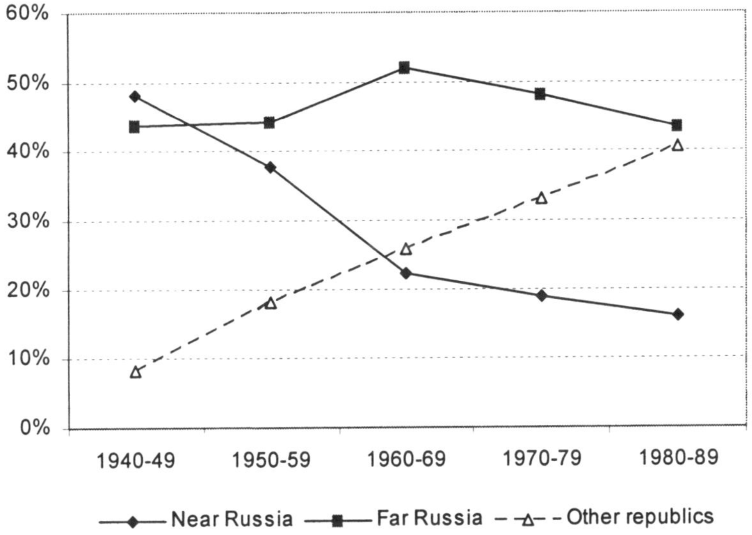

Figure 3.2 Region of childhood of immigrants
Source: Estonian Family and Fertility Survey (EFFS), 1994 (all figures)

The educational background of immigrants changed over time, as did the mechanisms of and reasons for immigration. In the 1940s and 1950s, immigrants with primary and basic education were dominant; beginning in the 1960s, more had secondary education (Figure 3.3). In the 1970s, the share of those with higher education increased considerably. These changes were partly caused by an increase in the general level of education, but the background of immigrants also played a role. The development of the

Estonian economy was characterized by a continuous demand for both skilled and unskilled labour in the 1950s and 1960s, but thereafter the need for industrial labour decreased.[23]

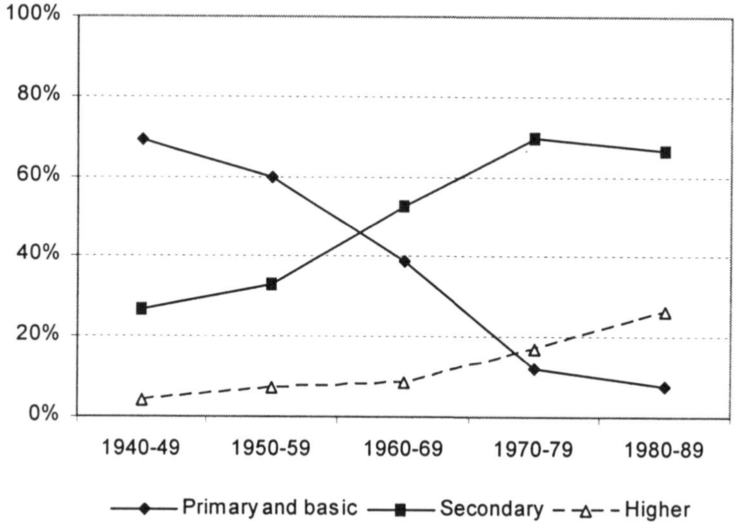

Figure 3.3 Level of education of immigrants

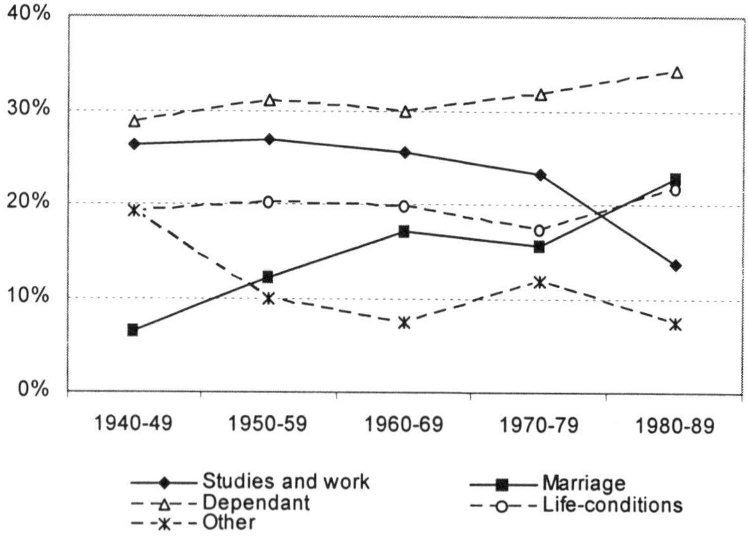

Figure 3.4 Reasons for immigration

The reasons for immigration were also subject to change. Labour migration decreased while migration related to family reunification became more important (Figure 3.4). In addition, the proportion of married women settling in Estonia with their husbands increased slightly.

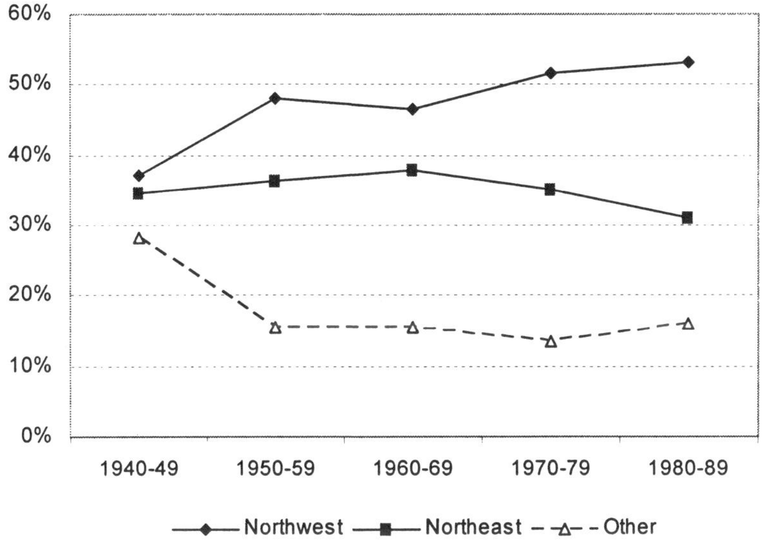

Figure 3.5 First residence of immigrants in Estonia

The socio-geographic composition of immigrants also changed. The most important type of immigration in the 1940s and the 1950s was rural-urban migration. Beginning in the 1960s, urban-urban migration became dominant; by the 1980s, urban-urban migration made-up four-fifths of all immigration. In addition, it must be mentioned that while rural-rural migration was common during the 1940s, the share of urban-rural migration slightly increased in the 1980s. Nine-tenths of all immigrants settled in urban areas. This figure was to some extent lower only among those who arrived in Estonia during the 1940s. Most of the immigrants settled in the capital of Tallinn and its surroundings in Northwest Estonia and in the fast-growing industrial cities of Northeast Estonia (in the region of Ida-Viru, including the cities of Kohtla-Järve, Sillamäe and Narva) during the post-war period (Figure 3.5). Those who settled elsewhere in Estonia were numerous only among the immigrants of the 1940s. Until the 1960s, immigrants settled in large numbers in both Northwest and Northeast Estonia. However, from the 1960s onward, the proportion of those who moved to Northwest Estonia increased, while the share of those who settled in Northeast Estonia decreased. These trends were consistent with the development of the Estonian economy. Extensive industrial growth dominated until the 1960s. Thereafter, investments into industry decreased, especially in Northeast Estonia.[24] Subsequently, economic development was directed toward Tallinn, which had preserved its earlier attractiveness as a capital and metropolis, with a rapidly developing service sector.[25]

The large post-war immigration to Estonia and the concentration of immigrants in two regions brought with it remarkable changes in the size and the structure of the Estonian population. In 1945, there were 854,000 people living in Estonia. By 1989, the country's population was 1,565,662 – 1.8 times larger. Immigrants composed 26 per cent of the total population and their share with the second generation was about 38 per cent.[26] When taken together, immigrants and their descendants made up more than four-fifths of the population in Northeast Estonia, and half of the population in Northwest Estonia, while elsewhere their numbers were considerably lower.[27] Thus, by the end of the Soviet period Northeast Estonia had become an area of high immigrant concentration. The proportion of natives and immigrants was equal in Tallinn, but elsewhere in Estonia the native population dominated. In everyday life this meant that Estonia was divided into regions where the Estonian language and culture dominated and others where Russian dominated.

The 1989 data on employment shows an over-representation of immigrants in the industrial and service sectors. Forty-seven per cent of immigrants and their descendants were employed in industry, 44 per cent in services, but only 10 per cent in agriculture. The corresponding figures for native population were 30, 42 and 27, respectively.[28] A more detailed analysis indicates that immigrants were clearly over-represented in mining and quarrying; electricity, gas and water supply; manufacturing; transport and communication. Immigrants also formed a majority of the labour force in public administration and finance. The occupational composition of immigrants and natives in Estonia did not differ significantly: immigrants were only slightly over-represented in manual jobs.[29]

Immigration to Estonia in Comparative Perspective

Labour migration from Southern to Western and Northern Europe dominated the European migratory system during the post-war period. This phenomenon began in the late 1940s, reached its peak in the 1960s,[30] and decreased in the 1970s.[31] Initially, labour migrants arrived in Western and

Northern Europe from countries on the European periphery, but later the migration hinterland widened to include North Africa and Asia.[32] Over time, the migration system changed as well. Labour migration was replaced by family reunification.[33] Economics and demographics were the prime factors underlying South-North migration. First, the economy of Western and Northern European countries developed quickly after the war. The motor of development was industry, which required a continuous supply of labour. The South, in turn, was more agricultural and had lower living standards. Second, there were important demographic differences. The generations born in the 1920s-40s were relatively large in Southern Europe because of a later demographic transition.[34] Precisely the opposite state of affairs could be found in Western and Northern Europe. In economic terms, then, a surplus of capital and a shortage of labour in the North and a deficiency of capital and glut of labour in the South helped catalyze South-North migration. Political factors were important. Countries suffering from labour shortages used immigration to solve the problem and negotiated bilateral contracts with countries offering labour. These administrative agreements shaped and directed migration streams.[35]

Changes in Southern European countries – most notably rapid industrial development and a concomitant improvement in living standards – led to a decrease in reserve labour, which in turn led to a widening of Northern Europe's migration hinterland.[36] The 1973 oil crisis and the decision to restrict labour migration caused a decrease in migration streams and led to changes in the migration regime. Deeper structural reasons, such as de-industrialization and the entry of Europe's post-war baby boom generation into the labour market also propelled this shift.[37]

It is not difficult to see that the trends noted with regard to Estonia were rather similar to those of Western and Northern European countries. In both instances, former emigration regions became immigration regions in the post-war period and, eventually, the migration hinterland widened and family reunification came on the heels of labour migration. The factors underlying migration flows also largely coincided. Estonia was economically one of the most developed regions in the Soviet Union and experienced rapid industrial development immediately after the war. Because of the early demographic transition, the cohort born in the 1920s-40s was small in Estonia. Immigrants arrived mainly from the rural areas of Russia where agriculture dominated and the working-age population was numerous. The migration hinterland widened as the labour reserve exhausted itself. In the 1970s, industrial growth in Estonia slowed, although employment was continuously offered by the service sector. This brought along a change in the background of immigrants and replaced labour migration with family reunification. Furthermore, immigration was heavily governed by state administrations in both cases.

However, the Estonian case also displays distinctive peculiarities. First, immigration was relatively large and the streams were numerous during the whole post-war period. Second, the largest amount of immigrants arrived in the late 1940s and early 1950s. Third, labour migration to Estonia lasted longer. Its share decreased in the 1970s, but the change was not as dramatic as in the Western and Northern European countries. Fourth, it must be mentioned that although most of the immigrants were employed in industry, some were also directed to state and governmental institutions.

What are some of the reasons behind these differences? It is clear that peculiarities of recent Estonian history were crucial. First, Estonia lost control over its economy after it lost its independence. The direction of post-war economic development was determined outside Estonia, according to the Estonian place in the Soviet regional division of labour. As Estonia had a developed (although partly damaged) infrastructure, as well as natural resources and pre-war experience in industry, the Soviet central authorities induced forced industrialization immediately after the war. Rapid and extensive industrial development required an abundant supply of labour. As this did not exist in Estonia, immigration from areas where the working-age population was numerous was used to fill gaps.

At the same time, it is interesting to note that although migration streams to Estonia were directly organized by central authorities in the 1940s and 1950s, since the 1960s decentralized migration became dominant. The incentive for migration came from the industrial enterprises established in Estonia.[38] Thus, it may be argued that immigration to Estonia was very similar to immigration patterns in West and North European countries in the 1960s. In addition to forced industrialization, two more factors resulting from Estonian peculiarities promoted the extraordinarily large immigration of the first post-war decade. First, numerous members of the Communist Party, Soviet elites and soldiers were directed to Estonia immediately after the war to secure Soviet authority in the occupied areas and to guarantee the functioning of state institutions. Second, 7 to 9 per cent of the Estonian population left in 1944 as refugees. The proportion of refugees was 10 to 15 per cent among the 15-35 age group and 15 to 20 per cent among those in their twenties. Thus, the escape of Estonians to the West before the end of the war deepened the labour problem in post-war Estonia, adding to the problems of low pre-war fertility and war casualties.

As a consequence of intensive immigration, the Estonian population changed considerably more in the post-war period than the populations of Western and Northern European countries. First, the Estonian population increased by 1.8 times from 1945 to 1989. Conversely, population growth due to immigration was modest in the Western and Northern European countries. Second, immigrants formed one-fourth of the Estonian population by the end of the 1980s, while their share was less than one-tenth in most Western and Northern European countries.[39] Third, in the industrial regions, cities were formed in Estonia where immigrants and their descendants became the dominant population. Fourth, the integration of immigrants remained considerably lower in Estonia than in the Western and Northern European countries. Only one-tenth of the immigrants had command of the Estonian language at the end of the Soviet period.[40] The low level of integration among the foreign-born population became a major issue after the Estonian state regained its independence in 1991.[41]

Consequences and Challenges of Post-war Immigration: Redefining Citizenship

Post-war labour migration not only changed the demographic and social fabric of Western Europe and Estonia, it also affected their respective notions of nationhood and posed new questions regarding the incorporation of immigrants into citizenship, challenging existing frameworks of minority-majority relations. Thus, the interrelation between nationhood and citizenship has emerged as a critical issue in both Western Europe and Estonia. Despite these similarities it is important to point out differences between the two cases. Perhaps most importantly, while immigrants into Western European industrial countries such as Belgium, Germany and the Netherlands were often precluded from immediately gaining citizenship,[42] immigrants to Estonia already possessed full (Soviet) citizenship rights upon arrival, as Estonia was a part of the Soviet Union. This changed with the decline and collapse of Soviet communism. Post-war immigrants to Estonia, usually Russian speakers, were suddenly confronted with a choice: they could either take on Russian citizenship and consider migrating to Russia, or they could become stateless and apply for naturalization in Estonia once independence was restored and a new citizenship and naturalization law was introduced.[43]

Unlike most other former Soviet republics, Estonia did not choose the so-called 'zero option' upon independence; that is, not all residents automatically became Estonian citizens. After intensive internal debates, Estonia decided to pursue a 'restoration policy', whereby the country had not gained but rather restored its independence. Citizenship was only granted to those inhabitants (including about 80,000 people of non-

Estonian ethnic origin) whose ancestors had already been Estonian citizens before the annexation of the country by the Soviet Union in 1940.[44] Thus, post-war immigrants did not automatically acquire Estonian citizenship. Latvia also instituted a restoration policy, while Lithuania granted citizenship to all residents automatically, including a relatively small number of post-war immigrants.[45]

Estonia's new naturalization procedure requires two years residence (five years for post-1990 immigrants) and successful completion of an Estonian language test.[46] Learning the Estonian language, however, has turned out to be a significant problem for many Russian-speaking immigrants and their descendants. As a result, about two-fifths are still stateless,[47] enjoying all social and civic rights, along with the right to participate in local but not national elections.[48] Recently, language requirements for citizenship have been relaxed as a consequence of international pressure. Moreover, children of stateless individuals born in Estonia after 1991 can receive citizenship after their parents have applied for it.[49]

For a long time, labour migrants in the West, particularly the first generation born outside the receiving countries, were deprived of citizenship. In the 1990s, processes tended to move in the direction of easier access to full citizenship rights for immigrants and their offspring. This trend has come to include hitherto restrictive states, such as Germany, where the 1999 reform of the citizenship law introduced *ius soli*. From 1 January 2000 onward, children of legally resident aliens born in Germany will be granted German citizenship and nationality at birth.[50] The new provisions also make naturalization easier for first generation immigrants. Interestingly, both Germany and Estonia have made passing a mandatory language test a condition for naturalization. Thus, one might surmise that corresponding challenges within Eastern and Western European immigration countries have led to similar responses, particularly with regard to the place of language as a measure of successful integration.

Conclusion

Post-war labour and family reunification migration has hitherto been associated with capitalist Europe. This chapter has noted that similar migration streams existed in socialist Eastern Europe as well, especially between the republics of the former Soviet Union. Comparable Western and Soviet migration trends were based on differences in the economic development and population structures of sending and receiving countries. Differences between the cases resulted from different political and economic systems, as well as differences in historical development and wartime experiences, in particular.

This study suggests several avenues for further research. First, I would emphasize the need for studies that compare European countries with different histories. These studies would allow us to clarify both universal and more context-dependent determinants of population settlement and migration. Second, from a geographical point of view, the foreign-born population in Estonia might be further examined in two respects. First, the settlement and mobility of immigrants in the multicultural cities of Western and Northern Europe and those of Estonia could be compared. For instance, we know that residential differences among immigrants and native populations also occurred in the Soviet Estonian cities.[51] However, levels of segregation and the mechanisms that contributed to such outcomes are still unclear. Second, the settlement patterns of the descendants of immigrants call for further investigation. It is important to determine whether residential differences between this group and the native population have decreased and, if so, to analyze the extent of this trend. This would provide a clearer picture of the level of the integration of immigrant descendants of the Soviet era and thus add to our knowledge of a post-socialist society under transition.

Notes

This research was supported by the Estonian Science Foundation (grant no 3983).

1 Salt and Clout, *Migration in Post-war Europe.*

2 Glebe and O'Loughlin, *Foreign Minorities in Continental European Cities.*

3 King et al., 'The Urban Dimension of European Return Migration'.

4 Compton, 'Migration in Eastern Europe', p. 210; Fassmann and Münz, 'European East-West Migration', pp. 523-525; Fassmann and Münz, 'Vergangenheit und Zukunft der europäischen Ost-West-Wanderung'.

5 Katus and Sakkeus, 'Foreign-born Population in Estonia', p. 6.

6 Estonia was a part of Russian Empire from 1710-1917, an independent state from 1918-40, occupied by the Soviet Union from 1940-41, by Nazi Germany from 1941-44, and again by the Soviet Union from 1944-91.

7 Nigol, *Eesti asundused ja asupaigad Wenemaal.*

8 Tooms, 'Opteerimisliikumine ja Eestisse jõudnud optandid'.

9 Kulu, *Eestlased maailmas*, pp. 74-77.

10 Laas, 'Rahvastiku ränded Eestis', p. 89.

11 Palli, 'Baltisakslased: ränne ja kihid'.

12 Angelus, 'Ümberasumine Saksamaale', p. 121.

13 Parming, 'Population Changes in Estonia, 1935-1970'.

14 Kulu, 'Eestlaste tagasiränne 1940-1989', pp. 132-133.

15 Parming, 'Population Changes in Estonia, 1935-1970'.

16 Rahi, *1949. aasta märtsiküüditamine Tartu linnas ja maakonnas.*

[17] Kulu, 'Eestlaste tagasiränne 1940-1989', p. 133.
[18] Sakkeus, 'Post-war Migration Trends in Estonia', p. 18.
[19] Katus, 'Demographic Trends in Estonia throughout the Centuries', pp. 57-58.
[20] Sakkeus, 'Post-war Migration Trends in Estonia', pp. 4-5.
[21] The data from the Estonian Family and Fertility Survey are used to describe the changes in the background of immigrants. The retrospective survey was carried out in 1994 among 5,021 women born between 1924-1973, including 1446 people (29 per cent) born outside Estonia.
[22] Katus, 'Demographic Trends in Estonia throughout the Centuries', pp. 57-59.
[23] Kliimask, 'Economic Transformation in the Post-socialist City', pp. 155-157.
[24] Cf. Roose, *Andmeohje ja geoinfosüsteemide rakendusi*, p. 29.
[25] Kliimask, 'Economic Transformation in the Post-socialist City', pp. 155-157.
[26] Katus and Sakkeus, 'Foreign-born Population in Estonia', p. 6.
[27] Ibid., p. 17.
[28] Puur, 'Economic Activity in Transition', pp. 297-299.
[29] Ibid., p. 299.
[30] Salt, 'International Labour Migration', pp. 87-92.
[31] Seifert, 'Admission Policy, Patterns of Migration and Integration', pp. 447-452.
[32] Salt, 'International Labour Migration', pp. 87-92; Salt, 'A Comparative Overview of International Trends and Types', pp. 441-443.
[33] Ibid., p. 433; Champion, 'International Migration and Demographic Change', pp. 658-659.
[34] Jones, *Population Geography*, p. 244.
[35] Cf. Leitner, 'International Migration and the Politics', p. 264; Seifert, 'Admission Policy, Patterns of Migration and Integration', pp. 443-446.
[36] Salt, 'International Labour Migration', pp. 88-89.
[37] Jones, *Population Geography*, p. 248.
[38] Mängel, 'Nekotoryye aspekty migratsionnoy politiki', pp. 12-13.
[39] Katus and Sakkeus, 'Foreign-born Population in Estonia', p. 16.
[40] Ibid., p. 22.
[41] Tammaru, *Venelased Eestis: ränne ja kohanemine*.
[42] Cf. Leitner, 'International Migration and the Politics of Admission'.
[43] Lauristin and Vihalemm, 'Recent Historical Developments in Estonia', p. 111.
[44] Smith, Aasland and Mole, 'Statehood, Ethnic Relations and Citizenship', p. 185; Vihalemm and Lauristin, 'Cultural Adjustment to the Changing Societal Environment', p. 286.
[45] Smith, Aasland and Mole, 'Statehood, Ethnic Relations and Citizenship', pp. 183-185.
[46] Cf. Smith and Wilson, 'Rethinking Russia's Post-Soviet Diaspora', p. 851.
[47] Statistical Office of Estonia, '2000 Population and Housing Census II', p. 8.
[48] Vihalemm and Lauristin, 'Cultural Adjustment to the Changing Societal Environment', p. 286.
[49] Cf. Citizenship and Migration Board, 'Citizenship'.
[50] Green, 'Beyond Ethnoculturalism?'; Hagedorn, 'Falling Borders'.
[51] Raitviir, 'Factorial Ecological Structure of Tallinn'.

References

Angelus, Oskar, 'Ümberasumine Saksamaale', in: Richard Maasing, Evald Blumfeldt, Hans Kauri and Vello Pekomäe (eds), *Eesti riik ja rahvas Teises maailmasõjas*, Stockholm, 1955, pp. 121-126.

Champion, Anthony G., 'International Migration and Demographic Change in the Developed World', *Urban Studies* 41 (1994): pp. 653-677.

Citizenship and Migration Board, 'Citizenship', http://www.mig.ee/eng_index.html, 2002.

Compton, Paul, 'Migration in Eastern Europe', in: John Salt and Hugh Clout (eds), *Migration in Post-war Europe. Geographical Essays*, Oxford, 1976, pp. 168-215.

EFFS (Estonian Family and Fertility Survey), *The Individual Level Data on 1067 Immigrant Females Arrived in Estonia as Adults (15 and older)*, Data File, Estonian Interuniversity Population Research Centre, Tallinn, 1994.

Fassmann, Heinz and Rainer Münz, 'European East-West Migration', *International Migration Review* 28 (1994): pp. 520-538.

Fassmann, Heinz and Rainer Münz, 'Vergangenheit und Zukunft der europäischen Ost-West-Wanderung', in: Heinz Fassmann and Rainer Münz (eds), *Ost-West-Wanderung in Europa*, Cologne, Vienna and Weimar, 2000, pp. 11-47.

Glebe, G. and John O'Loughlin (eds), *Foreign Minorities in Continental European Cities*, Stuttgart, 1987.

Green, Simon, 'Beyond Ethnoculturalism? German Citizenship in the New Millennium', *German Politics* 9 (2000): pp. 105-124.

Hagedorn, Heike, 'Falling Borders: Liberal Trends in German Citizenship Politics', http://www2.smu.edu/tower/Hagedorn.html, 2000.

Jones, Hue, *Population Geography*, second edition, London, 1990.

Katus, Kalev, 'Demographic Trends in Estonia throughout the Centuries', *Yearbook of Population Research in Finland* 28 (1990): pp. 50-66.

Katus, Kalev and Luule Sakkeus, 'Foreign-born Population in Estonia', *Eesti Kõrgkoolidevaheline Demouuringute Keskus, rahvastiku-uuringud* B 19, 1993.

King, Russell L., A. Strachan and J. Mortimer, 'The Urban Dimension of European Return Migration: The Case of Bari, Southern Italy', *Urban Studies* 22 (1985): pp. 219-235.

Kliimask, Jaak, 'Economic Transformation in the Post-socialist City. The Case of Tallinn', in: Martin Åberg and Martin Peterson (eds), *Baltic Cities. Perspectives on Urban and Regional Change in the Baltic Sea Area*, Lund, 1997, pp. 151-167.

Kulu, Hill, *Eestlased maailmas*, Tartu, 1992.

Kulu, Hill, 'Eestlaste tagasiränne 1940-1989. Lääne-Siberist pärit eestlaste näitel', *Publicationes Instituti Geographici Universitatis Helsingiensis* C 9, 1997.

Laas, Kaljo, 'Rahvastiku ränded Eestis', *Eesti Geograafia Seltsi Aastaraamat* 22 (1987): pp. 81-97.

Lauristin, Marju and Peeter Vihalemm, 'Recent Historical Developments in Estonia: Three Stages of Transition (1987-1997)', in: Marju Lauristin, Peeter Vihalemm, Karl E. Rosengren and Lennart Weibull (eds), *Return to the Western World*, Tartu, 1997, pp. 73-126

Leitner, Helga, 'International Migration and the Politics of Admission and Exclusion in Postwar Europe', *Political Geography* 14 (1995): pp. 259-278.

Mängel, Toivo, 'Nekotoryye aspekty migratsionnoy politiki v Estonskoy SSR za poslevoyennyy period', in: Kalev Katus (ed.), *Podhody k upravleniyu migratsionnym razvitiyem*, Tallinn, 1989, pp. 11-17.

Nigol, August, *Eesti asundused ja asupaigad Wenemaal*, Tartu, 1918.

Palli, Heldur, 'Baltisakslased: ränne ja kihid', *Eesti Kõrgkoolidevaheline Demouuringute Keskus, rahvastiku-uuringud* B 39, 1998.
Parming, Tönu, 'Population Changes in Estonia, 1935-1970', *Population Studies* 26 (1972): pp. 53-78.
Puur, Allan, 'Economic Activity in Transition: Population of Foreign Origin in Estonia in the 1990s', *Trames* 4 (2000): pp. 286-316.
Rahi, Aigi, *1949. aasta märtsiküüditamine Tartu linnas ja maakonnas*, Tartu, 1998.
Raitviir, Tiina, 'Factorial Ecological Structure of Tallinn', in: Jaan-Mati Punning (ed.), *Estonia: Geographical Researches*, Tallinn, 1988, pp. 136-148.
Roose, Antti, *Andmeohje ja geoinfosüsteemide rakendusi keskkonnaökonoomilistes hinnangutes Ida-Virumaa näitel*, Tartu, 1993.
Sakkeus, Luule, 'Post-war Migration Trends in Estonia', *Eesti Kõrgkoolidevaheline Demouuringute Keskus, rahvastiku-uuringud* B 15, 1991.
Salt, John, 'International Labour Migration: The Geographical Pattern of Demand', in: John Salt and Hugh Clout (eds), *Migration in Post-war Europe. Geographical Essays*, Oxford, 1976, pp. 80-125.
Salt, John, 'A Comparative Overview of International Trends and Types, 1950-1980', *International Migration Review* 23 (1989): pp. 431-456.
Salt, John and Hugh Clout (eds), *Migration in Post-war Europe. Geographical Essays*, Oxford, 1976.
Seifert, Wolfgang, 'Admission Policy, Patterns of Migration and Integration: The German and French Case Compared', *new community* 23 (1997): pp. 441-460.
Smith, Graham, Aadne Aasland and Richard Mole, 'Statehood, Ethnic Relations and Citizenship', in: Graham Smith (ed.), *The Baltic States: The National Self-determination of Estonia, Latvia and Lithuania*, New York, 1994, pp. 181-205.
Smith, Graham and Andrew Wilson, 'Rethinking Russia's Post-Soviet Diaspora: The Potential for Political Mobilisation in Eastern Ukraine and North-east Estonia', *Europe-Asia Studies* 49 (1997): pp. 845-864.
Statistical Office of Estonia, *2000 Population and Housing Census II*, Tallinn, 2001.
Tammaru, Tiit, *Venelased Eestis: ränne ja kohanemine*, Tallinn, 1999.
Tooms, Anton, 'Opteerimisliikumine ja Eestisse jõudnud optandid', *Eesti Statistika kuukiri* 5 (1922): pp. 5-22.
Vihalemm, Triin and Marju Lauristin, 'Cultural Adjustment to the Changing Societal Environment: The Case of Russians in Estonia', in: Marju Lauristin, Peeter Vihalemm, Karl E. Rosengren and Lennart Weibull (eds), *Return to the Western World*, Tartu, 1997, pp. 279-297.

Chapter 4

Minorities into Migrants: Emigration and Ethnic Unmixing in Twentieth-Century Romania

Rainer Ohliger and Cătălin Turliuc

Within the meta-story of ethnic unmixing and ethnic cleansing in Central and Eastern Europe, Romania epitomizes a prototypical case. The country was subject to virtually all the elements that mark the transformation of a previously multiethnic state into a more homogeneous entity. Border revisions, population exchanges, forced and voluntary migrations, internal displacement, deportations, pro-natalist population policies, steered internal migration, planned settlement policies as well as genocide all contributed to making Romania ethnically (and socially) largely homogenous. Thus, Romanian political elites increasingly fulfilled the ethno-national imperative of making nation and state congruent. Whereas nearly a third of the population of post-World War I Greater Romania was made up of minorities, only roughly 10 per cent of present day Romania's total population consists of minorities. Minority migration, the focus of this article, contributed greatly, though not exclusively, to this process.

State – Population – Minorities: Ethno-demographic Structures and Developments

With the end of the First World War Romania doubled its size and population by gaining territories mainly inhabited by Romanians from the imploding Austro-Hungarian Empire (Transylvania, Bukovina), Soviet Russia (Bessarabia) and Bulgaria (southern Dobrudja).[1] As a consequence, the enlarged Romanian nation-state very quickly went from being ethnically rather homogeneous to multiethnic. The newly gained territories were extremely diverse ethnically, with 30 to 60 per cent non-Romanian population. Altogether the newly incorporated territories were inhabited by 6.1 million ethnic Romanians and 4.5 million members of other ethnic and national minorities. Among the roughly 30 per cent of Romanians who belonged to a minority group, ethnic Hungarians were the largest, with 1.4 million people (9.1 per cent), followed by Jews (778,000; 4.9 per cent) and ethnic Germans (713,000; 4.5 per cent). In the interwar period these three groups made up around 60 per cent of Romania's minority population.[2] Moreover, interwar Romania was populated by Ukrainians (in Bessarabia and the Bukovina), Turks (in the Dobrudja) and Bulgarians (in the Dobrudja, in Bessarabia and in the Banat), as well as some smaller often dispersed minorities such as Czechs, Slovaks, Poles and Serbs. The census of 1930 registered 582,000 Ukrainians (3.2 per cent), 409,000 Russians (2.3 per cent), 366,000 Bulgarians (2.0 per cent), 154,000 Turks (0.9 per cent) and 105,000 Gagauz (0.6 per cent).

Table 4.1 Ethno-demographic composition of Romania's population since 1920 in thousands (percentage of total)*

	Romanians	Hungarians	Germans	Jews	Roma	Others	Total
1920	11,545	1,463	713	778	133	1,411	16,043
	(71.9)	(9.1)	(4.5)	(4.9)	(0.8)	(8.8)	(100.0)
1930	12,981	1,426	745	728	263	1,914	18,057
	(71.9)	(7.9)	(4.1)	(4.0)	(1.5)	(10.6)	(100.0)
1948	13,598	1,500	344	139	53	239	15,873
	(85.7)	(9.4)	(2.2)	(0.9)	(0.3)	(1.5)	(100.0)
1956	14,996	1,588	385	146	104	270	17,489
	(85.7)	(9.1)	(2.2)	(0.8)	(0.6)	(1.6)	(100.0)
1966	16,747	1,620	383	43	64	247	19,104
	(87.7)	(8.5)	(2.0)	(0.2)	(0.3)	(1.3)	(100.0)
1977	19,004	1,707	359	26	230	235	21,561
	(88.1)	(7.9)	(1.7)	(0.1)	(1.1)	(1.1)	(100.0)
1992	20,353	1,620	119	9	401	258	22,760
	(89.4)	(7.1)	(0.5)	(0.1)	(1.8)	(1.1)	(100.0)

* 1948 data is based on mother tongue, all other data on ethnicity (self-declaration).

Source: Ohliger, *Vom Vielvölkerstaat zum Nationalstaat*, p. 287, based on Romanian censuses 1930, 1948, 1956, 1966, 1977, 1992 (Recensămîntul populaţiei); data for 1920 is calculated and estimated by the author.

The number of Roma was most likely considerably under-enumerated. Non-settled Roma were usually not counted at all; others were either assimilated, unaware of their ethnic affiliation, or illiterate and thus unable to fill out the questionnaire. Still others posed as members of other ethnic groups to prevent possible discrimination. These reservations need to be kept in mind for all twentieth-century census data, particularly those collected during the Communist period.

Periods of Migration

Romanian migration history in the twentieth century can be divided into four analytically and chronologically distinct periods. During these periods, members of various ethnic groups emigrated and immigrated for different reasons, as outlined below:

1. 1920 to 1939: Romania as country of emigration and immigration.
2. 1940 to 1947: Period of border revisions and forced migration guided by the principle of ethnic homogenization.
3. 1948 to 1989: The Communist system of state-governed migration with 'preferential' exit options for members of ethnic minorities.
4. Since 1989-90: The system of newly opened borders and new migration control and restrictions.

During the interwar period, Romania was a country of immigration and emigration. First, in the early 1920s, former Hungarian state and administrative elites left Transylvania, which until 1919 had belonged to the Hungarian part of the Austro-Hungarian Empire. From post-revolutionary Soviet Russia around 100,000 (political) refugees immigrated, particularly to Bessarabia, which previously had been part of the Russian Empire. Additionally, in the 1920s overseas emigration of Romanian citizens played a minor role.

During the second period, Romania's migration system was dominated by forced migrations and population exchanges following border revisions which were imposed on the country by the Hitler-Stalin pact (1939) and the Second Vienna Award (1940). Romania had to cede the northern Bukovina and Bessarabia to the Soviet Union and the southern Dobrudja to Bulgaria. These border revisions foreshadowed future population transfers and forced migrations. Nazi Germany, moreover, used the situation to 'repatriate' parts of Romania's ethnic German population, as part of its plan of ethnic cleansing and population redistribution along ethnic lines (so-called *Volkstumspolitik*). Most ethnic Romanians left northern Bukovina in 1939-40 and many fled from Bessarabia after these territories were annexed by the USSR. Ethnic German residents of these territories, as well as from the

Dobrudja, were resettled in the so-called *Warthegau*, Polish territory annexed by Germany. In 1940, Bulgaria and Romania exchanged their co-ethnic populations between the southern and northern Dobrudja.

During the third period, that is, between the end of the Second World War and the collapse of Communism in 1989, Romania became a country of emigration. This period was dominated by state-controlled population and migration policies. From the late 1940s onwards, Romania developed into a closed society, which strictly controlled and limited the spatial mobility of its citizens. For ethnic Romanians, it was almost impossible to leave this system legally. However, members of ethnic and national minorities, Jews and Germans in particular, and to a lesser extent ethnic Hungarians, were partly exempted from these restrictions. The national-Communist Romanian regime established a 'barter system' of migration: Jews and ethnic Germans were granted the right of exit in return for economic advantages granted to Romania by Israel or West Germany. This profitable business of exporting Romanian citizens as commodities to Western states only ended with the revolution of 1989. However, the dominance of ethnic migration only ended in 1990-91, when emigration from Romania became predominantly shaped by temporary, cyclical and often irregular or illegal forms of migration.[3] Until 1990, migration mostly affected the country's ethnic minorities. These patterns of ethnic migration increasingly dissolved after 1991-92. However, the direction of the migration streams have remained similar, going predominantly from East to West, in particular to Western Europe, the United States and Canada.

Processes of political and social transformation led to considerable changes in Romania's migration system in the 1990s, when the fourth period of migration commenced. Three distinctive features have characterized the newly emerging migration era. First, freedom of movement became possible after the Communist system was toppled. This led to an upswing in ethnic migration, continuing and expanding the pattern established during the Cold War. Specifically, ethnic Germans and ethnic Hungarians migrated en masse to Germany and Hungary during the early 1990s. Moreover, freedom of movement also created opportunities for ethnic Romanians to leave for Western, mainly Western European, countries, particularly as asylum seekers. However, freedom of movement (and recognition as refugees) for Romanian citizens was limited almost immediately after the fall of the Communist system. From 1990 onward, a strict visa system was introduced by Western European countries, this time limiting freedom of movement for Romanians to the West. De facto legal emigration was thus made impossible for Romanian citizens, except for the couple of thousand who temporarily came to Western European states as labour migrants within a system of bilateral contracts. However, the legal restriction, i.e., the mandatory visa system for Western Europe (Schengen countries), was lifted beginning of 2002. Even so, leaving the country now requires a substantial financial deposit at the Romanian border and a valid return ticket.

Historical Patterns of Ethnic Migration: The Jews

Of the four quantitatively dominant historical ethnic minorities in Romania, two, namely Germans and Jews, have disappeared, mostly by way of emigration (as well as persecution during the Second World War and in its aftermath). Roma and ethnic Hungarians, however, mostly remained in the country, though they have played an important role in Romania's recent emigration history, i.e., from the late 1980s to the present.

Jewish Emigration after the Second World War (1944-45 to 1947)

According to official census data, the number of Romanian Jews decreased from 728,000 to 138,000 people between 1930 and 1948.[4] These numbers are, however, disputed. Critics argued that the censuses undercounted the number of Romanian Jews. It is worth noting that the census of 1948 neither included the northern Bukovina with roughly 70,000 Jews in 1930, nor Bessarabia with 206,000 Jews. Moreover, in the 1948 census ethnic groups were only counted according to mother tongue, so that Jews assimilated to the Hungarian or Romanian languages did not show up as such. (In 1930, only 70 per cent of the Romanian Jews declared Yiddish as their mother tongue.) It is also likely that many Jews were afraid of discrimination after their wartime experiences and thus declared themselves to be Hungarian or Romanian. In fact, the 1956 census showed a higher number of Jews than the 1948 figures (1948: 138,000, 1956: 148,000). Given that Israeli immigration statistics show that 122,000 Romanian Jews immigrated to Israel between 1948 and 1956, it is most likely that the number of Romanian Jews after the end of the Second World War was around 260,000. Quantitative data about the Romanian Jewry in the period after the war is disputed. In particular, the number of Jews who perished in German concentration camps, were shot by members of the Romanian army or killed during deportations and internments by Romanian officials, is still unclear.[5] Romanian Jews in northern Transylvania (who again became Hungarian citizens between 1940 and 1945) were deported to German concentration camps in 1944 and thus mostly perished.[6] Romania did not send its Jewish population to German death camps, but did establish its own network of work and internment camps in Transnistria, in which approximately 90,000 of the 150,000 deportees starved and died. As early as 1938, discriminatory laws against Jews were passed and state repression was implemented and often followed by spontaneous pogroms, such as those in Iaşi, Dorohoi and Bucharest in 1941. After 23 August 1944, when Romania changed sides in the war and King Michael and the democratic political forces arrested dictator Marshall Ion Antonescu, the situation of the Jewish population changed. The new political regime abrogated the previous racial legislation.[7]

However, by 1944 the number of pre-war Romanian Jews had been reduced by almost half, as a result of the war and political measures directed against the community. Estimates of surviving Jews in post-war Romania range from 356,000 to 430,000 survivors.[8] After the war, the great majority of the Jewish population was in profound economic distress and was seriously affected by former discriminatory legislation, deportation and all kinds of hardships connected with the war. After the historical experiences of Jews in Romania the intention to build a future there was not particularly pronounced, despite the fact that initially Jewish social life as well as Jewish parties and NGOs were re-established.[9] A 1952 report by the World Jewish Congress stated that:

> The constitution recognized Jews as equal citizens, and laws for restitution of property and lost positions were both enacted and enforced. The Jews worked for their rehabilitation with admirable vigor and diligence. Synagogues and religious and communal organizations were revived; hospitals and homes for the aged people were opened; dozens of schools were established; sixteen Jewish periodicals sprang up; Jewish businessmen rebuilt their firms relatively quickly.[10]

However, the initial recognition of equality was replaced by new discrimination once the Communist system was established. The early expectation that Jewish property confiscated by the Antonescu regime would be returned to its former owners soon proved to be an illusion. Moreover, recently acquired political opportunities were suddenly rescinded in 1946, when, under Communist pressure, the Jewish Party was dissolved 'voluntarily'. The Jewish Democratic Committee was taken over by 'progressive elements' within the Communist Party. In November 1947, the Jewish Democratic Committee held a conference at which 'purification' of Jewish public and political life was agreed upon. This 'purification', or rather persecution of political dissidents, was carried out with the direct aid of the police. As a result, the Grand Rabbi of Romania, Alexandru Şafran, fled to Switzerland on 23 December 1947. This served as an important signal for many Romanian Jews considering the prospects of emigration.

However, with regard to emigration, the Jewish community living in Romania was of two minds. The main group, due to a large number of reasons including the Holocaust, economic misery, persistent anti-Semitism and other ideological and political factors, was strongly Zionist and in favour of immediate emigration. The second, smaller group was actively involved in the process of building a new (Communist) polity and society in Romania.[11] Thus, the majority of Romanian Jews wanted to leave the country. And even before the end of the Second World War, emigration of Romanian Jews started, in particular to Israel and the United States.

The Romanian government established in August 1944 was a strong supporter of Jewish emigration to Palestine and facilitated it with all its means and powers. The British authorities of Palestine were strongly against this policy. As a result, a large illegal emigration occurred. In November 1944, Turkish ships were allowed to carry Jews to Palestine, but in the following January the Soviets stopped these transports from the harbour city Constanţa. Still, during 1945 almost 3,000 Jews left Romania by boat or train in order to establish themselves in Palestine. This occurred with the acceptance of the British authorities. Moreover, a much larger, though unspecified number of Jews emigrated illegally from Romania to Palestine. For instance, in April 1946 the police in Sălaj county noted that: 'in March 33 Jews tried to cross the border illegally and in April another 40. All of them were young, less than 25 years old and belonging to both sexes...'.[12] Nicolas Sylvain claims that at least 40,000 Jews left Romania between 1944 and 1948.[13] This claim is supported by holdings in Romanian archives.

Soviet authorities (established in Romania as an occupying force) successfully encouraged large numbers of Jews living in Bessarabia, now a part of the USSR, to emigrate to Romania. Many of the Bessarabian Jews moved to Romania in order to emigrate to Palestine.[14] Moreover, a significant number of Jews entered Romania from the neighbouring countries, in particular from Hungary hoping for better living conditions and easier opportunities to emigrate to Palestine. As a result, the Romanian population's traditional anti-Russian attitudes were imbued with a strain antisemitism. Many Romanians commented negatively on the Russians' practise of returning Jews to Romania without the territories they inhabited before the war.[15] By the end of 1944, more than 70,000 requests to leave for Palestine were registered by Romanian authorities. According to Eliezer Frenkel, a Jewish lawyer working in Romania in 1945,[16] there were two main groups of Jews requesting permission to emigrate. Almost 60,000 were Romanian citizens who had lived in Romania for a long time but were deprived of their economic status. A second group, also of about 60,000 people, were formed by Jewish refugees from other countries and former inmates of concentration camps who now wished to find new homes in Palestine. In June 1945, the Jewish Telegraphic Agency announced that more than 150,000 Jews were registered to leave Romania.[17]

Jewish Emigration 1948 to 1965

After the establishment of Israel in 1948, immigration became legal and was propagated and encouraged by the new state. According to Israeli immigration statistics, 41,000 Romanian Jews lived in Israel in mid-1948. From then on, their number increased rapidly. Between the foundation of Israel in May 1948 and 1951, 117,000 Romanian Jews emigrated to Israel. Israel was not always the migrants' final destination, but often only a transit point for those who intended to settle in the United States. For instance, in 1952, only 56,000 Israelis claimed to be born in Romania, despite the fact that almost 120,000 had immigrated there between 1948 and 1951. Thus, for more than 50 per cent of the immigrants, Israel was a country of transit,[18] though it is likely that many of these immigrants had migrated from Romania without having been born there. In the 1950s, Romania limited the possibilities for Jewish emigration. Only in 1961, when a bilateral agreement was concluded which provided economic benefits for Romania, did emigration recommence on a larger scale. By and large, the time between 1948 and 1965 was marked by three emigration waves. More than 213,000 Jews left Romania in this period; 118,000 between 1948 and 1952, 32,000 between 1958 and 1960, and 64,000 between 1961 and 1965. Jewish emigration was practically stopped between 1952 and 1958. Emigration of Romanian Jews during this broad period was based largely on inherently internal reasons, namely resurgent antisemitism within the Communist Party and the state. However, external 'pull' factors, such as the perception of better living conditions in Israel and the ideological allure of Zionism, also encouraged immigration to Israel.

Between 1948 and 1952, the situation of Romania's Jewish population was shaped by two factors: the internal evolution of the Romanian Communist regime and the Soviet Union's policy toward Israel. Antisemitism became a major internal force from 1948 onwards and culminated in May 1952, when a decisive 'purge' of the Romanian Communist Party was launched. The purge was orchestrated with Moscow's approval and involved the leading party figure, Ana Pauker, who became victim of the purge *as a Jew*. The purge took on a distinctly anti-Jewish character right from the beginning. Already in 1948, a campaign directed against Zionism and Jewish communal life had been initiated following the anti-Zionist turn of the Soviet Communist Party.[19] The Romanian Communist rulers quickly jumped on the bandwagon. Attacks were launched against Zionism, 'Jewish nationalism' and Jewish organizations in general. In December 1948, the *politbureau* of the Romanian Workers Party (the official name of the Communist Party at that time) published a resolution on minorities containing a special paragraph condemning Zionism and 'Jewish nationalism'. It was concluded that a thorough reorganization of the Jewish Democratic Committee itself was necessary, in order to 'liberate' it from Zionist elements. The ideological campaign and the accompanying repression ultimately destroyed all Zionist organizations, including the most influential Jewish newspaper with a pro-Communist attitude, *Unirea*.

The attack on Jewish communal life was accompanied by police repression against Zionist organizations and by a violent drive to eradicate any Zionist influence in Jewish life.[20] On November 3, 1948, police forces raided the offices of the Jewish National Fund and the Palestine Foundation Fund and arrested some of their leaders. In December, the headquarters and offices of Zionist organizations were shut down along with the clubs affiliated with them. Within three months there was not a single Zionist association left in the country. Previously more than 110,000 Jews had been involved in the activities of these organizations. In 1949, an estimated 750 Zionists were in Romanian camps and jails. Numerous arrests and trials in which Jewish Zionist leaders were persecuted also marked the period between 1950 and 1954. Many of them were allowed to leave for Israel after having served several years in prison.[21]

1948 marked the last year of independence for Jewish schools. The 1948 Constitution stipulated that the Jewish population be taught 'in its mother language'. However, the previously independent Jewish schools were simply absorbed into the general state school system and restructured according to a Russian pattern. The two Jewish theatres in Bucharest and Iaşi were nationalized in 1948 and 1949 during the anti-Zionist campaign. Jewish religious communities were reorganized under a new statute published in 1949.[22] According to this statute, only one Jewish community was allowed to exist in each town. It had to encompass all Jewish religious groups. The Jewish communities had to belong to only one central body, the Federation of Romanian Jewish Communities, which was to become the supreme administrative authority. A Supreme Rabbinical Council of twelve members, appointed by the Ministry of Religions on the recommendation of the Federation, was to be the highest spiritual authority. No rabbi or religious functionary could be put into office, no religious services of any kind could be carried out without the consent of the new administrative body whose leadership was in Communist hands. Thus, in the 1950s, the general atmosphere in Romania was hostile toward Jews and dominated by antisemitism. Permits for emigration were not issued until 1958.

When the policy regarding Jewish emigration was changed again in autumn 1958, more than 100,000 Jews applied for exit visas.[23] The consequences of an application for emigration were quite dramatic for the applicant. As soon as Jews applied, they lost their jobs and their positions were filled by non-Jews. Homes were expropriated upon emigration and became state property. Moreover, the administrative process of emigration was characterized by discrimination, bribery and corruption.[24]

The emigration waves of Jews in the late 1940s-early 1950s and in the late 1950s-early 1960s led to an almost complete disappearance of Jewish life in Romania. From among the more than 140,000 Romanian Jews living in the country in 1956, more than 100,000 had left for Israel or the United States ten years later. In 1966, the Jewish minority had shrunk to only 40,000 people. The number of Jews of Romanian origin in Israel, however, had increased to 200,000 by the beginning of the 1970s. As such, Romanian Jews accounted for 6 per cent of the total Israeli population. The aging Jewish population in Romania was not only further decimated by emigration, but also by natural decrease, as an effect of high mortality rates.[25] It shrank to 25,000 people in 1977 and to 9,000 in 1992.[26] In the 1980s, between 1,200 and 1,600 Romanian Jews emigrated to Israel annually. Since the beginning of the 1990s, this number has fallen to only a few hundred.[27] This process of continuous decline was however not unique to Romania; it characterized most of Europe, with the notable exception of France, where, despite losses incurred during the Holocaust, the Jewish population grew and became quantitatively more important than before the Second World War. This came as a result of postcolonial immigration from the Maghreb in the second half of the twentieth century.

Historical Patterns of Ethnic Migration: Ethnic Germans

The emigration of ethnic Germans from Romania occurred in three phases. First, by way of planned resettlement according to bilateral treaties in 1940, second by way of flight and deportation in 1944-45 following the retreat of the German army from Romania, and third by way of emigration from the late 1960s onward.

In 1940, the 200,000 ethnic Germans (1930 census) from the Bukovina, Bessarabia and the Dobrudja were nearly completely resettled in occupied

Polish territories such as the *Warthegau* and western Prussia, as well as Upper Silesia, Alsace-Lorraine, Bohemia and Moravia, the Sudeten area and Lower Styria.[28] The resettlement, negotiated between Berlin, Bucharest and Moscow, was interrelated with the planning of the Holocaust and the expulsion or enslavement of Poles as forced labourers. Ethnic Germans were mostly settled in previously 'emptied' Polish and Jewish villages and houses.[29] The withdrawal of German troops from Romania in 1944 was accompanied by the resettlement of ethnic Germans. Around 20,000 ethnic Germans from northern Transylvania and 66,000 from the Banat area fled westward.[30] Moreover, in January 1945, 70,000 ethnic Germans of working age were deported upon Soviet command as forced labourers to the Soviet Union. Some of the survivors returned to Romania between 1947 and 1949; some were released to the Soviet zone, some to the western zone of occupied Germany.[31]

The number of ethnic Germans in Romania decreased to less than half of the previous population between 1930 and 1948 as an effect of war and its consequences. In the 1948 census, only 340,000 persons claimed to belong to the German minority. Until the late 1960s, the stock of ethnic Germans in Romania remained nearly constant before large-scale emigration to Western Germany started. War and its consequences had not only led to a quantitative decrease, but also to a social, economic and political weakening of the formerly socially and economically comparatively middle-class minority.[32] Resettlement, flight and deportation considerably changed ethnic German social structures and milieus which had been intact until the late 1930s. Families were pulled apart, their members dispersed to different countries such as Austria, Germany, the United States and Canada on the one hand, and Romania on the other. The early expropriation of ethnic Germans in Romania already in 1945 (three years before the Communist measures of socialization/nationalization) and deportation to the Soviet Union speeded up the uprooting of the remaining members of the minority.

Family unification formed the basis for the planned migration of Romania's ethnic Germans after 1945. Until the end of the 1950s, during the heyday of the Cold War, some one thousand ethnic Germans succeeded in emigrating to Western Germany with the help of the Red Cross. Overall, 15,000 ethnic Germans emigrated from Romania to West Germany between 1950 and 1966.[33] However, only the establishment of diplomatic relations between Romania and the Federal Republic of Germany in 1967 and the era of detente provided the possibility for larger-scale emigration. From the early 1970s onward, an average of 8,000 ethnic Germans emigrated annually from Romania to West Germany. In 1978, when the

Federal Republic and Romania concluded a bilateral treaty regulating the emigration (the Schmidt-Ceauşescu Treaty), some 69,000 ethnic Germans had already left the country. The treaty fixed a number of 10,000 ethnic German emigrants per year. As compensation, the Federal Republic agreed to pay DM 8,000 per migrant. This was a pattern Romania had already successfully practised when the Jews had left the country: granting freedom of movement against economic benefits.

Since the 1980s, the emigration of ethnic Germans has developed its own dynamic. Continuous emigration split up families, villages and church parishes. The incentive to leave the country increased as a result of declining social and cultural structures. Emigration also had an effect on those who remained or intended to remain in Romania, since the social and cultural life of the minority could no longer be maintained. The mass exodus after the implosion of the Communist system in 1989, when within three years 150,000 of 250,000 ethnic Germans emigrated, thus had its own internal logic. It became a predominantly self-induced process.[34] After the end of this emigration wave, the minority has been reduced to approximately 30,000 to 40,000 people at the beginning of the twenty-first century. The remaining ethnic German group in Romania is strongly biased toward old age and will most likely vanish more or less completely within a generation or so.

Historical Patterns of Ethnic Migration: Ethnic Hungarians

The emigration of ethnic Hungarians occurred in three waves in the twentieth century. In contrast to the emigration of Jews and ethnic Germans, however, this emigration did not lead to the disappearance of the minority. The first phase of the Hungarian exodus started after the end of World War I. Through the Romanianization of the state administration, politics and cultural life in the formerly Hungarian territories, Hungarian elites lost their dominant role and partly also their professional existence. Moreover, the new Romanian government tried to legally and economically privilege the ethnically Romanian population in the newly gained territories. The promise of the Decrees of Alba Iulia of 1918 to establish and practise a tolerant minority protection was not or not fully realized after 1918.[35] The fight for cultural hegemony in Transylvania further alienated the Hungarian minority from the Romanian state and increased the inclination to emigrate.[36] According to official Hungarian data, 200,000 ethnic Hungarians left Transylvania between 1919 and 1924.[37]

The annexation of northern Transylvania by Hungary in 1940, by way of the Second Vienna Award, caused a re-migration of Hungarian state officials; however, this process was short-lived. In 1945-46, 125,000 ethnic Hungarians left Transylvania for Hungary. The third wave of Hungarian emigration started in the mid-1980s. Between 1985 and 1989 between 30,000 and 40,000 ethnic Hungarians left Romania for Hungary as an effect of economic misery in Romania and economic reforms and a better standard of living in Hungary. Romanian sources registered more than 32,000 legal ethnic Hungarian emigrants between 1985 and 1989. Hungarian and international sources speak of more than 40,000 emigrants before 1989.[38] The Romanian government responded to the increase of illegal emigration of ethnic Hungarians by closing the border and in 1988 even constructing a fence, but the project was abandoned within the year.[39] After the changes in 1989, the number of ethnic Hungarian emigrants increased again. Reinforced by anti-Hungarian riots, violently culminating in 1990 when ethnic Hungarians died in Tîrgu-Mureş, 22,000 Magyars left Romania by 1993. Since then, emigration of ethnic Hungarians has drastically decreased.[40] Only a couple of thousand have left the country each year legally. On the other hand, black labour markets in Budapest and the Romanian-Hungarian border areas have emerged and are served by ethnic Hungarians from Romania who benefit from the wage differentials between the two countries.[41]

Despite these emigration waves, according to official Romanian data 1.6 million ethnic Hungarians still live in Romania. Representatives of Hungarian associations even claim that the number is around two million. A major reason for a relatively and comparatively lower rate of emigration among ethnic Hungarians is not least their spatial concentration. For instance, the two administrative districts Harghita (1992 census: 84.7 per cent) and Covasna (75.2 per cent) in the very heartland of the Romanian nation-state have an ethnic Hungarian majority. Thus, not only everyday life, but also education and culture are predominantly Hungarian in these districts. Assimilation is not an issue or a danger for the minority populations of these regions.

Conclusion

The twentieth century has not been very kind to minorities in Central and Eastern Europe. They have often fallen victim to nationalist policies aimed at assimilating them or physically excluding them from their territories. Displacement, deportations, border changes, 'ethnic cleansing', expulsions and (forced) emigration, if not genocide, figured prominently among these measures. In this respect, the century certainly was an 'age of extremes'.[42]

In Central and Eastern Europe, the nations, at least theoretically, eventually inherited the state after the implosion of the multiethnic empires in 1918. This left minorities in many cases trapped within newly created or enlarged nation-states. The rise of nationalism during the twentieth century made minorities a prime topic of domestic and international concern. Within the triadic interrelation[43] of nationalizing nation-states, (potential) homelands or patron states and minority or diaspora groups, minority existence was transformed decisively. Most Central and Eastern European nationalizing nation-states pursued the goal of achieving ethnic purity within their borders. Conversely, minorities often aligned themselves with their putative mother countries or patron states, which exercised and implemented politics aimed at protecting and/or privileging their co-ethnic minorities in neighbouring or even more distant states. This special interrelation between minorities and their patron states had several consequences. First, homelands opened exit options for co-ethnic minorities. Thus, the opportunity to emigrate, find refuge and establish a permanent home in homelands emerged. Second, the exit option came with full political integration; that is, these immigrants were given homeland citizenship upon arrival. In the Romanian case, the country's German and Jewish minorities enjoyed the possibility of becoming full legal members of their respective patron states, Germany and Israel, for all of the post-World War II period. This exit option was a necessary, though not yet a sufficient precondition to spur minority migration.[44] Nationalist or discriminatory host state politics were needed to alienate minorities from their traditional settlement areas and thus make them prone to emigrate.

In the Romanian case the dynamic between minorities, the host state and national homelands was particularly important for two of the four largest minority groups, ethnic Germans and Jews, but only to a lesser extent for ethnic Hungarians (and not at all for Roma, who lacked a homeland or patron state to which they could have emigrated). The decisive legal and political changes happened right after the end of the Second World War. With the establishment of Israel and an Israeli policy granting citizenship to Jews all over the World ('Law of Return'), a homeland option was created for Romanian (and other) Jews. (West) Germany also offered the remaining ethnic Germans in Central and Eastern Europe citizenship. Romania, the third state actor on this stage, contributed by implementing a minority policy, which was, to say the least, inhospitable to minorities.[45]

Minority migration had considerable effects on both host and homeland societies. Patron states were confronted with the incorporation of co-ethnic immigrants and had to justify the privileged incorporation of these migrants vis-à-vis the native population which was not always receptive and welcoming. Though these co-ethnic immigrants were officially considered alike and easy to integrate, they often did not 'fit' into the homeland society or remained outsiders, thus once again becoming marginalized – the very status they wanted to rid themselves of via emigration. For countries of origin, in our case Romania, minority migration usually meant 'streamlining' the society's diversity and making it ethnically more homogeneous. In Romania, this process is more than obvious if one analyzes and compares the demographic figures throughout the twentieth century. However, while Romania might be a prototypical case, it is not an exception in Central and Eastern Europe. Most of the nation-states in this region of the world followed a demographic policy of engineering ethnic homogeneity by ethnically 'unmixing' their populations. The events of the 1990s have shown that this process has not yet become mere history.

Notes

1 The southern Dobroudja had already become Romanian after the end of the Second Balkan War in 1913.

2 Kolár, *Rumänien und seine nationalen Minderheiten*.

3 Diminescu, *Deplaşările oaşenilor in strainătate* and Diminescu and Lagrave, *Faire une saison*.

4 Zach, *Rumänien*, p. 404.

5 Ibid., p. 407.

6 In 1940, Romania lost 93,364 out of 295,049 sq. km of its territory and one third of its total population to Hungary, the USSR and Bulgaria. 58 per cent of Romanian Jews lived in these territories, 275,000 in Bessarabia and 150,000 in Northern Transylvania.

7 Benjamin and Stanciu, *Evreii din Romania între anii 1940-1944*.

8 Filderman and Manuila, *Regional Development of the Jewish Population in Romania* and Hilberg, *The Destruction of the European Jews*.

9 Turliuc, *Jewish Emigration from Romania 1945-1965*.

10 Open Society Archives (OSA), Box 279, Folder 1100, item No. 3711/52.

11 The relationships between Romanian Jews and the Romanian Communist Party is still a hotly debated and controversial issue in current Romanian historiography.

12 National Archives Bucharest (ANB), Inspectoratul general al jandarmeriei centrală, dosar 50/1946, vol. III, f. 92.

13 Sylvain, *Rumania*, p. 531.

14 ANB, Direcţia Generală a Poliţiei, dosar 3/1946, f. 444.

15 Fischer-Galati, *Communism and the Jewish Question in Romania*, p. 173.

16 Quoted by Sylvain, *op. cit.*, p. 530.

17 Şandru, *Imigrarea şi emigrarea evreilor* 1944-1948, p. 256.

18 *Statistical Abstract of Israel*, pp. 22 and 26.

19 Letter to Alexander R. in '*Pravda*', 21 September 1948.

20 OSA, Box 279, Folder 1100, item No.1015/51.

21 Ibid., *item No. 7503/55.*

22 *Monitor Oficial*, 12 July 1949.
23 OSA, Box 279, Folder 1100, item No.327/64.
24 Ibid., *item No. 3070/58.*
25 Kuller, *Opt studii despre istoria evreilor din Romania*, p. 12.
26 Wasserstein, *Vanishing Diaspora.*
27 Comisia Natională pentru Statistica, *Anuarul Statistic al României 1997*, pp. 150f.
28 Jachomowski, *Die Umsiedlung der Bessarabien-, Bukowina- und Dobrudschadeutschen*, pp. 150-197 and Kulischer, *The Displacement of Population in Europe*, p. 16f.
29 Aly, *Endlösung*, p. 59.
30 Statistisches Bundesamt, *Die deutschen Vertreibungsverluste*, pp. 474f. These numbers, however, are disputed.
31 Weber, *Die Deportation von Siebenbürger Sachsen.*
32 It should be noted that the plural 'minorities' is more precise as ethnic Germans in what became Romania after 1918 were not a coherent, but a historically, socially, economically and religiously very diverse group.
33 *Info-Dienst Deutsche Aussiedler.*
34 Sterbling, *Die Aussiedlung der Deutschen aus Rumänien*, pp. 66-74.
35 Illyés, *Nationale Minderheiten in Rumänien*, p. 100.
36 Seewann, *Migrationen und ihre Auswirkungen.*
37 Kulischer, *Europe on the Move*, p. 149 and Dövényi/Vukovich, *Hungary and International Migration*, pp. 187-206.
38 Comisia Natională pentru Statistica,, 150f.; Kendé, *Flüchtlinge aus Rumänien in Ungarn*; OECD, *SOPEMI 1995*, 142f.; OECD, *SOPEMI 1999.*
39 The Minority Rights Group, *Romania's Ethnic Hungarians*, p. 19.
40 Fullerton, Sik and Tóth, *From Improvization Toward Awareness?.*
41 OECD *op. cit.* 1995, p. 144; OECD, *op. cit.* 1999.
42 Hobsbawn, *Age of Extremes.*
43 Brubaker, *Nationalism Reframed.*
44 Turliuc, *The National Minorities of Romania.*
45 Kendi, *Minderheitenschutz in Rumänien.*

Archival Sources

National Archives Bucharest (ANB)
Inspectoratul general al jandarmeriei centrală, dosar 50/1946, vol. III, f. 92
Direcţia Generală a Poliţiei, dosar 3/1946, f. 444

Open Society Archives
Box 279, Folder 1100, item No. 3711/52
Box 279, Folder 1100, item No.1015/51
Box 279, Folder 1100, item No.327/64

References

Aly, Götz, *Endlösung. Völkerverschiebung und der Mord an den europäischen Juden.* Frankfurt/M., 1995.
Benjamin, Lya and Sergiu Stanciu (eds), *Evreii din Romania între anii 1940-1944.* Vol. I. Legislaţia antievreiască. Bucharest, 1993.

Brubaker, Rogers, *Nationalism Reframed. Nationhood and the National Question in the New Europe*. Cambridge, 1996.
Comisia Natională pentru Statistica (ed.), *Anuarul Statistic al României 1997*. Bucharest, 1998.
Diminescu, Dana, 'Deplaşările oaşenilor in strainătate, un nou model de migraţie', in: *Revista de Cercetări Sociale*, 3, 2 (1996): pp. 16-33.
Diminescu, Dana and Rosemarie M. Lagrave, 'Faire une saison', *Migrations/Etudes*, no. 91/1999.
Dövényi, Zoltan and Gabriella Vukovich, 'Hungary and International Migration', in: Heinz Fassmann and Rainer Münz (eds), *European Migration in the Late Twentieth Century: Historical Patterns, Actual Trends, and Social Implications*. Aldershot, 1994, pp. 187-206.
Filderman, Wilhelm and Sabin Manuila, *Regional Development of the Jewish Population in Romania*. Rome, 1957.
Fischer-Galati, Stephen, 'Fascism, Communism and the Jewish Question in Romania', in: Bela Vago and George O. Mosse (eds), *Jews and Non-Jews in Eastern Europe 1918-1945*. New York, 1974.
Fullerton, Maryellen, Endre Sik and Judith Tóth (eds), *From Improvization Toward Awareness? Contemporary Migration Politics in Hungary*. Budapest, 1997.
Hilberg, Raoul, *The Destruction of the European Jews*. Chicago, 1961.
Hobsbawm, Eric J., *Age of Extremes. The Short Twentieth Century 1914-1991*. London, 1994.
Illyés, Elemér, *Nationale Minderheiten in Rumänien. Siebenbürgen im Wandel*. Vienna, 1981.
Info-Dienst Deutsche Aussiedler 2000. Zahlen – Daten – Fakten. Bonn, 2000.
Jachomowski, Dirk, *Die Umsiedlung der Bessarabien-, Bukowina- und Dobrudschadeutschen. Von der Volksgruppe in Rumänien zur 'Siedlungsbrücke an der Reichsgrenze'*. Munich, 1984.
Kénde, Peter, *Flüchtlinge aus Rumänien in Ungarn*. Budapest, 1989.
Kendi, Erich, *Minderheitenschutz in Rumänien*. Munich, 1992.
Kolár, Otmar, *Rumänien und seine nationalen Minderheiten*. Vienna, Cologne and Weimar, 1997.
Kulischer, Eugene M., *The Displacement of Population in Europe*. Montreal, 1943.
Kulischer, Eugene M., *Europe on the Move. War and Population Changes 1917-1947*. New York, 1948.
Kuller, Hary, *Opt studii despre istoria evreilor din Romania*. Bucharest, 1997.
The Minority Rights Group, *Romania's Ethnic Hungarians. A Minority Rights Group Report*. London, 1990.
Monitor Oficial, 12 July 1949.
OECD (Organization for Economic Co-operation and Development), *SOPEMI. Trends in International Migration. Continuous Reporting System on Migration. Annual Report*. Paris, 1995.
OECD (Organization for Economic Co-operation and Development), *SOPEMI. Trends in International Migration. Continuous Reporting System on Migration. Annual Report*. Paris, 1999.
Ohliger, Rainer, 'Vom Vielvölkerstaat zum Nationalstaat. Auswanderung und Einwanderung von und nach Rumänien im 20. Jahrhundert', in: Rainer Münz and Heinz Fassmann (eds), *Migration in Europa. Historische Entwicklung, aktuelle Trends, politische Reaktionen*. Frankfurt/M., 1996, pp. 285-302.
Şandru, Dumitru, 'Imigrarea şi emigrarea evreilor 1944-1948', in: *Anuarul Institutului de Istorie "A.D. Xenopol"* Vol. XXXIV. Iaşi, 1996, pp. 234-262.

Seewann, Gerhard (ed.), *Migrationen und ihre Auswirkungen. Das Beispiel Ungarn, 1918-1995*. Munich, 1997.

Statistical Abstract of Israel 1951-52. Jerusalem, 1952.

Statistisches Bundesamt (ed.), *Die deutschen Vertreibungsverluste*. Wiesbaden, 1958.

Sterbling, Anton, 'Die Aussiedlung der Deutschen aus Rumänien: Motive, Randbedingungen und Eigendynamik eines Migrationsprozesses', in: Rainer Münz, Hermann Korte and Gert Wagner (eds), *Demographie aktuell, No. 5, Internationale Wanderungen*. 28. Arbeitstagung der Deutschen Gesellschaft für Bevölkerungswissenschaft 1994. Berlin, 1994, pp. 66-74.

Sylvain, Nicolas, Rumania, in: Peter Meyer et al. (eds), *The Jews in the Soviet Satellites*. Syracuse, NY, 1953.

Turliuc, Cătălin, 'Jewish Emigration from Romania 1945-1965', in: *Studia et Acta Historiae Iudeorum Romaniae*. Vol. VI. Bucharest, 2001, pp. 268-287.

Turliuc, Cătălin, 'The National Minorities of Romania during the "People's Democracy"', in: *Transylvanian Review*, 10 (2001): pp. 142-150.

Wasserstein, Bernard, *Vanishing Diaspora. The Jews in Europe since 1945*. Cambridge, MA, 1996.

Weber, Georg, *Die Deportation von Siebenbürger Sachsen in die Sowjetunion 1945-1949*. 3 Vol. Cologne, Vienna and Weimar, 1995.

Zach, Krista, 'Rumänien', in: Wolfgang Benz (ed.), *Dimensionen des Völkermords. Die Zahl der jüdischen Opfer des Nationalsozialismus*. Munich, 1991, pp. 381-409.

Chapter 5

Female Professional Immigration in Post-war Europe: Counteracting an Historical Amnesia

Umut Erel and Eleonore Kofman

At a time when skilled migration is being encouraged in Western European states, it would seem appropriate to examine our representations of the contributions and experiences of professional migrants, especially female professionals, in past flows to Europe. Immigrants are overwhelmingly represented as being unskilled and simply contributing to labour shortages in agriculture, manufacturing and low-level service sectors. The significance of female migrants in the labour force has in particular been occluded; the stereotypical image is of the female dependent of the male labourer who entered through family reunion after the stoppage of mass labour immigration in the mid-1970s. The reinterpretation of historical patterns of settlement and the use of qualitative sources shows that this image fails to reflect the reality of the period. Our knowledge of the situation in different countries is however still very partial. In the United Kingdom (UK) with its Irish and colonial flows, women from the Irish Republic and the Caribbean filled many of the intermediate professions, such as nursing and social work.[1] Commonwealth migrants from Australia, Canada and New Zealand are in the majority female and often highly skilled. In Germany, many Turkish women, as autobiographical and case study material reveals, sought emancipation;[2] many, however, did not find it in professional employment but were forced to take up unskilled work in factories. The de-skilling of those years continues today, as is the case with many of the highly qualified women who have come to Germany from Eastern Europe.[3] In this chapter we argue that professional and skilled women did migrate to the European Union countries in post-war years, though to varying degrees, as our comparison of Germany and the UK highlights. Many of these women were often forced to work in unskilled sectors, thus rendering the presence of skilled female migrants invisible. In the second section of the chapter, we illustrate the impact of migration on the professional trajectory of such women's lives through an examination of case studies of two women from Turkey in Germany and the UK.

Feminist Contributions to the Analysis of European Immigration

The first studies to incorporate women into analyses of international migration in European countries were written at the beginning of the 1970s by women of immigrant origin. Early feminist research on migration aimed to increase the visibility of women within migratory streams. Research carried out by Morokvasic in the mid 1970s was among the first to point out the extent to which migration represented not simply an enforced response to economic hardship by single, widowed or divorced women, but also a deliberate, calculated move on the part of individual gendered actors to escape from a society where patriarchy was an institutionalized and repressive force.[4] Since 1975, a number of conferences have focused on migrant women. However, despite a proliferation of studies, many scholars have perpetuated the stereotype of women as wives and mothers. Upon closer inspection, what quickly becomes apparent is the diversity in women's experiences; women were migrating for employment, as parts of households, or to join family members who had already migrated.

Different countries developed different emphases in the way they studied female migrants. In the UK, political economy approaches stressed participation and exploitation in the labour market.[5] It was difficult to ignore the labour market presence of Irish and Caribbean women who tended to occupy, to a higher degree than indigenous women, full-time jobs. In West Germany, although migrant women, especially amongst Yugoslavs and Greeks, participated to a greater extent in the labour market than indigenous women, there were few studies of their working lives. Between 1976 and 1980, the literature focused on Turkish women and three main themes emerged: the uncivilized stranger, the victim of patriarchal honour, and the experience of being 'twice rootless'.[6]

The first stocktaking occurred in the early 1980s, in the shape of the publication *Women on the Move*, with chapters by Abadan-Unat and Morokvasic on Europe. Around the same time, Phizacklea offered a structuralist analysis of labour migration in *One Way Ticket*. These analyses downplayed the non-economic factors influencing emigration. The lacuna was particularly important in the context of understanding women's migration because the reasons often included marital discord and physical violence, the impossibility or difficulty of divorce, and the prevalence of conservative social legislation and practices. Bretell and Simon subsequently edited a volume on migrant women, which emphasized cultural elements influencing migration, family life and reproduction and recognized a greater variety of migrant categories, including refugees.[7] A bibliography compiled by Taravella demonstrated that by the 1980s a variety of themes had been addressed, such as professional training, culture, adaptation, legal situation, health, etc.[8] Since then, studies of female migration have almost exclusively been based on case studies and biographical material. By the 1990s a large number of case studies had accumulated, some of which provide a more European-wide perspective.[9]

Most works that have explored female migration to Europe have been undertaken by sociologists.[10] Initially this led to an emphasis in the literature on the social construction of the labour market. More recent work has been heavily influenced by cultural analysis, with a focus on representations of migrants and on the meanings that they attach to their lived experiences, resulting in a relative neglect of new forms of migration and the changing structural factors and immigration legislation which has shaped migratory flows. The focus has shifted from the experiences of migrants to that of minorities, those with a more settled migrant status, and often children of migrants.

Recent years have witnessed an increase in work that draws on multiple sources and methods to develop cross-disciplinary approaches to the study of migration. Biographical studies and narratives are increasingly being incorporated into accounts of migration. There has also been a growth of interest in literature written by migrants which connects conditions in the homeland with the movement to the destination countries and describes migratory experiences as well as relationships with the dominant society.[11] This has become more significant with the burgeoning literature on diaspora[12] and transnationalism.[13] Autobiographical accounts of women across different generations are being used to understand the changing class and gender experiences.[14] Chamberlain used oral histories to demonstrate familial networks and the movements between the homeland and receiving countries.[15] Commemorative historiography has also come of age, as for instance, with the literature and documentaries that have traced and explored the history of Caribbean migration to the UK since the late 1940s. The new fields of interest and the accumulation of studies, including those which are Europe-wide, have yet to make any substantial impact on theorizations of migration or European studies of migration. A selection of key texts confirms this silence and the assumption that the only migrant who counts is male.[16]

What has emerged has been a diversity of categories of migration, new and traditional: labour (legal and undocumented), family reunion and formation, marriage, prostitution, asylum seekers and refugees. The effects of immigration policy on the status and exclusion of women from the labour market and social rights is also generating attention.[17] While there has been an increasing recognition of the rapidity and the significance of changes in migratory experiences in recent decades within Europe, and complex theorizations of these processes, there has been little attempt to acknowledge the explicitly gendered nature of these experiences in mainstream analysis.[18] On the whole, gender has rarely been considered a significant analytical category within the European literature on migration, which has remained gender blind. Migrants have been treated as asexual categories and feminists researching women have often focused on nationals rather than immigrant women. European research also fails to incorporate the recent meso-level of analysis in migration research,[19] which emphasizes the role of households and wider social networks in migration decisions.

Professional and Skilled Female Migrants

If gender issues in the development of European migrations have still not been adequately integrated, it is even more so for recognition of the presence of educated and professional women. It is virtually impossible to find much discussion of women or gender relations in studies of skilled migration, except for the occasional statistics on the gender breakdown of employment. While this might not have been surprising in the earlier period of the 1960s and 1970s, when fewer women participated in the higher education system and migrated independently, it surely must seem aberrant today. Even so, in some sectors, such as nursing and teaching, especially in primary schools, it was women who almost exclusively constituted the workforce several decades ago. In the UK, there was a considerable amount of skilled and professional migration, largely from the New and Old Commonwealth. Many students from the Commonwealth and beyond came to study and were subsequently able to switch their residence status. The diffusion of educational systems throughout the Commonwealth also meant that qualifications were recognized in the UK, unlike the situation in many other European states.

From the 1960s onward, many of the labour shortages were in welfare sectors, such as health, education and social work. Some of these were already feminized, others, such as doctors, began to increase their percentage of female professionals in subsequent decades. These sectors, especially in the metropolitan centres, were unable to recruit from the indigenous population. In the United Kingdom, both public hospitals and general medical practices came to rely on foreign doctors, who until the 1990s came predominantly from the Indian subcontinent. Supply teachers tended to be recruited from the Old Commonwealth. And unlike the situation in Germany and the Netherlands,[20] Caribbean social workers did not mainly deal with ethnic populations. The transfer of interest from brain drain to the relationship between skilled international migration and economic globalization has overlooked important and continuing migratory flows of welfare professionals. For example, the cosmopolitan composition of doctors is higher than in any other profession in both the US and the UK, where foreign doctors are employed in the lower echelons of the health service.

The European research agenda is heavily influenced by British research in its typologies of skilled migration[21] and its emphasis on the economic reasons for migration in the context of a human capital approach. The social dimension and its interaction with the economic have, in contrast, been weakly developed. Furthermore, attention has focused on transfers within multinational companies while in fact a far wider range of professional personnel are involved in international movements. Koser and Salt distinguished twelve categories, including corporate transferees, professionals, consultants, entertainers, business people, academics, researchers and students, as well as spouses and children of these categories.[22] While intra-company transfers have reinforced global reach and interaction, in effect the current emphasis on this group means that only a few of the categories listed by Salt are being intensively studied. Yet some of the understudied categories are worthy of attention. Large numbers of students, some of whom remain and take up professional employment, were attracted to high quality educational institutions in the UK, France and Germany. In many countries, including EU states such as Greece, there is insufficient provision across a range of disciplines and professional training and this has led to high levels of student emigration. France has the second highest foreign student population in the world after the USA. Indeed, 56 per cent of foreign students entering France in 1996 were women.[23]

Until the 1980s, it was much easier in many countries to switch from a student category to a work permit. As Ackers shows in her study of EU female migrants, many originally moved as students or to improve their linguistic ability and then stayed in the country either because they found work and/or married.[24] Researchers, unlike students, have found their rights to work facilitated in many countries. In France, for example, a number of Algerian researchers have benefited from assistance in securing refuge, while schemes for Eastern Europeans have been expanded.

Apart from the welfare professions, computing specialists are also very much in demand. This may only have reached the headlines in the summer 2000 with several European countries starting to confront shortages in this field. Germany announced 20,000 contracts for IT specialists, many of whom are likely to be recruited from Eastern Europe and India. Similarly France and the UK have announced that they will increase the number of permits in specified professional fields. British immigration policy is currently overturning the restrictions of the past 30 years, at least for skilled categories. This includes the traditional shortage areas of welfare professionals as well as information technology. However, we know little about the channels of immigration for the latter sector and the history of its development. There are a number of large recruiting companies in India which send IT specialists on projects throughout the world. The longer-term contracts (two years) are normally filled by men and operate within a corporate system. Shorter-term (three- to six-month) contracts have a higher female proportion, usually young single women.[25]

We might well ask why women are still so invisible and gender issues absent from the agenda on skilled migration. In a comprehensive review of the subject, Koser and Salt[26] comment that a recent trend in the mainstream literature has been to locate migration within a broader social and cultural context and that feminist discourses have been one of the contributing factors. This statement is taken no further nor the topic thought worthy of inclusion as a future issue for examination. The reticence toward gender issues is symptomatic of its painfully slow recognition in mainstream migration literature, despite the availability of numerous critiques of dominant theorizations and empirical studies undertaken by feminist scholars.[27] As we noted, women are still largely treated as dependants or as providers of unskilled labour. Yet skilled female migration is becoming more crucial as households increasingly rely on two incomes, and as women have entered higher education and gained a greater degree of independence. Increasingly, studies in traditional societies of immigration such as Australia, Canada and the United States are beginning to realize the significance of female skilled migration in professional flows. Many may enter not as part of the skilled quota, but in the context of family reunion. At the same time, research is seeking to highlight the problems faced by many women as a result of the inability to deploy their skills or receive appropriate training resulting from their status as dependants of principal applicants.[28]

The significance of social factors and the use of migration as a way out of social control and oppressive situations play a far more important role in female migration. Stalker calls this migration for social emancipation.[29]

The ability to migrate for these purposes is likely to be greater for the educated and those who have economic, social and cultural capital. For some it may mean a period of de-skilling before they are able to retrain and acquire the required linguistic skills. It is also often the fate of refugees whose qualifications are not recognized and need to find new ways of redeploying their knowledge or recycling themselves.[30] Nowadays many highly qualified women migrants are forced to accept employment as domestics and carers, occupations which are classified as unskilled.[31]

There are, of course, exceptions to the representation of women migrants as unskilled workers, including Morokvasic's study of migrant women entrepreneurs,[32] Bhachu's critique of a unidimensional view of Asian women[33] and Lutz's study of migrant women as community mediators in the welfare sector.[34] However, by concentrating on unskilled female migrants in Europe, feminist studies have oddly enough played a part in obscuring the visibility of skilled female migrants. The European research which, in the 1980s, put female migration on the agenda, wanted to demonstrate above all that women worked and were not confined to the home or domestic responsibilities.[35] Mainstream research has tended to assume that family reunion migrants did not work or, if they did, it was for pin money and in unskilled jobs. Even today we know very little about the employment patterns of women who are admitted as family migrants,[36] which in most European Union countries remains the single most significant form of legal immigration. There is evidence from one of the few large-scale studies of groups with high rates of family migration that the educational qualification of female migrants has been rising.[37] Indeed, the female migrant may be more highly educated than her male partner. It is essential that feminist research on international migration in Europe begins to pay attention to the migration of professional women. As we have pointed out, the welfare sectors have for a long time been more feminized than the financial world of inter-company transfers. The feminization of these sectors, whether it be in health, education or social work, has been growing.

Broadening the analytical framework and sectors of study is only one of the ways in which skilled migration and gender issues will be more fully incorporated. The narrowly economic bias of most research also precludes the exploration of the interplay of economic with social and cultural factors. As we noted previously, the role of social factors such as the household have been highlighted in recent theorizations of migration[38] and insights from other disciplines, such as cultural studies and ethnography, incorporated.[39] Sociology, too, which has been more attentive to gender relations and geographical mobility, has its place in the study of international skilled migration.[40] Approaches derived from these disciplines would allow the experiences of skilled female migrants and gender issues to be firmly located within a broader economic, social and cultural context. Biographical accounts, upon which we base our discussion of professional women's lives in the following section, are beginning to capture the diverse and contradictory aspirations, strategies and experiences of skilled and deskilled female migrants.[41] These methods can help us understand the repercussions of changing familial structures and the increasing participation of single and married women in professional occupations, whether they are indigenous or migrant women. They elucidate the relationships between reasons for migration, conditions in the country of origin, education, and economic, social and cultural capital and networks utilized in getting support. They also enable us to understand the relationship between subjectivity, agency and structures. In their life stories, the migrants elaborate on both the legal, institutional and economic structures they face and their ways of overcoming the obstacles they pose, as well as how they utilize the opportunities they present.

Professional Female Migrants in Germany and the United Kingdom

In this section we present some findings from a study on agency and subjectivity in the life stories of highly educated and professional women of Turkish background in Britain and in Germany.[42] The sample consisted of ten first- and second-generation interviewees. The interviewees' qualifications and the jobs they held were diverse (doctors, social workers, nursery nurses, entrepreneurs, scientists, health professionals), as were their routes of migration: some had migrated for study, some for family reunification, others as 'guestworkers', au pairs and refugees. Their professional trajectories were as diverse as the categories under which they migrated; thus some had followed educationally and professionally recognized and normalized routes, while others experienced various forms of skilling, de-skilling and re-skilling. Common issues that the interviewees faced included the recognition of their skills, whether acquired formally or informally. Interpersonal and institutionalized discrimination hampered access to jobs and means of attaining further qualifications. Many interviewees had to deal with overt and subtle forms of sexist and racist discrimination at the work place. While none of them gave up their careers because of this, it formed a further obstacle which they had to overcome. Social networks formed on the basis of shared ethnicity, political activism or class- and ethnicity-specific cultural activities were important for many interviewees, as they facilitated migration, provided access to jobs and improved information about and opportunities for further qualification.

This sample of interviewees is very specific in so far as it consists of divorced and single women only. While this need not indicate that professional and skilled work for migrant women cannot be combined with marriage, it can alert us to the differential impact of marital status on migratory and professional trajectories. For the mothers in the sample, childcare and financial independence constituted important factors in their professional and migratory trajectories.

The comparative dimension between Germany and Britain was chosen to highlight different dynamics of incorporation and differential racialization on individual women's lives.[43] The migration from Turkey to Britain has a different history than that to Germany. While there has been small-scale migration of students and professionals since the 1970s, the volume of migration has increased significantly in the late 1980s, with a large proportion of asylum seekers, including a large proportion of Kurdish migrants. In Germany, the migration from Turkey took place within the framework of 'guestworker' migration and from 1973 onwards, with the recruitment stop, largely took the form of family reunification, with an increase of asylum seekers in the 1980s.[44] In Germany, migrants from Turkey were for a long time constructed as the most distant ethnic group in both public discourses and social research. In contrast, their presence in Britain has passed largely unnoticed and they are positioned ambivalently as a 'white' ethnic minority within the predominant race relations paradigm.[45]

The study is exploratory and the sample is not intended to be statistically representative. Instead, these case studies show the diversity of a neglected category, namely professional migrant women from Turkey. This is particularly relevant since the academic and public discourses on migrant women from Turkey still seem to be locked into an Orientalist, or 'modernity-difference' binary hypothesis[46] that is blind to the experiences of highly educated and professional women in this group.

An in-depth analysis of the life stories of the subjects elucidates the interrelation of social factors involved in female skilled migration. Moreover, it demonstrates the usefulness of an approach that takes the subjectivity and resourceful agency with which migrant women negotiate institutional, legal and economic factors enabling and restricting their professional trajectories, seriously. The following two case studies of professional migrant women may serve as an example of how a biographical method can enhance our understanding of the interrelation of migrant women's gendered, ethnic and professional identities. The main emphasis is on the migration process and its effect on the interviewees' professional development. We argue that social and cultural capital, on the one hand, and institutional structures, such as immigration legislation and (mis)recognition of professional qualifications in the countries of immigration, on the other hand, form the restrictive and enabling framework for the women's professional development.

Nâlan

Nâlan is a 48 year-old first generation migrant living in Britain. She has a 17 year-old son. Although she was initially trained in computing, she worked in unskilled jobs for six years after migrating to Britain. She subsequently entered the field of social work and now works with women as a qualified social worker. She migrated to Britain in the early 1980s, after getting divorced. She found that life as a divorced single mother in Turkey was very difficult because of the numerous social sanctions against single women and economic difficulties.

Formal and Informal Educational Choices

Nâlan comes from an educated middle class family in Istanbul. Her professional and educational aspirations in her youth were determined by two important events in her life. The first was the early loss of both her parents, which traumatized her intensely. The event and its impact also prompted her older siblings with whom she grew up to not push her into pursuing academic achievements. The second event influencing her professional trajectory was her involvement in political groups, which meant that political activity was 'the most important thing' in her life at the time. This political involvement formed her own value system and Nâlan ruled out professional options she had previously considered attractive, such as acting, as 'a bourgeois thing'.

After leaving school she enrolled in vocational courses in computing which were very novel at the time and immediately found employment. Although she only had vocational qualifications, the specific conditions of supply and demand for her novel skills in an expanding area with little competition and her increasing experience provided her with job security and good working conditions. Despite Nâlan's initial politically motivated resistance to marriage, familial pressures and social control finally convinced her and her boyfriend to marry as a 'formality'. She continued working and was the breadwinner in the family, while her husband was finishing his studies. This continued after the arrival of their child.

Nâlan's independence was also curtailed by the fact that her in-laws provided her with necessary childcare; this arrangement provided them with a lever of social control. The 1980 military coup had a significant effect on her life as well, in that it made her previous political activity impossible and led to a dispersal of the social bonds with the old comrades. During this time, Nâlan started to get involved with the new women's movement, which was the first progressive political oppositional movement that could be organized at the time.[47]

Migration as a Way Out of Social Control

When she was divorced from her husband, Nâlan began to experience increasing social control through her brothers and her freedom of movement was restricted. Moreover, she began worrying about the future of her childcare arrangement with her in-laws in case she should engage in a new partnership. Her activism in the women's movement as well as contacts through her previous political activity gave her an opportunity to make connections with individuals in England. When a close friend living there suggested that she migrate, she gave up her flat and job, left her son in the care of her in-laws, and migrated to England. Despite the support of this friend, she experienced the initial period in England as very difficult. Her lack of knowledge of English made her feel especially vulnerable.

Nâlan felt she needed to learn English and at the same time earn money, since she could not be a burden on her friend. Another Turkish friend, whom she had come to know through their political organization 'took her by the hand' and helped her secure a job in a Turkish-owned textile factory, as a finisher.

> I started work the next morning at 8, looking forward to earning money and being able to find a flat of my own. But then I realized the bad working conditions, very unhealthy, the building was damp, no health and safety regulations were in place. We worked till ten at night, around four in the afternoon my feet began hurting very badly.

She worked in this factory for nearly a year. For her, the worst thing was the humiliating treatment of the workers. She gives an example of a relative of the owner also working in the factory:

> he was a real macho, always looking at the women from behind, at their bum and everything, disgusting. And I was working, putting something on

> the shoulders of the garments.... I had the things in a box. He passed and dropped the box. He didn't even say sorry or anything, he didn't have any manners at all. And he told me to pick them up. I looked at him and in that moment I would have liked to hit him on the head. But I didn't have anywhere else to go, I depended on this job.

Nâlan felt caught in a vicious circle; not knowing English, she could not access different employment opportunities. Moreover, at the time her residence status was irregular. Furthermore, the bad pay necessitated long working hours which made it impossible for her to attend language classes. The transnational social network acquired through her political organization and the women's movement was essential in supporting her in her migration and in giving her access to ethnically specific job networks. However, by being dependent on the ethnic community's economic niche because of her lack of English and an unclear immigration status, Nâlan could not exploit her professional skills. The textile factory as an economic niche for migrant newcomers in Britain has a long tradition. More recently, the Turkish-speaking community has occupied this niche. As Nâlan's and others' testimony shows, the benefit of an ethnic economic niche is very ambiguous for the workers. Unsafe and unhealthy working conditions and lack of job security, working regulations or workers' organization are often the trade-offs for being able to work in an undocumented or semi-documented way. Moreover, sexual harassment is commonplace.[48]

After a year, her boyfriend, also a computer specialist from Turkey, joined her and experienced some of the same problems. Living with her boyfriend allowed Nâlan to share the expenses and enabled her to quit the factory.

> We had rented a flat together ... and I started to go to school and worked in a café. At that time I didn't have problems with Immigration [and] I got a residence permit after three months, at the time it was easier I guess. ... When that happened I tried to bring my son over. I researched a bit and they told me you have to pay taxes, ... that's why I went to work in a hotel, which was the easiest work to get. ... I started to work as a chambermaid, to clean the rooms, change the bedding. I worked there for a year, then [my son] came. That was very hard work, also. For five years I was there, everyday I changed the bedding, it was very hard work ... they treated you very badly, not the workers but the guests. Very, very weird things. In general at a five star hotel it was men on business trips who stayed on their own. They left pornographic pictures in the bed, you open the bed and you find these pornographic magazines. Because they're paying a lot of money.
> U: They think they've got the right to humiliate people.
> N: Humiliate the people, macho people.

The necessity of bringing her son over as soon as possible made her accept documented and taxed but unskilled work that made her vulnerable to sexist harassment once again.

Going into Social Work

When her son arrived, Nâlan changed jobs so that her working hours were more compatible with her childcare arrangements. Working at a restaurant, she gained more practice and confidence speaking English.

> Once I had more confidence in myself, I started looking for other work. I started working as a sessional nursery worker. I also thought it had the advantage of having childcare included. I got the job through the job centre, and then went on to work at a girls' project. During that time I thought, while I am doing this work I might as well get a qualification.
> U: Was it easy for you to get into that kind of work, that girls' project…
> N: Well, to tell the truth, I told them a lie to get the job. I told them I had worked in a kindergarten in Turkey. A friend of mine in Turkey … wrote me a reference. Because actually working with children is not that difficult.
> U: Of course.
> N: Of course I had also started to get involved in … political movements here. Asylum, work… I had started to work as a community activist. Well you learn some things in political movements. I had learned a bit of jargon, I saw a lot of my friends [doing social work]… Before going to the job interview I had asked a friend of mine what they are likely to ask, how are they likely to put the questions, what kind of questions should I expect. She gave me a general idea, they'll ask this and this, you should answer like this.

Nâlan's improved English might have been instrumental in enabling her to look for other work. However, it is also crucial that she was freed from the pressures of having to earn a steady income in order to enable her son's immigration. Moreover, being able to fall back on her partner's financial resources in case the sessional nursery work did not meet her and her son's economic needs was crucial, too. Thus, a certain amount of economic and legal security was necessary to enable her professional mobility.

She achieved this mobility also because her political networks and her activism provided her with the social and cultural capital to succeed in the job interview. That is, the 'jargon' that she had acquired in her community activism enabled her to understand and reciprocate the interviewers' communication. Her networks with social workers enabled her to gain an insiders' view of the formal and informal mechanisms of access and closure. Apart from informal mechanisms of closure, such as knowledge of jargon, self-presentation and social networks, the need for a reference can be seen as an instance of formal professional closure. Here again, Nâlan's social capital in Turkey enabled her to surmount this difficulty.

Nâlan's move into a job in a project for Turkish girls raises another important issue of social and cultural capital. While migrant women's educational or professional qualifications are often not recognized, their linguistic and cultural competencies are beginning to be valued in social work contexts, thus creating a new, ethnicized and gendered professional niche. The problematic positioning of migrant women in social work professions working for an ethnic clientele has been pointed out by Lutz.[49] Often, their qualifications get underestimated and only their linguistic qualifications are recognized. Moreover, they are placed in the problematic position of mediator vis-à-vis the ethnic community they are supposed to represent: they are confronted with differential expectations on the basis of their group membership, both by the institutions they work for and its clients.

As Nâlan's professional experience grew, she decided to formalize her qualifications and started a university course in social work. During her studies, her field of interest shifted more specifically to women's projects. Now she works in this area, which also serves migrant women. She enjoys her work and sees it as politically and socially important. However, she also finds it is very stressful emotionally and notes that a lot of overtime is required.

Ayla

Ayla is 49 years old. She is a scientist, working in an international research institute in Germany. She comes from an urban middle class background that encouraged education and female employment. During her studies in England, she met her future husband, whom she joined and married in England in 1974 to do her PhD there. In 1978 they had a son. When she was divorced in 1982, she moved with her son to another country to work in a research project. Soon she realized that she could not take care of her son as a single working mother and sent him to Istanbul, where he lived with her parents until he finished primary school. In 1984, she got a job offer in her current workplace and moved to West Germany.

Education and Migration

Ayla was born and brought up in Istanbul. Her mother played an important part in Ayla's educational decisions. On the one hand, she provided a role model for a successful woman in a scientific academic profession. Here it is important to note that in Turkey there is a high proportion of women in academic posts throughout the disciplines and hierarchies. While this can be seen as a measure of gender equality in the academic labour market and of the success of the modernization of gender relations from above,[50] it is important to note that academic employment is financially a far less attractive option than employment in the private sector. This may be a reason contributing to the prevalence of women in academic posts.

Although there was no unanimous support for female education and employment in her family, Ayla's identification with the maternal family enabled her to construct for herself a cross-generational norm of female education and independence. Among the normative expectation with regards to education was going abroad to do her PhD. These normative expectations, of course, do not only depend on the familial attitude toward education, but also on the financial capacities of the family. Ayla makes clear that her decision to migrate to England was, on the one hand, related to her marriage to an English man; on the other hand, she considered going abroad for postgraduate study 'normal'.

Reflections on Being a Woman in the World of Research

Throughout the interview, Ayla emphasized her professional identity in her self-presentation, rather than her ethnic or gender identity. To Umut's introductory explanations of the research – i.e., 'What does it mean to be a woman from Turkey here...' – Ayla responded by separating out 'First of all what does it mean to live in Germany and to work in Germany as a woman'. This corresponds to an add-on approach to ethnicity and gender, not as articulating each other, but rather as two separate particularities. She emphasized that she has not encountered any difficulty in her field of work. That is, 'I don't encounter anything special let's say'. This juxtaposition of being treated 'special' as a woman and being treated like everybody else is to be found throughout the interview. It exemplifies how Ayla conceptualizes being a woman as a particularistic subject position, as opposed to a universalized, ungendered 'professional' subject position.

Despite this, Ayla recalls a job interview, where her ability to do hands-on technical work was questioned, thus challenging her professional authority on the basis of gender. Ayla singles out this moment in her career as 'the only time I had a comment because I was a *woman*'. This suggests that it was a memorable experience because it could have had a deep impact on her future professional life. However, by pointing out the singularity of the event, Ayla constructs the remainder of her working life as free of gendered restrictions and, ideally, as ungendered. This construction of discrimination as an isolated and exceptional event is a recurring motif.

Another positive meaning attached to being a woman had to do with the fact that her superior 'liked women'. In this sense, she feels being a woman was an advantage in her workplace. In fact, at a later point, Ayla remarks, that 'I always saw being a woman from all the advantageous sides'. In this way, she employs a voluntaristic model of identity in which specific identities can be chosen and emphasized or de-emphasized at will. This goes hand in hand with her deployment of a dominant discourse, conflating any gender- and ethnicity-sensitive approaches with a discourse of problems. This view is based on a normative assumption of ungendered, unethnicized social identities and relations as the universalist ideal. We would argue that such a universalist identity does not exist, but rather conceals the normalization of dominant subject positions.

While subscribing to an ungendered professional ideal, Ayla points out that her career strategy was non-threatening to her colleagues and superiors, because she did not aim for leadership positions. This could imply that one brings about the oppression one experiences by being too pushy. On the other hand, Ayla points out herself that there is a fine line between aiming for a higher position and wanting to do good and interesting work. It requires (gender-) specific emotional and self-representational work to be seen to be competent at the same time as not to seem threatening. Moreover, this can be interpreted as a female career strategy, thus contradicting the ideal of ungendered professional identities.

Mothering Responsibilities

The experience of mothering is one important point where Ayla's gender identity and her professional identity conflict. In retrospect, Ayla wishes she had taken time out from work to look after her son during his first years. When her son was born, Ayla brought a live-in childminder from Turkey. This enabled her to go back to work immediately because she was concerned about her prospects of future employment. Despite having a trustworthy childminder, recruited by her mother in Turkey, Ayla felt guilty for not looking after her son herself.

Although Ayla was not ambitious to gain a high position, she was keen to do interesting work. This differentiation, however, has its own pitfalls. As Ayla points out, to be given interesting work one has to be seen to be good at it, which is usually equated with holding a good position. Good positions are rarely available part-time; thus, this potential option for maximizing time with her son was foreclosed.

The feeling of not being able to fulfil the roles of mother and worker satisfactorily might be tied to the fact that these roles have been constructed as mutually exclusive and gendered (even if implicitly so).[51] Full-time work, the ability to work overtime and flexible hours implicitly construct the ideal worker as male, without family or other care responsibilities. Ayla may not conceptualize the experiences of work and mothering as interrelated at all. She emphasizes her effort to separate work and gender identities: 'you know, at least during my career I tried to forget that I was a woman, I tried to forget that I was Turkish – as far as the career is concerned now, and I tried... The main point was the work'.

This notion confirms the universality of an ungendered, unethnicized subject as the professional subject, whereas the particularities of being a woman or being Turkish are constructed as 'disturbances' of that professional subjectivity. This perspective does not take into account the interrelatedness of identities, and their location in social relations. Thus, the lack of caring responsibilities for male workers is only possible by delegating it to others, mainly women. This caring responsibility includes the physical and emotional reproduction of the male worker himself. So, unlike Ayla, who uses a universalist ideal of ungendered, unethnicized professional subjects, we interpret her experiences in her working life as structured through gender-specific experiences.

When Ayla divorced her husband, she migrated to another European country for a new job and did not take her childminder with her. Despite the availability of a kindergarten, she could not take care of her son alone, since her job required her to travel regularly. Therefore, she sent her son to her parents in Istanbul until he finished primary school. By that time she was working and living in Germany. The separation from her son was a very painful experience for her. This instance shows the importance of caring networks for facilitating women's migration:[52] the availability of a live-in childminder was crucial in enabling Ayla to continue working. This childminder was the daughter of her mother's domestic worker and actually herself only 13 years old. The mutual familial bonds between Ayla's and her childminder's family allowed Ayla to find affordable, trusted full-time childcare with the additional advantage that she could teach her son

Turkish. Thus, in this instance, Ayla's class positioning and ethnic resources facilitated her professional trajectory.

Conclusion

In Nâlan's life story the relevance of transnational networks for the initiation and support of migration become obvious. Moreover, the gender specific reasons for her migration, i.e., the increased social control faced after her divorce and her wish to support herself and her son financially without recourse to the unpaid childcare provided by the family of the child's father were shown. Nâlan's professional development was not only determined by gender and ethnicity, but also by her identification as part of oppositional, transnational social movements such as the women's movement and leftwing movements whose values she adopted. These social movements formed part of her social and cultural capital, which she could mobilize for geographical and professional mobility. It is important here to point out the specificity of these social networks and the cultural capital attached to them, as the existing literature tends to treat ethnic networks as rather unified and not as internally divided along lines of class, gender, sexuality and political positioning, as well as to other ethnic memberships. These are important insights to be gained from a qualitative, biographical approach that takes subjectivity into account.

Nâlan's migration took place outside of legal structures as an undocumented migrant. Because of this, her employment options were restricted to the very limited job opportunities of the ethnic economy. This de-skilling went hand in hand with an increased vulnerability to sexist harassment. Only through gaining legal documentation could she become occupationally mobile. This point alerts us to the role that migrants' agency plays in creating fluidity between the seemingly unconnected categories of skilled or undocumented migrants.

The priority of facilitating her son's immigration made her delay any attempt at re-skilling, which also involved financial risk-taking. This underlines the specific difficulties of migrant single mothers in (re)skilling, as this always involves financial risk taking, which is impossible without the security of social benefits (often unavailable to new immigrants), or the financial support of family and friends. Her professional move to social work, especially with migrant girls and women, is not accidental but can be seen against the backdrop of both local authorities' equal opportunities policies, and ethnically specific niches in social work.[53] Thus, Nâlan's professional trajectory demonstrates a de-skilling and a re-skilling, for which her own resourcefulness and her social networks were as important as the structural factors of immigration legislation, labour market segregation and the implicit normativity of a two-parent family, as demonstrated in her difficulty to earn enough money in Turkey.

Ayla's professional trajectory is more linear and appears to be more of a 'career story' than Nâlan's. She continuously worked in her own profession and her migrations seemed only motivated by personal and professional reasons, rather than constituting a way out of gender oppression. Ayla claims a universalist subject position for herself, which is contingent on material conditions. Thus, her financial positioning allowed her to pursue education abroad and gain an internationally recognized European professional qualification. Thus, as opposed to Nâlan's professional trajectory, the social and cultural capital at Ayla's disposal was transnationally validated.

Nevertheless, the ungendered professional identity Ayla claims for herself can be put into perspective considering the strains that mothering and working full-time put on her. This dilemma, we argue, cannot be solved without deconstructing the identity of an ungendered, unethnicized professional, since this very construct relies on the outsourcing of indispensable caring responsibilities to others. Ayla's capacity to use a childminder did not give her peace of mind. Even though Ayla tried to separate other identities from her professional sphere, the demands of her job infringed on her mothering responsibilities and her own ideal of good mothering. Thus, on the one hand, her position as a professional migrant working in an international institution seems to do away with gendered and ethnicized particularities. On the other hand, her caring responsibilities in the family reified her gendered position. Because dominant identities are unmarked, the cultural and social capital inherent in them may go unrecognized as such. However, the capacity to neutralize one's identity can often be seen as a manifestation of one's dominant positioning.[54]

Both these women are professional migrants from Turkey. Despite their divergent experiences, we feel it is important to recognize their qualifications and the impact migration has had on their professional trajectories. The obstacles to being recognized as a professional inherent in immigration control and the granting of work permits often go unrecognized when migrant populations, such as migrants from Turkey in Europe, are homogenized. In the study of professional and highly skilled migration, as opposed to migration of those viewed as unskilled labour, the relevance of social networks and the validation of cultural capital are rarely taken into account, as it is assumed that for professionals these are neutral. Our study points to the need to closely examine the class, gender and ethnic bases of constructing such neutrality. A universalist subject position has been re-inscribed into the lives of migrants that reproduces the ideal of the male breadwinner with his family responsibilities limited to the economic realm. The movements of these breadwinners, however, depend on wives, mothers, childminders or others' unnamed support. We hope to have highlighted the partiality of ungendered accounts of skilled migration. Even if these case studies themselves only provide partial and situated accounts, we hope to have suggested some important areas for further research which can be identified through the use of ethnicity- and gender-sensitive biographical methods.

Notes

1 Kofman, Phizacklea, Raghuram and Sales, *Gender and International Migration in Europe*; Walter, *Insider Outsider.*

2 Inowlocki and Lutz, 'Hard labour'; Seyhan, 'Scheherazade's Daughters'.

3 Friese, 'East European Women'.

4 Morokvasic, 'Birds of Passage'; see also Gray, 'Unmasking Irishness'.

5 Phizacklea, *One way ticket.*

6 Inowlocki and Lutz, 'Hard Labour'.

7 Simon and Bretell, *International Migration.*

8 Taravella, *Les femmes migrantes.*

9 Campani, 'Women Migrants'; Morokvasic, 'In and out of the Labour Market'; Kofman and Sales, 'Towards Fortress Europe?'; Lutz, 'The Limits of Europeanness'.

10 Idem; Brah, 'Difference'; Morokvasic, 'Birds of Passage'; Morokvasic, 'Entre Est et Ouest'; Phizacklea, *One Way Ticket.*

11 Brinker-Gabler and Smith, 'Writing New Identities'; King, Connell and White, *Writing across worlds.*

12 Anthias, 'Diasporas'; Brah, *Cartographies of Diaspora.*

13 Glick Schiller, Basch and Blanc-Szanton, 'Towards a Transnational Perspective'; Lawson, 'Arguments'.

14 Gabbaccia, *Seeking Common Ground*; Inowlocki, 'Grandmothers'.

15 Chamberlain, *Caribbean Migration.*

16 Collinson, *Europe*; King, *A New Geography*; Miles and Thränhardt, *Migration and European Integration*; Uçarer and Puchala, *Immigration.* Feminist scholars are beginning to rectify this situation, see for example Ackers' book on migrant women moving within the European Union (*Shifting Spaces*); Morokovasic, 'Entre Est et Ouest', and Koser and Lutz, *The New Migrations.*

17 Simon and Bretell, *International Migration*; Kofman and Sales, 'Migrant Women'.

18 Kofman, 'Birds of Passage'.

19 Boyd, 'Family and Personal Networks'; Goss and Lindquist, 'Conceptualizing International Labor Migration'; Miller Matthei, 'Gender and International Labor Migration'.

20 Lutz, *Obstacles to Equality.*

21 Gould, 'Skilled International Migration'; Salt, 'Migration Processes'; Todisco, 'Intellectual, Professional and Skilled Migrations'.

22 Koser and Salt, 'The Geography'.

23 In France the higher than average percentage of female students amongst Algerians compared to other North African groups is thought to stem from women seeking to escape from oppressive and dangerous conditions in their country, see Borgogno and Vollenweider-Andresen, 'Les étudiants étrangers'.

24 Ackers, *Shifting Spaces*.

25 Discussion with Parvati Raghuram.

26 Koser and Salt, 'The Geography', p. 294.

27 Ackers, *Shifting Spaces*; Bjeren, 'Gender and Reproduction'; Kofman, 'Birds of Passage'; Morokvasic, 'Birds of Passage'.

28 Man, 'The Experiences'.

29 Stalker, *The World of Strangers*.

30 Interviews conducted with Bosnian female refugees with professional qualifications in London and Paris, some of whom had managed to rebuild their careers after six or seven years in their new country. The study was part of an Economic and Social Research Council (UK) project 'Civic stratification, exclusion and migratory trajectories in three European states (1999-2001). The three researchers were Eleonore Kofman, Cathie Lloyd and Rosemary Sales.

31 See Anderson, *Doing the Dirty Work?*, on domestic workers in general, Andall, 'Migrant Women', and Escriva, 'Control' on domestic labour in Italy and Spain. Friese, 'East European Women' gives examples in Germany of highly qualified women, such as teachers and agricultural engineers, some of whom speak a number of languages, but who can only obtain domestic or cleaning employment. She highlights the increasing web of dependency between those able to capitalize on their education and those whose qualifications have been devalued by economic restructuring.

32 Morokvasic, 'Roads to Independence'.

33 Bhachu, 'New European women'.

34 Lutz, 'In between'.

35 Morokvasic, 'Birds of Passage'; Phizacklea, *One Way Ticket*.

36 Kofman, 'Birds of Passage'.

37 Tribalat, *Faire France*.

38 Portes, 'Immigration Theory'.

39 Brinkler-Gabler and Smith, *Writing New Identities*; King, Connell and White, *Writings across Worlds*.

40 Bonney and Love, 'Gender and Migration'.

41 Friese, 'East European Women'; Gray, 'Unmasking Irishness'; Seyhan, 'Scheherazade's Daughters'.

42 The wider study forms an Umut Erel's PhD project *Subjectivity and Agency in the Life Stories of Migrant Women from Turkey in Britain and Germany* (2002), at Nottingham Trent University under the supervision of Prof. Richard Johnson, Prof. Eleonore Kofman and Dr. Tracey Skelton.

43 Brah, 'Difference, Diversity, Differentiation'.

44 Many European estimates of Turkish-origin populations use figures derived from the Turkish Ministry of Work and Social Security in the absence of regular census figures (Manco, 'Turcs d'Europe'). In Britain, the number of migrants from Turkey was estimated to be almost 60,000 in 1996. In Germany, the number of Turkish citizens in 1999 was 2,053,564, accounting for 28.8 per cent of the foreign population.

45 This paradigm's focus on Black and Asian ethnic minorities pays insufficient attention to the diversity of racist discrimination including that based on immigration status, and linguistic, economic and social exclusions faced by other ethnic minority groups (Anthias and Yuval-Davis, *Racialized Boundaries*).

[46] Apitzsch, 'Frauen in der Migration'; Inowlocki and Lutz, 'Hard Labour'.
[47] Tekeli, 'Frauen in der Türkei'.
[48] Anthias, *Ethnicity, Class and Migration*.
[49] Lutz, *Welten verbinden*.
[50] Kandiyoti, 'Women and the Turkish State'.
[51] Tizard, 'Employed Mothers'.
[52] Hochschild, 'Global Care Chains'.
[53] Sales, *Migrant Women*.
[54] Anthias and Yuval-Davis, *Racialized Boundaries*.

References

Ackers, Louise, *Shifting Spaces. Women, Citizenship and Migration within the European Union*, Bristol, 1998.

Andall, Jaqueline, 'Migrant Women and Gender Role Definitions in the Italian Context' *Journal of Area Studies* 6 (1995): pp. 203-215.

Anderson, Bridget, *Doing the Dirty Work? The Global Politics of Domestic Labour*, London, 2000.

Anthias, Floya, *Ethnicity, Class and Migration: Greek Cypriots in Britain*, Aldershot, 1992.

Anthias, Floya, 'Diasporas: Beyond Ethnicity?' *Sociology* 32, 3 (1997): pp. 557-580.

Anthias, Floya and Yuval-Davis, Nira, *Racialized Boundaries*, London, 1992.

Apitzsch, Ursula, 'Frauen in der Migration', in: *Frauen in der Einen Welt*, Nr. 1 (1996): pp. 9-25.

Ausländische Wohnbevölkerung nach ausgewählten Staatsangehörigkeiten von 1994-1999, http://www.bundesauslaenderbeauftragte.de/fakten/tab2.htm.

Bhachu, Parminder, 'New European Women and New Cultural Forms. Culture, Class and Consumption among British Asian Women', in: Hedwig Rudolph and Mirjana Morokvasic (eds), *Bridging States and Markets. International Migration in the Early 1990s*, Berlin, 1993, pp. 225-242.

Bjeren, Gunilla, 'Gender and Reproduction', in: Tomas Hammar, Grete Brochman, Kristof Tamas and Thomas Faist (eds), *International Migration, Immobility and Development. Multidisciplinary Perspectives*, Oxford, 1997, pp. 219-46.

Bonney, Norman and Jill Love, 'Gender and Migration: Geographical Mobility and the Wife's Sacrifice', *Sociological Review* 39 (1990): pp. 335-348.

Borgogno, Victor and Lise Vollenweider-Andresen, 'Les étudiants étrangers France. Trajectoires et devenir', *Migrations Etudes* 79 (1998).

Boyd, Monica, 'Family and Personal Networks in International Migration. Recent Developments and New Agendas', *International Migration Review* 23 (1989): pp. 638-670.

Brah, Avtar, 'Difference, Diversity, Differentiation: Processes of Racialization and Gender' in: John Wrench and John Solomos (eds), *Racism and Migration in Western Europe*, Oxford, 1993, pp. 105-214.

Brah, Avtar, *Cartographies of Diaspora*, London, 1996.

Brinker-Gabler, Gisela and Sidonie Smith, *Writing New Identities: Gender, Nation and Immigration in Contemporary Europe*, Minneapolis, 1997.

Campani, Giovanna, 'Women Migrants: From Marginal Subjects to Social Actors', in: Robin Cohen (ed.), *The Cambridge Survey of World Migration*, Cambridge, 1995, pp. 546-550.

Chamberlain, Mary, *Caribbean Migration. Globalised Identities*, London, 1998.

Collinson, Sarah, *Europe and International Migration*, London, 1993.

Escrivá, Angeles, 'Control, Composition and Character of New Migration in South-West Europe. The Case of Peruvian Women in Barcelona', *new community* 23/1 (1997): pp. 43-58.

Friese, Marianne, 'East European Women as Domestics in Western Europe - New Social Inequality and Division of Labour Among Women', *Journal of Area Studies* 6 (1995): pp. 194-202.

Gabaccia, Donna (ed.), *Seeking Common Ground. Multidisciplinary Studies of Immigrant Women in the United States*, Connecticut, 1992.

Gaspard, Francoise, *Obstacles in Society to Equality of Opportunity for Immigrant Women. The Situation in France, Belgium, Italy and Spain*, Strasbourg, 1994.

Glick Schiller, Nina, Linda Basch and Christina Blanc-Szanton (eds), 'Towards a Transnational Perspective on Migration. Race, Class, Ethnicity and Nationalism Reconsidered', *Annals of the New Academy of Sciences*, New York, 1992.

Goss, Jonathan and Bruce Lindquist, 'Conceptualizing International Labor Migration. A Structuration Perspective', *International Migration Review* 29 (1995): pp. 317-351.

Gould, William, 'Skilled International Migration', *Geoforum* 19 (1988): pp. 381-386.

Gray, Brenda, 'Unmasking Irishness: Irish Women, the Irish Nation and the Irish Diaspora', in: John MacLaughlin (ed.), *Social Location and Dislocation and Irish Identities*, Cork, 1997, pp. 209-235.

Hochschild, Arlene, 'Global Care Chains and Emotional Surplus Value', in: Will Hutton and Anthony Giddens (eds), *On the Edge. Living with Global Capitalism*, London, 2000, pp.130-146.

Inowlocki, Lena, 'Grandmothers, Mothers and Daughters. Intergenerational Transmission in Displaced Families in three Jewish Communities', in: Daniel Bertaux and Paul Thompson (eds), *International Yearbook of Oral History and Life Stories: Between Generations*, Oxford, 1993, pp. 139-153.

Inowlocki, Lena and Helma Lutz, 'Hard Labour. The "Biographical Work" of a Turkish Migrant Woman in Germany', *European Journal of Women's Studies* 7 (2000): pp. 301-319.

Kandiyoti, Deniz, 'Women and the Turkish State. Political Actors or Symbolic Pawns?', in: Floya Anthias and Nira Yuval-Davis (eds), *Woman-Nation-State*. Houndmills, 1989, pp.126-149.

King, Russell (ed.), *A New Geography of Migration in Europe*, London, 1993.

King, Russell and Ian Shuttleworth, 'Education, Identity and Migration. The Case of Young Highly Educated Irish Emigrants, *Studi Emigrazione* 32, 117 (1995): pp. 159-176.

King, Russell, John Connell and Paul White, *Writings across Worlds: Literature and Migration*, London, 1995.

Kofman, Eleonore, '"Birds of Passage" a Decade Later. Gender and Immigration in the European Union', *International Migration Review* 33 (1999): pp. 269-299.

Kofman, Eleonore, 'Beyond a Reductionist Analysis of Female Migrants in Global European Cities. The Unskilled, Deskilled and Skilled', in: Marianne Marchand and Anne Sisson Runyan (eds), *Gender and Global Restructuring*, Routledge, 2000, pp. 129-139.

Kofman, Eleonore, 'The Invisibility of Female Skilled Migrants and Gender Relations in Studies of Skilled Migration in Europe', *International Journal of Population Geography* 6 (2000): pp. 45-59.

Kofman, Eleonore and Rosemary Sales, 'Towards Fortress Europe?', *Women's Studies International Forum* 15 (1992): pp. 29-39.

Kofman, Eleonore and Rosemary Sales, 'Migrant Women and Exclusion in Europe', *European Journal of Women's Studies* 5 (1998): pp. 381-398.

Kofman, Eleonore, Annie Phizacklea, Parvati Raghuram and Rosemary Sales, *Gender and International Migration in Europe*, London, 2000.

Koser, Khalid and Helma Lutz (eds), *The New Migrations in Europe. Social Constructions and Social Realities*, London, 1998.

Koser, Khalid and John Salt, 'The Geography of Highly Skilled International Migration', *International Journal of Population Geography* 3 (1997): pp. 285-303.

Lawson, Victoria, 'Arguments within Geographies of Movement. The Theoretical Potential of Migrants' Stories', *Progress in Human Geography* 24 (2000): pp. 173-189.

Lutz, Helma, *Welten verbinden. Türkische Sozialarbeiterinnen in den Niederlanden und der Bundesrepublik Deutschland*, Frankfurt a. M., 1991.

Lutz, Helma, 'In between or Bridging Cultural Gaps? Migrant Women from Turkey as Mediators', *new community* 19 (1993): pp. 485-494.

Lutz, Helma, *Obstacles to Equality. Opportunities in Society for Immigrant Women with Particular Reference to the Netherlands, the United Kingdom, Germany and the Nordic Countries*, Strasbourg, 1994.

Lutz, Helma, 'The Limits of Europeanness. Immigrant Women in Fortress Europe', *Feminist Review* 57 (1997): pp. 93-111.

Lutz, Helma, 'The Legacy of Migration. Immigrant Mothers and Daughters and the Process of Intergenerational Transmission', in: Chamberlain (ed.), *Caribbean Migration*, pp. 95-108.

Man, Guida, 'The Experiences of Women in Chinese Immigrant Families. An Inquiry into Institutional and Organizational Processes', *Asian and Pacific Migration Journal* 4 (1995): pp. 303-326.

Manço, Ural, 'Turcs d'Europe. De l'image tronquée à la complexité d'une réalité sociale immigrée', *Hommes et Migrations* 1226, July/August (2000), pp. 76-88.

Miles, Robert and Dietrich Thränhardt (eds), *Migration and European Integration*. London, 1995.

Miller Matthei, Linda, 'Gender and International Labor Migration. A Networks Approach', *Social Justice* 23, 3 (1996): pp. 38-53.

Morokvasic, Mirjana, 'Birds of Passage are also Female', *International Migration Review* 18 (1984): pp. 890-910.

Morokvasic, Mirjana, 'Roads to Independence. Self-employed Immigrants and Minority Women in Five European States', *International Migration* 29 (1991): pp. 407-420.

Morokvasic, Mirjana, 'In and out of the Labour Market. Immigrant and Minority Women in Europe', *new community* 19 (1993): pp. 459-484.

Morokvasic, Mirjana, 'Entre Est et Ouest, des migrations pendulaires', in: Mirjana Morokvasic and Hedwig Rudolph (eds), *Les Nouvelles Mobilités en Europe*, Paris, 1997.

Phizacklea, Annie (ed.), *One Way Ticket. Female Labour Migration*, London, 1983.

Portes, Alejandro, 'Immigration Theory for a New Century. Some Problems and Opportunities', *International Migration Review* 31 (1997): pp. 799-827.

Sales, Rosemary, *Migrant Women, Citizenship and Political Action*, 2000, unpublished manuscript.

Salt, John, 'Migration Processes among the Highly Skilled in Europe', *International Migration Review* 26 (1992): pp. 484-505.

Seyhan, Azade, 'Scheherazade's Daughters. The Thousand and One Tales of Turkish-German Women Writers', in: Gisela Brinker-Gabler and Sidonie Smith (eds), *Writing New Identities. Gender, Nation, and Immigration in Contemporary Europe*, Minneapolis, 1997, pp. 230-248.

Simon, Rita James and Caroline Brettell (eds), *International Migration: The Female Experience*, New Jersey, 1986.

Stalker, Peter, *The World of Strangers. A Survey of International Labour Migration*, Geneva, 1994.
Taravella, Louise, *Les femmes migrantes. Bibliographie analytique internationale (1965-1983)*, Paris, 1984.
Tekeli, Şirin, 'Frauen in der Türkei der 80er Jahre', in: Ayla Neusel, Şirin Tekeli and Meral Akkent (eds), *Aufstand im Haus der Frauen. Frauenforschung aus der Türkei*, Berlin, 1991, pp. 27-48.
Tizard, Barbara, 'Employed Mothers and the Care of Young Children', in: Anne Phoenix, Anne Woollett and Eva Lloyd (eds), *Motherhood: Meanings, Practices and Ideologies*, London, 1991, pp. 178-194.
Todisco, Enrico, 'Intellectual, Professional and Skilled Migrations', *Studi Emigrazione* 30 (1993): pp. 574-590.
Tribalat, Michèle, *Faire France. Une enquête sur les immigrés et leurs enfants*, Paris, 1995.
Uçarer, Emek and Donald Puchala (eds), *Immigration into Western Societies: Problems and Policies*, London, 1997.
UNESCO (ed.), *Women on the Move: Contemporary Changes in Family and Society*, Paris, 1986.
Walter, Bronwen, *Insider Outsider: Whiteness, Place and Identity of Irish Women*, London, 2000.
Wrench, John and John Solomos (eds), *Racism and Migration in Western Europe*, Oxford, 1993.

PART III
MIGRATION AS A POLITICAL AND SOCIAL CHALLENGE

Chapter 6

The Political Consequences of Forced Population Transfers: Refugee Incorporation in Greece and West Germany

Triadafilos Triadafilopoulos

The proliferation of often violent ethnic conflicts in Eastern and Southeastern Europe since the end of the Cold War has prompted some scholars and journalists to advocate compulsory population exchanges as means of settling such disputes.[1] In particular, Yugoslavia's brutal disintegration and descent into war prompted many to question the validity of preserving multinational regimes in the face of nationalist challenges. The logic behind such positions is straightforward: if groups can no longer live together, it is preferable to facilitate their separation along territorial and demographic lines, rather than risk suffering the potentially horrendous consequences associated with trying to force their continued coexistence. In the words of Chaim Kaufmann, a leading proponent of partition and 'engineered ethnic unmixing':

> Stable resolutions of ethnic civil wars are possible only when the opposing groups are demographically separated into defensible enclaves.... [T]o save lives threatened by genocide, the international community must abandon attempts to restore war-torn multi-ethnic states. Instead it must facilitate and protect population movements to create true national homelands.[2]

Kaufmann and others cite the 1923 Greek-Turkish exchange of populations and the post-World War II compulsory transfer of ethnic Germans from Eastern Europe as examples of the type of solutions the international community ought to emulate.[3] They argue that in both cases, compulsory population transfers led to interstate peace and the successful incorporation of the expellees. Hence, the Greek-Turkish and German examples might serve as 'blueprints' for contemporary decision-makers grappling with similar kinds of conflicts.

Advocates of population transfers imply that refugees produced by population transfers can be inserted into the correct national slots like so many matched pegs.[4] They exhibit little interest in probing the domestic consequences of such policies and instead accept nationalist interpretations of these events as constituting moments of national renewal and unification. This is problematic, for even a cursory examination of the Greek and West German cases reveals that the incorporation of 'kin' groups into receiving societies is a complicated and contingent proposition. The transfer of substantial numbers of refugees inevitably places serious burdens on receiving states and these burdens upset existing social and political structures. Where such structures are already under stress – as they often are in post-conflict situations – the result may be further instability.

Indeed, the protracted incorporation of refugees in interwar Greece deepened pre-exchange political cleavages and contributed to the eventual breakdown of the country's democratic regime. The support of disaffected urban refugees was also a key source of strength for the Greek left during the years of Axis Occupation (1941-44) and Civil War (1946-49). It was only after the defeat of the Greek Communists in the Civil War and the subsequent entrenchment of a staunchly conservative, anticommunist social order that Greece's 'refugee problem' ceased to be a source of political instability.

Most contemporary observers argued that the incorporation of a vast number of destitute refugees would also hinder West Germany's post-war reconstruction.[5] Yet while the immediate post-war years were indeed problematic, West Germany fared relatively better than Greece with regard to its incorporation of refugees. This difference in outcomes naturally leads one to ask why this was the case. The answer put forward in this chapter is relatively straightforward: the difference in outcomes was due in large part to West Germany's atypical post-World War II settlement and extremely rapid political and economic reconstruction. West Germany benefited from the convergence of a unique set of circumstances, including the Allied occupation, Marshall Plan aid, European economic integration and prudent statesmanship of its mainstream politicians. These factors helped West Germany to diffuse its refugee problem before it could develop to the extent that it had in Greece. However, the fact that such a unique constellation of factors were needed to bring about a relatively successful outcome in the German case illustrates how difficult it is to incorporate refugees produced by population transfers.[6]

The chapter begins by briefly summarizing events leading up to the decisions made in favour of compulsory uprooting in Lausanne and Potsdam and comments on the mechanics of the resulting population transfers. I then assess the impact of these population transfers in Greece and West Germany, paying particular attention to the politicization of divisions between refugees and locals. In both cases, shared nationality gave way to pronounced cultural differences and sharp boundaries separating the two groups. The refugees' dire economic condition, alienation, and demands for compensation fuelled their discontent and compelled them to seek redress through political mobilization. Differing historical circumstances and variations in the structure of each country's political, economic, and legal institutions shaped the refugees' political action, leading to further instability in Greece and the comparatively more rapid, if still complicated, incorporation of refugees in West Germany. The chapter's conclusion summarizes the insights drawn from the foregoing comparison of the Greek and West German cases and relates them to contemporary debates regarding the efficacy of population transfers.

Lausanne and Potsdam: Sanctioning the 'Unmixing of Peoples'

The Greek and German refugee experiences had their roots in internationally sanctioned mass population transfers. In each case, the transfers were aimed at eliminating national minorities from neighbouring states, thereby improving the chances of establishing durable post-war settlements.[7] The compulsory exchange of the Muslim population of Greece and the Greek Orthodox Christian population of Turkey was effected on the basis of the Convention Concerning the Exchange of Greek-Turkish Populations, signed by Greece and Turkey at the Lausanne Conference on 30 January 1923. The Convention came on the heels of Greece's defeat by Turkish nationalist forces in 1922. Greece had been granted jurisdiction over the city of Smyrna (Izmir) and its hinterland under the Treaty of Sèvres, signed on 10 August 1920.[8] After consolidating its control over Smyrna, the Greek army advanced into the Anatolian interior and was routed by Kemal Ataturk's forces and forced to retreat. Turkish forces pushed the Greeks back to the coast and into Smyrna and Ataturk entered the city in September 1922. By late 1922, Fridtjof Nansen, the League of Nation's High Commissioner for Refugees, reported that approximately 900,000 refugees from Asia Minor had entered Greece in the weeks following the fall of Smyrna. The Lausanne Convention Concerning the Exchange of Greek-Turkish Populations acknowledged and extended the unofficial uprooting of the preceding months. Under the terms of the Convention, approximately 150,000 remaining Turkish nationals of Greek Orthodox religion were transferred from Turkey to Greece and approximately 350,000 Greek nationals of the Muslim religion remaining in Greece were forced to leave their homes and settle in Turkey. The Convention barred the return of all those who had fled either country since the Balkan Wars (1912-13).[9]

It is important to note that many of the 'unmixed' on both sides did not want to leave their homes, and that many of those who did flee wanted desperately to return once the war had ended.[10] The Convention's sponsors purposefully ignored the wishes of both these groups and proposed instead the 'rationalization' of demographic patterns in the Near East. As such, the Convention set an important precedent in modern diplomatic conduct.[11] The compulsory and permanent nature of the uprooting ensured that state interests would be given priority over the rights of local populations.

The decision to forcibly remove ethnic German minorities from Eastern Europe at the close of the Second World War grew out of a similar logic. As has been noted:

> The very wide adherence to the principle of population transfers among leaders of the Western democracies was attributable in part to a rather optimistic appraisal of the results of the Greek-Turkish population exchange.... While a few leading politicians deplored the transfers, a majority gradually exhibited a peculiar euphoria over the conceptual simplicity of the solution.[12]

Public statements made by leading Western politicians in the months leading up to the end of World War II tend to confirm this position. In a speech before the British Parliament in 1944, Churchill maintained that:

> expulsion is the method which so far as we have been able to see, will be most satisfactory and lasting. There *will be no mixture of populations to cause endless trouble*, as has been the case in Alsace-Lorraine. A clean sweep will be made. *I am not alarmed by the prospect of the disentanglement of the populations, nor even by these large transferences which are more possible in modern conditions than ever before.*[13]

Similarly, Roosevelt believed that the Allies 'should make some arrangements to move the Prussians out of East Prussia the same way the Greeks were moved out of Turkey after the last war'.[14]

During the fall of 1944, Soviet troops pushed westward through Poland and Germany toward Berlin, prompting a flood of German civilians to flee ahead of their advance. Thousands of others were forcibly expelled from

Poland and Czechoslovakia in the course of 'wild' expulsions.[15] At the Potsdam Conference (17 July-2 August 1945), the United States, Great Britain, and the Soviet Union formally agreed to place German territories east of the Oder-Neisse line under Polish and Soviet administration and consented to Czechoslovakia, Poland, and Hungary's calls for the expulsion of their German minorities. Section XIII of the Potsdam Protocol stipulated that the United States, Britain and the Soviet Union would

> recognize that the transfer to Germany of German populations, or elements thereof, remaining in Poland, Czechoslovakia and Hungary, will have to be undertaken. They agree that any transfers that take place should be effected in an orderly and humane manner.[16]

On 20 November 1945, the Allied Control Council for Germany approved a schedule for the transfer of 6.5 million (ethnic) Germans from Czechoslovakia, Poland and Hungary.[17] By April 1947, 10.5 million refugees were registered in the four Allied occupation zones with the majority concentrated in Schleswig-Holstein, Lower Saxony and Bavaria – rural, agricultural provinces in the British and American zones of occupation.[18] While there is no consensus as to precisely how many died during the course of the expulsions, Ahonen suggests that up to 1.5 million persons may have perished en route to Germany.[19] Regardless of the precise casualty figure, there is no gainsaying that the uprooting was extremely costly in terms of the suffering inflicted upon the expellees.

Impact upon Arrival: Cultural Differences and Social Exclusion

Greece: 1923-1928

The flight of the refugees from Turkey signalled the end of the *Megali Idea*: the Greek nationalist dream of retaking Constantinople and creating a Greater Greece patterned after the Byzantine Empire.[20] As a result of the exchange of populations, the vast majority of Greeks inhabited the same country and were bound by the borders of a single state. Consequently, cultural and linguistic differences that had been blurred by distance and submerged in the fiction of a homogeneous 'imagined community' were revealed.

It soon became evident that the arriving Greeks of Asia Minor, Thrace and the coasts of the Black Sea were quite different from the Greeks of 'Old Greece'.[21] Many of the refugees had little or no consciousness of being Greek. League of Nations officials on the scene noted that the refugees displayed a bewildering variety of languages, dialects, customs and loyalties.[22] These cultural differences were seized upon by native Greeks who saw the refugees as a threat to their economic interests and the purity of the Greek nation. Locals referred to the refugees as '*Tourkosporoi*' (Turkish seed) and '*giaourtovaftesmeni*' (baptized in yogurt).[23] Indeed, the 'Greekness' of the refugees was essentially denied at the time by a large proportion of the locals.[24] In Mavrogordatos's words,

> The invidious distinction between refugees and natives provided the basis for the most salient cleavage in interwar Greek society, which truly dominated the politics of the period.... [T]he distinction was then often characterized as *fyletike*, which ... should be translated as 'ethnic'.[25]

The refugees assisted in the crafting of boundaries separating their lifeworld from that of the natives. As Hirschon has noted, the refugees drew from the ideational resources of their pre-exchange heritage to craft a positive identity that contrasted their cosmopolitanism, religious devotion and worldliness to the locals' parochialism and backwardness.[26] This positive identity influenced the refugees' perceptions of local institutions and norms, including those in the sphere of politics. Many of the more influential and prominent refugees had fled from cosmopolitan centres such as Constantinople (Istanbul) and Smyrna (Izmir), where their engagement in commercial activities had exposed them to liberal and republican ideas. These refugees viewed Greece's hereditary monarchy as a throwback to an unenlightened world.[27]

The boundaries separating refugees (*prosphyges*) and the 'Old Greeks' (*Palioelladites*) were particularly pronounced in urban centres such as Athens and Thessaloniki.[28] Between 1920 and 1928 the combined population of Greece's five largest cities increased from 12.6 per cent to 21.3 per cent of the country's total population.[29] This seemingly 'uncontrolled' urban expansion caught many of the inhabitants of Old Greece by surprise.[30] Henry Morgenthau described the impact of the refugees' arrival in stark terms:

> [Athens] had been almost somnolent before this irruption [sic]. It had been living the staid life of an orderly capital, where business had grown into established channels and where life had settled into an easy and familiar routine. Overnight all this was changed. Now the streets thronged with new faces. Strange dialects of Greek assailed the ear. The eye was caught by outlandish peasant costumes from interior Asia Minor. Sidewalks were crowded. Avenues that had been pleasantly ample were now filled with peddlers' carts of refugees who were now trying to make a living by selling a few strings of beads.... The great rock of the Acropolis ... looked down

> upon as strange a sight as it had seen since the days when Phidias was adorning the Parthenon at its summit.[31]

The urban refugees' alienation was compounded by their lack of adequate housing and meagre job prospects.[32] Consequently, cultural differences were reinforced by economic and material hardships. In Pentzopoulos's words:

> The [material] conditions prevailing among the newcomers further widened the gap between the two communities. The poverty, the unhealthy makeshift tin barracks, the hungry faces were stumbling blocks to any impulsive fraternization; many natives were genuinely repelled by this misery.[33]

The experiences of refugees settled in rural areas were relatively better. About 90 per cent of the approximately 670,000 rural refugees were settled in the 'New Lands' of Macedonia and Thrace.[34] More than 50 per cent of this cohort was given the land, homes, livestock and tools of exchanged Turks and Bulgarians.[35] The other half benefited from prime minister Eleftherios Venizelos's drastic land reform policies, which resulted in the summary expropriation of large estates in Macedonia and Thrace.[36] Furthermore, the rural refugees did not have to face the enmity of the Old Greeks in quite the manner as their urban counterparts. The New Lands still possessed sizable minority populations despite the unmixing that had marked the years since the Balkan Wars. Consequently, the rural refugees were deemed to be a 'Hellenizing force', which would finally tip the demographic scales in Greece's favour.[37] The presence of other ethnic groups (Jews, Vlachs, Roma, Slav-Macedonians, Pomaks, Chams) affirmed the Greekness of the rural refugees and blunted conflicts between themselves and native Greeks in the region. However, as Karakasidou has noted, even in the New Lands, locals distinguished themselves from the recently arrived refugees.[38]

Germany: 1945-1948

As in the Greek case, the expulsion of German minorities from Eastern Europe brought hitherto dispersed groups into close proximity with one another. Germans were suddenly confronted with putative members of the *Volk* whose dialects, manners and cultural patterns often differed markedly from their own.[39] The refugees 'were strangers ... and both they and their neighbours began to discover that the concept of a "Greater Germany" was more of a myth than a goal that could be realized'.[40]

The sheer number of refugees overwhelmed the local inhabitants and worsened pre-existing shortages in housing, foodstuffs, clothing, heating material, household equipment and other commodities.[41] Hundreds of thousands of refugees were forced to live in barracks, camps, dance halls, temporary relief shelters and hastily converted schools.[42] The strain on resources, coupled with the refugees' poverty and cultural heterogeneity gave rise to growing disaffection among the local population. Locals saw the refugees as 'destitute outsiders who brought nothing and took much.... They had no connection to the community, and in the meagre living conditions of the first post-war years, became a burden'.[43] Refugees were branded 'Polacks' and deemed to be shiftless and lazy. Their very status as Germans was often rejected on the grounds that they failed to conform to distinctly local ways of life. In the words of one disgruntled native:

> The influx of refugees brings the danger that our People (*Volk*) loses its genuine and original character and is mixed up with a character foreign to our land and our customs.... It is no exaggeration to say that popular life in the villages of the Heide [the northern plains] is the healthiest and happiest conceivable with regard to religion as well as culturally, economically, and socially, but now the axe is being laid to the roots of the old tree.[44]

Among the natives, negative opinions of the newcomers were widely held.[45] The refugees 'were regarded as a latent threat to the natives' world, to the traditional ways of doing things, ways that had not been questioned by anyone for a long time, if ever'.[46]

The locals' enmity was mirrored in the refugees' recognition of their displacement and loss of material, social, and professional foundations.[47] Their distress was neatly captured in a survey carried out in March 1945 by the British occupying forces. The survey recorded that 72 per cent of the refugees polled stated that their relationship with the native population was 'bad'. Refugee respondents noted that their relationship with locals was marred by the natives' selfishness and penchant for treating them as 'a lower class of being'.[48] The results of another poll taken four years later revealed that 85 per cent of those questioned would have preferred to return to their homelands if permission to do so was granted.[49]

Reports from observers in Germany at the time tend to corroborate the refugees' view that they were being mistreated. Journalists and others on the scene noted that refugees were usually given the most uncongenial jobs for which they often neither had training nor aptitude. Refugees were also often the first to be fired when workers had to be laid off, particularly during the first few years of the post-war period.[50]

The refugees' disillusionment propelled them to form groups founded on their shared experience. These Homeland Societies (*Landsmannschaften*) helped foster a more positive refugee self-image.[51] The Societies rendered some material aid, arranged social gatherings and broached refugee issues in meetings with political officials. Perhaps more importantly, they also provided the refugees with a sense of agency and voice which enabled them to advance their interests as a distinct group with specific goals and requirements, most notably a desire for equality and the right of return.[52] These sentiments were manifested in a number of newspapers and other publications written, distributed and read by the refugees.

In short, as in the Greek case, a distinct refugee consciousness surfaced among the German expellees. The refugees differentiated themselves from the local population and advanced a unique set of grievances based on their interests and needs.[53] The establishment of refugee organizations would soon be followed by more explicitly political mobilization.

The Politics of Refugee Incorporation

Greece: 1928-1950

The task of settling approximately 1.5 million refugees after ten years of intermittent war and political crisis mobilized international assistance, which culminated in the establishment of the League of Nations sponsored Refugee Settlement Commission (RSC), in November 1923.[54] The Commission answered calls for humanitarian assistance in the years immediately following the disaster in Asia Minor. It also succeeded in settling many refugees in rural areas. By 1930 – the year of the Commission's dissolution – 145,758 families had been settled on farms in Macedonia and Thrace.[55]

Despite the work of the RSC, the bulk of the refugees, both urban and rural, remained lodged at the bottom of Greek society. Refugees continued to be shunted into exclusively refugee villages and urban neighbourhoods and derided by locals for their cultural heterogeneity. Many locals also took issue with the refugees' affiliation with the Liberal Party (*Kommu Fileleftheron*) and its leader Eletherios Venizelos.[56]

The origins of 'refugee Venizelism' stretched back to the beginning of the First World War.[57] Venizelos's pro-Entente, pro-war platform was considered to be in accord with the interests of the Asia Minor Greeks, who feared the increasingly hostile nature of Turkish nationalism. Conversely, for many Orthodox Christians in Asia Minor, anti-Venizelist neutrality stood for inaction and the abandonment of 'unredeemed Greeks'.[58] The Asia Minor catastrophe coincided with anti-Venizelist rule and solidified the refugees' association with Venizelos and the Liberal Party.

The Venizelist parties recognized the importance of the refugee vote and worked to integrate the newcomers into their organizations.[59] Refugees were deemed to be an integral part of the Venizelist camp and refugee candidates ran on the Liberal Party's ticket in local and national elections.[60] Refugee associations and newspapers, such as *Prosfygikos Kosmos* (Refugee World), also became an important part of the broad network of Venizelist partisan organizations.[61]

The Venizelists' embrace of the refugees evoked even greater hostility to the newcomers from conservative anti-Venizelists. Anti-Venizelists went so far as to demand the exclusion or segregation of the refugees from the political process.[62] For instance, they initially refused to accept the refugees' right to vote and, having lost that argument, insisted on the institution of separate refugee electoral colleges, similar to those created for Muslims and Jews.[63] Although the demand was rejected, it deepened divisions between refugees and natives.

The conservative backlash against the refugees reached its pinnacle in the election of 1928: anti-Venizelists accused the refugees of depriving the native majority of its legitimate political power and used the mainstream press to heighten awareness of the refugee 'menace'.[64] Native supporters of Venizelos were characterized as unthinking dupes who had lost sight of their interests as natives.

Venizelos's decisive victory in 1928 forced some conservative politicians to reconsider their strategy toward the refugees. Venizelos' brokering of the Ankara Convention in June 1930 also gave conservatives a convenient pretext for changing tactics and aggressively courting the refugee vote. Under the terms of the Convention, Greece and Turkey agreed to drop all claims for refugee compensation.[65] This was meant to inculcate a spirit of friendship and goodwill between the two states. The debate over the ratification of the Ankara Convention led to a partial split among refugee politicians: while most refugee deputies submitted to Liberal Party discipline, a sizable minority denounced the Convention as a sell-out and severed their ties to the party. The People's Party sought to capitalize on this by forcefully attacking the Convention and siding with the refugees on the issue of compensation.[66] By 1933 a broad range of conservative, pro-Royalist parties had fused under the banner of the 'United Opposition', whose rallying cry was 25 per cent compensation for 'our refugee brothers'![67]

This strategy proved to be effective. The Venizelists lost 20 out of 21 seats in Athens by less than 2000 votes.[68] Following the election, however, the United Opposition failed to honour its 25 per cent promise and the right quickly reverted to its more customary anti-refugee rhetoric and policies. This was manifested in the government's redrawing of electoral districts in Athens and Thessaloniki to diminish the weight of the refugee vote in those cities.[69]

Anti-refugee sentiment picked up after the election and reached a near fever pitch following the failed Venizelist coup of March 1935.[70] Conservatives used the situation to purge the armed forces and civil service of Venizelists. They also restored the monarchy and sent Venizelos into exile in Paris, where he died on 18 March 1936. The declining fortunes of the Liberal Party caused many of the more radical refugees to abandon mainstream politics altogether. Consequently, increasing numbers of them turned to the Communist Party of Greece (KKE).[71]

Communist Party organizers recognized the unique opportunity made available to them by the decline of the Liberals and set about reworking their platform to make it more palatable to refugee voters. The KKE's traditional opposition to Venizelist irredentism had limited its popularity with refugee voters in the past. The KKE had also alienated the refugees by taking the side of 'native' workers in the cities and ethnic minorities in the countryside. Indeed, the party had denounced the settlement of refugees in Macedonia and Thrace as a scheme designed to forcibly alter the ethnic composition of the New Lands.[72] After the Venizelists' failed 1935 coup, the KKE dropped its policy for an independent Macedonia and began to address itself as the unabashed party of the refugees. The refugees were courted as a coherent group, without concern for their internal differentiation or class distribution.[73] The dire economic conditions, which wracked Greece throughout the 1930s, prompted many poor, indebted urban refugees to shift their allegiance to the KKE.

The growing popularity of the KKE among the refugees and other sectors of the population manifested itself in the results of the December 1935 election. The voting resulted in a hung parliament, with the Venizelists winning 143 seats to the anti-Venizelists' 141. The KKE-dominated Popular Front (*Laiko Metopo*) held the balance of power with its 15 seats. News of both the Populists' and Liberals' negotiations with the Communists prompted a strong reaction from the staunchly anticommunist armed forces.[74] The Minister of War, General George Papagos, warned the two main parties that the army would not tolerate any coalition with the Communists. Shortly after the death of caretaker Prime Minister, Konstantinos Demertzis, the King appointed the staunch anti-Communist General Ioannis Metaxas as his replacement.

Metaxas used mounting incidences of labour unrest in Greece's towns and cities as a pretext for suspending parliament, restricting freedom of the press and declaring martial law.[75] A military dictatorship was formally established on 4 August 1936. Metaxas declared that only a strong, extra-parliamentary government could save Greece from political ruin. The dictatorship was ostensibly instituted to preserve the state from both Communism and party faction.[76] Metaxas' 'collectivist nationalism' aimed at eliminating societal conflicts and inculcating a sense of 'national mindedness'. In so doing it eliminated Greece's democratic regime and the civil and political rights of the country's citizens. This drove the KKE and many of its remaining supporters, refugees and natives alike, underground.

The Axis occupation of Greece and subsequent Civil War transformed the country dramatically. Poor urban refugees formed an important part of the Communist insurgency. The victory of the Right after almost four years of fratricidal civil war ushered in a fundamentalist anti-Communism that pervaded the post-war period.[77] While a majority of urban refugees continued to support parties of the left through the 1950s and 1960s, they no longer held the kind of political leverage that they enjoyed during the interwar period. Mass emigration to Western and Northern Europe, North America and Australia reduced their numbers and the ideological divisions fostered by the Civil War shifted the support of many refugees to the parties of the Centre and Right. Furthermore, the conservative orientation of the post-war Greek political regime worked to limit the power of the organized left and its adherents. In short, the refugees 'ceased to constitute a single, politically cohesive ... social group'[78] and the 'refugee problem' receded as a source of political instability.

Germany: 1949-1960

As in Greece, the German refugees' discontent was channelled into the local political party system. Initially, there was very little that they could do to improve matters. Fearing that the refugees might destabilize an already tense situation, the American, British and French occupying forces expressly refused to license any political group or party dedicated primarily to the advancement of refugee interests.[79] The Allies feared that the refugees 'might provide a reservoir of votes for parties that would combine social radicalism with a foreign policy prepared to take large risks to win back homes they had left behind in the East'.[80] Consequently, local residency requirements were used to prevent refugees from participating politically at the state (*Land*) level up until 1948.[81]

The pace of refugee organizing accelerated after the passage of the western zones' currency reform in 1948. The currency reform hurt refugees and other have-not groups disproportionately and led to heightened levels of discontent.[82] The refugees pressed for greater political participation and by 1949 succeeded in organizing a cross-zone political movement made up of delegates from all types of refugee groups.[83] The introduction of West Germany's Basic Law in May 1949 guaranteed freedom of association for all German citizens and soon thereafter the nascent national movement along with many of the refugee Homeland Provincial Societies grouped themselves under the banner of the United East German Provincial Societies (*Vereinigte Ostdeutsche Landsmannschaften*).[84]

After the first federal elections of August 1949, the American military government formally delegated its responsibility for licensing political parties to the new Bonn government. This sparked the creation of the first and most important refugee party in West Germany: the Block of Expellees and Victims of Injustice (*Bund der Heimatvertriebenen und Entrechteten* – BHE).[85] The BHE appealed to refugees and other victims of the war and military occupation and promised to address their material and social hardships. The party also affirmed the refugees' 'right to self-determination' and championed calls for the return of lost homelands. In short, 'a massive organized system of expellee pressure groups began to make itself felt'.[86]

The amalgamation of the refugee groups at the national level was precisely what the Western Allies had hoped to avoid. There was a genuine fear that the refugees' desire to regain lost homelands could seriously hinder Germany's post-war reconstruction and European stability, more generally. In a 1949 report, the United States High Commissioner for Germany noted that:

> Unfavorable conditions of refugee life are beginning to have serious political repercussions within Germany and may vitally and adversely affect the international political situation.... The repeal of the United States Military Government law requiring licenses of political parties [has] opened the way for ... more vociferous and definite demands on the part of the refugees for political expression.[87]

In the same year, the British Military governor wrote a memorandum to Britain's Foreign Secretary, Ernest Bevin, warning him that:

> The loss of self-respect which these people [the refugees] have undergone and the discontent which their mode of life engenders lays them open to the temptations of nationalist agitation and provides ready made material for the first unscrupulous leader that comes to power. Paradoxically enough, though the refugees as a class owe their miseries in large measure to the policy of the Soviet Union in Germany and Eastern Europe, the conditions in which they live make them easy prey to communist blandishments.[88]

The Allies' fears were heightened after the BHE campaigned and won 23 per cent of the votes cast in the July 1950 state (*Land*) election in Schleswig-Holstein. The BHE emerged as the second largest party in the state, after the German Social Democratic Party (*Sozialdemokratische Partei Deutschlands*, SPD).[89] Its fifteen seats in the state legislature ensured that no government in Schleswig-Holstein could be formed without its support. Indeed, it eventually formed a coalition government with the CDU. The BHE went on to win seats in state legislatures in Württemberg-Baden, Hesse and Bavaria.

In the second federal election of 1953, the BHE secured 27 seats in the *Bundestag*, giving the party a prominent place on the national stage. And yet, the 1953 election also marked the peak of the party's success. In the subsequent federal election of 1957, the BHE failed to secure *any* seats in the *Bundestag*. In the space of four short years, the threat of radical refugee politics that seemed so real in the years immediately following the end of the war had all but receded. This paradoxical turn of events was due to a number of factors that together made West Germany's post-war reconstruction atypical.

First, it is important to note that after assuming responsibility for the handling of the refugee problem in 1949, the Bonn government took steps to quicken the incorporation process. A Ministry for Expellees (*Ministerium für Vertriebene*) was established and charged with coordinating all governmental refugee assistance organizations and programmes. These organizations helped the refugees deal with housing needs, employment and general social welfare.[90] The 1949 Refugee Settlement Act (*Flüchtlingssiedlungsgesetz*) eased refugees' demands for housing by providing special inducements, such as tax exemptions, to individuals selling or leasing land to refugees. A refugee bank was also established to re-finance loans granted to refugees by local banks and, in 1952, the Equalization of Burdens Act (*Lastenausgleichsgesetz*) was passed in an effort to provide restitution to refugees.

While these measures were important, they did little to palliate the refugees, as is evinced by the economic plight of the refugees as late as 1951 and the success of the BHE in the 1953 election. Arguably, the single most important factor contributing to the relatively rapid incorporation of Germany's refugee population was the 'economic miracle' (*Wirtschaftswunder*) that lifted the country from the mid-1950s onwards. Foreign intervention facilitated West Germany's rapid economic recovery. Marshall Plan aid freed indigenous investment capital, which was used to reinvigorate Germany's ailing industries. As a result, industrial production tripled between 1949 and 1959. This rapid expansion led to a sharp drop in unemployment, as more and more workers were drawn into Germany's factories. Indeed, unemployment fell from about 9 per cent in 1949 to a mere 1 per cent ten years later, despite an overall increase in the active labour force from 13.6 to 19.6 million.

Furthermore, the corporatist social compact the Allies also helped forge played an important role in diffusing potential conflicts between workers and their employers. This was particularly important with regard to wages, as workers effectively agreed to practice wage restraint in return for jobs and security. Finally, moves aimed at ensuring West Germany's quick entry into the revamped capitalist global economy helped propel the economic miracle forward by shifting the focus of the economy toward exports. Early moves toward European economic integration also played an important role in this regard. The cumulative effect of West Germany's economic reconstruction was astonishing. By 1953, the average living standard in West Germany was higher than it had been in 1938; by 1961, the country had become the world's third largest industrial producer.[91]

West Germany's economic recovery allowed Bonn to compensate the refugees for their wartime losses.[92] The growth of German heavy industry, building trades and manufacturing also eased tensions caused by high levels of refugee unemployment.[93] In short, Germany's economic recovery allowed it to

> turn its expellee liability into a prime asset. The phenomenal *Wirtschaftswunder* made possible by the influx of dollars rested no less on the availability of skilled workers who had ... been unemployed. At once two important ends were achieved – rapid economic recovery and the integration of millions of expellees.[94]

Another key to Germany's diffusion of its refugee crisis lay in its mainstream political parties' co-opting of the BHE. The CDU and SPD lured prominent refugee politicians away from the BHE, and refugee voters turned to the larger catch-all parties after they accepted the refugees' demands for equal treatment.[95] The CDU/CSU also created a special body responsible for formulating refugee policy for the Christian Democrats. On the foreign policy front, the CDU, SPD and Free Democratic Party (*Freie*

Demokratische Partei – FDP) all exhibited varying degrees of support for the refugees' calls for the eventual unification of pre-war Germany and the return of their 'lost homelands'. In its 1952 *Action Programme*, the SPD stated that:

> Settlement of German territorial and border questions must await a peace treaty. This settlement must not be prejudiced by prior agreements between governments of individual parts of Germany and the Occupation Powers. Detachment of lands that belonged to Germany in 1937 has not created a new law but a new injustice. The Social Democratic Party of Germany does not recognize this state of affairs either in the East or in the West.[96]

In short, West Germany's mainstream parties purposefully kept alive the refugees' dream of return, knowing full well that such a return was highly unlikely given the exigencies of Cold War geopolitics. This strategy succeeded in diffusing more radical refugee politics. However, as Ahonen has convincingly argued, it also constrained the mainstream parties' options toward their Eastern Bloc neighbours throughout the early years of the Cold War.[97] Hence, while the danger of refugee radicalism no longer threatened the stability of the regime, the refugees continued to influence West German politics throughout the post-war period, particularly in the area of foreign policy.

Conclusion

Proponents of mass population transfers suggest that the process of matching peoples, territories, and states provides the surest means of settling ethno-nationalist disputes. The analysis presented in this chapter problematizes this assumption by illustrating that the incorporation of refugees produced by engineered ethnic unmixing is fraught with risks and uncertainties. As noted, refugees created by such flows do not necessarily identify with the political unit in which they are inserted: in both Greece and West Germany, refugees formed distinct identities and pressure groups that drew in large part on their status as outsiders. Their identity was not given; rather, it was constructed according to their material conditions, cultural dispositions, dialects and relationships with local populations. In short, one of the assumptions upon which partition and unmixing is based – that there are mutually exclusive identities that can be mapped onto coherent political entities – is false.

The politicization of divisions between locals and refugees was also considered in this chapter. In Greece, the refugees' arrival onto the political scene 'posed a social challenge that strained the tolerance of the natives [and] changed the face of party politics beyond recognition'.[98] The refugees' impact on the existing social order contributed to the profound changes that swept Greek politics and society in the interwar period. The refugees' turn to radical politics following Venizelos's death and the decline of the Liberal Party lifted the fortunes of the Greek left and contributed to the polarization of Greek society which culminated in the Civil War of 1946-49.

Many feared that the influx of refugees into West Germany at the close of World War II would lead to a similar outcome. As noted above, a unique set of circumstances, including the Allied occupation, the Marshall Plan and, most importantly, West Germany's rapid economic recovery, converged and allowed the Federal Republic to diffuse its refugee crisis before it could develop to the extent that it had in Greece. However, West Germany's success was not a foregone conclusion; indeed, many felt that it had all the makings of a monumental disaster. It is worth pausing to consider what might have transpired if West Germany had not benefited from Marshall Plan aid and other forms of foreign technical and material assistance that poured into the country as foreign powers worked to establish it as a bulwark against Soviet Communism. West Germany's ability to move the refugees into the labour market and out of refugee camps quickly was key to its success. But how many countries can reasonably hope for similar levels of foreign assistance? The failure of the international community to honour its commitments in Bosnia-Herzegovina, Kosovo and elsewhere would suggest that outcomes resembling the Greek case are more likely in any future post-transfer situations.

In sum, proponents of population transfers must consider the consequences of their preferred solutions on receiving states. The difficulties raised by the partition of territories and forced transfer of peoples do not end once refugees are inserted into 'national homelands'. Rather, the stability of these states may be imperilled and this, in turn, is likely to hamper economic reconstruction and democratization efforts. The Greek and German cases suggest that engineered ethnic unmixing is likely to create as many problems as it seeks to solve. Hence, its utility is suspect.

Notes

I thank Renée Hirschon, Adamantia Pollis, Aristide Zolberg, Jane Cowan, Patrick Hossay, Peter Benda, Shaun Young, Catherine Frost, Tobias Vogel, James Ingram, Fiona Adamson, John Nagl, Carola Weil and the participants of the Berlin Workshop on

Assimilation, Diasporization and Representation – particularly Pertti Ahonen, Rainer Münz, Rainer Ohliger and Karen Schönwälder – for comments on earlier drafts of this chapter. Financial support from the Social Sciences and Humanities Research Council of Canada is gratefully acknowledged.

[1] See Kaufmann, 'Possible and Impossible Solutions to Ethnic Wars'; Kaufmann, 'When All Else Fails'; Pape, 'Partition: An Exit Strategy for Bosnia'; O'Hanlon, 'Turning the Cease Fire Into Peace'. For critical responses to the partition/unmixing argument see Kumar, 'Partition's Troubled History' and Kumar, *Divide and Fall: Bosnia in the Annals of Partition*.

[2] Kaufmann, 'Possible and Impossible Solutions to Ethnic Wars', p. 137.

[3] Kaufmann, 'When All Else Fails', p. 125, n. 12.

[4] This presumption is not limited to proponents of population transfers. As Eftihia Voutira has noted in 'Population Transfers and Resettlement Policies in Interwar Europe', 'a common assumption that lingers is the belief that people uniting across borders will be welcomed by their kith and kin whom they share common origins, culture and heritage, and, more rarely, language. Certainly these are important factors; but they do not constitute sufficient conditions for successful integration', p. 123.

[5] See Neumann, 'The New Crisis Strata in German Society'. Neumann referred to the refugees as the 'number one' crisis stratum in Germany – i.e. the single most important social group with regard to stability/instability (p. 25). For an intriguing consideration of how the threat of refugee radicalism was perceived by American occupation officials in the early post-war period, see Schraut, 'Zwischen Assimilationsdiktat und Fürsorgeverpflichtung'.

[6] These conditions applied specifically to West Germany, which serves as the sole focus of this chapter. For discussions of the situation in East Germany see Ther, *Deutsche und polnische Vertriebene*; and Hoffman and Schwartz, *Geglückte Integration*.

[7] For a useful discussion of European minorities and their relation to nation-states in the twentieth century see Arendt, *The Origins of Totalitarianism*; especially chapters 6, 8 and 9. Also see Zolberg, 'The Formation of New States as a Refugee-Generating Process'; and Keeley, 'How Nation-States Create and Respond to Refugee Flows'.

[8] The Treaty of Sèvres allowed Turkey to maintain sovereignty over Smyrna until 1925, at which time the region could be annexed to Greece if the local population so requested. Turkey never ratified the Treaty. See Clogg, *A Concise History of Greece*, pp. 95-96.

[9] One of the consequences of defining nationality via religious affiliation was that many Greek-speaking Muslims and Turkish-speaking Orthodox Christians were tranferred to linguistically alien homelands. Many contemporary observers were struck by the fact that the 'Greek' refugees they encountered spoke fluent Turkish but little or no Greek; much the same occurred in Turkey.

[10] 'When I arrived among the settlers [in Greece] as late as 1928, quite a number were still hoping that the Turks would let them go back; a few of the wilder spirits hoped that the Greeks might reconquer part of Anatolia; and more than one of the older folk plaintively insisted that they didn't want to be buried here [in Greece] but wanted "to be taken home"'. Mitrany; *The Effect of the War in Southeastern Europe*, p. 253.

[11] Koufa and Svolopoulos, 'The Compulsory Exchange of Populations', p. 287, note 9.

[12] Zayas, *Nemesis at Potsdam: The Expulsion of the Germans from the East*, p. 8. Also see Zayas de, *The German Expellees: Victims in War and Peace*, p. 80.

[13] House of Lords, *Parliamentary Debates*, column 1098; emphasis added.

[14] United States, Department of State, *Foreign Relations of the United States*, p. 15. Also see Sherwood, *Roosevelt and Hopkins*, p. 710. Another high ranking American, Sumner Wells, argued that 'the minority problems cannot be solved through frontier and territo-

rial adjustments alone. Populations must be transferred under international control, even though in some cases such transfers may involve a million human beings'; Wells, *Where are We Heading?*, p. 127.

15 Schulze, 'The Refugee Population in Western Germany After World War II', p. 290.

16 Claude, *National Minorities: An International Problem*, p. 115. According to Claude, by agreeing to the terms of section XIII, 'the great powers ... acquiesced in the expulsion of the native German population of the eastern provinces by Polish authorities, and thus confirmed the view that the Potsdam decision had as its corollary the elimination of Germans from the area tentatively assigned to Poland'. Also see Friedrich, 'The Peace Settlements with Germany – Political and Military', pp. 121-122.

17 Kulischer, *Europe on the Move*, p. 282.

18 Bouman, Beijer and Oudegeest, *The Refugee Problem in Western Germany,* p. 13; Schulze, 'The Refugee Population in Western Germany After World War II', p. 293. The Allies' goal of securing 'an equitable distribution' of refugees 'among the several zones of occupation' was spoiled by France's refusal to admit refugees into its zone of occupation, among other factors. See Connor, 'German Refugees and the Bonn Government's Resettlement Programme', p. 337.

19 Ahonen, 'Expellee Organizations and West German Ostpolitik, 1949-1969', p. 20.

20 See Augustinios, 'The Dynamics of Modern Greek Nationalism'; and Augustinios, 'Hellenism and the Modern Greeks'.

21 Mavrogordatos, *Stillborn Republic*, p. 193. See also Karakasidou, *Fields of Wheat, Hills of Blood*, pp. 147-149; and Pentzopoulos, *The Balkan Exchange of Populations*, pp. 208-209.

22 Pentzopoulos, *The Balkan Exchange of Populations*, p. 101. 'Some presumably Greek rug-makers from one resettled village refused even to incorporate Greek designs into their rugs, so outraged were they at having such a label applied to them; according to one relief worker, "they were wedded to Turkey. They sulked at the idea of attempting to do anything Greek"'.

23 This rather novel slur (*giaourtovaftesmeni*) referred to the refugees' penchant for adding yogurt to their cuisine. It is interesting to note that today, yogurt based dishes such as *tzatziki* have been appropriated as 'national' foods in contemporary Greece.

24 Pentzopoulos, *The Balkan Exchange of Populations*, p. 211.

25 Ibid.

26 Hirschon, *Heirs of the Greek Catastrophe*, pp. 30-33.

27 Pentzopoulos, *The Balkan Exchange of Populations*, p. 175.

28 An estimated 615,000 refugees were settled in cities and towns. See Mears, *Greece Today: The Aftermath of the Refugee Impact*, pp. 299-300.

29 Mazower, *Greece and the Interwar Economic Crisis*, p. 47.

30 Ibid.

31 Morgenthau, *I Was Sent to Athens*, p. 50.

32 Hirschon notes that public investment in housing failed to meet the needs of a sizable portion of the urban refugee population well into the 1950s, thirty years after the refugees' arrival in Greece: Hirschon, *Heirs of the Greek Catastrophe*, p. 43.

33 Pentzopoulos, *The Balkan Exchange of Populations*, p. 211.

34 Mavrogordatos, *Stillborn Republic*, p. 187.

35 The Treaty of Neuilly signed by Greece and Bulgaria on 27 November 1919, allowed for the voluntary exchange of minorities between the two countries. See Ladas, *The Exchange of Minorities: Bulgaria, Greece, and Turkey*, pp. 27-49.

36 Mazower, *Greece and the Interwar Economic Crisis*, pp. 74-79.

37 Pentzopoulos notes that '[t]he colonization policy of the Greek government was implemented with due consideration to national security. While it is true that Mace-

donia, and to a lesser extent Thrace, offered many advantages for the inexpensive and immediate rehabilitation of the refugees, the number of persons settled there exceeded any figure justified by economic arguments', *The Balkan Exchange of Populations*, p. 36.

38 Karakasidou, *Fields of Wheat, Hills of Blood*, p. 161.

39 Bouman, Beijer, and Oudegeest noted that differences in dialect, customs, and religion often led to friction between refugees and locals. In their words, '[t]he native population ... shows clearly its contempt for the intrusive and noisy manners of the foreigners. The refugees feel themselves strengthened thereby in their inclination to remain apart. ... Differences in dialect exert the strongest influence on the attitudes of the socially lower groups [of refugees]', *The Refugee Problem in Western Germany*, p. 3. Here it is important to emphasize the confluence of differences in culture, language/dialect, and class in the formation of boundaries between refugees and locals and note the similarities with the Greek case.

40 Schoenberg, *Germans from the East*, p. 38.

41 Schulze, 'The Refugee Population in Western Germany After World War II', p. 298. Also see Heller, 'Economic Policy and Political Equilibrium in Postwar Germany', p. 59.

42 Bouman, Beijer and Oudegeest, *The Refugee Problem in Western Germany*, p. 19.

43 Hackett, 'Transforming Identities and Changing Contexts', p. 43.

44 Cited in the original German by Schulze, 'The Refugee Population in Western Germany After World War II', p. 305.

45 Ibid., p. 302.

46 Ibid., p. 305.

47 Schulze, 'Growing Discontent: Relations between Native and Refugee Populations', p. 344.

48 Public Opinion Research Office/Political Division CCG Bielefeld 67 HQ CCG BAOR 15, Report No. 11: German Housing Conditions, Refugees and Some Other Problems Relating Thereto, PRO: FO 105/1857. Cited in Schulze, 'The Refugee Population in West Germany After World War II', p. 314.

49 Schechtman, *The Refugee in the World: Displacement and Integration*, p. 27.

50 *The New Statesman and Nation*, 9 September 1949.

51 Carey, 'Political Organization of the Refugees and Expellees in West Germany', p. 193. See also Ahonen, 'Domestic Constraints on West German Ostpolitik', p. 33; and Schoenberg, *Germans from the East*, p. 75. It is important to note that a complex array of organizations based on the refugees' place of residence in West Germany emerged alongside and competed with the *Landsmannschaften*. See Ahonen, 'Expellee Organizations and West German Ostpolitik, 1949-1969', pp. 32-37.

52 Ibid., p. 194; Hackett, 'Transforming Identities and Changing Contexts', p. 46.

53 Ther, 'The Integration of Expellees in Germany and Poland after World War II', p. 787; Ther, *Deutsche und polnische Vertriebene*.

54 The Commission had four members: two were appointed by the Greek government, one by the Council of the League of Nations. The fourth member, and chairman of the Commission, was a United States national representing a variety of relief organizations operating in Greece. For a detailed account of the work of the Refugee Settlement Commission see Société des Nations, *L' Établissement des Réfugiés en Grèce*.

55 Dakin, *The Unification of Greece 1770-1923*, p. 139.

56 Ibid.

57 Mavrogordatos, *Stillborn Republic: Social Coalitions and Party Strategies in Greece, 1922-1936*, p. 199.

58 Ibid.

59 Legg, *Politics in Modern Greece*, p. 209.

60 Pentzopoulos, *The Balkan Exchange of Populations*, p. 186.

61 In marked contrast to the German case, very little has been published on the organization and influence of refugee organizations in Greece. One hopes that future research will address this deficiency.

62 Pentzopoulos, *The Balkan Exchange of Populations*, p. 203.

63 Ibid.

64 See Mavrogordatos, *Stillborn Republic*, p. 204.

65 For the full text of the Ankara Convention (in French) see Ladas, *The Exchange of Minorities*, pp. 817-830.

66 Mavrogordatos, *Stillborn Republic*, p. 211.

67 Ibid., p. 212.

68 Ibid., pp. 212-213. Although the United Opposition won only 46.19 per cent of the popular vote, (as compared to 46.32 per cent for the Venizelist coalition) this translated into a 136-110 advantage in terms of seats. Dakin, *The Unification of Greece 1770-1923*, p. 152.

69 Mavrogordatos, *Stillborn Republic*, p. 213; Dakin, *The Unification of Greece 1770-1923*, p. 154.

70 The coup was organized by a group of Venizelist officers with the connivance of Venizelos himself. The prime motive was to block a feared purge of republicans in the armed forces and the restoration of the monarchy. See Clogg, *A Concise History of Greece*, p. 113.

71 Legg, *Politics in Modern Greece*, p. 128.

72 Mavrogordatos, *Stillborn Republic*, p. 219.

73 Ibid., p. 222.

74 Dakin, *The Unification of Greece 1770-1923*, p. 155.

75 Ibid., p. 159-160.

76 Sarandis, 'The Ideological Character of the Metaxas Regime', p. 149.

77 Tsoucalas, 'The Ideological Impact of the Civil War', p. 331.

78 Mavrogordatos, 'The 1940s: Between Past and Future', p. 44.

79 Rodgers, *Politics After Hitler*, pp. 107-111; Lee, 'CDU Refugee Policies and the Landesverband Oder/Neisse', pp. 131-149.

80 Kitzinger, *German Electoral Politics*, p. 9. Also see Carey, 'Political Organization of the Refugees and Expellees in West Germany', p. 195; and Neumann, *Der Block der Heimatvertriebenen und Entrechteten 1950-1960.*

81 Carey, 'Political Organization of the Refugees and Expellees in West Germany', p. 196.

82 See Connor, 'The Refugees and the Currency Reform'.

83 Schoenberg, *Germans from the East*, p. 73.

84 Ibid., p. 75.

85 Ibid., p. 76; Carey, 'Political Organization of the Refugees and Expellees in West Germany', p. 206.

86 Schoenberg, *Germans from the East*, p. 78.

87 Ibid., p. 79.

88 Schulze, 'The Refugee Population in Western Germany After World War II', p. 314.

89 The BHE received 307,000 votes as compared to the SPD's 360,000. See Carey, 'Political Organization of the Refugees and Expellees in West Germany', p. 207.

90 Schwarz, *Refugees in Germany Today*, p. 114.

91 For background see Maier, 'The Two Postwar Eras and the Conditions for Stability in Twentieth Century Western Europe'; Katzenstein, *Policy and Politics in West Germany: The Growth of a Semi-Sovereign State.*

92 Balfour, *Germany: The Tides of Power*, p. 151

93 Schechtman, *The Refugee in the World: Displacement and Integration*, p. 35.
94 Zayas, *Nemesis at Potsdam: The Expulsion of the Germans from the East*, p. 52.
95 Kitzinger, *German Electoral Politics: A Study of the 1957 Campaign*, p. 10.
96 Schoenberg, *Germans from the East*, p. 246.
97 See Ahonen, 'Domestic Constraints on West German Ostpolitik' and 'Expellee Organizations and West German Ostpolitik, 1949-1969'.
98 Veremis, '1922: Old Themes, New Challenges', paper presented at the Conference on the 1923 Compulsory Exchange of Populations between Greece and Turkey. Oxford, England, September 1998. On file at the Refugee Studies Programme, University of Oxford (UK).

References

Ahonen, Pertti, 'Domestic Constraints on West German Ostpolitik: The Role of the Expellee Organizations in the Adenauer Era', *Central European History* 31 (1998): pp. 31-64.

Ahonen, Pertti T., *Expellee Organizations and West German Ostpolitik, 1949-1969*, PhD, Yale University, 1999.

Arendt, Hannah, *The Origins of Totalitarianism*, New York, 1948.

Augustinios, Gerasimos, 'The Dynamics of Modern Greek Nationalism: The "Great Idea" and the Macedonian Problem', *East European Quarterly* 4 (1973): pp. 444-453.

Augustinios, Gerasimos, 'Hellenism and the Modern Greeks', in: Peter F. Sugar (ed.), *Eastern European Nationalism in the 20th Century*, Washington, D.C., 1995, pp. 163-204.

Balfour, Michael, *Germany: The Tides of Power*, London and New York, 1992.

Bouman, P.J., G. Beijer and J.J. Oudegeest, *The Refugee Problem in Western Germany*, The Hague, 1950.

Carey, Jane P.C., 'Political Organization of the Refugees and Expellees in West Germany', *Political Science Quarterly* LXVI (1951): pp. 191-215.

Claude, Jr., Inis L., *National Minorities. An International Problem*, Cambridge, Massachusetts, 1955.

Clogg, Richard, *Parties and Elections in Greece: The Search for Legitimacy*, Durham, NC, 1987.

Clogg, Richard, *A Concise History of Greece*, Cambridge, 1992.

Connor, Ian, 'The Refugees and the Currency Reform', in: Ian D. Turner (ed.), *Reconstruction in Post-War Germany: British Occupation Policy and the Western Zones, 1945-1955*, Oxford, 1989, pp. 301-326.

Connor, Ian, 'German Refugees and the Bonn Government's Resettlement Programme: The Role of the Trek Association in Schleswig-Holstein, 1951-3', *German History* 18 (2000): pp. 337-361.

Dakin, Douglas, *The Unification of Greece 1770-1923*, London, 1972.

Friedrich, Carl J., 'The Peace Settlements with Germany – Political and Military', *Annals of the American Academy of Political and Social Science* 257 (1948): pp. 119-142.

Hackett, Beatrice N., 'Transforming Identities and Changing Contexts: Ethnic German Refugees and Expellees 1945-1990', in: Pamela A. DeVoe (ed.), *Selected Papers on Refugee Issues*, Committee on Refugee Issues, American Anthropological Association, Washington, D.C., 1992, pp. 40-55.

Heller, Walter, 'Economic Policy and Political Equilibrium in Postwar Germany', in: Hans J. Morgenthau (ed.), *Germany and the Future of Europe*, Chicago, 1951, pp. 58-75.

Hirschon, Renée, *Heirs of the Greek Catastrophe: The Social Life of Asia Minor Refugees in Piraeus*, Oxford, 1989.
Hoffman, Dierk and Michael Schwartz (eds.), *Geglückte Integration? Spezifika und Vergleichbarkeiten der Vertriebenen-Eingliederung in der SBZ/DDR*, Munich, 1999.
House of Lords, *Parliamentary Debates*, vol. 130, Fifth Series, London, 1944.
Karakasidou, Anastasia, *Fields of Wheat, Hills of Blood: Passages to Nationhood in Greek Macedonia, 1870-1990*, Chicago, 1997.
Katzenstein, Peter J., *Policy and Politics in West Germany: The Growth of a Semi-Sovereign State*, Philadelphia, 1987.
Kaufmann, Chaim, 'Possible and Impossible Solutions to Ethnic Wars', *International Security* 4 (1996): pp. 136-175.
Kaufmann, Chaim, 'When All Else Fails: Ethnic Population Transfers and Partitions in the Twentieth Century', *International Security* 2 (1998): pp. 120-156.
Keeley, Charles B., 'How Nation-States Create and Respond to Refugee Flows', *International Migration Review* 30 (1998): pp. 1046-1066.
Kitzinger, Uwe, *German Electoral Politics: A Study of the 1957 Campaign*, London, 1960.
Koufa, Kalliopi K. and Constantinos Svolopoulos, 'The Compulsory Exchange of Populations Between Greece and Turkey: The Settlement of Minority Questions at the Conference of Laussane, 1923, and its Impact on Greek-Turkish Relations', in: Paul Smith (eds.), *Ethnic Groups in International Relations: Comparative Studies on Governments and Non-Dominant Ethnic Groups in Europe, 1850-1940*, vol. V, New York, 1991, pp. 275-308.
Kulischer, Eugene, *Europe on the Move*, New York, 1948.
Kumar, Radha, 'Partition's Troubled History', *Foreign Affairs* 1 (1997): pp. 22-34.
Kumar, Radha, *Divide and Fall: Bosnia in the Annals of Partition*, London and New York, 1997.
Ladas, Stephen P., *The Exchange of Minorities: Bulgaria, Greece, and Turkey*, New York, 1932.
Lee, Sabine, 'CDU Refugee Policies and the Landesverband Oder/Neisse: Electoral Tool or Instrument of Integration?', *German Politics* 8 (1999): pp. 131-149.
Legg, Keith R., *Politics in Modern Greece*, Stanford, 1969.
Maier, Charles, *In Search of Stability: Explorations in Historical Political Economy*, Cambridge, 1987.
Maier, Charles, 'The Two Postwar Eras and the Conditions for Stability in Twentieth Century Western Europe', in: Charles Maier, *In Search of Stability: Explorations in Historical Political Economy*, Cambridge, 1987.
Mavrogordatos, George T., *Stillborn Republic: Social Coalitions and Party Strategies in Greece, 1922-1936*, Berkeley, Los Angeles and London, 1983.
Mavrogordatos, George T., 'The 1940s: Between Past and Future', in: John O. Iatrides and Linda Wrigley (eds.), *Greece at the Crossroads: The Civil War and Its Legacy*, University Park, PA, 1995, pp. 31-47.
Mazower, Mark, *Greece and the Interwar Economic Crisis*, Oxford, 1991.
Mears, E. G., *Greece Today: The Aftermath of the Refugee Impact*, Stanford, 1929.
Mitrany, David, *The Effect of the War in Southeastern Europe*, New York, 1973.
Morgenthau, Henry, *I Was Sent to Athens*, Garden City, 1929.
Neumann, Franz, *Der Block der Heimatvertriebenen und Entrechteten 1950-1960. Ein Beitrag zur Geschichte und Struktur einer politischen Interessenpartei*, Meisenheim am Glan, 1968.
Neumann, Sigmund, 'The New Crisis Strata in German Society', in: Hans J. Morgenthau (ed.), *Germany and the Future of Europe*, Chicago, 1951, pp. 25-39.

O'Hanlon, Michael, 'Turning the Cease Fire Into Peace', *Brookings Review* 1 (1998): pp. 41-44.

Pape, Robert A., 'Partition: An Exit Strategy for Bosnia', *Survival* 4 (1997-98): pp. 25-28.

Pentzopoulos, Dimitri, *The Balkan Exchange of Populations and its Impact Upon Greece*, Paris and The Hague, 1962.

Rodgers, Daniel E., *Politics after Hitler: The Western Allies and the German Party System*, London, 1995.

Sarandis, Constantine, 'The Ideological Character of the Metaxas Regime', in: Robin Higham and Thanos Veremis (eds.), *The Metaxas Dictatorship: Aspects of Greece, 1936-1940*, Athens, 1993, pp. 144-177.

Schechtman, Joseph B., *The Refugee in the World: Displacement and Integration*, New York, 1963.

Schoenberg, Hans W., *Germans from the East. A Study of their Migration, Resettlement and Subsequent Group History since 1945*, The Hague, 1960.

Schraut, Sylvia, 'Zwischen Assimilationsdiktat und Fürsorgeverpflichtung: Die amerikanische Besatzungsmacht und die Flüchtlinge', in: Mathias Beer (ed.), *Zur Integration der Flüchtlinge und Vertriebenen im deutschen Südwesten nach 1945: Bestandsaufnahme und Perspektiven der Forschung*, Sigmaringen, 1994, pp. 77-94.

Schulze, Rainer, 'Growing Discontent: Relations between Native and Refugee Populations in a Rural District in Western Germany after the Second World War', *German History* 7 (1989): pp. 332-350.

Schulze, Rainer, 'The Refugee Population in Western Germany After World War II: The Case of Lower Saxony (*Niedersachsen*)', in: Goran Rystad (ed.), *The Uprooted: Forced Migration as an International Problem in the Post-War Era*, Lund, 1990, pp. 289-330.

Schwarz, Leo W., *Refugees in Germany Today*, New York, 1957.

Sherwood, Robert E., *Roosevelt and Hopkins*, New York, 1948.

Société des Nations, *L'Établissement des Réfugiés en Grèce*, Geneva, 1926.

Ther, Phillip, 'The Integration of Expellees in Germany and Poland after World War II: A Historical Reassessment', *Slavic Review* 55 (1996): pp. 779-805.

Ther, Philipp, *Deutsche und polnische Vertriebene. Gesellschaft und Vertriebenenpolitik in der SBZ/DDR und in Polen*, Göttingen, 1999.

Tsoucalas, Constantine, 'The Ideological Impact of the Civil War', in: John O. Iatrides (ed.), *Greece in the 1940s: A Nation in Crisis*, Hanover, NH, 1981, pp. 319-342.

United States, Department of State, *Foreign Relations of the United States*, vol. 3, 1943.

Veremis, Thanos, *1922: Old Themes, New Challenges*, unpublished ms., Refugee Studies Programme, Oxford, 1998.

Voutira, Eftihia, 'Population Transfers and Resettlement Policies in Interwar Europe: The Case of Asia Minor Refugees in Macedonia from and International and National Perspective', in: Peter Mackridge and Eleni Yannakakis (eds.), *Ourselves and Others: The Development of a Greek Macedonian Cultural Identity Since 1912*, Oxford and New York, 1997, pp. 111-132.

Wells, Sumner, *Where are We Heading?*, New York, 1946.

Zayas, Alfred-Maurice de, *Nemesis at Potsdam: The Expulsion of the Germans from the East*, Lincoln and London, 1989.

Zayas, Alfred-Maurice de, *The German Expellees: Victims in War and Peace*, New York, 1993.

Zolberg, Aristide R., 'The Formation of New States as a Refugee-Generating Process', *Annals of the American Academy of Political and Social Science* 467 (1983): pp. 24-38.

Chapter 7

Why Governments Do Not Learn: Colonial Migrants and Gypsy Refugees in the Netherlands

Wim Willems

We can identify many patterns in the behaviour of policy-makers and governments. This chapter will focus on five of them, which I derive from the field of post-war migration to the Netherlands. To prove my points I will elaborate upon the history of colonial migrants from what is now Indonesia, but before 27 December 1949 used to be the Dutch East Indies.[1] In the decades following the Second World War the colonial European community in that part of the world was forced by the changing political tide to leave a society which started to look upon them as a category of strangers.

I will proceed to examine whether the Dutch government gained any useful experiences for the time of the decolonization of Surinam in the 1970s, when it was the government's policy to admit and accommodate all would-be migrants who had once been fellow members of the Dutch Empire. Third, I will test my findings in relation to policy during the same years towards a specific group of non-colonial refugees, i.e., foreign Gypsies.

Five Assumptions about Government Policy

My first hypothesis is that governments, from top to bottom, almost always react to what happens instead of anticipating it. Policy takes shape in response to largely unforeseen or unexpected events and as a consequence policy makers rather frequently find themselves reacting to events. There are three reasons why this is so: first, policy commitments and their implementation do not always fit together well; second, the interests of the various parties involved are often diametrically opposed; and, third, as a result of decentralized responsibilities, policy is never homogeneous. While policy-makers can brim over with resolutions, in their execution they are dependent on actors and processes not always amenable to control from above. Conflicts of interest in the international arena, as well as differences in outlook, responsibilities and vested interests among departments at the national level or between central and local governments, often impede the formulation of a unified policy. Since such jockeying often takes place behind the scenes and out of public scrutiny, the proportion of problematic negotiations usually remains opaque to those involved, for example to migrants, as well as to outsiders.

My second hypothesis predicates that policy makers and those who do their bidding have short memories. Whoever scrutinizes government policy over a somewhat longer time span now and then comes in for a surprise at how rapidly acquired knowledge fades away again. It seems as if within a single governmental period – four years in the Netherlands – memory withdraws into the archives.

My third hypothesis is that migrants are seldom judged on their merits. Not only are stereotypes often decisive, governments are often led by wishful thinking. One of the consequences of this state of affairs is that the dynamics of migration are systematically underestimated.

Although it may sound contradictory to what appears above, my fourth postulate asserts that the idea that the Netherlands is a tolerant country – albeit comparatively – is not entirely false. The notion that coloured Dutch from the East Indies have become identified as a racial group and are therefore not socially accepted, as the Dutch anthropologist John Schuster argued not so long ago, strikes me as indefensible.[2] That is not to say that in the fifties and subsequent decades the Netherlands was free of racism, prejudices or negative stereotypes where newcomers from then Indonesia were concerned. Rather, I wish to point out that in postcolonial Netherlands the authorities were sensitive to the social code 'Thou shalt not discriminate'. Political receptivity for the spirit of the times meant that every potential mechanism of exclusion sooner or later had to yield to the authority of the national self-image.

Fifth, whoever wishes to follow the logic of governments, instead of concentrating on the written intentions, would do well to study who bore financial responsibility for what. He who wishes to get to the bottom of a policy should follow the money. Neither reason nor the twisted path of argumentation or invocation of principles offers a solution. The answer to the following question, however, does: Who is presented with the bill?

Policy is Reactive

The history of colonial migration from the East Indies and later Indonesia to the Netherlands serves to illustrate my first hypothesis. In the early 1950s a fierce parliamentary struggle was waged by the central authorities in order to pass a resolution that would enable them to apply pressure on municipalities to make housing available to the Dutch Indies' repatriates.[3] This resulted in the Repatriate Housing Law, a temporary measure to ease the housing shortage among persons 'repatriated' from Indonesia, Surinam and the Dutch Antilles. Provincial inspectors of the Social Welfare Services, who facilitated the first phase of the integration process in the name of the Ministry of the Interior, acquired the authority to intervene wherever municipalities refused on unacceptable grounds to allow the state to requisition residences intended for repatriates.

Why did municipalities behave so apprehensively? In the first decades after the Second World War the housing shortage was Public Enemy No. 1 in the Netherlands. The last thing cities and towns needed was a stream of newcomers. They were having a hard enough time supplying their own registered population with a roof over their heads. With memories of their experiences under German occupation still fresh, they were not receptive to the proposal, handed down from above, to limit their autonomy. Yet, in the end, the government won out. The crisis was too acute. True, it took seven months to sway parliament, but the emergency act was renewed without difficulty until 1955. During this period 6,737 families of repatriates, altogether some 25,000 persons, were assisted with housing. Inspectors rarely had to resort to imposing their authority. On, at most, twenty occasions they were obliged to requisition a dwelling. In addition, after 1952, invoking regulations about priority housing rights, authorities assigned half of the total housing units which the government could claim for state employees to repatriates. All in all, this involved some 5 per cent of the residences which fell under the housing act.

Until 1963, the housing of repatriates always, in one form or another, entailed a policy of compulsion with compensation for municipalities who trailed almost invariably behind the facts.[4] Experience taught that in the first instance, for example, a quarter of the repatriates followed the path to The Hague, an unsettling situation for the city council, which led them to complain of their predicament to the central government. Due to a combination of war damage in parts of The Hague and the expansion of state services, which brought with it a formidable population growth, the city believed that in the early 1950s it could no longer provide houses for new arrivals from the then Indonesia. Whoever had no residence permit could from then on expect to be turned out of his house. At least that was the city's strictly worded intention, although nothing much ever came of the resolution.[5] Hundreds of eviction orders may have been served, but in practice no one was banned from the city. If one managed to find a place to live in The Hague, chances were he or she would be able to stay.

In other words, unruly reality seldom allows itself be tamed from above. Moreover, conflicts of interest prove a considerable hindrance to any homogeneous policy. With regularity the parties concerned find themselves compelled to modify their stance. Thus it has been shown that during the first half of the 1950s the Dutch government was not particularly generous and warm-hearted towards some groups of Indonesian-Dutch who wanted to migrate to their unknown fatherland and claimed state funds to support them.[6] When, despite lack of help and often wholly through their own devices, migrants succeeded in reaching the Netherlands, they became automatically eligible for all the reception facilities provided by this same government. Such stratification of policy generates contradictions that make it difficult to anticipate developments in relation to each other.

Policy-makers Have Short Memories

A somewhat dramatic example of my second hypothesis is the discussion about material losses suffered during the Second World War by the Dutch Indies' community. In the summer of 1951 the Ministry of Overseas Affairs asked Mr. N.S. Blom, then Secretary of State for Foreign Affairs and previously, during the Japanese invasion, Minister of Justice in the Dutch East Indies, to let his light shine on this issue. Blom did not bother to undertake an extensive inspection of relevant files, but improvised, mining his own memory. He thought he recalled that the problem was acute after the outbreak of hostilities with Japan. In the State Mobilization Council it was then agreed that Justice would take on responsibility for war victims and the possessions they left behind, while Economic Affairs would occupy itself with material losses. That led to a War Compensation Act, which the People's Council had adopted in February 1942. As far as material loss was concerned, Blom recalled that at the time it was constantly emphasized that absolutely no responsibility to indemnify rested on the state. Something would of course have to be arranged, but individuals had no right to make any claims on the state.

This was the position zealously maintained by the Ministry of Colonial Affairs in exile in London during the war years whenever claims were made. Blom still remembered the case of the BPM oil company which demanded compensation for a ship the marines had requisitioned and that was later destroyed by enemy fire. At the time the claim was denied. The idea was only to pay out if the money would go to the reconstruction of things useful to the community. The government never went much further in its concessions. Because the case had been handled at least ten years earlier, Blom concluded by encouraging further investigation: 'Perhaps it's still possible to find somewhere in Indonesia evidence on the aforementioned budgetary post. That would make it possible to determine whether my memory misleads me, and, if so, to what extent'.[7] The investigation only began in earnest in subsequent months; then documents were procured which were carefully examined.[8] The memories of the policy-makers involved proved to be shaky and limited and were no longer taken as a point of departure for the development of new policies. Thus, the claims were finally taken seriously and the archival files considered as the only justifiable source for historical reconstruction.

The Dynamics of Migration are Underestimated

The third hypothesis requires further explication, for it is connected to definitions of the category 'Indo' (coloured Dutch from the Indies), and thus with decisions on the right to migrate to the Netherlands. In the early 1950s the designation 'Dutch' was not sufficient to entitle anyone to migrate. Especially the passage and assimilation of 'those with their roots in the former colony' remained controversial. Whoever fit this description could expect a reluctant, if not hostile response from the authorities. The criteria for selection of migrants from Indonesia shifted and were an ongoing subject of controversies and discussions, though different camps of thought were not clearly demarcated.

The military comprised a category which illustrates particularly well the confusion prevailing within the ranks of the government.[9] In the spring of 1950, it proved necessary to charter no fewer than seven British ships to accommodate the removal of Dutch migrants from Indonesia. There were 25,000 citizens on the rolls to make the journey whose births and upbringing indicated an indisputable orientation to the Netherlands. They were welcome, plain and simple. Feelings towards the estimated 14,000 soldiers of the former Dutch colonial army and their families, in all some 45,000 persons, were more complicated. Questioning divulged that roughly 5,000 of these military personnel belonged to the category of people with their roots in the Asian society. The government considered giving them a premium if they chose to face the future in their land of origin. For the others, those who originally were at home in the Netherlands and served permanently in the colonial army, possibilities were explored for their transfer to the royal army in the Netherlands. Sifting had to occur in Indonesia. It was expected that (sub)officers could move into the royal army without problems, albeit at a lower rank. Corporals and their inferiors were likely to fall out of the military boat. In the selection process, for both the royal army and the voyage to the Netherlands, it made no difference whether someone was European-Dutch or of mixed origin. There were still no clear guidelines for drawing such distinctions. The concepts of 'leavers' as opposed to 'stayers' (in the former colony) were also inadequate indicators, for before the war so-called full-blooded Dutchmen had also been recruited in the colony for the local army, whereas especially Indo-Europeans were signed on in Holland. Where the military was concerned, origin and place of birth were insufficient criteria to exclude anyone from repatriation. Only a lump sum of money and limited transport capacities might, as the government hoped, prevent them from too hastily deciding to depart.[10]

Thus, at the start of the 1950s priority was given to slowing the influx of repatriates. Temporary accommodation in camps cost too much money, there was a chronic shortage of housing and the labour market was far from flourishing. This attitude was shared by both the Dutch government and the Coordination Commission for the Repatriated.[11] But soldiers from the former colonial army, just like pensioners and the self-employed, had a right to a free passage to the Netherlands. Considering the situation carefully, we see that the only would-be travellers who could be culled from those waiting to go were Dutch-Indies who in normal times would most likely have remained in the new republic of Indonesia, but who now sold their belongings to raise the fare to Holland. They were regarded by members of the commission as incapable of accepting the political changes in Indonesia, although it seemed much better for them to opt for the status of an Indonesian citizen. It was assumed that they were strongly attached to their Dutch nationality and felt superior to Indonesians and believed they had only the Netherlands to fall back on. It appeared dubious whether these low-level civil servants could adapt readily in the Netherlands, but those who retained Dutch citizenship in Indonesia soon found themselves out in the street. Those who were not civil servants lived under constant threat. If they paid for their journey themselves, the government could hardly refuse to admit them. On the grounds of their function, state employees could even insist on transportation to Holland. And that, in large numbers, is precisely what they did.

In the meantime the Dutch government began to sound the alarm anew.[12] To their minds the High Commissioner in Jakarta was too generous in advancing funds to needy Dutchmen for their voyage. The housing crisis in the Netherlands had in the interim grown more acute. The arrival of discharged Moluccan soldiers from the former colonial army and their families, some 12,500 people, and the shaky financial position of the country, made it necessary to shut the tap still further. It was time to draft even stricter guidelines. Until that moment the four categories generally admitted were the poor, reuniting family members, those with medical conditions and persons seeking personal safety. Anyone without paid work and not enough savings to live on in Indonesia was deemed poor, and was permitted to come to the Netherlands, so long as he or she could provide evidence of potential housing and could pay for their own living expenses, possibly with the support of family. Those claiming to satisfy this criterion were generally given the benefit of the doubt, except persons with Asian roots. The accuracy of the information provided by the latter had to be verified. The intention was to allow as few paupers as possible to migrate. It cost less to help them survive in their land of origin with social welfare from the Commission. The same was true for people wanting to rejoin their families in Holland. The Ministry of Overseas Affairs zealously checked their data. For the poor who were ill, a medical authority had to prescribe their transport. Should the patient be the head of a family, the rest could go with him. It also happened that people had to leave to seek a safe haven in the Netherlands. In such instances the state paid for their voyage.

None of the four categories left very much room for attempts to reduce the number of persons eligible to migrate. The only remaining possibility to curb the influx of the poor was to curtail stipends advanced to those who were not oriented to Holland. To monitor this the Ministry of Overseas Affairs was dependent on the decisions handed down by the department of the High Commissioner in Jakarta (the most important Dutch representative in Indonesia). They, however, provided absolutely no indication of the category the indigent belonged to. Apparently, in Indonesia at that moment they found drawing such distinctions problematic. As long as Jakarta was tied to The Hague's apron strings, something had to happen. Sharper control, to the extent possible, and more specific definition of the terms used were demanded.[13] Yet in guidelines distributed to seven regional commissions, the High Commissioner left it at that. The decisive principle remained whether the wish to migrate was born of necessity. In practice such a point of departure offered little concrete to hold on to. This was no less true of the overlapping descriptions 'not oriented to the Netherlands' and 'with roots in Indonesia'. The Commissioner was very well aware that differences in interpretation were unavoidable. Some were of the opinion that a person had the right to make the voyage if, with family help in the Netherlands, he could fit in, or was engaged in a steady correspondence with his or her father-in-law who already lived there. Others believed that being born in Holland should be decisive. After a great deal of quibbling, the following shadowy definition emerged:

> Persons oriented to the Netherlands are those who, measured by an objective standard, will, with reasonable certainty, upon migration to the Netherlands feel at home without (much) difficulty in the special sphere and circumstances, in other words, those who belong here.[14]

Nothing became any clearer, for 'feeling at home' could hardly be called a precise criterion. The motivation to prevent people from leaving derived in practice from, above all, negative arguments. The departure of people to the Netherlands who did not belong there was said to have resulted in their bitter disappointment and regrets about having made the decision too lightly. The High Commissioner indeed recognized that the 'lower class Indo-Dutch' saw themselves obliged by circumstances to get away from Indonesia as soon as possible, but, because they had no idea of what awaited them in the Netherlands, they easily ended up working against their own interests. Thus, in a certain sense they had to be protected against themselves. For to be stuck for the rest of their lives in Holland, experience taught, proved an alarming prospect. The moral decay they were exposed to as a group in Indonesia was certainly not counteracted by departure to the Netherlands; rather it was intensified.[15] What had to be done was to construct a dam to contain the suffering caused by unnecessary relocation. It was in this spirit Dutch representatives in Indonesia were to work.

It was thus first and foremost financial and societal considerations which, on the Dutch side, led to further reduction of the number of repatriates – at least on paper, for, as already noted, three-fourths of the needy simply arrived without any government support. In discussions of qualifying criteria, which became characterized by an increasing subtlety, money played an invisible leading role. Financial injections for Dutch paupers in Indonesia cost less than their reception and accommodation in the Netherlands. The state, however, had but a small arsenal of weapons where the selection process was involved. Only through a painfully meticulous administrative process was it possible to determine whether would-be migrants truly were in a life-threatening situation, were physically unwell, had family members or the chance of a normal livelihood in the Netherlands.[16] As they shied away from introducing such a procedure, the authorities remained focused on a category as murky as 'oriented to Indonesia', a desperate move to sustain the illusion of having some grip on a movement which had its own dynamics. In decisions on who belonged to this category, neither racial, nor phenotypical, nor biological characteristics played a role. Which is not to say that all kinds of things might not have infiltrated civil servants' minds. Just as irrelevant, on the whole, were origin and birth. What did make themselves felt were social class and (previous) status. Vocational qualifications and curriculum vitae were even more important. At the start of the 1950s 'oriented to the Netherlands' meant no more than having a family there or a demonstrable prospect of employment.

Dutch Policy is Comparatively Tolerant

It is true that during the first half of the fifties the government tried to implement a policy of discouraging Dutch with Asian roots to migrate to the Netherlands. But when John Schuster argues that this was a manifestation of virulent racist ideas circulating in those days, he goes too far.[17] Given that between 1945 and 1968 some 300,000 so-called repatriates came to the Netherlands and that it was only during the period 1951 to 1955 when (only partly successful) tactics were set in operation to keep some potential migrants where they were, it is inadequate to qualify Dutch policy as racist. Restrictive strategies were drafted behind the scenes, but they provoked resistance at the time and were challenged by the Churches and other social organizations.[18] The media in the 1950s did perhaps present the coloured Dutch from the Indies as 'symbolic foreigners', as Schuster asserts,[19] but widespread 'cold feet' towards this category of compatriots from overseas soon disappeared. If we compare these attitudes to far more deeply ingrained mechanisms of rejection, such as those which continue to affect relations with Jews and so-called Gypsy groups, they appear relatively harmless. Politicians and other authorities made it clear in public that people from the former colony indeed belonged to the Dutch nation and had the right to settle in the Netherlands. After only about ten years they were cited as the classic example of newcomers who smoothly found their way within Dutch society. Schuster is highly suspicious of how Prime Minister W. Drees *cum suis* invoked the tolerance and hospitality of the Dutch people, suggesting we should 'read' this as a dishonest appeal to a national fiction.[20] He thinks the appeal was false because it denied the reality of small disturbances which broke out, minor discrimination and other forms of painful exclusion. But whatever may have gone through the Prime Minister's mind, his public speeches can justifiably be interpreted as an adequate and responsible response to widespread fears in the face of tens of thousands of newcomers. People need to be encouraged or urged to behave in a morally acceptable fashion. The conduct of the authorities was adequate in so far as racial antagonism was conspicuous for its absence.

Money Determines Policy

To prove my fifth and last hypothesis, dozens of examples from the treatment of the decolonization issue could be quoted. If, in the following, I refer to the half-hearted support for the migration of former colonial soldiers to the Netherlands, this is a more or less arbitrary choice.[21] In July 1949, Prime Minister Drees had declared in the cabinet that the colonial army was a Dutch-Indies organ and therefore had to undergo a transition to become part of the United States of Indonesia (USI). This standpoint provoked staunch criticism, for the soldiers involved had since 1945 maintained close ties to the Dutch armed forces who had fought for years against the freedom fighters of the newly declared republic of Indonesia. This 'fusion' could not be dissolved, and placing the colonial army in the hands of its former foe – the Indonesian army that had struggled for independence – would be outrageous. At most, individual colonial soldiers were to be allowed to join the ranks of the Indonesian forces. Compulsion was absurd. Yet the premier stuck to his guns and insisted that especially Indonesians serving in the former colonial army had little desire to come to Holland. Giving them free choice could have dire financial consequences for the Dutch treasury. Financial considerations were the Prime Minister's major concern.[22]

In this context, categorization also played a role. Some government members found that *Dutch* soldiers from the former colonial army who returned should *under certain circumstances* be able to take advantage of guarantees then being drafted. Nonetheless they wished to embark on negotiations about the decolonization process at the Round Table Conference (RTC) in 1949 – between Indonesia and the Netherlands – with a couple of intransigent points of departure. First, the colonial army had never been a Dutch organ. Thus, after transfer of sovereignty the army must not cost the Netherlands another penny. Second, there should not be a whisper breathed about voluntary absorption within the Indonesian services. Before this was agreed upon, the Dutch military commission reacted with fury and months of bitter debate ensued.[23]

The Prime Minister threw all his weight into the balance. To offer army personnel the alternative of migration to the Netherlands would lead to financial ruin. It would moreover play into the hands of the Indonesians at the decolonization conference, providing them with an argument for disowning responsibility for military debts. Another point was that it was none other than the colonial army itself that provided in his eyes a countervailing force against the military forces in non-republican areas of the new Indonesian state, a kind of guarantee against the outbreak of civil war. An obligatory shift of colonial army allegiance to independent Indonesia was therefore, in a certain sense, a necessity, also to protect Dutch interests in Indonesia.

Drees's outspoken point of view provoked an equally sharp rebuttal. Colonial army Major General D.R.A. van Langen cautioned that unless the legal position of the Indonesian personnel of the Indies branch of the army was formulated clearly, chaos could be the result. It would reinforce the sense of an overhanging threat, which could easily lead to resignations on a grand scale, refusals to enter military service, underground resistance, turncoats and banditry. His rhetoric seems to have struck a responsive chord in most members of parliament, and new rounds of discussion were held.[24] On the eve of the transfer of power from the Dutch to the Indonesians, it was resolved that liquidation of the colonial army would proceed under the aegis of the Dutch government, but from 1950 the financial burden would be borne by the Indonesian budget.

The Expensive Lessons of Indonesia Applied to Surinam

The preceding account of problems prompts the question what the Dutch government learned during the decolonization of Indonesia that it could profitably apply during the events leading up to Surinam's independence on 25 November 1975, especially concerning the flow of migration which the transfer of sovereignty had set in motion. After the Second World War, steadily more Surinamese moved to Holland,[25] searching for a way to improve their lives, or brought from Surinam to work in factories, hospitals, nursing homes or offices. From the 1960s onward, the aim to climb the social ladder motivated people from all social and ethnic groups to migrate. It partly acquired the character of chain migration: family members, acquaintances and friends arranged for those left behind to come and join them, paying their way and providing a welcoming nest upon arrival. From the newcomer's point of view, it seemed at first as if the trees in the Netherlands grew all the way to heaven. In these years it was pretty easy to find work, work that paid better than jobs in Surinam. In Holland illness, invalidity or retirement did not mean impoverishment.

Migration was legally supported by the Commonwealth Treaty of 1954, which bestowed the same rights on Surinamese and Antillians as were enjoyed by so-called indigenous Dutch. While in the past Creoles (people with 'black roots') were the ones to migrate as pioneers, during the late 1960s two planes full of Hindustanis (who had migrated from India as indentured labourers at the end of the nineteenth century) from rural areas took off daily from the Zanderij airfield to alight at Amsterdam-Schiphol.[26] They had a real fear thrown into them when the Creole nationalists exploited their election victory of September 1973 to open negotiations with the Dutch Prime Minister, J. M. den Uyl, about independence for Surinam. Dutch threats to put a stop to migration had the opposite effect of what was intended. Inhabitants of Surinam with vague migration plans hastily left before Surinam under Creole leadership would dominate their lives.

When, in 1974, it became definite that Surinam would become independent, the migration swelled to vast proportions. The Great Crossing seemed irresistible. Some 80,000 Surinamese people settled in 1974 and 1975 in the distant 'fatherland'. The date of independence signalled the first levelling off of the migration curve. For five more years the door to the Netherlands was left ajar; thereafter a visa was required. As a consequence, up until the close of the 1980s, additional tens of thousands of Surinamese came to seek their fortune in Holland. The catastrophic results of this mass exodus and brain drain for Surinam's infrastructure are still being felt today.

How did the Netherlands, and in particular the government, respond to the surging stream of migrants? As the 1960s passed, Surinamese were ever more visible: on trams, in office canteens, on the football field. An image widespread in those days portrayed the Surinamese male as an uneducated Negro who could not succeed in society and almost automatically remained dependent on welfare payments, and landed in the world of criminality and prostitution. Such stereotypes were partly influenced by the coincidence of the arrival of Surinamese people with that of labour migrants from Mediterranean coastal areas. In a certain sense people began to regard the Surinamese newcomers also as (temporary) foreign workers. The rapid rise in migration after 1970 conjured images in the minds of politicians of a marginal group in society whose rampant increase could not be stopped. This explains why migration occupied a central place in political discussions between the two countries. On the Dutch side, the fear existed that the welfare state, in particular the system of social support, would attract their former fellow commonwealth members from Surinam and the Antilles with a magnetic power.

At the time, the Netherlands did not consider itself an immigration country. It once observed as much explicitly in a government memo entitled 'Foreign Workers' (1970). Extant policy was the concern of the Ministry for Social Work, which for a long time also coordinated the assistance provided to Dutch from the Indies and to Moluccans. The Foreigners Law provided the Ministry of Justice with an instrument to restrict migration, although it was useless where Surinamese who had Dutch citizenship were concerned. Even so, after 1972 voices calling for restricting migration from Surinam increased in volume. The media suggested that a stop was imminent. An advisory commission appointed to study the question of migration from Surinam concluded that in the light of the Royal Statute it was not possible to pass measures which would treat Dutch, Surinamese and Antillians differently. Not only the ever-accelerating migration, but fear of having to intervene in civil unrest in Surinam, inclined the government to find ways to extricate itself from the statute's provisions. The wish to get rid of a neo-colonial image of the Netherlands also played a part. Others emphasized the financial blood-letting involved.

This trend dovetailed neatly with the more robust nationalistic striving of Surinamese intellectuals, above all those of black origin. They were bent on independence, even if Surinam's Prime Minister H. Arron announced the wish somewhat reluctantly. Consistent with the decolonization process in Indonesia, in the case of Surinam the Netherlands was determined to confer Surinamese citizenship on as many people as possible. In August 1974 talks began on nationality. The Netherlands proposed that, regardless of how long they may have lived in the Netherlands, all persons with a Surinamese father (or, where paternity was unknown, a Surinamese mother) would lose their Dutch nationality. The Surinamese negotiators refused to accept such an insulting and racially-based provision as a workable point of departure. In the end the most obvious solution was found acceptable, i.e., Surinamese in the Netherlands retained a Dutch passport, as well as the right to opt for Surinamese nationality. The former colonial power made the extremely far-reaching concession that the traffic of people between Surinam and the Netherlands would be free for five years following independence. After that the government would require visas.

The rapid implementation of independence was for cabinet, parliament and public opinion clearly a manifestation of the wish to put an end to Surinamese migration to the Netherlands. Thanks to the political ferment and high emotions surrounding independence, however, the result was until 1980 more migration than before. What happened was exactly what people had been afraid of: As long as the door to Holland stood open, even if only a crack, it drew people by suction. Dutch politicians, pinned in between their flexible attitude towards the movement for independence on the one hand and their wish to control the volume of human traffic between both countries on the other, were truly startled by this spectacular turn of events. In a practically immediate response, they brought forward a plan to make additional funds available to bolster the Surinamese economy. It never seems to have penetrated the minds of the responsible officials that the migration in question was at no time primarily economically motivated but rather a flight from looming political uncertainty and ethnic unrest.[27] It sufficed the government to lavish funds on the *Tenasu* foundation, established to facilitate return migration and to cling to the idea that in the long run most Surinamese migrants would go back of their own accord. The desire to return home, actually expressed by many newcomers, was, upon close examination, influenced above all by the surroundings in which they lived in Holland.[28] In fact, it was in some ways similar to the Surinamese drive to achieve independence, which also never itself enjoyed much support on the grassroots level. It was more a matter of ideology than practice – statistics indicate as much. With difficulty and only after 1980, once the Surinamese political system had turned into a military dictatorship, Dutch attitudes towards Surinamese immigration became more realistic. With the publication of a Memo on Minorities in 1983 the government, for the first time, conceded that post-war immigrants, including former fellow commonwealth members, had come to stay.

The Refugee as Foreigner

In order to penetrate to the heart of policy regarding the entry and reception of colonial migrants, comparison is necessary with a group of refugees without historical ties to the Netherlands. For this purpose it is useful to examine the policy the government adopted in the post-war context towards foreign Gypsies (nowadays designated as Roma), who were legalized as residents between 1978 and 1980.[29] In 1969, for the first time in a long while, Gypsies from Eastern Europe began to arrive, especially from former Yugoslavia. In contrast to Belgian and Scandinavian Gypsies who came on sporadic (family) visits, they expressed the wish to settle permanently. In the 1970s various other small groups of Yugoslav, but also Hungarian and Czechoslovak Gypsies followed. The image of these newcomers which central and local authorities shared exhibited parallels with thinking from the previous century.[30] By definition Gypsies were considered undesirable aliens. However aware one might have been of the pitiful circumstances in which they lived, the opinion prevailed that they had come to the Netherlands to milk the favourable social welfare system and that with their asocial and criminal behaviour, they were a nuisance to the population.

The Dutch authorities acknowledged that as refugees – or in contemporary terminology, potential asylum seekers – they were disadvantaged, but they wished to take no responsibility for this. The Ministry of Justice was, to be sure, familiar with the centuries-long persecution of groups which belonged to this category of foreigners, climaxing in the atrocities of the Second World War, but this never induced the government to consider conferring on them the status of refugees entitled to sanctuary. Common policy dictated getting rid of them as quickly as possible. When that proved a bit difficult, the tactic of keeping them moving was adopted. This entailed continuously urging them to move on (often from municipality to municipality) in the hope that at last they would leave the country, while providing them with a bare minimum of facilities. This policy amounted to making their stay in the Netherlands as unpleasant as possible. Consistent with its attempt to prevent settlement, the ministry was constantly on the alert to thwart volunteers, sympathizers and the media who would champion the Gypsies' cause. Experience taught that the more visible Gypsies became in the public eye, the harder it was to shake them off.

The legalization of some 500 foreign Gypsies in a number of steps between 1978 and 1980 flew in the face of usual policy. Although governments carried on as before when it came to new illegal Gypsies, policy towards the group of 500 was modified, including an entitlement to residence which the Ministry of Justice, under pressure, recognized. The fundamental point of departure of policy nevertheless remained – and still remains today – the strict application of regulations for aliens so that, for those who are legally unified with their families or married with non-residents, a residence permit can be blocked for years. A number of arguments were used to legitimize this restrictive policy towards Gypsies. First was the need to forestall any *specific suction effect*, i.e., attracting ever-increasing numbers of Gypsies to the Netherlands. Second, it was the aim to avoid a *general suction effect*, the attraction of droves of other categories of undesirable aliens. Third was the desire not to set a *specific precedent* that might enable other Gypsies to claim for themselves the special position (an unlimited residence permit) accorded to the first group. Fourth, the government was determined to avoid setting a *general precedent*, which might encourage other aliens to apply for such special status.[31]

This standpoint should be placed in the context of the generally restrictive policy the Netherlands maintains with respect to admitting foreigners, expressed in, among other documents, the above-mentioned Memo on Minorities. Going back a long way, this policy has aimed at limiting immigration even in periods of cyclical prosperity. Exceptions are made only for those sorely needed in the labour market, for refugees and for asylum-seekers. Foreigners who do not live up to the official ideal of beauty – that is, who are not considered likely to contribute to the economy but seem likely instead to be a burden – have their papers stamped: unwanted. And these are precisely the very associations which the image of the Gypsy summoned – and even today summon – to mind. It was accordingly far from surprising that the foreigners from Yugoslavia who arrived in Amsterdam in 1971 were confronted almost immediately by a restrictive policy. By virtue of their openly itinerant way of life, their moving about with wives and children in caravans or tents, they were a perfect match of the traditional image of the Gypsy.

Why then were they legalized seven years later? The Secretary of State in the Ministry of Justice is the figure who bears political responsibility for possible changes in policy. Driven by both practical and humanitarian motives – the Gypsies could not be expelled without public protest and Holland's international image was at stake – between 1973 and 1977 two of them successfully used their room to manoeuvre. In an interview, one former Minister told me that the legalization of some 15,000 foreign workers announced in 1975 had made the acceptance of a comparatively small group of Gypsies easier.[32] In a certain sense the legalization of foreign Gypsies took place in the wake of the great 'general amnesty'. Groups of sympathizers, lawyers and the media played a decisive role in the process. It was time for a political gesture.

Under later politicians (between 1977 and 1984) the clock was set back. In contrast to their predecessors, they were far more inclined to go along with the standpoint of the directorate of the department concerned with the affairs of foreigners, where the received opinion was that 'regularization' of foreign workers had generated enormous frustration. The Ministry of Justice's agreement to attempts to achieve an international solution within the Council of Europe turned out, upon closer scrutiny, to be largely a matter of deceptive appearances. However, the Ministry of Justice did not stop pointing at the continued efforts of the Netherlands to achieve an international solution, as a way of justifying in court its restrictive policy towards later groups of Gypsy refugees. The absence of any international answer to 'the nomad problem' left the road clear for Justice to apply normal alien policy to Gypsies and, citing general policy towards minorities, to reject out of hand any special treatment. The idea persisted that a separate, i.e., more flexible, Dutch policy towards Gypsies would lead to the unbridled influx of hundreds of thousands of them – a quantitative estimate which was easy to deflate, although the Ministry of Justice was not prepared to do so.[33]

Just like the Dutch from the East Indies, after gaining admission from the central government Gypsies were distributed among a number of municipalities that were to shelter them and promote their integration. Their placement was preceded by months of insistence by the central government. As a rule, resistance yielded to the persuasive power of far-reaching (financial) concessions and the portrayal of Gypsies as groups which were prepared to adapt to their new situation at all costs. There is no doubt that spokesmen for the Gypsy groups themselves made a lot of promises. The Ministry of Social Welfare, still responsible for the reception of newcomers, promised to meet the expenses incurred. An interdepartmental 'steering committee' would provide guidance.

In reality things took a different turn. Year after year there was no consultation at the national level. The Ministry of Social Welfare – which, in 1980, handed over its coordinating function to the Ministry of Internal Affairs – single-handedly provided the necessary bureaucratic support. Once the decision was made, most 'host' municipalities took on their task with verve and went ahead to implement truly effective measures. Unfortunately the good will and an unmanageable reality were seldom a good match. After the first year, three municipalities were certain integration was a failure, and old recalcitrance once more raised its head. In the early 1980s, as other 'host' locations also began to make no secret of their dissatisfaction with the Gypsy integration project, a call for firmer intervention arose which drowned out the cautious, hopeful news from other municipalities. The introduction of a control model then became national policy, with extra funds for the police to make sure things ran smoothly. In 1986, it became apparent that the host municipalities practically unanimously regarded integration as an illusion and social counselling as a stop-gap measure. They saw the forceful maintenance of law and order as the only way to manage the problems that had emerged. This development gave a boost to the strict, restrictive policy that Justice was pursuing. As a category of refugees, Gypsies were even less welcome than before and the prevailing negative stereotype, and attendant stigma, were confirmed in their entirety.

What effects and implications did such a policy of applying stigma to the Gypsies have? I differentiate four, which are probably also applicable to the category of refugee or asylum-seeker in general.[34] First, persons to whom the label 'Gypsy' was attached ceased to be judged by individual characteristics but rather by supposed group traits. Second, suspicions and accusations are sufficient to turn away foreign Gypsies, to expel them, to register them. Third, the newcomers in question experienced difficulty escaping from the stigma of being undesirable aliens and potential criminals. Voices to the contrary from optimistic municipalities were invariably ignored. Fourth, a great deal of political and administrative time, attention and money is expended on a comparatively small minority group. As with colonial migrants, policy governing admission and reception was reactive. The mishandling of integration and the difficulties encountered during attempts to achieve it reflected poorly on both Gypsies already settled here and those who aspired to take up residence. They were and remained undesirable aliens.

Drawing Up the Balance

What does the academic account look like when we compare the mechanisms which played a role in the admission and reception of the Dutch from the Indies, Surinamese migrants and foreign Gypsies? First, there are the items which make it clear in hindsight that little profit accrued from hard lessons. In every relevant period, policy continued to be a reaction to events, so that the government was always trailing behind the facts.[35] Such lack of anticipation not only prevented a coherent approach; it also had important consequences for the private lives of residents in the Netherlands who came from (former) Dutch colonies. Perhaps the worst mistake was to suppose that political developments would have few direct social consequences for people who lived in Dutch enclaves overseas. The idea prevailed that, after all, those born and raised there or those who came from families which had lived there for generations felt so inextricably bound up with the land and society of their birth that they would soon enough realize that their future lay in the new republic or the independent Surinam. What was insufficiently appreciated was that people, because their education in the colonies was in Dutch, in part identified with Dutch culture, language and history (including the royal house). Moreover, it was overlooked that what was Dutch about them came under pressure in the new political configuration.

As a consequence of the underestimation of colonial migration and its dynamics, Dutch governments were constantly obliged to revise their statistics and to retroactively adjust policy to reality. In the ten years preceding the independence of Surinam, juggling of statistics was endemic. The cry for regulation of entry into Holland – a policy which the Ministry of Justice had been demanding since the 1950s – steadily increased in volume.[36] In the early 1960s, a work group was set up in order to, in the government's terminology, consider the problem of asocial Surinamese and Antillians, no more of whom the government wished to see coming to the Netherlands. As in the instance of foreign Gypsies, they emphasized the dangers of a suction effect and of setting precedents. Only people who were worthy were welcome. But, as with the category 'having roots in the Indies', the government ultimately had few tools at hand to apply a rigorous system of selection to Surinamese wanting to cross over. They were all Dutch: they could not be turned into aliens with a wave of the hand. No official entry code could exist that did not entail drawing distinctions among groups – this awareness kept all concerned watchful. To escape accusations of paternalism or of neo-colonial sentiment, as occurred during the decolonization of Indonesia, the Netherlands waited for selection procedures according to origin that would be sanctioned by the Surinamese government.

In the Netherlands, the government, usually behind the scenes of public life, has always tried to discourage and forestall the settling of newcomers. Their premise was that migration was a phenomenon that required no management and that, even after the Second World War, no immigration policy was needed. It was believed that colonial migrants would wish to stay in their places of origin or, like labour migrants from Mediterranean coastal regions, would move back home again as soon as the socio-political situation there was stable. Only a trickle of refugees or asylum-seekers was admitted out of humanitarian considerations. We should see the large-scale legalization of foreign workers in this light – and the small-scale legalization of 500 foreign Gypsies. Even today, the Dutch government – and not only the government – adheres to two basic tenets: The first is that people are better off staying in their country of birth because in the Netherlands they will go under and fail to feel at home. The second is that it is harmful for the Netherlands to take in large groups of newcomers with a deviant background for they will not be able to integrate readily and this will destabilize society.

The time has come to move from the credit to the debit of the ledger in which the balance is drawn up and to reveal what the Netherlands learned from the migration of the Dutch from the Indies. It was a step forward in the 1970s when, right from the start, policy emphasis was placed on having a widespread and well-maintained apparatus to receive newcomers, a social network to facilitate integration. It had proven effective for hundreds of thousands of Dutch from the East Indies; thus it would be of essential importance for the waves of Surinamese arriving (it was hoped only temporarily) without enthusiasm. The approach, as far as we know, leaned less heavily in the direction of state care and assimilation than in the 1950s, when hardly anyone thought to challenge the Dutch model. Twenty years later the ruling dictum advised: Provide guidance where adaptation to operational matters is needed, but hands off minority social and cultural identities. Pressure for total conformity is no longer official policy. Drawing on past experiences, the Dutch government did not behave obstructively during the transition to independence. Dutch citizens overseas were not put under pressure to become Surinamese. Implementation of policy determining who would be admitted to Holland was colour-blind, recognizing no subcategories for which entry was made more difficult. The government harboured considerable anxiety that, abroad or at home, they would be accused of neo-colonialism. In the view of some observers, fear of discriminating became too much of a guideline in the course of events.

During both decolonization processes Dutch governments could in no way get around the fact that by law colonial migrants belonged to the Dutch nation and thereby to the larger Dutch socio-cultural community. Whatever stereotypical fears and perceptions slunk about in the minds of government employees, in implementing policy it was their duty to submit to historical and legal reality. Successive cabinets and governments had to acknowledge that the label 'Dutch' covered many more varieties of humans than they perhaps deemed desirable. We saw how newcomers were let in reluctantly and under the pressure of extreme forces. Once admitted, and with the notion of their rapid return dismissed, the position of newcomers socialized by the Dutch language, culture and history was never again subject to debate. Tolerance and acceptance set the political and ideological tone. In the course of the next decades, critical or full-blown negative perceptions of Dutch with Asian roots or black Surinamese newcomers as population groups that would never feel at home in the Netherlands faded. Indeed, they no longer had a point, for these new Dutch whose formative years were spent in the colonies had in the meantime, with their offspring, found a niche in the state on the North Sea.

The world of difference which nationality or acknowledged citizenship makes becomes apparent when we compare what happened with the group of foreign Gypsies. They were considered only and exclusively as aliens, even after their integration into Dutch society was under way. Existing prejudices against 'roving groups' were simply strengthened by their being admitted and legalized and by subsequent policy to promote their integration, in which neither side placed much confidence. Neither in state policy nor public opinion are Gypsies, even the Sinti who have lived in the Netherlands for some generations, ever looked upon or recognized as members of the Dutch community. The legal distinction, although dating from long ago, continued to be decisive for the state's attitude and behaviour towards groups of Gypsy refugees arriving at the border. As newcomers they remained aliens. In that respect, Dutch governments did not learn their lesson from the past.

Notes

1 On 1 January 1991 there were 229,000 persons of Surinamese origin in the Netherlands: mostly Creoles, followed by 85,000 Hindustanis, 23,000 Javanese and 2,500 Indians. The number of Antillians was 76,000, the Moluccans numbered 42,000 and the Dutch of (partial) Indonesian ancestry, 480,000. See Beets, 'Een aanzet tot de demografie van Indische Nederlanders'.

2 Following the lead of British literature on the subject Schuster has elaborated on this theory of racialization in his doctoral dissertation *Poortwachters over immigranten*, pp. 81-116.

3 The emergence of the 'Wet Huisvesting Gerepatrieerden', *Staatsblad*, 22 December 1950, complete with all amendments and the responsible minister's argumentation, was

analyzed for the first time by parliamentary historian Ramakers, 'Hier is een schuld te voldoen!'.

[4] Ibid., p. 116.

[5] Cottaar, *Ik had een neef in Den Haag*, pp. 94-95.

[6] Such a policy of discouragement was mentioned for the first time in Cottaar and Willems, *Indische Nederlanders*, pp. 141-152; and examined more deeply in an unpublished study by Gielen and Hommerson, *De boot afgehouden?* In my recently published book *De Uittocht uit Indië* I have devoted extensive attention to this material.

[7] Memorandum dated 10 August 1951 from Mr. N.S. Blom to J.J. Rombach, Cabinet Director of Ministry of Affairs Overseas. In the name of State Secretary L. Götzen, Rombach thanked him in a letter dated 17 Aug. for his important contribution (Internal Archives of the Ministry of Foreign Affairs, code 3, 1945-1954, inv. 584).

[8] Internal memo dated 22 October 1951 from the cabinet of Ministry of Affairs Overseas concerning 'supposed agreements' (National Archives, Ministry of Colonial Affairs, 2.10.36.15, box 14).

[9] The following derives from a letter, plus notes dated 24 April 1950 from the Minister of the Affairs Overseas to W. Drees, Minister-President, for discussion in the cabinet (National Archives, Cabinet of the MP, 2.03.01, inv. 3260).

[10] Ibid.; article 32 of the *Regelingen betreffende de onder Nederlands bevel staande landstrijdkrachten in Indonesië na de Souvereiniteitsoverdracht* [Regulations concerning military forces under Dutch command in Indonesia after the transfer of sovereignty] decreed that this military personnel: a) would in part join the Indonesian army; b) in part enlist in the armed forces of the Commonwealth of the Netherlands; c) also was earmarked for leaving the services.

[11] What follows is from the *Verslag van de vierde vergadering van de CCG*, under the chairmanship of the Secretary-General of the Ministry of Affairs Overseas, 17 July 1950 (National Archives, Cabinet of the MP, 2.03.01 inv. 3122).

[12] From an internal memo dated 18 April 1951 from the Ministry of Overseas Affairs, division SAZ, Mr Rombach to Boerstra [National Archives, Ministry of Welfare Work (MaWe), inv. 473].

[13] Secret note dated 15 December 1951 from the High Commissioner to regional commissions in Bandung, Surabaja, Semarang, Palembang, Medan, Makassar and Bandjirmasin (National Archives, MaWe, inv. 527).

[14] Ibid., 5.

[15] Ibid., 6. Derived from a citation of the State Secretary for Overseas Affairs in his advice to the RAVI about 'the Indo-European problem' on 10 September 1951.

[16] Ibid., 7. In appeals for selection, Indonesians also demanded family reunions with people such as sisters, cousins, nephews and adopted children who, according to the official guidelines, were not relatives of the first degree. These were not encompassed within the official guidelines. In such cases social necessity had to be demonstrated in order to qualify for a favorable judgement.

[17] Schuster, *Poortwachters over immigranten*, p. 101.

[18] Cf. Willems, *De Uittocht uit Indië*, in which I have examined in depth different strands of government policy and also the position and actions of churches and social organizations in the 1940s, 1950s and 1960s.

[19] Schuster, *Poortwachters over immigranten*, pp. 221-222, 263-266.

[20] Ibid., pp. 111-116.

[21] Parliamentary discussion of the future of the colonial army is described in Maas and Clerx, *Parlementaire Geschiedenis van Nederland na 1945*, pp. 534-537, 603-607.

[22] Ibid., pp. 534-535.

[23] Ibid., p. 536. The State Secretaries of War and of the Marines presided over the Military Commission. They soon found support from the Commission of Nine for their standpoint that the colonial army was a component of the Dutch military and that therefore 'moral, political and military considerations made it unacceptable' to permit the colonial army to merge into the Indonesian military apparatus.

[24] Ibid., p. 537.

[25] The most important survey of this research field is Oostindie's, *Het paradijs overzee.* Nevertheless the material in this section comes from one of my previously published articles, 'Migranten op golven van de dekolonisatie'.

[26] An analysis of the influence of Surinamese pioneers, both Creoles and Hindustani, in a city such as The Hague can be found in Cottaar, *Ik had een neef in Den Haag*, pp. 112-135.

[27] Oostindie and Klinkers reach the same conclusion in their study *Knellende Koninkrijksbanden.*

[28] See, for example, Bovenkerk, *The Sociology of Return Migration.*

[29] For a policy analysis, see Willems and Lucassen, *Ongewenste vreemdelingen.* For an historical survey of attitudes and behavior in the Netherlands towards groups with itinerant vocations, see Cottaar, Lucassen and Willems, *Mensen van de reis.* Books which focus on the broader socio-historical context in Western Europe are Willems, *In Search of the True Gypsy,* and Lucassen, Willems and Cottaar, *Gypsies and Other Itinerant Groups.* I am aware of the fact that diverse groups have been labeled 'Gypsies', such as Sinti and Roma in the Netherlands, and that these groups organize themselves under this label. Until quite recently, however, in policy statements the term 'Gypsies' has been used. To avoid confusion I adopt this nomenclature.

[30] Lucassen offers an historical analysis of the history of so-called Gypsy groups in the Netherlands, in his book *'En men noemde hen zigeuners'.*

[31] Willems and Lucassen, *Ongewenste vreemdelingen*, p. 157.

[32] The interview with Zeevalking took place on 17 May 1990 at his home in Rijswijk. As a result of this 'regularization' widespread public discussion of the treatment of foreigners began for the first time. A social climate was created that also was favorable to increased attention for the position of foreign Gypsies.

[33] Willems and Lucassen, *Ongewenste vreemdelingen*, p. 96.

[34] Ibid., p.174.

[35] Oostindie and Klinkers reach the same conclusion in their recently published book (*Knellende Koninkrijksbanden*). They write on Surinam: 'In this extremely complex context Dutch policy was primarily reactive and remained ambivalent'.

[36] See also Schuster, *Poortwachters over immigranten*, pp. 133 on 'the numbers game'.

Archival Sources

Ministry of Foreign Affairs, Internal Archives
  Code 3, 1945-1954

National Archives, The Hague
  Cabinet of the MP
  Ministry of Colonial Affairs
  Ministry of Welfare Work (MaWe)

References

Beets, Gijs C., 'Een aanzet tot de demografie van Indische Nederlanders' [A Preliminary Approach to the Demography of the Indonesian-Dutch], in: Wim Willems and Leo Lucassen (eds), *Het onbekende vaderland. De repatriëring van Indische Nederlanders (1946-1964)* [The Unknown Fatherland. The Repatriation of Indonesian-Dutch (1946-1964)], The Hague, 1994, pp. 67-79.

Bovenkerk, Frank, *The Sociology of Return Migration, a Bibliographical Essay*, The Hague, 1974.

Cottaar, Annemarie, *Ik had een neef in Den Haag. Nieuwkomers in de twintigste eeuw* [I Had a Nephew in The Hague. Newcomers in the Twentieth Century], Zwolle, 1998.

Cottaar, Annemarie and Wim Willems, *Indische Nederlanders. Een onderzoek naar beeldvorming* [Dutch from the East Indies. Research on Images], The Hague, 1984.

Cottaar, Annemarie, Leo Lucassen and Wim Willems, *Mensen van de reis. Woonwagenbewoners en zigeuners in Nederland 1868-1995* [Travelling People. Caravan Dwellers and Gypsies in the Netherlands], Zwolle, 1995.

Gielen, Corine and Maureen Hommerson, *De boot afgehouden? Het Nederlandse beleid ten aanzien van de repatriëring van Indische Nederlanders op Rijksvoorschotbasis, 1949-1959* [Keep off the boat? Dutch Policy towards the 'Repatriation' of the Dutch from the Former East Indies], Nijmegen and Scherpenzeel, 1985 (not officially published).

Lucassen, Leo, *'En men noemde hen zigeuners'. De geschiedenis van Kaldarasch, Ursari, Lowara en Sinti in Nederland, 1750-1944* ['They Were Named Gypsies'. The History of Kaldarash, Ursari, Lovara and Sinti in the Netherlands], Amsterdam and The Hague, 1990.

Lucassen, Leo, Wim Willems and Annemarie Cottaar, *Gypsies and Other Itinerant Groups. A Socio-Historical Approach*, London and New York, 1998.

Maas, P.F. and J.M.M.J. Clerx, *Parlementaire Geschiedenis van Nederland na 1945* [Parliamentary History of the Post-war Netherlands]. Deel III, Het Kabinet Drees-Van Schaik (1948-1951), Band C, Cold War, Decolonization and Integration, Center for Parliamentary History, Nijmegen, 1996.

Oostindie, Gert, *Het paradijs overzee. De 'Nederlandse' Caraïben en Nederland* [The Paradise Overseas. The 'Dutch' Caribbean and the Netherlands], Amsterdam, 1997.

Oostindie, Gert and Inge Klinkers, *Knellende Koninkrijksbanden. Het Nederlandse dekolonisatiebeleid in de Caraïben, 1940-2000*, Three volumes [Galling Bonds in the Kingdom. The Dutch Policy of Decolonization in the Caribbean], Amsterdam, 2001.

Ramakers, Jan, 'Hier is een schuld te voldoen! Het huisvestingsbeleid voor repatrianten, vergeleken met joodse vluchtelingen' [Here Is a Debt to Be Paid. The Housing Policy for Repatriates, Compared to Jewish Refugees], in: Wim Willems and Leo Lucassen (eds), *Het onbekende vaderland. De repatriëring van Indische Nederlanders (1946-1964)*, The Hague, 1994, pp. 108-120.

Schuster, John, *Poortwachters over immigranten. Het debat over immigratie in het naoorlogse Groot-Brittannië en Nederland* [Gatekeepers on Immigrants. The Debate on Immigration in Post-war Great Britain and The Netherlands], Amsterdam, 1999.

Willems, Wim, 'Migranten op golven van de dekolonisatie' [Migrants on the Waves of Decolonization], *Leidschrift* (issue on the theme 'Migration and Acceptance') 11, December (1995): pp. 49-66.

Willems, Wim, *In Search of the True Gypsy. From Enlightenment to Final Solution*, London and Portland, 1997.

Willems, Wim, *De Uittocht uit Indië. De geschiedenis van Indische Nederlanders, 1945-1995* [The Exodus from Indonesia. The History of Indonesian-Dutch, 1945-1995], Amsterdam, 2001.
Willems, Wim and Leo Lucassen, *Ongewenste vreemdelingen. Buitenlandse zigeuners en de Nederlandse overheid: 1969-1989* [Unwanted Aliens. Foreign Gypsies and Dutch the Government: 1969-1989], The Hague, 1990.

Chapter 8

The Norwegian Encounter with Pakistanis: Diversities and Paradoxes on the Road to Norway's Immigration Stop

Hallvard Tjelmeland

In 1967, the first ten Pakistanis arrived in Norway. Within a short period of time, Pakistanis became visible on the streets and in the media, and it was in relation to this group that the ability of Norwegian culture to face up to the challenges of international migration was put to the test. In the following years, labour migration from the Third World would be so closely associated with Pakistanis that in order to describe perceived problems relating to immigration, it became common to refer to 'the Pakistani problem'.[1] Norway's decision to close its borders in December 1974 was partly due to a new migratory movement from the 'Third World' which – while small in numbers – challenged Norwegian ideals of cultural homogeneity and social equality.

On the Periphery of European Migration

For a long time, Norwegians lived in a state of innocence as regards international migration. In the early post-war period, the number of foreign citizens residing in the country amounted to just under 16,000 persons, or half of one per cent of the population.[2] In the years immediately following the war, Norway received 600 Jews from transit camps in Germany and Poland, as well as some early Cold War refugees – mainly Czechs – from the Eastern Bloc. By 1950, former Displaced Persons from German prison camps in Norway and from transit camps elsewhere in Europe, together with Cold War refugees, numbered about 2,000 people altogether.

In the mid-1950s, the Nordic countries became a single labour market and common passport area.[3] Thus, in the early decades after the Second World War the majority of immigrants in Norway came from other Nordic countries and were people who did not represent any kind of cultural or social challenge in a period of full employment. Labour migration from southern to northern Europe, which began in the 1950s and soon also reached the far north, presented more of a challenge. But this migration was limited in extent: In 1960 there were only about 1,000 people from Italy, Spain and Yugoslavia in Norway, and there was practically no net immigration from these countries in the 1960s. Altogether, right up to 1967 more people left than entered Norway, thus making it a country of net emigration. In the early 1970s foreigners still formed only 1.3 per cent of the workforce, far less than in other European countries.[4] There was, however, a shift in the composition of the foreign workforce during this period. While in 1952 about three-quarters of all foreign workers had been immigrants from the Nordic countries, in 1967, when for the first time after the Second World War immigration exceeded emigration, their share had dropped to just over half. However, if we include those who came from other European countries and North America, immigrants from the industrialized world still accounted for 95 per cent of all foreigners. Only one in twenty was from the Third World.[5]

In 1967, foreigners constituted only about one per cent of the total workforce, which in fact represented a clear decline since the early 1950s. Given that Norway participated in the international economic boom, that there was great demand for workers all over Europe and large-scale migration from the south to the north, this is extraordinary. The small number of foreign workers was not due to a particularly restrictive immigration policy. On the contrary, Norway had in fact a relatively liberal immigration policy. In practice, from 1957 onward anybody who wanted to work in Norway could freely enter the country. Unlike other northern European industrialized nations, including Germany and neighbouring Sweden, Norway did not respond to the labour shortage by actively encouraging the immigration of 'guestworkers'. Official policy, passed unanimously by the Norwegian parliament (*Storting*) as late as 1969, held that no obstacles should be placed in the way of foreigners wanting to work in Norway. Apparently, Norway was simply not attractive to immigrant workers.

And yet Norway was not entirely unaffected by European population movements, and Norwegian attitudes to the 'others' were challenged. According to Norwegian self-perceptions and their image abroad, Norwegians are liberal in their attitudes to other cultures. In the media, in politics and in popular movements, evidence can be found of a strong commitment to combating all forms of racial discrimination in other countries, such as the southern states of the USA and South Africa. Norwegians generally supported foreign aid, and it was no longer acceptable to publicly express racist attitudes toward Jews or people of African extraction, as had been the case before the war and before the world had seen what racially based politics could lead to. Traditional biological racism became the exclusive domain of the extreme right wing and smaller magazines and newspapers. During the 1950s and 1960s, there was also a slight shift toward accepting claims that the largest minority group in Norway, the Sami, had a right to maintain their own culture – which represented a move away from the ruthless Norwegianization policy this group had been subjected to up to 1945.[6]

However, these were only tiny steps toward an acceptance of ethnic pluralism. It was still widely held that minorities and newcomers had to adjust to the norms of the majority. Policies aimed at groups of refugees Norway took in during the Cold War, especially Czechs and Hungarians, sought to assimilate them as quickly as possible; this entailed making them culturally Norwegian. And even if most refugees themselves wanted to blend into Norwegian society as smoothly as possible, they often found it virtually impossible. They never truly experienced being 'one of us'. They remained strangers.[7] The small number of dark-skinned people in the country might experience anything from intense staring to paternalistic goodwill or even open racism. Bill Caldwell, an African-American who had known Norway from as early as 1959 and had worked as a journalist in Oslo since 1963, said that Norway 'participates in the same form of racial discrimination as is found in the rest of the Western world'.[8] He found the same mix of condescending kindness which after two drinks would change to conventional western racial hatred; the same unkind stares from neighbours who regarded people of a different skin colour as intruders; and, in one case, outside a movie theatre, experienced what he referred to as 'symptoms of mob psychology'. His pessimistic conclusion was that 'Norway is a better breeding ground for racial hatred than people are willing to admit'.

During this period in Norwegian history – that is, up to the 1970s – the feeling of community was at its strongest, and the Norwegian nation-state was consolidated as never before, culturally, socially and economically. The experience of five years of occupation during the Second World War had created a strong feeling of community, which was reproduced in the collective tradition by a strong myth of heroic resistance against the occupants and their collaborators.[9] Furthermore, in the two decades after 1945, the social democratic Norwegian Labour Party ruled the country on the basis of a class compromise that secured support for the establishment of a strong welfare state that was supposed to eliminate regional and social inequality. This strengthened the values of equality and cultural as well as social community. In this situation, people of a completely different cultural background who had no desire to become Norwegian arrived in the country.

The Arrival of Pakistanis

In 1967, Pakistanis were first registered as a nationality in Norwegian statistics. Over the next three years, not more than approximately 100 arrived annually, but this was enough for their presence to be noticed. In the summer of 1971 the head of the Government Office of Immigration said in an interview with the newspaper *Aftenposten* that 'immigration (from Pakistan) started in October 1968. Suddenly, we saw the arrival of nine or ten people on a Pakistani bus which had driven all the way from Karachi'.[10] Arnulf Emil Jørundstand remembered this event in spite of the fact that in 1968 he had had to deal with about 6,000 work permit applications, of which about 700 were from southern Europe and the Third World, that is, from people considered foreign workers at the time.[11] Probably he referred to an incident that in November 1968 received broad coverage in the newspaper *Arbeiderbladet.* As was then assumed, a group of Pakistanis had been smuggled into the country by 'a London gang specialized in smuggling foreign workers into Norway for certain economic favours'.[12] At this stage the number of Pakistanis was not high enough to warrant much attention. There were, for instance, far more immigrant workers from Morocco at the time. Most of them took unskilled jobs in industry and the service sector, especially in hotels and restaurants and, with the help of relatives and other people, also managed to find some form of accommodation. Mekhtar Ahmed, from Harabunabad in western Pakistan, was probably a typical representative of these very first Pakistanis. At the time he was interviewed by *Arbeiderbladet* in June 1967, he had been in the country for about six months and was working as a driver for the manufacturing company NEBB in Oslo. He had to make do with a room in a hostel which was so expensive that he had little money left to send to his wife and six sons in Pakistan.

Toward the end of the 1960s, when the first Pakistanis arrived, the sometimes idyllic picture of life in Norway had begun to crack. Even the presence of immigrants of European origin was a challenge to many

Norwegians. Newspapers and magazines reported that Italians and other southern Europeans had been harassed on the streets, in taxi queues and in restaurants – usually by drunken Norwegians, but also by respectable citizens in broad daylight. It was perceived as particularly provocative when these 'dagoes' (South Europeans) were seen with Norwegian girls, and a particularly unsavoury stew of xenophobia and misogyny was the result. In the summer of 1967, gang fights between Italian and Norwegian men erupted in Stavanger, in West Norway, because natives resented the immigrants' contacts with 'their' women. 'Norwegian citizens go at them like enraged animals when these Italians so much as look at the girls', a reader's letter to the magazine *Aktuell* reported.

In spite of such incidents, Pakistanis were not initially met with hostility. Instead, the predominant response was concern about their living conditions and their exploitation. The first political reactions to the new labour immigration to Norway came from the Norwegian Hotel and Restaurant Workers' Association, the federation representing workers in one of the sectors most likely to attract the newcomers. The association was concerned that employers might use the increased availability of workers to reduce salaries and offer employees poorer conditions. In February 1969, the front page of *Arbeiderbladet*, the main Labour Party paper, reported that 'foreigners cleaned hotels for NOK 5.50 an hour', i.e., only half the normal wages in the hotel sector. The story referred to three Pakistanis working at 'a provincial Norwegian hotel', where conditions for employees were generally poor. *Arbeiderbladet* claimed that conditions were better and more orderly in Oslo, where most of the foreigners working in hotels and restaurants lived (1,300 altogether).[13] The principle demands of the labour union were compulsory union membership, that employers should be responsible for ensuring that their employees had proper accommodation and that foreigners should be offered language courses and other information that would enable them to adapt to working in Norway.[14] According to *Arbeiderbladet*, the chairman of the union, Eivind Strømmen, said at the national convention in June 1969 that he regarded the foreigners 'as enriching Norway, but that we must also make sure that foreigners do not have the effect of pushing wages down rather than being colleagues'. From the fall of 1968, the Hotel and Restaurant Workers' Association in particular urged the Norwegian Federation of Trade Unions (LO) to develop an active policy on the new worker immigration.

Not before the summer of 1970 did the media seriously take up the problems the new immigrant workers faced in their encounter with

Norwegian employers and the housing market. *Arbeiderbladet* carried huge headlines about a large group of Turks who had been shamelessly exploited by a firm in Drammen, and *Dagbladet* wrote of Pakistanis who had been evicted from a hostel following that newspaper's story about exorbitant rents. Around the same time, *Aktuell* wrote that immigrant workers had become 'a pariah caste in our society today'. In an interview, Pakistani Bahis Ahmad, who worked in a kitchen in Blindern on the university campus, said that it had taken him seven months to find himself a place to live, and that it had also taken some weeks to find a job. When asked whether he had managed to make contact with Norwegians, he answered diplomatically: 'How can I say anything about Norwegians? Look at my hand. It has five fingers. Every finger is different. That's how it is with Norwegians as well'. In their attitudes to Pakistanis and other groups from the Third World, ordinary Norwegians did not exhibit the same awareness of differentiation. Pakistanis were regarded as a fairly homogeneous group of people who lacked education and technical skills, and it seemed natural that they would mainly take the lowest paid and least skilled jobs.

Panic Measures: The Shift Toward Restrictions

As concern over the increase in the number of foreign workers grew, the authorities gradually started to take action – following the examples of neighbouring countries, such as Sweden and Denmark. The Norwegian Aliens Act of 1956 was an enabling act, which gave the administration the power to adjust immigration policy to changes in the labour market and the international situation. Until the early 1970s, people could apply for a work permit after having found work in Norway. From 1 January 1970, Norway followed Danish practice in requiring individuals to secure a work permit before entering the country. Early 1970 also saw the introduction of stricter rules concerning foreigners' duty to report their whereabouts to the authorities. At the same time, however, arguments holding that foreigners should earn the same wages and enjoy the same working conditions as Norwegians were advanced. There was no sign of any panic. The Norwegian economy was going at full blast and the low-paying industries had problems finding enough workers. When a committee was established to examine Norwegian immigration policy in the fall of 1970 ('The Danielsen Committee'), the underlying premise was that there should be no major changes to the liberal practices approved by the *Storting* as recently as the previous year.

It was nevertheless clear that there was some concern at the higher political levels. In August 1970, the Ministry of Justice stated that to prevent 'foreigners who were unable to adapt' from getting into the country, 'a certain standard' had to be required of them when it came to 'personal matters'.[15] The Director General of the Directorate of Labour, Reidar Danielsen, pointed out that other countries had introduced tighter restrictions than Norway, and that this 'might mean that the least suitable workers will come here'.[16] 'And we're not interested in that', he added. The decisive shift occurred in the spring of 1971. The previous winter had seen a sharp increase in the number of Pakistanis seeking work, following Denmark's introduction of a moratorium on immigration and stricter rules for acquiring work permits. Norway was at the time probably the country with the most liberal rules for labour immigration in northern Europe. During that spring 600 Pakistanis entered Norway, most of them going to the capital, Oslo. They quickly garnered the full attention of the media. Dramatic conditions were described in large headlines in all the Oslo papers in the summer of 1971. *Arbeiderbladet* attacked 'people-smuggling' and a 'slave trade' (8 June 1971), and reported that unemployed Pakistanis warned others against coming to Norway. *Dagbladet* reported that 'hundreds of Pakistanis' were seeking jobs in Oslo (21 May 1971) and that there was 'intense fear and apathy among the immigrant workers' (19 June 1971). On 4 June the newspaper *VG* proclaimed in huge headlines that 'financial sharks have tricked 300 Pakistanis into coming here' and, in even larger type: 'They must starve in Norway'. In July the largest headline type available announced the presence of 'grotesque racial hatred in Oslo'.

The background to the headlines was real enough. The arrival of a large number of Pakistanis within a brief period of time, to a city experiencing a housing shortage, created enormous social problems. Most Pakistanis entered Norway on tourist visas, without jobs, and sometimes spent weeks or months trudging from one employer to another looking for work. When they had landed a job, they had to leave the country again – most went to Hamburg – to apply for work permits. And even then they were not certain of getting one. A study by sociologist Aud Korbøl of 635 Pakistanis who had applied for work permits between 1 April and 1 July 1971, revealed that one-fifth of the applicants were turned down because they could not prove that they had jobs and proper accommodation. The application process took 25 days on average, but it could take up to three months, and when an application was turned down the applicant had to contact the authorities again to deal with the matter, thereby incurring new expenses for accommodation and travel. Many had fallen deeply into debt in order to come to Norway. The fear of not obtaining a work permit and of being expelled from the country with large debts to family or agents made many foreigners willing to accept almost anything in terms of working and living conditions.

The sudden change in immigration patterns coupled with the feeling that restrictions in the immigration policies of the neighbouring countries had created a difficult situation, led to a form of panic among the authorities, the foreign workers themselves and probably also the general public. This panic paved the way for the formation of some very strange alliances on the issue of immigration policy. In record time, measures were introduced to reduce immigration. The committee formed in the fall of 1970 had a mandate to propose immediate action. An immigrant worker from the hotel and restaurant sector, the Portuguese José Carlos Santos, was now appointed as an additional member of the committee. The committee proposed the introduction of a stricter immigration policy. Their main idea was to change the regulations so that applications for work permits had to be submitted to a Norwegian embassy or consulate in the country of which the applicant was a citizen or the country where he or she had lived for the previous six months. A transition period of ten days was introduced for those already in Norway and those who already had contracts. The shortness of this transition period created much chaos and confusion in itself. The new regulations came into effect from 7 July 1971.

The impression of panic is reinforced by the fact that these measures came just a few weeks after the country's biggest selling newspaper, *Aftenposten*, had written that 'Norway ought to take in more foreign workers' (21 May 1971). Moreover, the measures were introduced just after an interview with the Director General of Labour, Reidar Danielsen, in *Tønsberg Blad*, in which Danielsen argued that: 'Apart from the northernmost parts of the country, there is a general shortage of labour in this country, and in my opinion Norway should have a liberal attitude as regards opening its borders to foreign workers'.[17]

There can be no doubt that the measures were primarily a reaction to increased Pakistani immigration, and that they probably worked most effectively against the weakest of them. It is estimated that during the summer of 1971 nine out of ten individuals were turned away at the external borders of the Nordic passport area.[18] In 1971, mainly before the introduction of the new restrictions, the number of Pakistani workers had risen to 990 (from 110 in 1970). During 1972, the increase levelled off somewhat and the figure reached 1,240. Pakistanis had then become by far the largest non-Western nationality in Norway. Although the Pakistani population no longer grew as rapidly as before, it proved difficult to stem altogether what at the time was considered a flood. In February 1972, the Minister of Local Government Oddvar Nordli indicated that there should be more emphasis on the employment situation, and that foreign workers had to be prevented from becoming 'guestworkers' in the sense of being a workforce allowed into the country in good times and being thrown out again when times got bad.[19] Gradually, the authorities started checking whether immigrant workers were getting the same wages and working conditions as Norwegians – which was a requirement for issuing a work permit. From January 1973, foreign workers were required to know a European language, on the grounds that this was necessary in order to adapt to Norwegian conditions. The language test was to be taken at a Norwegian consulate in the applicant's home country, a procedure that allowed for considerable arbitrariness.[20] In spite of various measures to make immigration more difficult, the number of Pakistani nationals increased year by year. In January 1975 there were 3,772 Pakistani citizens in Norway, compared to 212 five years earlier, and by then they comprised one-third of immigrants from the Third World.

'Close the Borders': Curious Alliances in Favour of Restrictions

The number of foreign residents thus kept rising in spite of the stricter immigration policy. The restrictions were always one step behind those introduced by the most important European host countries. Furthermore, the authorities did not manage to solve the problems the new groups faced. The first accommodation many of them got in Oslo was in Majorstua School, which was a 40-day emergency provision for 300 to 400 foreign workers, mostly Pakistanis. Later a former police academy served as a temporary solution. It housed 150-200 homeless immigrants, with up to 20 people in each room. The building had no kitchen or bathrooms, no hot water and only two toilets. This temporary arrangement lasted two years. During this period, Oslo municipality made no progress in solving the acute housing needs of the city's new taxpayers.[21] The Pakistanis were thus left to fend for themselves on the private housing market, which was full of unscrupulous landlords willing to exploit the weakness of foreign workers at a time when a permanent address was a requirement for getting a work and residence permit. In a series of articles in *Dagbladet* in the fall of 1974

– later published as a book with the title *Vi er så gode så: fra mine Fremmedarbeidernotater* ['Aren't We Nice? From my Foreign Worker Notes'] – Gunnar Bull Gundersen provided moving accounts from the slums that existed in many parts of Oslo, and of the racist attitudes facing those in need of accommodation.

The Danielsen Committee tabled its findings in December 1972. By then, belief in a liberal immigration regime had vanished. A majority, including the representatives of the Norwegian Federation of Trade Unions and the Norwegian Employers Federation, would have been happy to see more attention paid to the employment situation and favoured the introduction of tighter controls; a minority preferred more drastic action and demanded a temporary moratorium on immigration. This was justified with reference to the negative consequences of labour migration for both the countries of origin and the host countries. The minority wanted the moratorium on immigration to last until the problems of the new immigrants had been solved.[22] The representative of the foreign workers belonged to the minority, and it was this view that won the day when the *Storting* voted in December 1974 to introduce a temporary moratorium on immigration from 1 February 1975.

The immigrant representative, Carlos Santos, had not been appointed by the immigrant workers themselves, but by the Norwegian Federation of Trade Unions. Nevertheless, his views were largely in line with those expressed when the immigrant workers started to speak up in the spring of 1971. The acute problems that arose in the spring and summer of 1971 did not affect a passive, unorganized group. As early as April, a committee for immigrant workers had been set up with a large Pakistani majority. In November, the *Fremmedarbeiderforeningen* (FAF) [Foreign Workers Association] was set up as an umbrella organization for all the national organizations of foreign workers – probably the only organization of its kind for foreign workers in Europe. From the beginning, the Pakistanis were the dominant ethnic group in the organization. One of the founders, the Palestinian Elias Chammas, appeared in a front-page story in *VG* at the end of July 1971 appealing to the authorities to close the borders to immigrant workers 'with immediate effect' until the problems of those already in the country had been solved. The FAF later upheld this view. The most important objections the organization had to the moratorium when it came into effect was the dispensations it permitted, which ensured that experts and key personnel for the expanding oil sector could enter the country, thus introducing a discriminatory element into immigration policy. The FAF acted with considerable confidence on the Norwegian political stage, combating discriminatory treatment in the housing and labour markets on the grounds that foreigners represented a necessary supplement to the Norwegian workforce. In 1973, they held their own Labour Day demonstration, and in 1974 an FAF committee entered into discussions with the Norwegian Federation of Trade Unions.[23] The demand for a moratorium on immigration was a result of their experience with Norway's labour and housing markets. The logic of their reasoning was not unlike that of associations of trade unions like the Norwegian Musicians' Union and Norwegian Hotel and Restaurant Workers' Association, which had for years been working for immigration control. Simply put, they argued that an influx of foreign workers would weaken the position of those workers already in the country.

It might seem something of a paradox that immigrant workers were in favour of closing the borders, albeit temporarily. It is no less astonishing in retrospect that the most powerful arguments against a liberal immigration policy came from those most sympathetic to the cause of foreign workers, the political left. The first person on the left to engage in the debate was Socialist People's Party politician and sociologist Ottar Brox, who in a 1967 column in the magazine *Liberalt Perspektiv* had already laid the foundation of what would become the most important arguments of the left. In his view, the immigration of cheap labour from the Third World solved a problem for both the powers that be in the Third World and the capitalists of the industrialized world. Inviting workers to take up poorly paid jobs with conditions so bad that Norwegian workers did not want them, weakened the strategic position of all wage-earners.[24] The new Maoist movement, which was a marked expression of the New Left in Norway, expressed its opposition toward a liberal immigration policy from a very early stage: 'Close the borders' was, for instance, one of the front-page headlines of their newspaper, *Klassekampen* (Class Struggle), in August 1971. Many young sociologists developed an interest in the problems of foreign workers and attacked liberal immigration policies in Norway as well as in the EEC. Several topical books were published which criticized Norwegian racism and denounced the government for being passive and applying immigration regulations in a discriminatory fashion. The short-term solution they advocated was to close the borders. The books had titles such as *Den billige arbeidskraften* [Cheap Labour] (Ragnar Kvam Jr., 1971), *Det norske herrefolket* [The Norwegian Master Race] (Knut Evensen, 1971) and the previously mentioned 'Aren't We Nice? From my Foreign Worker Notes' (Gunnar Bull Gundersen). Opinions on migration policy did not follow the usual political divides.

From an early stage, the radical-liberal newspaper *Dagbladet* demanded that the borders be closed, while the conservative paper *Aftenposten* favoured open borders – as did the Norwegian Employers' Federation. These differences in the newspapers' views on immigration policy were not reflected in their general attitudes to foreigners. A study of four newspapers for the years 1971, 1973, 1975 and 1978 shows that the two conservative papers *VG* and *Aftenposten* expressed somewhat more negative attitudes toward immigrants than the liberal paper *Dagbladet* and the social-democratic *Arbeiderbladet*, although attitudes were altogether positive in all four.[25] In general, pluralist attitudes were stronger on the left, while their egalitarian attitudes led to stronger reactions to the growing inequality immigration brought with it.

Political scientist Espen Thorud has suggested that Norway's opposition to the EEC explains why the Norwegian left, unlike the left in other European countries, around 1970 held restrictive attitudes to immigration. This, however, is not convincing. It is true that this early immigration from the Third World, with the Pakistanis as by far the largest and most visible group, coincided with the run-up to the referendum on Norwegian membership of the EEC in the fall of 1972. Poor conditions for immigrant workers in the EEC and the possibility of increased immigration if Norway was to join, were points made in the debate. However, the political conclusion that immigration had to be regulated had been reached before the debate on Norwegian membership of the EEC opened, and attitudes to the immigration moratorium act changed very quickly once it had been passed – when the EEC question was closed in the Norwegian debate. Analyses of the function and the position of foreign workers in Western capitalist societies did not diverge from what were mainstream left-wing attitudes in Europe at the time, although political conclusions differed.[26] For part of the Norwegian left, the critical attitudes of the early 1970s to international labour migration can also be considered as a reflection of a critical, anti-capitalistic attitude to *domestic* labour migration. Migration from countryside to town was considered as weakening the strategic positions for ordinary people at both places. The left-wing demand for a temporary immigration stop was partly founded on a fear of growing inequality and the emergence of a new underclass. Both on the left and among Norwegians in general, an ideology of equality went hand in hand with a strong confidence in the ability of the state to solve problems and create equality. Stopping immigration was considered a tool the state could use in order to solve practical problems for the newcomers and to prevent a new kind of inequality.

If we turn to the other extreme of the political spectrum another peculiarity can be noted. It seems that during this period no basis existed for a political mobilization against foreign workers and for an immigration policy based on racist or xenophobic grounds. This distinguishes Norway from, for instance, the United Kingdom, where Enoch Powell successfully fuelled hostility against immigration, and Switzerland, where in 1970 and 1974 only small majorities in two referendums prevented immigrant workers from being expelled. When in July 1970 an advertisement in *Aftenposten* announced that a new party was to be launched under the banner of 'forbidding foreign workers to live and work in Norway', nothing came of it. When the right-wing populist Progress Party was founded in 1973, opposition to immigration was not among the fourteen 'we are tired of' statements which formed its founding manifesto,[27] and during the election campaign that all foreigners were not a target. This changed in the 1980s, when opposition to immigration became one of the main issues for this party, while opposition to a restrictive immigration policy became increasingly important for the entire left.

Changing Communities

Norwegian attitudes to immigration thus present a somewhat confusing picture. On the one hand, there was a policy-shift from wide-open to closed borders. On the other hand, people at the heart of the political system changed their attitudes toward foreigners and accepted a greater degree of pluralism. As late as 1970, the head of the Government Office of Immigration stated that it was a political aim that foreign workers should be assimilated into Norwegian society, i.e., they should become like Norwegians. But in the 1972 report on immigration, which formed the basis for later immigration policy, it was pointed out that the newcomers had a right to maintain their own culture and language. As the report stated, integration rather than assimilation should be the aim – a shift in attitudes which was strongly influenced by the younger immigration researchers and the impulses they had picked up from the European debate on immigration, particularly that in Sweden. On the one hand, the borders were now closed, or to be more precise, they were closed for immigrants from the Third World. While about 200 Pakistanis had been given work permits in the last six months before the immigration stop, only a handful received work permits over the next few years. The number of work permits granted to western European and American citizens, however, remained at the same level or even increased.[28] On the other hand, government policy on family reunification allowed for continued Pakistani immigration, so that Norway now has one of Europe's largest Pakistani immigrant populations. Indeed, only two other European countries (Great Britain and Germany) have more inhabitants with Pakistani citizenship than Norway.[29] Pakistanis constitute the largest non-European immigrant group in Norway, and the second largest group overall – slightly less numerous than Swedes, but more so than Danes. In 2000, Pakistanis (immigrants and their children) numbered 22,831 persons.[30] Family reunification completely changed the social and gender composition of the Pakistani group in Norway, which developed from a population of young males into a differentiated community. We also have to take into consideration that Pakistanis, more than other immigrant groups, are geographically very concentrated, with over 80 per cent living in the area of the capital, Oslo.

If the Norwegian picture was complex, it was no less so on the Pakistani side. Norwegians tended to see the first Pakistanis as a weak, homogeneous mass, lacking in education and aptitude for anything but the least skilled jobs in industry and the service sector. Attitudes expressed by the staff of employment agencies and the office of immigration also sprang from such preconceptions. A study conducted by sociologist Aud Korbøl of the 276 Pakistanis in Norway as of 31 March 1971 – i.e., before the start of the main wave of immigration – showed that nine out of ten had eight years of schooling or more, while one-fifth had 12 years or more. There is no doubt that those who came to Norway generally had a substantially higher level of education than the average in their home country.[31] It is likely that the educational level rose further after an English language requirement had been introduced in 1973. As a recent MA thesis by Kristin Wist shows, between 1970 and 1980 the proportion of Pakistanis without any education dropped from a quarter to practically nil, while the number of people with university education rose from barely one in 25 to one in five. In 1980, more than half of the Pakistanis had secondary schooling, while that had only been the case for less than one-fifth ten years earlier.[32] Korbøl's 1971 study also showed that the work experience that the Pakistanis had amassed in their own country was more differentiated than the conventional picture allowed, with a relatively large proportion of white-collar workers. Both Korbøl and Wist conclude that the Pakistani immigrants came from relatively good conditions in their home country, from the rural and urban middle classes. Many must have experienced a dramatic drop in status. Wist shows that 94 per cent of the small number of Pakistanis in Norway in 1970 worked in industry and the service sector, and we know from other sources that they had the heaviest and worst paid jobs within these sectors. Over time, however, Pakistanis experienced a form of 'diagonal social mobility' and did not become a permanent underclass. That is to say, their position as a group has generally improved with regard to work and income, accommodation and education; however, this happened within those social domains in which they were already established.[33]

The Pakistani community gradually changed their attitudes to life in Norway. There is no doubt that originally Pakistanis came to Norway in order to earn money and then return to Pakistan. The closing of the borders and rise of family reunification changed this. During the second half of the 1970s, 86 per cent of the Pakistanis who came to Norway ended up staying in the country. Almost from the very beginning, they developed their own institutions. The *Fremmedarbeiderforeningen* [Foreign Workers Association] has already been mentioned. There was also a plethora of welfare organizations, and a religious community developed, which led to the establishment of the first mosque in Norway in 1974.[34] The organizations represented a community that was as socially, religiously and politically diverse as the host country, Norway.

Conclusion: From Culture Shock to Uneasy Pluralism

After a liberal immigration regime in the 1950s and 1960s, the authorities applied the brakes in the early 1970s. On the one hand, we might regard this as an extension of the more restrictive policies that had taken hold in other northern European countries immediately prior. The almost panicked introduction of the new restrictive regulations in 1971 must also be seen as a result of a fear of unmanageable social and cultural problems prompted by increased immigration from non-western countries. In light of the much higher immigration in the years after 1971, the intense public focus on the marked increase in Pakistani immigration seems alarmist and almost comical. There were two to some extent peculiarly Norwegian reasons for this. First, there was a widespread feeling that Norwegians constituted a homogeneous cultural community in which the only national minorities of any size were peripheral in relation to Oslo, the hub of the national media and political institutions. Second, the principles of the welfare state and equality enjoyed strong support in Norway and members of the trade union movement and the Norwegian left feared that importing workers from the Third World would create a new underclass and therefore give rise to greater inequality. This also explains why many critical, left-wing social scientists entered into an alliance with the liberal centre to demand that the borders be closed temporarily.

The period between the first tightening of immigration policy in 1970 to the introduction of the moratorium in 1975 also witnessed the breakthrough of cultural pluralist thinking in relation to the integration of foreigners into Norwegian society – from assimilation to integration on the basis of maintenance of the immigrants' own cultures. After the introduction of the moratorium on immigration, Norway passed through the same phases as the rest of Europe: first a phase of family reunification, and then, from the early 1980s onward, a large increase in the numbers of refugees and asylum-seekers. Norwegian culture did not remain unaffected by this encounter with cultures very different from what were considered Norwegian norms. Nor did the immigrant cultures. From being a country on the very periphery of the flow of international migration in the 1950s and 1960s, Norway became a country with an immigrant population of about the European average. During the course of this transformation, Norway developed policies that were in line with the emerging European norm: doors closed to the outside world, increased acceptance of multiculturalism internally.

Notes

1. The title of an article by Aud Korbøl, the foremost immigration researcher in this early phase, is symptomatic: 'Norsk innvandringspolitikk – norsk pakistanerpolitikk?' ['Norwegian immigration policy – Norwegian Pakistani policy?']. A count of the number of stories about immigration in four Oslo newspapers for the years 1971, 1973, 1975 and 1978 revealed that Pakistanis were the subject of 60 per cent of those stories which mentioned nationality, even though this group, as late as 1980, only constituted barely 5 per cent of the population with foreign citizenship. Vaage, 'Innvandringssituasjonen – pressens beskrivelse og folks oppfatning'.
2. *Norwegian Official Reports: Historisk statistikk*, table 3.10. On the other hand, the proportion of the Norwegian population born abroad was three times as high, 1.7 per cent, ibid., Table 3.11.
3. An exception was made for Finnish citizens in Troms and Finnmark. This decision was based on security considerations, i.e., fear of espionage on behalf of the Soviet Union. This thinking goes back to the period before the war, when there was a fear of a 'Finnish threat' to Norway, which was, among other things, connected to the existence of a minority of Finnish extraction in Norway, the *Kvens*. Bergh and Eriksen, *Den hemmelige krigen*, p. 203-205.
4. *Norwegian Official Reports 1973: No. 17: Innvandringspolitikk*. Not included here are foreigners employed in the Norwegian merchant marine, who in the 1950s and 1960s were as numerous as foreigners working in Norway.

5 *Norwegian Official Reports: Historisk Statistikk*, 1994.

6 Nevertheless, it was only in the 1980s that the Sami, who mainly live in northern Norway, were finally recognized as a separate people with the rights of indigenous peoples according to international conventions. Other minorities, such as *Kvens*, travellers, Gypsies and Jews had to wait until the late 1990s for such pluralistic attitudes to afford them the status of national minorities.

7 *Norwegian Official Reports 1986: No. 8: Flyktningers tilpasning til det norske samfunn.*

8 *Aktuell*, 28/1969.

9 Eriksen, *Det var noe annet under krigen*.

10 Korbøl, 'Den kritiske fasen. Del 1', p. 54.

11 *Norwegian Official Reports 1973: No. 17*, p. 54.

12 *Arbeiderbladet*, 19 January 1968.

13 *Arbeiderbladet,* 11 February 1969.

14 Thorud, 'Norsk innvandringspolitikk og arbeiderbevegelsen', pp. 112-117.

15 Ibid., p. 60, also *Norwegian Official Reports 1973: No. 17.*

16 *Dagbladet,* 7 August 1970.

17 Quoted in Korbøl, 'Den kritiske fasen. Del 1', p. 66.

18 Korbøl, 'Den kritiske fasen. Del 4', p. 17.

19 *Dagbladet*, 12 February 1972.

20 *Dagbladet,* 10 January 1973, Korbøl, 'Den kritiske fasen. Del 4', p. 76.

21 Cf. Ophaug, 'Innvandrere – hvor skal de bo'.

22 Thorud, 'Norsk innvandringspolitikk og arbeiderbevegelsen', p. 121.

23 Kjeldstadli, 'En organisasjon som passer på dem den passer for'.

24 Brox, 'Hvem trenger fremmedarbeiderne, og hva trenger de?' [Who needs the foreign workers, and what do they need?].

25 Vaage, 'Innvandringssituasjonen – pressens beskrivelse og folks oppfatning', p. 8.

26 Cf., for instance, Castles and Kosack, 'The Function of Labour Immigration in Western European Capitalism' – a pilot study for Castles and Kosack, *Immigrant Workers and Class Structure in Western Europe*; Cinanni, *Emigration und Imperialismus*. These books were also referred to in the Norwegian literature on immigration issues.

27 Iversen, *Fra Anders Lange til Carl I. Hagen,* p. 24. For the first three years, the party was called Anders Lange's Party, after its charismatic founder.

28 Bø, 'Norsk innvandrings- og asylpolitikk', p. 161.

29 Carling, 'Arbeidsinnvandring og familiegjenforening 1967-1980', p. 28. The number of Pakistanis doubled during the first five years after the moratorium, ibid., p. 89.

30 Central Bureau of Statistics, 'Befolkningsstatistikk. Innvandrerbefolkningen', 1 January 2000.

31 Korbøl, 'Den kritiske fasen. Del 1', pp. 36, 45. Here there are, of course, problems concerning critical attitudes toward sources. The immigrants could be interested in exaggerating their educational background. Korbøl sees immigrant workers as a part of a reserve army of industrial workers, which is functional for the upper classes of both the country of origin and the host country.

32 Wist, 'Pakistanere og indere i Norge på vei oppover?'.

33 Ibid., p. 113.

34 Vogt, *Islam på norsk,* p. 15. Cf. Ahlberg, 'New Challenges – Old strategies'.

References

Ahlberg, Nora, '"New Challenges – Old Strategies". Themes of Variation and Conflict among Pakistani Muslims in Norway', *Transactions of the Finnish Anthropological Society*, no. 25, Helsinki, 1990.

Bergh, Trond and Knut E. Eriksen, *Den hemmelige krigen. Overvåking i Norge 1914-1997* [The Secret War: Surveillance in Norway 1914-1997], vol. 2, Oslo, 1998.

Bø, Bente P., 'Norsk innvandrings – og asylpolitikk' [Norwegian Immigration and Refugee Policy], in: Thomas H. Eriksen (ed.), *Flerkulturell forståelse* [Multicultural understanding], Oslo, 1997, pp. 153-157.

Brox, Ottar, 'Hvem trenger fremmedarbeiderne, og hva trenger de?' [Who Needs the Foreign Workers, and What Do They Need?], *Liberalt Perspektiv 7* (1967): pp. 125-129.

Carling, Jørgen, 'Arbeidsinnvandring og familiegjenforening 1967-1980' [Worker Immigration and Family Reunification], in: Research Council of Norway, *Kulturstudier*, no. 4, Oslo, 1999.

Castles, Stephen and Godula Kosack, 'The Function of Labour Immigration in Western European Capitalism', *New Left Review* 73 (1972): pp. 3-21.

Castles, Stephen and Godula Kosack, *Immigrant Workers and Class Structure in Western Europe*, London, 1973.

Central Bureau of Statistics, 'Befolkningsstatistikk. Innvandrerbefolkningen' [Population Statistics. The Immigrant Population], 1 January 2000.

Cinanni, Paolo, *Emigration und Imperialismus*, Munich, 1970.

Eriksen, Anne, *Det var noe annet under krigen. 2. verdenskrig i norsk kollektivtradisjon* [It Was Different during the War. Second World War in Norwegian Collective Tradition], Oslo, 1995.

Iversen, Jan M., *Fra Anders Lange til Carl I. Hagen. 25 år med Fremskrittspartiet* [From Anders Lange to Carl I. Hagen. 25 Years of the Progress Party], Oslo, 1998.

Kjeldstadli, Knut, 'En organisasjon som passer på dem den passer for' [An Organization that Watches over Those it Caters for], in: Inger Bjørnhaug et al. (eds), *I rettferdighetens navn* [In the Name of Justice], Oslo, 2000, pp. 127-147.

Korbøl, Aud, *Den kritiske fasen. Om innvandringa til Norge fra Pakistan og de pakistanske fremmedarbeidernes situasjon i Norge*, Del 1, Rammebetingelser [The Critical Phase. On Immigration to Norway from Pakistan and the Situation of Pakistani Migrant Workers in Norway, Part 1, General Background], ISF Oslo, 1974.

Korbøl, Aud, *Den kritiske fasen. Om innvandringa til Norge fra Pakistan og de pakistanske fremmedarbeidernes situasjon i Norge*, Del 4, Om kampen for tilværelsen [The Critical Phase. On the Immigration to Norway from Pakistan and the Situation of Pakistani Migrant Workers in Norway, Part 4, The Struggle to Survive], ISF Oslo, 1974.

Korbøl, Aud, 'Norsk innvandringspolitikk – norsk pakistanerpolitikk?' [Norwegian Immigration Policy – Norwegian Pakistani Policy?], *Sosiologi i dag* 7 (1977): pp. 19-33.

Norwegian Official Reports 1973: No. 17: Innvandringspolitikk [Immigration Policy], 1973.

Norwegian Official Reports 1986: 8: Flyktningers tilpasning til det norske samfunn [How Refugees Adapt to Norwegian Society], 1986.

Norwegian Official Reports: Historisk statistikk 1994 [Historical Statistcs 1994].

Ophaug, Elisabeth, *Innvandrere – hvor skal de bo? Kommunal og statlig boligpolitikk i Oslo overfor innvandrere og flyktningar 1970-1995* [Immigrants – Where Should They

Live? Municipal and State Housing Policies in Oslo in Relation to Immigrants and Refugees 1970-1995], unpublished MA thesis in history, University of Oslo, 1999.
Thorud, Espen, *Norsk innvandringspolitikk og arbeiderbevegelsen. Fra åpne dører til innvandringsstopp* [Norwegian Immigration Policy and the Labor Movement. From Open Doors to Moratorium], MA thesis in political science, Oslo, 1985.
Vaage, Odd F., *Innvandringssituasjonen – pressens beskrivelse og folks oppfatning* [The Immigration Situation – Media Descriptions and Popular Perceptions], Oslo, 1985.
Vogt, Kari, *Islam på norsk. Moskeer og islamske organisasjoner i Norge* [Islam in Norwegian. Mosques and Muslim Organizations in Norway], Oslo, 2000.
Wist, Kristin Kolbeinstveit, *Pakistanere og indere i Norge på vei oppover? Om pakistanere og indere i norsk arbeidsliv fra 1960-tallet til 2000* [Pakistanis and Indians in Norway – On the Way up? On Pakistanis and Indians Working in Norway from the 1960s to 2000], MA thesis in history, University of Oslo, 2000.

Chapter 9

Gendered Policies – Gendered Patterns: Female Labour Migration from Turkey to Germany from the 1960s to the 1990s

Esra Erdem and Monika Mattes

In the migration literature, migrant women and their experiences often remain invisible and get subsumed under those of men. This misperception arises out of a long tradition according to which mainly migrant men are assumed to be economically active.[1] Particularly with respect to Turkish[2] female migrants, the culturalist stereotypical construct of the economically inactive, isolated, dependent and oppressed woman dominates popular and academic discourse.[3] Official publications on the employment of the migrant population reinforce the notion that economic inactivity among Turkish women is culturally given and voluntary.[4] The ascribed characteristics used in the construction of stereotypical representations are attributed to the migrants' cultural origins, which are taken as determining their destiny.[5]

This article attempts to correct this misperception through a feminist reading of post-war migration history. The high inactivity rate among Turkish migrant women is situated in a broader historical context, and it will be argued that German immigration and labour market policies since the 1960s have had differential consequences for the lives and the labour market position of migrant men and women. Through the case study of female migration from Turkey, we will show the ways in which socio-economic processes and political practices of West German society have interacted. The focus of the article is the labour market, and the gender- and ethnicity-specific patterns in its operation. We will show how gendered patterns in worker recruitment have shaped Turkish women's participation in the German labour market from the 1960s onwards. The centrality of West German immigration policies and of structural changes in the economy for shaping the lives of Turkish women is thereby rendered visible.

Recruitment Policies

As a result of the labour shortage associated with the economic boom in West Germany, from the mid-1950s onwards, the state initiated and promoted the immigration of foreign workers. Between 1955 and 1968, the federal government signed agreements with eight Mediterranean countries – specifically, Italy (1955), Spain and Greece (1960), Turkey (1961), Morocco (1963), Portugal (1964), Tunisia (1965) and Yugoslavia (1968) – to facilitate the recruitment of so-called *Gastarbeiter* ('guestworkers'), many of whom were women. The share of women in the 'foreign employee' category was 23 per cent in 1965 and rose to nearly 30 per cent by 1973. Among labour migrants from Turkey, the share of women was relatively low: 13 per cent in 1965 and 24 per cent in 1973. But in absolute terms, there was a rapid increase in the number of female labour migrants from Turkey. In 1962, i.e., one year after the German-Turkish agreement for worker recruitment had been signed, only around 1,500 Turkish women were employed in West Germany. In 1973, there were 129,000, making them the second largest group of female migrant workers after the Yugoslavs.[6] This push in the recruitment of female workers from Turkey can only be understood if the overall context of the German recruitment system and the shift in the labour market are taken into consideration.

By 1959-60 full employment had been reached on the female labour market in the Federal Republic. From the mid-1950s onwards, it had become clear that the West German labour force would shrink in the medium run due to longer periods spent in education and the introduction of conscription. This was also and, not least, a demographic echo effect from the losses in the Second World War and the abrupt end of East-West migration between the two Germanies after the building of the Berlin Wall in 1961. In the context of the government's family policy it was not considered desirable to make up for the gap in the labour force by mobilizing non-working housewives and mothers for full time jobs.[7] It was equally difficult to fill vacancies posted through the employment service with unemployed German women. In sectors of the labour market with a high share of female employees, such as the textile industry, hotels and restaurants, in hospitals and canteens, etc., employers were desperately looking for workers.[8] An increasing number of companies placed requests for foreign female employees through the employment service.

In mid-July 1961, an agency was set up in Istanbul by the German employment service for the specific purpose of recruiting workers from Turkey. In September 1963, an Ankara branch was added. Initially, it was thought that recruitment from Turkey would be fairly modest in numbers and limited to skilled male workers.[9] The decision to also recruit female workers was probably related to the lack of success in placing female workers from the other recruitment countries. While unskilled men could be recruited in sufficient numbers and without encountering major problems in all Mediterranean countries, until the mid-1960s it was generally more difficult to recruit female workers. The Southern European countries were mostly interested in sending young, unemployed, unskilled men abroad, thus exporting unemployment and preventing potential social conflicts. The recruitment of women, on the other hand, was a delicate matter, especially in Catholic Mediterranean countries. In Italy, therefore, German efforts to recruit women remained relatively unsuccessful. The German recruitment agencies set up in Greece and Spain, on which companies with a high proportion of female workers had initially pinned their hopes, were completely overwhelmed by the requests for placements. The Federal Employment Service (*Bundesanstalt für Arbeit*), which organized the recruitment of foreign workers, remarked in its 1961 report that 'there is a large demand for foreign female employees in the German economy', half of which could not be met through successful 'placements that actually took place'.[10]

As a result of the difficulty in covering the demand of German firms for Spanish and Greek female employees, female recruitment from Turkey began to gain significance. Firms were advised by the employment offices to place their requests for female 'guestworkers' with the Istanbul office because of the shorter processing time. Sometimes, after long waiting periods, employers replaced their requests for female employees from Greece or Spain with requests from Turkey.[11] As a result, processing times for requests for female workers from Turkey increased as well, but most likely the worker profile demanded by the employers caused the greatest difficulty in the recruitment process. Demands for female workers who were single or had no children could rarely be fulfilled.[12] Due to the traditionally young age of marriage, the high number of children and the low level of qualifications among Turkish women, the German recruitment office initially considered their chances to be recruited as slim.[13] They did not appear to correspond to the picture of the ideal 'female guestworker', who was supposed to be young, single, without children and if possible literate.[14] In order to be able to process the growing pile of requests, the German job centres asked the employers to take into consideration the social reality of Turkey and to consider employing Turkish women who did not fit this ideal 'guestworker' profile.[15] Illiterate women were foremost recruited for work in cleaning services, for seasonal work in the hotel and restaurant sector, or in the food processing industry.[16] Illiterate men, on the other hand, continued to be excluded from the recruitment process.[17]

More than 90 per cent of female migrant workers were recruited for unskilled jobs. Among Turkish migrant women, the share of skilled workers was somewhat higher: 21 per cent in 1966 and 14 per cent in 1968, due to the qualified dressmakers, seamstresses and spinners who were recruited to work in the low paying textile and clothing industries.[18] In the early 1970s, most female workers from Turkey were engaged in the electronics industry. In the textile and clothing industries they made up the largest contingent among migrant workers.[19] In northern West Germany they could also be found in highly unattractive jobs in the fishing and food processing industries. In services, the cleaning sector was dominated by Turkish female employees. In 1972, for example, they were the largest migrant group employed in the cleaning industry.[20]

Similar to the agreements with other countries, the German-Turkish agreement for labour recruitment designated a long bureaucratic and selective procedure for the recruitment of workers.[21] West German employers placed a request with their local job centre, in which they listed the desired characteristics of the job candidate such as nationality, gender, marital status, age, occupational qualifications and the physical and psychological prerequisites for the job. The job centre would then send the request to the German recruitment agency in the respective country, in this case the agency in Istanbul. From there it would be forwarded on to the head office of the Turkish employment exchange, which in turn contacted the local job centres in which the potential migrants were registered. Selected candidates travelled to Istanbul at their own expense and presented themselves at the German recruitment agency, which made further selections among candidates. All potential migrants had to undergo qualificational and medical tests. The rigorous health tests carried out by German doctors were central to this process. Only the healthiest were supposed to migrate to Germany. Pregnant women and women who had a large number of children were excluded from recruitment.[22] Candidates who passed these tests were handed a job contract for signature. For all recruited workers, a so-called 'authorization card' (*Legitimationskarte*) replaced the residence and work permit for one year.

The advantages of migrant women over German women were their young age, the health-based selection and the fact that they were willing to work full-time. Most were assigned to work shifts, to do piecework and to work on assembly lines in the above-mentioned industries, in jobs that took a toll on their health, and which German women refused to work at. The Federal Employment Service described the employers' demands in the electronics industry as follows:

> They require mostly younger mobile full-time workers who adjust quickly to the modern methods of production as well as to shift work etc. and who are also capable of maximum results. Standards are high as regards skilfulness, the ability to concentrate, quick reactions and the willingness to adjust to internal restructuring. Foreign workers are less likely to suffer from impairments which would stand in the way of these demands of the employers. They represent a group already selected for their good health and they generally belong to younger and medium age groups. They do not have to consider family obligations and therefore do not object to shift work.[23]

The German recruitment agency had to select women who could physically and psychologically bear these working conditions. For the recruitment of assembly workers doing delicate work in the electronics industry and in some branches of metal processing there were special vision tests. In these industries, automation and rationalization required the assembly of ever smaller parts by hand and with the magnifying glass. The job candidates also had to provide proof of the agility of their hands and fingers. The so-called 'Southerners' were supposed to be particularly suitable for the assembly of small parts because of the presumption that they had small hands.[24] And many Turkish female employees of Siemens attended courses organized by the company in Istanbul, which served the purpose of testing the suitability of job candidates prior to the official tests by the recruitment agency.[25]

No doubt the West German recruitment policy helped to sustain and stabilize a hierarchical and gender-segregated labour market. This can also be seen in the wages offered to migrant women. The recruitment agreements merely specified that migrants be paid the standard wages prevailing in Germany. In 1961 a leaflet posted in the German recruitment agency informed observers that the average gross wage was DM 2.00-2.80 per hour for men and DM 1.50-1.70 for women.[26] The reference was to the low-wage groups in the German labour market, which prevailed in sectors with a high share of female workers and where wages were up to 30-40 per cent lower than men's. These gender-specific wage differentials were a regular part of pay agreements and quite common in all industries until the late 1960s. In female-dominated sectors of the labour market, the employment of 'guestworkers' kept wage costs low, especially in the insufficiently unionized branches such as the hotel and restaurant services, cleaning and health care. As a result, migrant women from Turkey and other recruitment countries remained stuck in poorly paid, unskilled jobs on the lowest level of the qualificational hierarchy.

The number of Turkish women seeking employment in Germany rose rapidly from the mid-1960s onwards. As the group of migrants with the highest growth rate, already in 1965, Turkey accounted for the second-largest group of female recruits (behind Greek women; Spaniards occupied third rank). Yet, until the recession in 1966-67 it remained difficult for the German recruitment agency to match the rising demand for migrant workers. It was only with the 1966-67 economic slump that a shift took place in the recruitment policy. The numbers recruited were dramatically reduced, and the agency in Ankara was closed down. Employment offices in Germany were instructed to make an effort to fill vacancies with unemployed Germans across the country before placing a request with the recruitment agency abroad. Since the manufacturing sector's demand for workers had vanished in the economic crisis, for the first time it became possible for the German recruitment agency to place workers for the poorly paying service jobs, which migrants had largely avoided until then.[27] After the recession, the number of recruited Turkish women rose again, exceeding 20,700 in 1969 – a number that the German recruitment agency optimistically declared to have been 'seemingly unattainable a few years ago, but [was] now opening favourable perspectives for the future'.[28] Following a temporary decline in labour demand in the early 1970s due to economic factors, the number of recruited Turkish women rose to roughly 24,000 in 1973, the year that recruitment was stopped.[29]

Among Turkish migrant women there was a high share who lived apart from their partners. According to the Representative Survey of 1968, 29 per cent of Turkish migrant women were single, divorced or widowed. For men the figure was only 18 per cent. If we add the number of Turkish women who had left their husbands behind in Turkey, the share rises to 48 per cent.[30] Among married women, there were many pioneers who came to the Federal Republic before their husbands and then tried to reunite the family in Germany.[31] In the case of some Turkish female migrants, emigration to Germany had been preceded by internal migration from rural to urban areas. While the majority had not been part of the labour force in Turkey, a large proportion of city dwellers who were recruited for unskilled work nevertheless had educational and/or vocational training. Some had finished high school, others even had a qualification in nursing or dressmaking.[32]

In the early years, more than half of the Turkish female workers came from the more developed western regions of Turkey: Istanbul, Thracia and Western Anatolia. Of the male migrants, on the other hand, a higher proportion came from Central and Eastern Anatolia. The reason lies in the so-called 'open contingent' (*offenes Kontingent*) recruitment procedure, according to which the Turkish job centres forwarded the application of every suitable female migrant to the German recruitment agency straightaway. The aim was to satisfy the high excess demand for female workers. Thus, unlike their numerous male counterparts, female migrants from large cities did not have to wait long to emigrate. Men, on the other hand, were subject to the 'queuing principle' (*Reihenprinzip*). Their recruitment was dependent on how much time had passed since their application and on their region of origin. Since the 1960s the Turkish government tried to recruit from all regions proportional to the size of their population. As a result, the share of men from Central and Southern Anatolia increased.[33]

Among the strategies of the Federal Employment Service used to increase the share of female migrants, was the recruitment of married couples.[34] This approach met with a positive response in Turkey as many young women were already married and preferred emigrating together with their husbands. The German recruitment agency contacted married applicants waiting to emigrate, and told them that they had good prospects 'to receive preferential treatment with regard to emigration if their wives emigrated with them'.[35] Among the Turkish population the interest in employment in Germany was exceptionally high. The recruitment of married couples turned out to be an outlet for unskilled and married potential labour migrants who, by 1973, were faced with waiting periods of up to seven years.[36]

Apart from the state-led recruitment procedure, it was possible for migrants to enter Germany with either a visa and job promise obtained from abroad or as tourists. Unfortunately, immigration statistics that disaggregate according to immigration status are not differentiated by gender. Generally speaking, however, the involvement of the state, i.e., the Federal Employment Service, in the recruitment of workers was much higher in Turkey then in other countries.

The Economic Cycle and Immigration Policies After 1973

The worker recruitment programme, which had dramatically increased the number of Turkish women in Germany, was ended in November 1973 by a decree of the German Labour Ministry. In the decree it was argued that the anticipated rise in unemployment due to the oil shock necessitated an end to foreign worker recruitment. Indicative of the unease that rapid immigration caused beyond the economic sphere is the fact that even after the economy assimilated the effect of the oil shock and growth picked up, worker recruitment did not resume.[37]

The end of labour migration left family reunion and asylum as the only legal channels for immigration from Turkey. However, complementary to the end of worker recruitment, migrants who had entered Germany after November 1974 ceased to be eligible for work permits. The purpose of these measures was to limit competition in the labour market and to make immigration less attractive. Women from Turkey, who had migrated relatively late were hit particularly hard by these measures. Female dependence on the male breadwinner increased and families' plans for returning to Turkey were thwarted. The desperate situation of women who had been unaware of the fact that they would face these restrictive regulations or who had hoped that they would soon be reversed, and who were now unable to seek employment has been documented in detail by a government commissioned study.[38]

The change in immigration and labour market policy combined with the recession to radically decrease Turkish women's employment rate, which dropped by 20 per cent within two years (from 62 per cent in 1973). Employment stagnated while the population of working age increased, due to continuing immigration under the family reunion provisions.[39] In other words, the West German government's immigration policy at the time was geared toward allowing the entry and settlement of new migrants while taking a non-integrationist stance by refusing new migrants access to the labour market. Given the fact that these newcomers to the labour market were to a large extent female these immigration policies were bound to have long-term implications for gender processes in the migrant community. Even earlier migrants who should have been able to apply for work were often discriminated against. As one unemployed Turkish woman who had migrated to Germany in 1973 put it: 'The job centre does not provide me with work. When I go and demand work, they bang the door in my face'.[40]

In 1977, in the midst of the economic recovery period, the work permit policy was altered so that from that point onwards migrants who had entered Germany before 1977 became eligible for work permits. And finally, in 1979, at the height of the boom, the policy was replaced with a three-year waiting period for newly arrived migrants.[41] But throughout, the priority entitlement of domestic workers for jobs (*Inländerprimat*) remained in place.[42] The implications for Turkish women's insertion into the German economy are quite clear: Basically, they were stuck with the few jobs that could not be filled by domestic workers. The number of employed Turkish women increased slightly in this period, however the effect was too weak to halt the continuing decline in the employment rate. Furthermore, whatever gains they made during the boom were soon lost in the recession following the second oil shock in 1979.

The direct link between economic processes and immigration policies in the 1970s, on the one hand, and migrant women's employment rate, on the other, emerges clearly from a government-commissioned representative survey (Table 9.1). While the employment rate dropped dramatically among the post-1974 migrant women from Turkey and Yugoslavia, that of recent Italian migrants – who as European Community members were not subject to restrictive immigration regulations – remained much more stable.

Table 9.1 Migrant women's labour force participation by year of immigration

Year of Immigration	Percentage of migrant women who by 1980 had at some point taken up employment in Germany (by country of origin)		
	Turkey	Yugoslavia	Italy
1977-1979	9.5	12.5	51.4
1975-1976	29.2	40.0	51.4
1974	51.2	80.0	66.7
1973	59.5	79.2	48.3
1971-1972	71.1	79.1	55.0
1966-1970	82.0	88.4	55.7
1961-1965*	59.3	n/a	66.1

* The relatively low employment rate of migrants of the 1961-1965 period is somewhat puzzling in view of known migration histories. It may reflect a sampling problem in the survey, as there were relatively few female migrants from Turkey at that time.

Source: Mehrländer et al., *Situation der ausländischen Arbeitnehmer und ihrer Familienangehörigen in der Bundesrepublik Deutschland: Repräsentativuntersuchung '80*, table 172, p. 340.

At the time, less than 5 per cent of the interviewed Turkish women indicated that they were not interested in getting a job. The most cited reason for non-employment was the lack of a work permit (24 per cent), followed by childcare and household related responsibilities (21 per cent and 13 per cent respectively); another 10 per cent cited the inability to find a job. Merely 9 per cent of non-employed women reported that their family was opposed to their taking up paid employment.[43] According to the survey, three-quarters of the Turkish women who were not employed at the time (in 1980) had never worked in Germany. And it is not surprising to find that 60 per cent of these women had immigrated to Germany between 1974 and 1980. Clearly, immigration policies played an important role in dividing the diasporic community into working and non-working women, and in constructing the stereotype of the dependent, isolated Turkish woman whose life revolves around the household and who does not participate in the labour market.[44]

The fact that the effects of easing labour market restrictions on immigrants slowly raised labour force participation is born out in the 1985 survey on the same theme: The percentage of non-employed Turkish women who had never worked in Germany was down to 60 per cent in just five years (from 76 per cent in 1980). Similar to the earlier survey, only 3 per cent stated that they were not interested in getting a job. Among the main reasons for non-employment, the lack of a work permit, childcare and household duties continued to rank high (14 per cent each), but the inability to find a job became the major reason why Turkish women did not work (19 per cent).[45] Non-employment continued to be strongly concentrated among the post-1973 migrants. Among women who had migrated to Germany after 1977, lack of a work permit remained the most important reason for economic inactivity.[46]

By 1995, we see how these developments appear to have triggered a process that has led a significant proportion of Turkish women to withdraw from the labour market and resign themselves to their role as housewives.[47] Thus, among Turkish women interviewed that year, the most often cited reasons for non-employment were household duties (36 per cent) and childcare responsibilities (34 per cent). The lack of a work permit or inability to find a job were only mentioned by a minority of women.[48]

The Labour Market for Women with Fewer Qualifications

If immigration policies in the 1970s substantially reduced the employment rate of Turkish women, the economic trends in the 1980s and 1990s have put them at further disadvantage. Their concentration in manufacturing and in jobs with low qualificational requirements has led to non-employment, as the German economy has been moving to service jobs, many of which require formal qualifications.[49]

Due to the pattern of worker recruitment described above, female Turkish employment for a long time remained highly concentrated in the manufacturing sector. Even in 1979, the share of industrial employment in total female Turkish employment was as high as 74 per cent, as opposed to 34 per cent for all women in Germany.[50] The disappearance of manufacturing jobs led to widespread unemployment. The fact that in 1985, 43 per cent of non-employed Turkish women were registered unemployed, and that close to 60 per cent of non-employed women with job experience had worked for more than five years is indicative of an economic restructuring process, the side effect of which is unemployment among vulnerable groups of workers.[51]

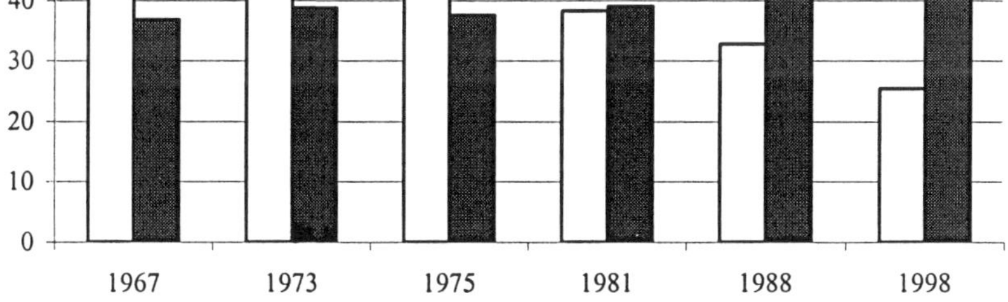

Figure 9.1 Female dependent employment as percentage of female population aged 15-64

Sources: Statistisches Bundesamt, *Ausländer*; *Amtliche Nachrichten der Bundesanstalt für Arbeit*, various years.

By 1998, services accounted for 65 per cent of total employment among Turkish women (78 per cent for all women in West Germany).[52] While this structural shift in the economy coincided with increased employment chances for German women, the employment rate of Turkish women has continued to decline (see Figure 9.1). It can therefore be concluded that Turkish women have been particularly hard hit by deindustrialization.[53] Besides the concentration in manufacturing, Turkish women have suffered due to the lack of qualifications. In 1968, 95 per cent of Turkish women worked in low-skill jobs not requiring a formal qualification. By 1985, the share was still as high as 78 per cent.[54]

As Glyn reports, in OECD countries 'the rise in labour force participation has been strongest among the better educated women'.[55] Indeed, in West Germany as a whole, there was a difference of 25 percentage points in the employment rate of the least educated and most educated quarter of the female population of working age (i.e., age 15 to 64) in 1995,[56] and the trend in the late 1990s has been toward a decline in the employment rate of less educated women.[57] Turkish women mirror such trends: Those with jobs are better educated than the employees of former years and there is a clear upward trend in the share of skilled Turkish employees.[58] Those with no qualifications, in contrast, are dropping out of (or never enter) the labour force. Hence, it can be said that the low employment rate of Turkish women reflects the characteristics of the German job market for women with low educational attainments rather than being an expression of Turkish cultural traditions.

Conclusions

This chapter has shown that West German immigration and labour market policies of the last forty years have had gender-specific effects on migrants from Turkey. A feminist perspective that analyses Turkish women's participation in the labour market within the context of these policies is therefore crucial to understand Turkish women's position on the labour market today. The first section of the article noted how the gender segmentation of the labour market, which had been endangered through labour shortage, was stabilized through the recruitment of female migrant workers. This emerges particularly clearly in the recruitment of Turkish women for the female-dominated low-wage sectors of the West German labour market in the 1960s and 1970s. It is therefore not surprising that the employment rate of Turkish women was significantly above that of

German women until 1973. Turkish female workers were on average younger than German women, and in contrast to the latter, were also willing to work full-time.

Up to the 1973 recruitment stop, engagement in paid work was the main reason why Turkish women migrated to Germany. However, as the second part of the article shows, the restrictive work permit policies of the post-1973 period played a significant role in reducing the employment rate of Turkish women and consigning them to their role as housewives at a time when German women were encouraged to take up paid employment. As such, they can be seen as an example of the constitution of difference as a social relation and its organization 'into systematic relations through economic, cultural and political discourses and institutional practices'.[59] Furthermore, the economy-wide shift of employment away from manufacturing and toward services has negatively affected women with inadequate or no occupational qualifications. The recent increase in non-employment among Turkish women mirrors this trend in the German labour market.

To conclude, the fact that today only a minority of Turkish women are engaged in paid work cannot simply be ascribed to their culture, as discourses using stereotypical representations of Turkish women tend to do. While there are differences between German and migrant women, as Räthzel reminds us,[60] these should be analysed in terms of the differential positions these two groups of women occupy in hegemonic structures and discourses and their differential access to hegemonic systems,[61] of which immigration policies are an important part.

Notes

We would like to thank Alev Deniz, Andrew Glyn, Ceren Özselçuk, Maliha Safri and participants at the workshop 'The Politics of Immigration in Contemporary Capitalism' at the Marxism 2000 conference in Amherst as well as participants at the conference out of which this book developed for comments and many extremely helpful suggestions on earlier versions of this chapter.

1 Economic activity is defined in the economics literature as engagement in paid work or the active search for paid work.

2 We use the term 'Turkish' to mean 'from Turkey' rather than 'of ethnic Turkish origin'. Although far from being ideal, we hope that this qualifier prevents the reading of the term as a signifier for the negation of ethnic diversity in Turkey.

3 Toksöz, 'Immigrantinnen aus der Türkei', pp. 57-66.

4 Cornelsen, for example, notes that economically inactive women who migrated after 1973 have lowered the employment rate among the adult female migrant population.

According to Cornelsen less than half of Turkish migrant women of working age are willing to take a job ('Erwerbstätigkeit der ausländischen Bevölkerung', p. 88).

5 Räthzel, 'Weltweite Frauensolidarität gegen nationale Großmachtpolitik und Alltagsrassismen?', p. 209.

6 Bundesanstalt für Arbeit, *Ausländische Arbeitnehmer. Erfahrungsbericht 1972/73*, Statistik, p. 71.

7 At the same time, the labour shortage in 1959/60 served as a signal to push through part-time employment as a new model for the participation of married women and mothers in specific sections of the labour market. See von Oertzen, *Teilzeitarbeit und die Lust am Zuverdienst*.

8 Bundesarchiv Koblenz (BAK), B 119/2308: Quartalsberichte zur Entwicklung der Frauenerwerbstätigkeit 1960 der Landesarbeitsämter Südbayern, Nordrhein-Westfalen und Baden-Württemberg.

9 Initially, recruitment was supposed to be restricted to the regions of Baden-Württemberg, North-Rhine-Westphalia and Hamburg, where a large number of Turkish workers were already employed. See Hauptstaatsarchiv Niedersachsen, Nds. 1310 Acc. 136/82 Nr. 727: Bundesanstalt für Arbeitsvermittlung und Arbeitslosenversicherung (BAVAV) an Landesarbeitsämter Baden-Württemberg, Nordrhein-Westfalen, Hamburg, und nachrichtlich an die anderen, 14 July 1961; ibid.: BAVAV to the regional employment offices on 13 October 1961.

10 All quotations are our own translation. *Erfahrungsbericht BAVAV 1961*, p. 14.

11 Staatsarchiv Nordrhein-Westfalen (StA NRW), BR 1134/711, p. 114: BAVAV to regional employment offices on 7 October 1964; BAK B 119/3017: Landesarbeitsamt Niedersachsen, Erfahrungsbericht 1966; BAK B 149/6239: correspondence between the food processing firm Gifhorn and Ministerialdirigent Fittges from the Bundesarbeitsministerium on 27 July 1964 and 10 August 1964.

12 StA NRW, BR 1134/711, p. 144: BAVAV to regional employment offices on 12 May 1965.

13 BAK B 119/3017: Erfahrungsbericht 1966 der Deutschen Verbindungsstelle in der Türkei.

14 Especially the documents of the regional employment offices on the recruitment and employment of migrant workers suggest that in the early phase of recruitment this projection substantially dominated the discourse of employers and employment offices on female 'guestworkers'.

15 StA NRW, BR 1134/710, p. 142: BAVAV to regional employment offices on 10 October 1962, and BR 1134/710, p. 145: BAVAV to regional employment offices on 11 November 1962; BR 1134/711, p. 150: BAVAV to regional employment offices on 30 June 1965.

16 BAK, B 119/4036, p. 227: Wochenbericht der Deutschen Verbindungsstelle in der Türkei vom 25. April bis 2. Mai.

17 StA NRW, BR 1134/711: BAVAV to regional employment offices on 26 July 1968.

18 BAK B 119/3017: Erfahrungsbericht 1966 der Deutschen Verbindungsstelle in der Türkei, and B 119/3018: Erfahrungsbericht 1968 der Deutschen Verbindungsstelle in der Türkei.

19 Bundesanstalt für Arbeit, *Ausländische Arbeitnehmer. Erfahrungsbericht 1972/73*, pp. 89, 91.

20 Ibid., p. 91.

21 See Eryilmaz, 'Wie geht man als Arbeiter nach Deutschland?' and Manfrass, 'Die Beziehungen zwischen der Bundesrepublik', in particular pp. 264-270.

22 On the pregnancy of migrant women see Mattes, 'Zum Verhältnis von Migration und Geschlecht', pp. 300-301.

23 Amtliche Nachrichten der Bundesanstalt für Arbeit, vol. 15, 1970, p. 908. 'Sie verlangten weitgehend jüngere bewegliche Ganztagskräfte, die sich rasch den modernen Fertigungsmethoden, auch hinsichtlich Schichtarbeit usw. anpassen und ein Höchstmaß an Leistung erbringen können. An Geschicklichkeit, Konzentrationsfähigkeit, schnelles Reaktionsvermögen und Bereitschaft zur Anpassung an innerbetriebliche Umstellungen werden hohe Forderungen gestellt. Beeinträchtigungen, die diesen Vorstellungen der Betriebe entgegenstehen, treten bei ausländischen Arbeiterinnen weniger auf. Diese sind gesundheitlich ausgesucht, gehören meistens jüngeren und mittleren Jahrgängen an..., haben durchwegs keine Rücksicht auf häusliche Bindungen zu nehmen und scheuen daher auch keine Schichtarbeit'.

24 The big electrotechnical company AEG employed dressmakers because they were supposed to be particularly suitable for delicate assembly work. See Eberhard Seidel-Pielen, *Unsere Türken. Annäherung an ein gespaltenes Verhältnis*, Berlin 1995, p. 88, cited after Ottens, 'Geschlechterrollenorientierungen türkischer MigrantInnen', p. 111.

25 BAK B 119/3017: Erfahrungsbericht 1966 der Deutschen Verbindungsstelle in der Türkei, and B 119/3018: Erfahrungsbericht 1968 der Deutschen Verbindungsstelle in der Türkei.

26 Politisches Archiv des Auswärtigen Amtes (AA), Ref. V, 1327: Bundesministerium für Arbeit (BMA) to the Auswärtige Amt on 17 October 1961, Appendix: Merkblatt über die allgemeinen Lebens- und Arbeitsbedingungen in der Bundesrepublik für Türken (Stand Juni 1961).

27 StA NRW BR 134/711: BAVAV to regional employment offices on 8 October 1966.

28 BAK, B 119/3013: Erfahrungsbericht 1969 der Deutschen Verbindungsstelle in der Türkei.

29 Bundesanstalt für Arbeit, *Ausländische Arbeitnehmer. Erfahrungsbericht 1972/73*, p. 57.

30 Bundesanstalt für Arbeit, *Ausländische Arbeitnehmer. Erfahrungsbericht 1968*, p. 21.

31 Eryilmaz, 'Die Ehre der Türkei', pp. 135-136.

32 Ottens, 'Geschlechterrollenorientierungen türkischer MigrantInnen', p. 111.

33 BAK, B 119/4036: Wochenbericht der Deutschen Verbindungsstelle in der Türkei vom 10.-17. April 1969; B 119/3013: Erfahrungsbericht der Deutschen Verbindungsstelle in der Türkei 1969. See also Manfrass, 'Die Beziehungen zwischen der Bundesrepublik', p. 266.

34 Bundesanstalt für Arbeit, *Ausländische Arbeitnehmer. Erfahrungsbericht 1964*, p. 22.

35 BAK, B 119/4035: Wochenbericht der Deutschen Verbindungsstelle in der Türkei, as of 17 to 23 July 1964 and 24 July 1964.

36 Manfrass, 'Beziehungen', p. 264.

37 Since the 1990s, a new labour migration regime involving Central and Eastern Europe has come into existence (see Erdem, 'Labour and Non-labour Immigration in the 1990s'). And, currently, a highly charged debate is continuing regarding possible future immigration to fill job vacancies and ensure demographic stability in Germany.

38 Bundesministerium für Jugend, Familie und Gesundheit, *Situationsanalyse nichterwerbstätiger Ehefrauen ausländischer Arbeitnehmer in der Bundesrepublik Deutschland*. For a short time, it was possible to get a work permit for employment in certain

industries facing extreme labour shortage such as hotels and restaurants or food processing, which have high concentrations of female workers and are known for the low pay and poor working conditions that prevail. But soon the latter measure was reversed.

Migrant youth with qualifications were, in principle, eligible for work. However, they were subject to the so-called *Inländerprimat*, which gives domestic workers (i.e. anyone who either does not need a work permit to work in Germany or who has a long-term permit) priority access to jobs. As Dohse, *Ausländische Arbeiter und bürgerlicher Staat*, documents, the state enforced this regulation quite rigorously, turning down work permit applications by young migrants who had been offered jobs by employers. In their case, although they had residence rights they did not have any rights pertaining to the labour market; the public employment offices thus functioned to *deter* them from working rather than finding jobs for them. Since migrants had no voting rights, these measures had no political repercussions.

39 Amtliche Nachrichten der Bundesanstalt für Arbeit, vol. 21, 1976, pp. 1162 and 1168.

40 Bundesministerium für Jugend, Familie und Gesundheit, *Situationsanalyse nichterwerbstätiger Ehefrauen ausländischer Arbeitnehmer in der Bundesrepublik Deutschland*, p. 44 (own translation).

41 Today there is a two-year waiting period for migrants from Turkey.

42 Trommer and Köhler, *Ausländer in der Bundesrepublik Deutschland*, p. 159. This policy continues to be practised today.

43 Mehrländer et al., *Situation der ausländischen Arbeitnehmer*, tables 315, 316.

44 According to the survey, the desire to reach the family's savings target faster does not play a substantial role in women's wish to pick up employment at this point in time. Rather, the desire to earn money and to be more independent and to make new acquaintances appear as the main motivating forces for seeking employment. This could be read as indicative of the settlement process. (Mehrländer et al., *Situation der ausländischen Arbeitnehmer*, table 317).

45 König, Schultze and Wessel, *Situation der ausländischen Arbeitnehmer*, tables 314, 318, 321, 324.

46 Ibid., table 326. On this question, no data is available for 1985 that is disaggregated by nationality, but given the high share of Turkish women in the sample this should not be the source of much bias.

47 Seventy-two per cent of non-employed women reported never to have worked in Germany (Mehrländer, Ascheberg and Ueltzhoeffer, *Situation der ausländischen Arbeitnehmer*, table 89).

48 Ibid., table 138. Also, 22 per cent reported that their families were against their seeking employment. While there is no disaggregation of these statistics by age, it is possible that students in full-time education could be partly responsible for this high percentage. Although 30 per cent of non-employed Turkish women had immigrated within two years of the survey (table 82) and were highly unlikely to be eligible for a work permit, only 3 per cent explicitly give this as the reason for non-employment. Furthermore, 44 per cent indicated that they were not interested in finding a job (table 95).

49 The absence of large numbers of low skill, badly paid service jobs such as prevail in the United States should be mentioned in this context.

50 Statistisches Bundesamt, *Ausländer*.

51 König, Schultze, and Wessel, *Situation der ausländischen Arbeitnehmer*, table 322.

52 Statistisches Bundesamt, *Ausländer*.

53 In their study of the Berlin manufacturing industries in the 1980-1987 period, Gillmeister, Kurthen and Fijalkowski found that Turkish female workers were particularly badly hit by job loss in manufacturing through a combination of factors such as dismissal based on seniority rules, the closing down of parts of production with high concentration of Turkish workers, discrimination and some firms' movement to three-shift production as a result of which women were substituted by male workers (*Ausländerbeschäftigung in der Krise*).

54 König, Schultze and Wessel, *Situation der ausländischen Arbeitnehmer*, table 55/1.

55 Glyn, 'Unemployment and Inequality', p. 200.

56 Glyn and Salverda, 'Employment Inequalities', table 2. Of the quarter of the female population with the lowest educational level only 45 per cent were employed compared to 70 per cent for the quarter with the highest educational level.

57 In 1995, 40 per cent of women aged 25-64 with less than upper secondary education were working; by 1998 this figure was down to 37.8 per cent (OECD Employment Outlook, 1998 and 2000 editions, table D).

58 Mehrländer, Ascheberg and Ueltzhoeffer, *Situation der ausländischen Arbeitnehmer*, table 43(3).

59 Brah, *Cartographies of Diaspora*, p. 117.

60 Räthzel, 'Weltweite Frauensolidarität gegen nationale Großmachtpolitik und Alltagsrassismen?', p. 215.

61 Brah, *Cartographies of Diaspora*, p. 215.

Archival Sources

Bundesarchiv Koblenz (BAK)
  B 119 Bundesanstalt für Arbeit (from 1969), re. Bundesanstalt für Arbeitsvermittlung und Arbeitslosenversicherung;
  B 149 Bundesministerium für Arbeit und Sozialordnung, re. (up to 1957) für Arbeit.
Hauptstaatsarchiv Niedersachsen (HstA Nds.)
  Hannover: Nds. 1310.
Politisches Archiv des Auswärtigen Amts (AA)
  Bonn: Ref. V Rechtsabteilung.
Staatsarchiv Nordrhein-Westfalen (StA NRW)
  Schloß Kalkum: BR 1134.

References

Amtliche Nachrichten der Bundesanstalt für Arbeit, various years.

Brah, Avtar, *Cartographies of Diaspora: Contesting Identities*, London, 1996.

Bundesanstalt für Arbeit, *Ausländische Arbeitnehmer. Beschäftigung, Anwerbung, Vermittlung. Erfahrungsberichte 1961 bis 1972/73*, Nürnberg, different years.

Bundesministerium für Jugend, Familie und Gesundheit, *Situationsanalyse nichterwerbstätiger Ehefrauen ausländischer Arbeitnehmer in der Bundesrepublik Deutschland*, Bonn, 1977.

Cornelsen, Carsten, 'Erwerbstätigkeit von Ausländern 1988', *Wirtschaft und Statistik* 2 (1990): pp. 85-94.

Cornelsen, Carsten, 'Erwerbstätigkeit der ausländischen Bevölkerung', *Wirtschaft und Statistik* 3 (1996): pp. 147-155.

Dohse, Knuth, *Die staatliche Regulierung der Ausländerbeschäftigung in der ökonomischen Krise*, Berlin, 1996.

Dohse, Knuth, *Ausländische Arbeiter und bürgerlicher Staat*, Königstein, 1981.

Erdem, Esra, *Labour and Non-labour Immigration in the 1990s: A Case Study of Germany*, paper presented at the workshop 'Beyond Fortress Europe?', ECPR Joint Sessions, 14-19 April 2000.

Eryilmaz, Aytaç, 'Wie geht man als Arbeiter nach Deutschland?', in: Aytaç Eryilmaz and Mathilde Jamin (eds), *Fremde Heimat. Eine Geschichte der Einwanderung aus der Türkei*, Essen, 1998, pp. 93-119.

Eryilmaz, Aytaç, 'Die Ehre der Türkei', in: Aytaç Eryilmaz and Mathilde Jamin (eds), *Fremde Heimat: Eine Geschichte der Einwanderung aus der Türkei*, Essen, 1998, pp. 133-137.

Gillmeister, Helmut, Hermann Kurthen and Jürgen Fijalkowski, *Ausländerbeschäftigung in der Krise*. Beiträge zur Sozialökonomik der Arbeit 21, Berlin, 1989.

Glyn, Andrew, 'Unemployment and Inequality', in: Tim Jenkinson (ed.), *Readings in Macroeconomics*, Oxford, 2000, pp. 196-213.

Glyn, Andrew and Wiemer Salverda, 'Employment Inequalities', in: Mary Gregory, Wiemer Salverda and Stephen Bazen (eds), *Labour Market Inequalities: Problems and Policies of Low-Wage Employment in International Perspective*, Oxford, 2000, pp. 35-52.

König, Peter, Günther Schultze and Rita Wessel, *Situation der ausländischen Arbeitnehmer und ihrer Familienangehörigen in der Bundesrepublik Deutschland: Repräsentativuntersuchung '85*, Bonn, 1986.

Manfrass, Klaus, 'Die Beziehungen zwischen der Bundesrepublik und den einzelnen Herkunftsländern im Zeichen der Arbeitskräftewanderung. Das Entstehen neuer Beziehungsstrukturen im staatlichen und gesellschaftlichen Bereich', in: Reinhard Lohrmann and Klaus Manfrass (eds), *Ausländerbeschäftigung und internationale Politik. Zur Analyse transnationaler Sozialprozesse*, Munich/Vienna, 1974, pp. 255-334.

Mattes, Monika, 'Zum Verhältnis von Migration und Geschlecht: Anwerbung und Beschäftigung von "Gastarbeiterinnen" in der Bundesrepublik 1960-1973', in: Jan Motte, Rainer Ohliger and Anne von Oswald (eds), *50 Jahre Bundesrepublik – 50 Jahre Einwanderung. Nachkriegsgeschichte als Migrationsgeschichte*, Frankfurt a. M., 1999, pp. 285-309.

Mehrländer, Ursula et al., *Situation der ausländischen Arbeitnehmer und ihrer Familienangehörigen in der Bundesrepublik Deutschland: Repräsentativuntersuchung '80*, Bonn, 1981.

Mehrländer, Ursula, Carsten Ascheberg and Joerg Ueltzhoeffer, *Situation der ausländischen Arbeitnehmer und ihrer Familienangehörigen in der Bundesrepublik Deutschland: Repräsentativuntersuchung '95*, Berlin, 1996.

OECD, *Employment Outlook*, Paris, 1998 and 2000.

Oertzen, Christine von, *Teilzeitarbeit und die Lust am Zuverdienst. Geschlechterpolitik und gesellschaftlicher Wandel in Westdeutschland 1948-1969*, Göttingen, 1999.

Ottens, Svenja, 'Geschlechterrollenorientierungen türkischer MigrantInnen im Spannungsfeld zwischen Herkunftsbindungen und kulturellen Neudefinitionen', *Zeitschrift für Frauenforschung* 16 (1998): pp. 106-123.

Räthzel, Nora, 'Weltweite Frauensolidarität gegen nationale Großmachtpolitik und Alltagsrassismen?', in: Brigitte Fuchs and Gabriele Habinger (eds), *Rassismen und Feminismen*, Vienna, 1996, pp. 198-216.

'Statistische Umschau: Bevölkerung', *Wirtschaft und Statistik* 12 (1975): pp. 813-815.

Statistisches Bundesamt, *Ausländer*, Fachserie 1, Reihe 2, Wiesbaden, various years.

Toksöz, Gülay, 'Immigrantinnen aus der Türkei', *Beiträge zur feministischen Theorie und Praxis* 29 (1991): pp. 57-66.

Trommer, Luitgard and Helmut Köhler, *Ausländer in der Bundesrepublik Deutschland*, DJI Materialien, Munich, 1981.

Chapter 10

Constructing Boundaries in a Multicultural Nation: The Discourse of 'Overforeignization' in Switzerland

Damir Skenderovic

Switzerland is generally seen as a prototype of the multicultural nation. To many, the country's history is a testament to the integrative force of multiculturalism, which has been able to bind together the German-, French-, Italian- and Rhaeto-Romance-speaking populations. Somewhat paradoxically, however, the long-term persistence and extraordinary influence of a strong anti-immigrant movement in the country is exceptional within Europe. In September 2000, Swiss voters rejected a popular initiative directed once again against the presence of foreigners. But the fact that 36.2 per cent voted in favour of the proposal to limit the number of foreigners to 18 per cent of the population illustrates how controversial the issue is.[1] Apparently, in Switzerland a widespread acceptance of immigration has thus far not been achieved. Answers to the new challenges for national identity in a democratic multicultural state have yet to be found.

This chapter outlines main features of the discourse of 'overforeignization' (*Überfremdung*) in Switzerland and demonstrates its persistence throughout the twentieth century. It then proceeds to present explanations of the emergence of xenophobia by emphasizing the role of political parties. It will be argued that anti-immigrant parties had considerable influence on immigration policies because they could rely on discourses already present in Swiss society. One of these discourses concerns the way Swiss see their nation and national identity. Contrary to the widespread assumption that Switzerland has to be seen as a classical example of state-nation (*Staatsnation*) and will-nation (*Willensnation*), this chapter argues that, with regard to immigration and citizenship policies, Switzerland more closely resembles models of cultural nation (*Kulturnation*) and ethnic nation (*Volksnation*). Finally, the chapter offers some explanations as to why Swiss multiculturalism is barely considered as an integration model for new minorities in an immigration society, despite its history as an incorporating force binding the 'native' minorities.

'Overforeignization' as a Socio-cultural Code

For any study of Swiss immigration policy and the discourse of exclusion directed toward foreigners, it is crucial to take a closer look at the term 'overforeignization' (*Überfremdung*).[2] In the sense of a sociocultural code, the term expresses the perception and exclusion of socially segregated groups that are culturally distinguished and demarcated. 'Overforeignization' implies the notion that there is a menacing danger from those who are of foreign origin and culture. Its discourse is the expression of xenophobic attitudes and patterns of thought, and it intends to exclude non-members of the national community. The 'stranger' (*der Fremde)* is perceived as a category, based on stereotypes, and not as an individual. Referring to a static and essentialist definition of culture, lifestyle and social group, 'overforeignization' assumes homogeneity of 'the others' who are cast in opposition to 'us'. The discourse of 'overforeignization' appeals to people's emotions and fears and operates in a dialectical manner: On the one side, there is the assumption that one's own identity and group is threatened; on the other side, the notion of 'overforeignization' establishes and reinforces one's own identity by pointing to differences and distinctions from 'the other', the foreigner.

The discourse of 'overforeignization' in Switzerland is unique in Europe for its persistence throughout the twentieth century. The term 'overforeignization' was already used before the First World War, when some intellectuals and politicians warned of cultural, economic and political 'overforeignization' by mainly German immigrants.[3] State authorities also began to apply the term, which appears, for instance, in a report on measures to combat 'overforeignization', published in 1914 by the Federal Department of Foreign Affairs (*Eidgenössisches Politisches Departement*). But it was only after the First World War that the term began to circulate in the general public and became an important feature in newspapers and political debates. It was then that the notion of 'overforeignization' began to have a significant impact on immigration legislation.[4] During the 1930s, 'overforeignization' acquired a central place in the national discourse, serving as a vigorous tool of argumentation in the restrictive refugee policy directed above all against Jewish refugees.[5]

In the early 1960s, the term 'overforeignization' was revived, and became the ideological and discursive hallmark of the anti-immigrant political movement.[6] However, at that time, criticism of Switzerland's relatively liberal immigration policy came from two sides: on the one hand, there were the new political groups from the so-called 'Movement against Overforeignization' (*Anti-Überfremdungsbewegung*); on the other, the left-wing parties and the trade unions. Both seized upon economic arguments to frame their arguments. In fact, already in the late 1950s, the latter had emphasized the danger of too many foreign workers in Switzerland. State authorities also embraced the discourse of 'overforeignization', as, for instance, the 1964 report of a state commission appointed to examine the policy on foreign labour shows with its statement that Switzerland 'is acutely threatened by overforeignization'.[7] Moreover, by the mid-1960s the notion of cultural 'overforeignization' – assuming that Swiss cultural identity was threatened by immigrants from the south of Europe – began to be evoked in the political discourse. Issues such as integration policy and immigrant culture were increasingly highlighted, indicating a shift in focus from arguments based on economic concerns to questions of culture and identity.

Examining this revival of anti-immigrant discourse, it should be taken into account that during the 1960s left-wing parties and trade unions supported demands to reduce immigration rates by applying not only economic and labour-market arguments but also by pointing to an assumed danger of 'overforeignization'.[8] Some scholars argue that Social Democrats and trade unionists accepted a broader ideological discourse grounded in notions of the national community and elected to refer to Switzerland as a special case (*Sonderfall*), a discourse which drew a heavy line separating the nation from both the outside world and non-Swiss citizens and residents.[9] This was due to the political and institutional integration of large segments of the Swiss Left into the 'consociational system',[10] which occurred mainly during the 1930s and 1940s.[11] In addition, most Social Democrats and trade unionists showed strong support for the so-called 'spiritual national defense'. Established during the 1930s, this ideological and cultural concept of 'Swissness', widely acclaimed by the polity and public, aimed to strengthen the country's independence from the surrounding totalitarian regimes by emphasizing the Swiss peculiarities and the distinctness of the Swiss people.[12]

When in the first half of the 1960s the anti-immigrant parties started to set forth their views on immigration policy, their targets were the so-called 'guestworkers' (*Gastarbeiter*) or 'foreign workers' (*Fremdarbeiter*), citizens of southern European countries like Italy, Spain, and Portugal. At the end of the 1970s, as the country received the first larger groups of refugees from Indochina, the anti-immigrant parties began to focus on asylum policy. The most important topic in their argumentation became the reference to the non-European '*Kulturkreis*' or 'cultural sphere'. In order to revive fears of 'overforeignization', the political parties referred to phenotypical characteristics and the 'visible presence' of the asylum seekers; in addition to fears about the supposedly increasing competition on the job market, the conflict of culture was emphasized as the main problem.

Thus, during the 1980s and 1990s 'overforeignization' was still a buzz-word in debates about immigration and asylum. The issues of political asylum and refugee policy were debated within an already politicized and polarized field, which had been prepared over the two preceding decades by the discussion of 'overforeignization'. In the 1980s and 1990s, however, there was an important difference. The concentrated attention on asylum seekers concerned relatively few individuals compared to the 'question of foreign workers' in the 1960s and 1970s. But it was nevertheless predestined to become a key area in the revival of the question of 'overforeignization'.

The 'Movement against Overforeignization'

Until the 1980s, the 'Movement against Overforeignization' was principally a grouping of three parties: the National Action (founded in 1961), Vigilance (1964) and the Swiss Republican Movement (1971).[13] In national and cantonal elections, the parties achieved some notable successes. Between 1971 and 1987, their electoral support in elections to the National Council was generally between 2 and 8 per cent. Although the 'Movement against Overforeignization' was composed of splinter parties, it could count on considerable support at the ballot box from Swiss voters. The anti-immigrant parties made great use of the instruments of direct democracy; during a period of 30 years (1970-2000), they were actively involved in twelve popular initiatives and referenda on policies regarding immigration and foreigners (see table 10.1).[14]

In June 1970, the first vote on a popular initiative by an anti-immigrant party was a political milestone for the young movement. The aim of the initiative was to limit the percentage of foreigners in Switzerland to 10 per cent of the population, which would have meant that more than one-third of the foreign population would have had to leave the country. The initiative led to an extensive public debate, and the turnout was over 74 per cent, the highest since 1947. With 54 per cent voting against it, the proposal was narrowly defeated, but in more than one-third of the cantons a majority of voters accepted the initiative.

Table 10.1: Popular initiatives and referenda of the anti-immigrant movement on policies toward foreigners, 1970-2000

Year	*Initiative or Referendum*	*Initiator*	*% of vote*
1970	Init. 'Against overforeignization'	NA	46.0
1974	Init. 'Against overforeignization and overpopulation'	NA	34.2
1977	Init. 'Against overforeignization'	REP	29.5
1977	Init. 'For limitation of naturalizations'	NA	33.8
1982	Ref. against the legislation on foreigners	NA	50.4
1983	Ref. against the facilitation of certain naturalizations	NA	55.2
1984	Init. 'Against selling out of the homeland'	NA	48.9
1988	Init. 'For limitation of immigration'	NA	32.7
1994	Ref. against the antiracism-law	Ad hoc Com.	45.4
1995	Ref. against the law facilitating foreigners' ability to buy real estate	SD	53.6
1996	Init. 'Against illegal immigration'	SVP	46.3
2000	Init. 'For control of immigration'	Ad hoc Com.	36.2

NA=National Action, REP=Swiss Republican Movement, SD=Swiss Democrats, SVP=Swiss People's Party, Init.=Initiative, Ref.=Referendum
Source: http://www.admin.ch/ch/d/pore/va/index.html

In the second half of the 1970s, after a number of election defeats, it seemed that the anti-immigrant parties would not recover politically. But from the mid-1980s onward, a second phase of the anti-immigrant movement commenced. It diversified and new parties and factions came into being. The Swiss Automobile Party, known as Swiss Freedom Party since 1994, was founded in 1985 as a reaction to the increasing success of ecological issues. By the start of the 1990s, the party was becoming more and more concerned with immigration policy and launched a number of strongly xenophobic campaigns against asylum seekers. With the League of Ticino, founded in 1991, the anti-immigrant movement received support from a primarily regionalist party which used populist discourse to challenge the established parties in the canton of Ticino. National Action, renamed Swiss Democrats in 1990, remained a very active anti-immigrant party through the 1990s.

Since the 1990s, the anti-immigrant parties have undergone major changes.[15] The Swiss People's Party (SVP) assumed the legacy of the 'Movement against Overforeignization' and succeeded in driving the splinter parties out of the political landscape; today, the anti-immigrant movement is concentrated in one established party. The SVP considerably increased its share of the vote in the National Council, while during the same period the Swiss Democrats and the Freedom Party lost much ground. In October 1999, the National Council elections turned into a sensational success for the Swiss People's Party, which won 22.6 per cent of the vote and became the strongest Swiss party. Within the national SVP, which is a member of the government coalition, the Zurich cantonal section has augmented its influence since the 1990s by promoting a political agenda containing mainly contentious issues such as immigration policy and European integration, themes taken from the splinter anti-immigrant parties.[16]

The latest example of the persistent mobilizing force of the anti-immigrant political actors is the popular initiative in the year 2000, which aimed to impose a constitutional limit on the percentage of foreigners in Switzerland.[17] It resembles the popular initiative of 1970, which also sought to introduce a strict quota in order to reduce immigration. During the campaign, opponents of the proposal – in fact a large majority of the Swiss polity – emphasized the negative economic effects of reducing immigration rates, and pointed to the importance of foreigners as a labour force in various sectors of the Swiss economy (construction, tourist industry, public health service, etc.).[18] It is striking that arguments against the initiative hardly ever stressed the fact that Switzerland is an immigration society, and deliberately avoided considering further social or political implications of an integrative immigration policy.

During the last 40 years, the anti-immigrant parties have had a substantial impact on public opinion and political decisions surrounding issues of Swiss immigration policy.[19] Especially in the German-speaking part of Switzerland, many protagonists of the anti-immigrant parties took part in the process of shaping political opinion and decision-making. For instance, earlier anti-immigrant campaigns facilitated matters for the federal government when in the middle of the 1970s it was able to push through, with scant opposition, restrictions on what had been relatively liberal immigration policies. Andreas Wimmer argues that 'it can also be proven from the Swiss case that the change in course, for example, of immigration policy and the official definition of basic political problems occurred only as *reactions* to nationalist and xenophobic social movements'.[20]

Features of Exclusion

The exclusionist discourse of Swiss anti-immigrant parties contains a set of various features and arguments, which aim at identifying and categorizing immigrants and foreigners. As early as the 1960s and 1970s, anti-immigrant positions in debates on immigration relied on the conception of culture as an unchangeable constant in individuals and societies. Essentialist notions of culture, values and ways of life were set forth, for example, in the debates on integration and, as it was called in the 1960s and 1970s, 'assimilation'. Thus, the anti-immigrant parties rejected the concept of 'assimilation' of foreigners or just argued that it was impossible. The immigrants, they claimed, would never really be assimilated, especially considering their national pride in deeply rooted traditions, a pride that is, according to them, inborn as a basic inherited characteristic.

During the 1980s and 1990s, when the asylum seekers – first non-Europeans and later Europeans from the Balkans – became the new targets of the anti-immigrant campaigns, culture and cultural difference became the main discursive features. The anti-immigrant movement now greatly emphasized an assumed cultural and ethnic distance from the Swiss culture and nation.[21] The immigrants' cultures and ways of life were seen as distinctive characteristics which were immutable and uniform. Politicians from the anti-immigrant movement stressed the fundamental incompatibility between cultures that would clash. They combined an 'ethnopluralist' view, which highlights cultural differences and the separate development of different cultures, with the claim that the refugees should stay in or at least return to their homelands.[22] In this view, there is no possibility of overcoming cultural difference.

This sort of discourse of exclusion directed toward foreigners corresponds to what, since the 1980s, scholarship on racism describes as the concept of neoracism.[23] As studies on the *Nouvelle Droite* in France demonstrate, the New Right contributed to a large extent to the important and politically fruitful doctrinal shift that occurred with the redefinition of racism.[24] In contrast to inegalitarian racism, neoracism exalts the 'right to be different' and thus pretends to support egalitarian assumptions, but emphasizes a presumed incommensurability of different cultural identities. Culture, whether attributed to a nation, ethnic identity or '*Volk*' (people), is viewed as a static and natural category, and it becomes the determining feature of differentiation. Neoracists substantiate their position with an essentialist notion of culture or way of life. Cultural unity and ethnic homogeneity are seen as basic conditions for the preservation of one's own identity or group.

Moreover, as the neoracist position uses the slogan 'right to be different' in order to preserve ethnic and cultural identity and difference, the homogenization of the group within, as well as its isolation from the outside, become important objectives. Following this line of argument, neoracism joins ethnopluralism in its purpose of segregation. Often, in the place of explicit exclusion and under the pretext of multicultural motivation, cultural exclusion within the society is pursued in order to maintain the symbolic distance between social groups. This important theme of the New Right represents a trap into which antiracist discourses of multiculturalism may fall, due to the fact that culture and ethnicity can become deterministic categories and thus promote the segregation of ethnic and culturally defined minorities.[25]

Since the 1980s, the reference to theoretical discussions of xenophobia as a natural characteristic of human beings has been another feature of anti-immigrant discourses in Switzerland. On this matter, the theoretical work of the New Right has some direct impact as it helps to legitimize a number of theorists and authors who claim that human beings are naturally distant, mistrustful and even frightened of 'strangers'. In their view the mistrustful relation to foreigners has to be seen as an anthropological constant which gives us the notion of a 'homo xenophobicus'.[26] Moreover, presupposed human instincts for territory and aggression would naturally lead to repulsive attitudes toward foreigners. Some representatives of anti-immigrant parties have embraced this point of view, and have frequently referred to human sociobiology and ethology to support their arguments.

This kind of research presents socio-affective behaviour patterns of individuals as indelible marks of the animal side of human beings.[27]

Finally, during recent years, debates on multiculturalism, citizenship and integration policy have significantly intensified in Switzerland, and some of the above-mentioned features of an exclusionist discourse can be found here. On this matter, the Swiss People's Party and particularly its Zurich section play an important role. In their view multiculturalism poses a threat to the Western value system, ultimately leading to the decline of Swiss culture: 'Multiculturalism means the decline of culture. As history shows the cohabitation of people of different nationality, race, skin colour and religion created problems at all times and in all countries and was conflict-ridden.'[28] Thus, the recently increasing rejection of a multiculturalism, which would address the questions of how to incorporate the new immigrant minorities, draws on features that were already used in the discourse of 'overforeignization'. Immigrants, now particularly from non-European countries or the Balkans, are perceived as fundamentally different and not able to integrate into the so-called host society due to their national origin and immutable culture. Moreover, when representatives of anti-immigrant parties assert that there is an anthropological fear of 'the other' and that xenophobia should be seen as a 'normal' human attitude of self-demarcation and self-defence, they denounce multicultural coexistence and cohabitation of people from different origins and cultures as an unrealisable project for society.

Xenophobia and the Perception of Crises

As has been noted above, there is a cyclical tendency in Switzerland to thematize a so-called 'foreigner problem' and to conjure up a threat of 'overforeignization'. Two general observations can be made regarding what may have triggered this cycle. First, it appears that the topic of too many foreigners could emerge when there was no noticeable rise in immigration.[29] During the 1920s, for instance, the notion of 'overforeignization' began to influence public debates and political decision-making, while the percentage of foreign residents in Switzerland dropped continuously (1910: 14.7 per cent; 1920: 10.4; 1930: 8.7). Second, periods of intense mistrust of foreigners did not correlate with times of economic crisis or recession. During the 1960s and in the beginning of the 1970s, demands for a restrictive immigration policy were widely espoused by the public, while the economic situation was very good and the oil crisis and the economic slump had not yet happened. Although the percentage of immigrants living in Switzerland had increased significantly since 1950 (1950: 6.1 per cent; 1960: 10.8; 1970: 17.2), during this period of full employment immigrant workers did not represent a real threat to Swiss workers in the job market. A recent study also strongly supports the argument that the percentage of foreigners in a particular area does not correlate with the degree of xenophobia among the local Swiss population.[30]

The emergence of the discourse of 'overforeignization' and of xenophobic attitudes can be interpreted 'as ways of reassuring the national self and its boundaries, as attempts at making sense of the world in times of crisis'.[31] The 1920s, for instance, were a period when Swiss society, traumatized like all countries in post-war Europe, went through a general crisis of social and political life.[32] The appeal to the notion of nation as a closed and homogeneous community seemed especially attractive as a way of calming longings for clarity, stability, and safety. The national community was strengthened in such a way that a strong sense of 'us' emerged, with clear boundaries set against the outside world and, internally, against foreigners. During the 1960s and 1970s, intensified modernization and apparently unlimited economic growth had major effects on society. Many were worried about the dissolution of traditional alignments of social life and about social disintegration. For many, it was a critical time of accelerated sociocultural transformations, where events such as the 1968 protests were signs of an insecure future and a society in disorder. The urge both to strengthen the collective identity and to demarcate non-members from the national community, apparently a reaction to a widely perceived insecurity, served as an aid to self-orientation.

However, it would be wrong to interpret the rise of the discourse of exclusion as primarily a result of modernization or socio-economic changes. It seems more likely that *perceptions* of social crisis, as well as subjective dimensions, are of relevance in explaining why some are attracted by exclusionist demands and xenophobic attitudes. In other words, many individuals *believe* themselves to be threatened by the challenges of modernity.[33] Thus, it is crucial to focus on political actors and social elites, who are of great importance in the construction of shared categories.[34] Political actors considerably influence the public and the institutional construction of patterns of perceptions of 'us' and 'them'. Additionally, institutional settings of the political system give the political actors specific power to actively intervene in the regulation of social conflicts.

In Switzerland, the tools of direct democracy provide distinctive political opportunity structures for the anti-immigrant movement. By launching initiatives and referenda, the movement not only continuously thematizes and expounds the 'foreigner problem', but also regularly puts strong pressure on the immigration policymaking of the government and established political parties. Nevertheless, it is also necessary to consider Switzerland's 'discursive opportunity structures', which provide symbolic resources to the anti-immigrant movement.[35] One has to examine how far anti-immigrant parties can mobilize within an ethnocultural framing of Swiss national identity and use ethnic and cultural counter-concepts to the widely assumed idea of the Swiss nation as a community bounded solely by political and civic components.

Framing the Discourse: Switzerland as *Kulturnation*?

Notions of nation continue to depend on the two classic concepts of state-nation (*Staatsnation*) and cultural nation (*Kulturnation*).[36] On the one hand, the concept of cultural nation emphasizes the symbolic feeling of group belonging, kinship and a collective identity that draws on real or constructed cultural and historical commonalties. On the other hand, the concept of state-nation highlights a sense of voluntarily belonging to a political community, and considers common citizenship as the foundation of nationhood. Thus, one can distinguish between ethnocultural nationalism and civic nationalism. While the former uses cultural and historical references, the latter stresses membership in the political community. But one has to be aware of some analytical weaknesses of this definitional antithesis, as the notion of civic nationalism and nationhood, although strongly referring to the political community and the state embodies historical, cultural and ethnic ingredients as well.[37] This distinct conception of nation, combining civic and ethnocultural components, is of great importance for the examination of the various references employed to define the Swiss nation.

For many scholars, Switzerland, with its federal state created in 1848, is the classic example of a state-nation founded on political will. Hans Kohn insisted as early as 1956 that the Swiss nation had been created 'on the basis of democracy and federation'.[38] Karl Deutsch speaks of Switzerland as 'a paradigmatic case of political integration'.[39] Even Benedict Anderson describes the historically late creation of the Swiss nation as an act of political will and rational choice.[40] Thus, numerous studies focus on the creation and development of the constitutional and institutional framework of the federal state that guarantees Switzerland's cohesion as a state-nation. The institutional mixture of the three key elements – direct democracy, federalism, and neutrality – is seen as the basic pillar of national identity.[41] According to Jürgen Habermas, one can legitimately claim that there is a strong 'constitutional patriotism' (*Verfassungspatriotismus*) in Switzerland.[42] Furthermore, after the Second World War, the firm integration of the Social Democratic Party into the consociational political system and a period of economic growth strengthened the political and social cohesion of the Swiss nation. The consensus politics of the parties led to a stable political peace with the national welfare state as a guarantor of the prosperity the economy had brought.

During recent years, however, investigations of the ethnic grounds of Swiss nationhood have increasingly preoccupied scholars. It became crucial, particularly with respect to immigration and citizenship policies, to examine discourses and institutional arrangements that imply notions of Switzerland as a culture- and even ethnic nation. Hanspeter Kriesi, for instance, argues that: 'the ethnic or communitarian element of the Swiss nation is tied to the local or cantonal level. Just as they have jealously tried to guard their political prerogatives, the cantons have also tried to retain the right to define the national identity of their citizens. ... Thus, the predominately *civic nationalism at the federal level* goes hand in hand with a predominately *ethnic nationalism at the cantonal and local level*'.[43] This point of view is also exemplified by the fact that local authorities play a decisive role in the rather restrictive naturalization procedure.[44] To obtain Swiss citizenship, one must prove one's cultural and social integration into Swiss society and particularly into the local community. Immigrants aspiring to Swiss citizenship have to show that they have fully adapted to customs and traditions of the country and accepted its social norms and culture codes. As a result, the restrictive manner of the ethnic-assimilationist model of Swiss '[c]itizenship laws based on *ius sanguinis* and tortuous naturalization procedures have made the Swiss system resemble Walzer's "tyranny" at most levels'.[45]

As far as national identity is concerned, many Swiss view themselves as members of a national group held together by common historical experiences and a common mentality. The continuous construction of national ideas and myths contributes to, as Didier Froidevaux calls it, 'an ethnic construction relying on a perception of Switzerland as an exceptional or insular case'.[46] In this respect, history is an especially powerful force for integration and possesses above all great symbolic value. Historical references are mainly to the period of the 'Old Confederation' that preceded the establishment of the federal state, and they emphasize a shared historical and geographical experience. References to the Alps' function as a national shield and a shelter and symbol of a peaceful and romantic life are often used as a means of expressing national history and feelings.[47] In literature and historical writings the main elements of the Swiss people's collective mentality are commonly described as love of liberty, the desire for independence, a rootedness in the native soil and a strong capability for defence of their lands.[48] Moreover, Swiss national identity, as it is built upon demarcation and defence against the outside world and stabilized through the belief that there are external threats to the country, should primarily be described as a 'negative identity'.[49] Some of the Swiss national myths, for instance, refer to fights of liberation from foreign powers (Wilhelm Tell) or to the strong will to defend the country against foreign invaders (Second World War). In a similar way, neutrality, a longstanding doctrine of Swiss foreign policy, is utilized by many to demarcate the country from the external world and thus reinforces the country's isolated position.

The Anti-immigrant Movement: Both Beneficiary and Supplier

The anti-immigrant movement and its discourse of 'overforeignization' found its ground in the longstanding and widely accepted national discourse characterized by references to both Switzerland as a state-nation and as a cultural nation. Thus, with its national categories and symbols the movement refers in its exclusionary discourse toward foreigners not only to the constitutional bases of the federal state, but also to language, culture and historical origins.

First, the anti-immigrant movement makes reference to Switzerland as a state-nation and to a distinct Swiss political culture. As its discourse on immigration shows, it does not trust foreigners to know and accept the rules of a democratic system. Following this line of argument, the movement emphasizes that foreigners in general come from states without longstanding democratic traditions and lack experience and competence in dealing with direct democracy. In its words, only the native Swiss are able to deal with the institutions of direct democracy and the historically proven traditions of the Swiss state.

Second, and more importantly in terms of immigration policy, in its continual references to the loss of Swiss culture and its peculiarities, the anti-immigrant movement follows essentialist notions of Switzerland as a cultural nation. It emphasizes that the country and the people are deeply rooted in a culture whose characteristics do not change throughout the entire life of a human being or indeed the whole history of a country. Representatives of the movement speak of the '*Volkscharakter*' and individual national character. With its essentialist view on nationhood, citizenship and the concept of nation, the anti-immigrant movement has joined the discourse of the New Right.

Furthermore, the anti-immigrant movement is embedded in a current that some scholars refer to as a new nationalism in Western democracies.[50] This new nationalism is principally characterized by interior exclusion and discrimination. It is directed against non-members of the nation inside the country, and thus constructs divisions within the population. In this respect, there is also a growing importance of the notion of nation perceived primarily as an exclusive welfare state, a welfare state that is considered a national achievement and an expression of solidarity reserved for the '*Volksgemeinschaft*'.[51] In this way, the feeling of belonging to a national community gains a concrete component of vested interest, as the exclusive national community replaces the inclusive social community. The anti-immigrant movement reinforces this development by using national characteristics and myths constructed and deployed to build a self-referential feeling of collective identity, which appeal across social classes.

Therefore, without doubt, the anti-immigrant movement not only benefits from these common notions of Swiss national identity, but, by constructing boundaries of 'the other', also supplies and strengthens beliefs in a homogeneous and exclusive national community. During the last 40 years, the movement has distilled a form of 'Helvetic nationalism' from a number of different elements of national ideology. It took up features of national identity, widely accepted in Swiss society and politics, and gave them a radical expression. By pointing to the rootedness and exclusiveness of Swiss national identity, the anti-immigrant movement contributed considerably to the construction of national identity, which relies on ethnic and cultural references, and thus to the reinforcing of the concept of 'Swissness'. Moreover, by launching initiatives and referenda concerning immigration policies, the movement caused public debates on national identity in regular intervals.

Essentialist notions of nation and culture also play a significant role in debates on multiculturalism, which have intensified considerably during recent years. By pointing to cultural components as deterministic and immutable categories, defined indistinctly by history, origin or mentality, the anti-immigrant movement emphasizes a presumably cultural distance between 'native' and immigrant populations. Although Swiss multiculturalism has its particular significance and tradition, it is interesting to see that the anti-immigrant movement's culturalist discourse could profit from a specific concept of multiculturalism developed within a widely accepted discursive and symbolic frame referring to Switzerland as an ethnic and cultural nation.

The Paradoxes of Swiss Multiculturalism

Swiss often refer to their own multiculturalism as an important feature of their national identity. To many, Switzerland is the example of the successful functioning of a multicultural nation, and the heterogeneity of the country, with its distinct cultural, linguistic and religious groups, symbolizes a unique achievement. The federal state brings together four distinct regions with their own languages and cultures. The longstanding co-operative relationship between previously antagonistic Catholic and Protestant factions is taken as further evidence of the integrating capacity of Swiss society and politics. Some also argue that because of the multicultural experience, large sections of the population would show great respect and understanding toward minorities as well as toward different cultures and ethnic groups.[52] In this respect, the notion of Switzerland as state-nation, bound together by civil rights, political will and institutional arrangements, provides the foundation of Swiss multiculturalism.

During the last few years, however, the language debate in Switzerland has intensified and become a crucial question mark in relation to the political and cultural cohesion of the country. Some scholars have pointed out that, in everyday life, relations between the culture and language factions are becoming more and more difficult. Referring to the Belgian example, some argue the centrifugal force generated by the antagonism between the cultural and linguistic groups will be *the* challenge of the future for Switzerland. In view of the reinforcement of language blocks, particularly between the German- and the French-speaking parts of the country, and the increasing ethnicization of politics, Urs Altermatt talks about the danger of the 'Belgianization' of Switzerland.[53]

Furthermore, the notion of Swiss multiculturalism appears to be a meaningful paradox, particularly with regards to today's immigration society.[54] Although the linguistic, religious and cultural differences make it rather difficult to define specific and common characteristics of a Swiss identity, many reduce the diversity by defining an 'essence' of the Swiss nation, and point to the uniqueness of 'Swissness'. Thus, in spite of the heterogeneous and multicultural composition of the country, many Swiss assume homogeneity of their national community where people of foreign origin seem not to fit in. In addition, while Switzerland is widely considered to be a paradigmatic case of political integration in a multicultural society, offering a framework for co-operation between different ethnic and cultural groups, the country, as a matter of fact, exclusively relies on an 'indigenous multiculturalism'[55] that integrates only native minorities. Swiss multiculturalism and its institutional settings fail to provide inclusive opportunity structures for immigrants and to develop open attitudes toward new minorities.[56] As the controversial debates on integration and citizenship issues show, the challenge of the new multiculturalism with foreign residents is rather difficult to meet.

Within the field of immigration and integration polices, there are two possible explanations for why the country's own multicultural experience did not serve as an efficient counter-model to the ideas and campaigns of the anti-immigrant movement and its discourse of 'overforeignization'. First, it must be conceded that the indigenous multiculturalism brought the four language regions only partly together, and it always remained a fragile model of integration. In fact, multiculturalism was primarily handled as a matter of institutional accommodations, and, in everyday practice, it involved only a limited cultural exchange between the distinct language populations. Second, the above mentioned paradox of the double-edged notion of national identity, relying both on civic and ethnocultural components, resulted in two competing approaches to multiculturalism: while indigenous multiculturalism implied the reference to Switzerland as state-nation, held together by political will and civil rights, the notion of Switzerland as an ethnic and cultural nation was used to reject the new multiculturalism by emphasizing the ethnocultural differences of foreign residents in Switzerland.

Notes

Parts of the findings used in this chapter result from the research project, 'Racism and Politics in the Nineties' (1997-1999; no. 5004-047786), which was part of the Priority Programme 'Switzerland: Toward the Future' and funded by the Swiss National Science Foundation. I wish to express special gratitude to Urs Altermatt, director of the project, with whom I led together the research at the Institute of Contemporary History, University of Fribourg. Moreover, I would like to thank Martin A. Schain and the Center for

European Studies, New York University, for providing a stimulating environment to write this chapter. Last but not least, I want to thank Rita Matus, Vanessa Nornberg, Hanna Schissler, and Christina Späti for their comments on previous drafts.

1 In 2000 the percentage of foreigners in Switzerland was 19.3 per cent. But if all the foreigners living more than twelve years in Switzerland became naturalized, the percentage of foreigners would be reduced by almost half; see Piguet and Wanner, *Die Einbürgerungen in der Schweiz*, p. 30.

2 For instance, see Skenderovic, 'Fremdenfeindlichkeit'; Tanner, 'Nationalmythos und "Überfremdungsängste"'.

3 On the origins of the notion of 'overforeignization', see Jost, *Die reaktionäre Avantgarde*, pp. 89-109; Garrido, *Le début de la politique fédérale*, pp. 7-11.

4 See Arlettaz and Arlettaz, 'Die schweizerische Ausländergesetzgebung'; Gast, *Von der Kontrolle zur Abwehr*, pp. 185-279.

5 In recent years, historical research has emphasized the crucial role the notion of 'overforeignization' played for antisemitism in Switzerland during the 1920s and 1930s; see Altermatt, *Katholizismus und Antisemitismus*, pp. 131-136, 172-202; Mächler, 'Kampf gegen das Chaos', pp. 364-374.

6 See Misteli and Gisler, 'Überfremdung'; Romano, 'Vom Sonderfall zur Überfremdung'; Ebel and Fiala, *Sous le consensus, la xénophobie*; Windisch, *Xénophobie*.

7 *Das Problem der ausländischen Arbeitskräfte*, p. 137 (translation: D.S.).

8 During recent years, historical research somewhat increased its concern about these aspects of Swiss immigration policy, insisting that the Social Democrats and trade unions contributed to a large extent to the revitalization of the discourse of 'overforeignization' during the 1960s; see D'Amato, *Vom Ausländer zum Bürger*, pp. 214-220; Misteli and Gisler, 'Überfremdung'; Romano, 'Vom Sonderfall zur Überfremdung'. However, a coherent and empirically grounded overview, which would also allow comparative considerations, is still missing. Although a study published in 1976 investigates in a broader way the trade unions' positions on labour immigration, it lacks the necessary conceptual and analytical examination of the notion of 'overforeignization' (Riedo, *Das Problem der ausländischen Arbeitskräfte*). A recent edited volume on Swiss trade unions does not provide any in-depth analysis of the trade unions' immigration policy (Armingeon and Geissbühler, *Gewerkschaften in der Schweiz*).

9 See Romano, 'Vom Sonderfall zur Überfremdung'; Romano, 'Links oder rechts'.

10 Lijphart, 'Typologies of Democratic Systems'.

11 In 1937, the signing of the 'peace agreement' was an important step of trade unions from a strategy of confrontation to a policy of cooperation; and in 1943, the Social Democrats had for the first time a representative in the federal government. The vigorous demarcation by the Social Democratic Party from the Communist left was a further integrative move since it came up to the ideological and political expectations of the centrist and right-wing power holders. The political integration process of the left found its fulfilment in the grand coalition which has governed Switzerland since 1959.

12 See Mooser, 'Spiritual National Defense'; Skenderovic, 'Fremdenfeindlichkeit'.

13 See Altermatt, 'Xenophobie und Superpatriotismus'; Pitterle, *The Limits of Interdependence*.

14 The Swiss political system has two instruments of direct democracy at the national level: The popular initiative (*Volksinitiative*) grants any citizen or group of citizens able to obtain 100,000 signatures the right to propose constitutional amendments which must then be considered by parliament and be submitted to a referendum. The *referendum*,

meanwhile, needs 50,000 signatures and obliges the government to submit major legislation or international treaties to the people for their approval.

15 On these recent developments and transformations of the Swiss anti-immigrant parties, see Skenderovic, *The Swiss Radical Right in Perspective*; Husbands, 'Switzerland: Right-Wing and Xenophobic Parties'.

16 In 1999, the city section of Zurich released a brochure on immigration policy. A section in a chapter entitled 'Mass immigration thanks to left wing policy' states that: 'We have to cope with a movement of immigration which consists of mostly non-educated, professionally unqualified persons who are only rarely ready to work and who come from another, non-Western European cultural sphere'; Swiss People's Party, *Konzept für eine Zürcher Ausländerpolitik*, p. 11 (translation: D.S.).

17 A small committee composed of politicians from various right-wing parties launched the popular initiative without the direct support of the SVP. In fact, some notorious politicians from the SVP opposed the initiative mainly for economic reasons. Nevertheless, the party conventions of the Swiss People's Party, as well as of the radical-right splinter parties, endorsed the initiative and asked voters to approve it. See *Neue Zürcher Zeitung*, 21 August 2000; 28 August 2000; *The New York Times*, 25 September 2000.

18 See for instance, *Neue Zürcher Zeitung*, 3 August 2000; 22 August 2000; *Tages Anzeiger*, 4 August 2000; *Le Temps*, 4 September 2000.

19 See Ireland, *Policy Challenge*, pp. 165-202; Linder, 'Migrationswirkungen', pp. 147-148.

20 Wimmer, 'Explaining Xenophobia', p. 26. Patrick Ireland draws a similar conclusion when he writes: 'In typically Swiss fashion, authorities took into consideration what was a substantial minority position.' (Ireland, *The Policy Challenge of Ethnic Diversity*, p. 174).

21 For instance, see Fröhlich and Müller, *Überfremdungsdiskurse*.

22 See Fischer, 'Ethnopluralismus, Multikulturalismus und interkulturelle Erziehung'; Terkessidis, *Kulturkampf*, pp. 46-131.

23 For instance, see Balibar, 'Is There a "Neo-Racism"'; Barker, *The New Racism*. Some authors, however, warn against a conflation of the concepts of racism and neoracism and prefer to differentiate them analytically (Priester, *Rassismus und kulturelle Differenz*, pp. 24-26; Bader, *Rassismus, Ethnizität, Bürgerschaft*, pp. 67-71). They maintain that the culturalist rhetoric of neoracism is distinct from racism as it 'reifies culture conceived as a compact, bounded, localized, and historically rooted set of traditions and values transmitted through generations by drawing on an ideological repertoire that dates back to the contradictory 19th-century conception of the nation-state' (Stolcke, 'Talking Culture', p. 4).

24 See Taguieff, *Sur la Nouvelle droite*; for the United States and Britain, Ansell, *New Right, New Racism*.

25 See Radtke, 'Lob der Gleich-Gültigkeit'; Taguieff, *La force du prejugé*.

26 Stolcke, 'Talking Culture', p. 5.

27 The human ethology research school surrounding Konrad Lorenz and his disciples such as Eibl-Eibesfeldt has been arguing for so-called neo-instinctivism. According to their way of thinking, the rejection of the foreigner has to be seen as an instinctive and natural reaction of human beings. After comparing different cultures they maintain the thesis that sceptical reactions and mistrust toward 'strangers' is part of the genetic heritage of the genus and not a result of social life and culture. See Seifert, 'Das Argument der menschlichen Natur'; Antweiler, 'Eibl-Eibesfeldts Thesen zu einer multiethnischen Gesellschaft'.

28 *Schweizerzeit*, 3 March 2000 (translation: D.S.).
29 See Imhof, 'Die Semantik des Fremden'; Wimmer, 'Der Appell an die Nation'.
30 See Armingeon, 'Fremdenfeindlichkeit in der Schweiz'.
31 Wimmer, 'Explaining Xenophobia', p. 27.
32 See various articles in the edited volume: Ernst and Wigger, *Die neue Schweiz?*
33 This conclusion can also be drawn from the research on voters and supporters of the radical right; for instance, see Minkenberg, 'The Renewal of the Radical Right'; Karapin, 'Explaining Far-Right Electoral Successes in Germany'.
34 For an excellent account of the constructivist character of categories such as 'race', 'ethnicity' or 'ethnic group', see Dittrich and Radtke, 'Einleitung'.
35 See Koopmans and Statham, 'Ethnic and Civic Conceptions'.
36 This differentiation goes back to the historian Friedrich Meinecke, who pointed out the distinct development of nations and nation-states (Meinecke, *Weltbürgertum und Nationalstaat*). Meanwhile, many scholars add a third type which is the ethnic nation or *Volksnation* based on descent and ethnic criteria (see Delannoi and Taguieff, *Théories du nationalisme*). There is, however, a similarity between the concepts of ethnic nation and cultural nation.
37 For a critical account of some current theoretical and conceptual inconsistencies and weaknesses in the research on nationalism, see Brubaker, 'Myths and Misconceptions'.
38 Kohn, *Nationalism and Liberty*, p. 77.
39 Deutsch, *Die Schweiz als ein paradigmatischer Fall politischer Integration*.
40 Anderson, *Imagined Communities*, pp. 135-139.
41 For instance, see Sciarini, Hug and Dupont, *Example, Exception or Both?*, pp. 4-8.
42 Habermas, 'Staatsbürgerschaft und nationale Identität'.
43 Kriesi, 'Introduction: State Formation', p. 17; emphasis in original.
44 See D'Amato, *Vom Ausländer zum Bürger*, pp. 59-60; Centlivres, *Devenir Suisse*.
45 Patrick Ireland refers to Michael Walzer's 1983 book *Spheres of Justice*; Ireland, *The Policy Challenge of Ethnic Diversity*, p. 270. As the annual OECD-report on international migration demonstrates, during the period 1988-97 the naturalization rate in Switzerland was about 1 per cent. During the same period, countries such as the Netherlands or Sweden had a nearly 6 per cent naturalization rate; see OECD, *Trends in International Migration*, p. 81.
46 Froidevaux, 'Construction de la nation', p. 58.
47 For a very good examination of the role the Alps and the Alpine myth played until the Second World War for the construction of Swiss national identity and the naturalization of the Swiss nation, see Kaufmann and Zimmer, 'In Search of the Authentic Nation'. Nonetheless, although there is little research done on references made in the post-war era to the Alps as a national symbol in political discourses, the two authors argue that 'the Alps may have lost a degree of symbolic significance [...] at the discursive level of national ideology. This is especially true with regard to the naturalization of the nation'. Kaufmann and Zimmer, 'In Search of the Authentic Nation', p. 506, note 29.
48 For instance, see Marchal and Mattioli, *Erfundene Schweiz*.
49 See Kriesi, *Le système politique Suisse*, pp. 12-21.
50 See Delanty, 'Beyond the Nation-State'; Judt, 'The New Old Nationalism'.
51 See Wimmer, 'Der Appell an die Nation'; Demirovic, 'Die Transformation des Wohlfahrtsstaats'.
52 Klaus Armingeon suggests that the respect for cultural and language rights as well as for freedom of religion and conscience may be seen as a reason for the weakness of radical-

right parties in Switzerland; Armingeon, 'Der Schweizer Rechtsextremismus', pp. 54-55. For a review of this argument, see Skenderovic, *The Swiss Radical Right*.

53 Altermatt, *Das Fanal von Sarajevo*, pp. 145-155. On the distinctive Swiss combination of a multicultural and differentialist strategy with regard to language policy, see also Altermatt, 'Multiculturalism, Nation State and Ethnicity', p. 81.

54 For some perspicacious reflections on the paradox of Swiss multiculturalism, see Kury, 'Wann ist man ein Schweizer?' Der Wandel der Einbürgerungsnormen im 20. Jahrhundert', *Neue Zürcher Zeitung*, 15/16 April 2000.

55 Skenderovic, 'Nation, Nationalismus und politische Parteien', p. 178.

56 As a prominent example one may take the recent book of Wolf Linder on Swiss democracy, in which he presents Switzerland's historical and institutional arrangements as possible solutions for conflicts in multicultural societies. Nevertheless, he argues that to 'integrate foreigners in the same way as the native minority groups of the past will be much more difficult for Swiss society. It will take more effort than simple peaceful coexistence. Contrary to the past, it will mean the integration of non-European cultural patterns, values, religious beliefs and mentalities. Switzerland has less space and less uncommitted resources than larger countries have to devote to such a multicultural experiment', Linder, *Swiss Democracy*, pp. 35-36.

References

Altermatt, Urs, 'Xenophobie und Superpatriotismus. Die populistische Anti-Überfremdungsbewegung in der Schweiz der sechziger und siebziger Jahre', in: Österreichische Gesellschaft für Zeitgeschichte (ed.), *Faschismus in Österreich und international. Jahrbuch für Zeitgeschichte 1980/81*, Vienna, 1982, pp. 167-193.

Altermatt, Urs, *Das Fanal von Sarajevo. Ethnonationalismus in Europa*, Zurich, 1996.

Altermatt, Urs, 'Multiculturalism, Nation State and Ethnicity: Political Models for Multi-Ethnic States', in: Hanspeter Kriesi et al. (eds), *Nation and National Identity. The European Experience in Perspective*, Chur/Zurich, 1999, pp. 73-84.

Altermatt, Urs, *Katholizismus und Antisemitismus. Mentalitäten, Kontinuitäten, Ambivalenzen*, Frauenfeld/Stuttgart/Vienna, 1999.

Anderson, Benedict, *Imagined Communities. Reflections on the Origin and Spread of Nationalism*, second ed., London/New York, 1991.

Ansell, Amy E., *New Right, New Racism. Race and Reaction in the United States and Britain*, New York, 1997.

Antweiler, Christoph, 'Eibl-Eibesfeldts Thesen zu einer multiethnischen Gesellschaft: Ein Kommentar', *Zeitschrift für Ethnologie* 114 (1989): pp. 21-26.

Arlettaz, Gérald and Silvia Arlettaz, 'Die schweizerische Ausländergesetzgebung und die politischen Parteien 1917-1931', in: Aram Mattioli (ed.), *Antisemitismus in der Schweiz 1848-1960*, Zurich, 1998, pp. 327-356.

Armingeon, Klaus, 'Der Schweizer Rechtsextremismus im internationalen Vergleich', *Swiss Political Science Review* 1, 4 (1995): pp. 41-64.

Armingeon, Klaus, 'Fremdenfeindlichkeit in der Schweiz in international vergleichender Perspektive', in: Rupert Moser (ed.), *Die Bedeutung des Ethnischen im Zeitalter der Globalisierung. Einbindungen – Ausgrenzungen – Säuberungen*, Bern/Stuttgart/Vienna, 2000, pp. 219-237.

Armingeon, Klaus and Simon Geissbühler (eds), *Gewerkschaften in der Schweiz. Herausforderungen und Optionen*, Zurich, 2000.

Bader, Veit-Michael, *Rassismus, Ethnizität, Bürgerschaft. Soziologische und philosophische Überlegungen*, Münster, 1995.

Balibar, Etienne, 'Is There a "Neo-Racism"?', in: Etienne Balibar and Immanuel Wallerstein, *Race, Nation, Class: Ambiguous Identities*, London, 1991, pp. 17-28.

Barker, Martin, *The New Racism. Conservatives and the Ideology of the Tribe*, London, 1981.

Brubaker, Rogers, 'Myths and Misconceptions in the Study of Nationalism', in: John Hall (ed.), *The State of the Nation: Ernest Gellner and the Theory of Nationalism*, Cambridge, 1998, pp. 272-306.

Centlivres, Pierre (ed.), *Devenir Suisse. Adhésion et diversité culturelle des étrangers en Suisse*, Geneva, 1990.

D'Amato, Gianni, *Vom Ausländer zum Bürger. Der Streit um die politische Integration von Einwanderern in Deutschland, Frankreich und der Schweiz*, Münster/Hamburg/London, 2001.

Das Problem der ausländischen Arbeitskräfte. Bericht der Studienkommission für das Problem der ausländischen Arbeitskräfte, ed. by the Bundesamt für Industrie, Gewerbe und Arbeit, Bern, 1964.

Delannoi, Gil and Pierre-André Taguieff (eds), *Théories du nationalisme*, Paris, 1991.

Delanty, Gérard, 'Beyond the Nation-State: National Identity and Citizenship in a Multicultural Society – A Response to Rex', in: *Sociological Research Online* 1, 3 (1996) (http://www.socresonline.org.uk/socresonline/1/3/1.html).

Demirovic, Alex, 'Die Transformation des Wohlfahrtsstaats und der Diskurs des Nationalismus', in: Bundesministerium für Wissenschaft, Forschung und Kunst (ed.), *Fremdenfeindlichkeit. Konflikte um die groben Unterschiede*, Vienna, 1995, pp. 125-157.

Deutsch, Karl W., *Die Schweiz als ein paradigmatischer Fall politischer Integration*, Bern, 1976.

Dittrich, Eckhard J. and Frank-Olaf Radtke, 'Einleitung. Der Beitrag der Wissenschaften zur Konstruktion ethnischer Minderheiten', in: Eckhard J. Dittrich and Frank-Olaf Radtke (eds), *Ethnizität. Wissenschaft und Minderheiten*, Opladen, 1990, pp. 11-40.

Ebel, Marianne and Pierre Fiala, *Sous le consensus, la xénophobie. Paroles, arguments, contextes (1961-1981)*, Lausanne, 1983.

Ernst, Andreas and Erich Wigger (eds), *Die neue Schweiz? Eine Gesellschaft zwischen Integration und Polarisierung (1910-1930)*, Zurich, 1996.

Fischer, Gero, 'Ethnopluralismus, Multikulturalismus und interkulturelle Erziehung', in: Helmut Reinalter, Franko Petri and Rüdiger Kaufmann (eds), *Das Weltbild des Rechtsextremismus. Die Strukturen der Entsolidarisierung*, Innsbruck/Vienna, 1998, pp. 243-259.

Fröhlich, Hans and Bernhard Müller, *Überfremdungsdiskurse und die Virulenz von Fremdenfeindlichkeit vor dem Hintergrund internationaler Migrationsbewegungen*, University of Zurich, 1995.

Froidevaux, Didier, 'Construction de la nation et pluralisme suisses: idéologie et pratiques', in: *Swiss Political Science Review* 3, 4 (1997): pp. 29-58.

Garrido, Angela, *Le début de la politique fédérale à l'égard des étrangers*, Lausanne, 1987.

Gast, Uriel, *Von der Kontrolle zur Abwehr. Die eidgenössische Fremdenpolizei im Spannungsfeld von Politik und Wirtschaft 1915-1933*, Zurich, 1997.

Habermas, Jürgen, 'Staatsbürgerschaft und nationale Identität', in: Jürgen Habermas, *Faktizität und Geltung. Beiträge zur Diskurstheorie des Rechts und des demokratischen Rechtsstaats*, Frankfurt a. M., 1992, pp. 632-660.

Husbands, Christopher T., 'Switzerland: Right-Wing and Xenophobic Parties, from Margin to Mainstream?', *Parliamentary Affairs* 53 (2000): pp. 501-516.

Imhof, Kurt, 'Die Semantik des Fremden in sozialen Krisenphasen', in: Hans-Rudolf Wicker et al. (eds), *Das Fremde in der Gesellschaft: Migration, Ethnizität und Staat*, Zurich, 1996, pp. 199-214.

Ireland, Patrick R., *The Policy Challenge of Ethnic Diversity. Immigrant Politics in France and Switzerland*, Cambridge/London, 1994.

Jost, Hans-Ulrich, *Die reaktionäre Avantgarde. Die Geburt der neuen Rechten in der Schweiz um 1900*, Zurich, 1992.

Judt, Tony, 'The New Old Nationalism', *The New York Review of Books*, 26 May 1994, pp. 44-51.

Karapin, Roger, 'Explaining Far-Right Electoral Successes in Germany. The Politicization of Immigration-Related Issues', *German Politics and Society* 16, 3 (1998): pp. 24-61.

Kaufmann, Eric and Oliver Zimmer, 'In Search of the Authentic Nation: Landscape and National Identity in Canada and Switzerland', *Nations and Nationalism* 4 (1998): pp. 483-510.

Kohn, Hans, *Nationalism and Liberty: The Swiss Example*, London, 1956.

Koopmans, Ruud and Paul Statham, 'Ethnic and Civic Conceptions of Nationhood and the Differential Success of the Extreme Right in Germany and Italy', in: Marco Giugni, Doug McAdam and Charles Tilly (eds), *How Social Movements Matter*, Minneapolis, 1999, pp. 225-251.

Kriesi, Hanspeter, *Le système politique Suisse*, Paris, 1995.

Kriesi, Hanspeter, 'Introduction: State Formation and Nation Building in the Swiss Case', in: Hanspeter Kriesi et al. (eds), *Nation and National Identity. The European Experience in Perspective*, Chur/Zurich, 1999, pp. 13-28.

Lijphart, Arend, 'Typologies of Democratic Systems', *Comparative Political Studies* 1 (1968): pp. 3-44.

Linder, Wolf, 'Migrationswirkungen, institutionelle Politik und politische Öffentlichkeit', in: Walter Kälin and Rupert Moser (eds), *Migrationen aus der Dritten Welt. Ursachen und Wirkungen*, Bern/Stuttgart, 1989, pp. 145-157.

Linder, Wolf, *Swiss Democracy. Possible Solutions to Conflict in Multicultural Societies*, second ed., London, 1998.

Mächler, Stefan, 'Kampf gegen das Chaos – die antisemitische Bevölkerungspolitik der eidgenössischen Fremdenpolizei und Polizeiabteilung 1917-1954', in: Aram Mattioli (ed.), *Antisemitismus in der Schweiz 1848-1960*, Zurich, 1998, pp. 357-421.

Marchal, Guy P. and Aram Mattioli (eds), *Erfundene Schweiz. Konstruktionen nationaler Identität*, Zurich, 1992.

Meinecke, Friedrich, *Weltbürgertum und Nationalstaat. Studien zur Genesis des deutschen Nationalstaates*, Munich/Berlin, 1908.

Minkenberg, Michael, 'The Renewal of the Radical Right: Between Modernity and Anti-modernity', *Government and Opposition* 35 (2000): pp. 170-188.

Misteli, Roland and Andreas Gisler, 'Überfremdung. Karriere und Diffusion eines fremdenfeindlichen Deutungsmusters', in: Kurt Imhof, Heinz Kleger and Gaetano Romano (eds), *Vom Kalten Krieg zur Kulturrevolution. Analyse von Medienereignissen in der Schweiz der 50er und 60er Jahre*, Zurich, 1999, pp. 95-120.

Mooser, Josef, '"Spiritual National Defence" in the 1930s: Swiss Political Culture between the Wars', in: Georg Kreis (ed.), *Switzerland and the Second World War*, London/Portland, 2000, pp. 236-260.

OECD, *Trends in International Migration*. Continuous Reporting System of Migration, Annual Report 1999, Paris, 1999.

Piguet, Etienne and Philippe Wanner, *Die Einbürgerungen in der Schweiz. Unterschiede zwischen Nationalitäten, Kantonen und Gemeinden, 1981-1998*, ed. by the Bundesamt für Statistik, Neuenburg, 2000.

Pitterle, Kenneth J., *The Limits of Interdependence. The Development of the Swiss New Right as an Oppositional Force to Switzerland's Regional and Global Interdependence*, Ann Arbor, MI, 1981.

Priester, Karin, *Rassismus und kulturelle Differenz*, Münster, 1997.

Radtke, Frank-Olaf, 'Lob der Gleich-Gültigkeit. Zur Konstruktion des Fremden im Diskurs des Multikulturalismus', in: Uli Bielefeld (ed.), *Das Eigene und das Fremde. Neuer Rassismus in der Alten Welt?*, second ed., Hamburg, 1992, pp. 79-96.

Riedo, René, *Das Problem der ausländischen Arbeitskräfte in der schweizerischen Gewerkschaftspolitik von 1945-1970*, Bern/Frankfurt a. M., 1976.

Romano, Gaetano, 'Links oder rechts oder Gemeinschaft oder Gesellschaft? Zur Konfusion politischer Unterscheidungen öffentlicher Kommunikation', in: Mario König et al. (eds), *Dynamisierung und Umbau. Die Schweiz in den 60er und 70er Jahren*, Zurich, 1998, pp. 265-275.

Romano, Gaetano, 'Vom Sonderfall zur Überfremdung. Zur Erfolgsgeschichte gemeinschaftsideologischen Denkens im öffentlichen politischen Diskurs der späten fünfziger und der sechziger Jahre', in: Kurt Imhof, Heinz Kleger and Gaetano Romano (eds), *Vom Kalten Krieg zur Kulturrevolution. Analyse von Medienereignissen in der Schweiz der 50er und 60er Jahre*, Zurich, 1999, pp. 55-93.

Sciarini, Pascal, Simon Hug and Cédric Dupont, *Example, Exception or Both? Swiss National Identity in Perspective*, EUI Working Paper, no. 32, San Domenico, 1997.

Seifert, Franz, 'Das Argument der menschlichen Natur in der Einwanderungsdebatte veranschaulicht am Beispiel Irenäus Eibl-Eibesfeldt', *Österreichische Zeitschrift für Politikwissenschaft* 25 (1996): pp. 193-206.

Skenderovic, Damir, 'Nation, Nationalismus und politische Parteien. Die Schweiz – keine Insel in Europa', in: Csaba Szaló (ed.), *On European Identity: Nationalism, Culture & History*, Brno, 1998, pp. 131-179.

Skenderovic, Damir, 'Fremdenfeindlichkeit', in: *Historisches Lexikon der Schweiz*, Bern, 2000.

Skenderovic, Damir, *The Swiss Radical Right in Perspective. A Reevaluation of Success Conditions in Switzerland*, paper presented at the Workshop 'Democracy and the New Extremist Challenge in Europe' of the ECPR Joint Sessions of Workshops in Grenoble, 6-11 April 2001 (http://www.essex.ac.uk/ecpr/jointsessions/grenoble/papers/ws14/damir.pdf).

Stolcke, Verena, 'Talking Culture. New Boundaries, New Rhetorics of Exclusion in Europe', *Current Anthropology* 36 (1995): pp. 1-24.

Swiss People's Party of the city of Zurich (ed.), *Konzept für eine Zürcher Ausländerpolitik* , Zurich, 1999.

Taguieff, Pierre-André, *La force du préjugé. Essai sur le racisme et ses doubles*, Paris, 1987.

Taguieff, Pierre-André, *Sur la Nouvelle droite. Jalons d'une analyse critiques*, Paris, 1994.

Tanner, Jakob, 'Nationalmythos und "Überfremdungsängste". Wie und warum die Immigration zum Problem wird, dargestellt am Beispiel der Schweizer Geschichte des 19. und 20. Jahrhunderts', in: Udo Rauchfleisch (ed.), *Fremd im Paradies. Migration und Rassismus*, Basel, 1994, pp. 11-25.

Terkessidis, Mark, *Kulturkampf. Volk, Nation, der Westen und die Neue Rechte*, Cologne, 1995.

Wimmer, Andreas, 'Der Appell an die Nation. Kritische Bemerkungen zu vier Erklärungen von Xenophobie und Rassismus', in: Hans-Rudolf Wicker et al. (eds), *Das Fremde in der Gesellschaft: Migration, Ethnizität und Staat*, Zurich, 1996, pp. 173-198.

Wimmer, Andreas, 'Explaining Xenophobia and Racism: A Critical Review of Current Research Approaches', *Ethnic and Racial Studies* 20 (1997): pp. 17-41.

Windisch, Uli, *Xénophobie? Logique de la pensée populaire*, in collaboration with Jean-Marc Jaeggi and Gérard de Rham, Lausanne, 1978.

PART IV
INDIVIDUAL AND COLLECTIVE IDENTITIES

Chapter 11

The Role of Discourse in the Construction of an Emigré Community: Ukrainian Displaced Persons in Germany and Austria after the Second World War

Volodymyr Kulyk

It is nowadays widely acknowledged among social scientists that identity, both individual and collective, is a social construct. In this view, an individual's sense of belonging to a given collectivity is constantly produced and reproduced by social practices, which can thus be seen as creating and/or maintaining that collectivity. Further, it is increasingly recognized that the primary instrument of this creation and maintenance of identity is discourse. In any society, elites use various forms of discourse to present the social relations which secure their dominance as the most reasonable and natural, rooted in the historical tradition or objective laws. The existence of the respective nation and its status as a primary source of identification for its members are generally presented as natural. At the same time, there are usually alternative discourses employed by counter-elites or other social groups, which try to delegitimize and deconstruct the dominant discourse and the social relations it supports. The ensuing competition between the dominant discourse and its rivals causes a permanent reshaping of the discourses and, therefore, of the nation itself.[1]

An alternative discourse may challenge established social borders and the prioritization of identities. In multiethnic states, leaders of an ethnic group often strive to implant the priority of belonging to the group in the consciousness of its members. If successful, this entails the creation of a new nation and often leads to a redrawing of political boundaries. But there are also situations where collective identities are adjusted to a change of political boundaries, or to other disruptions of the correspondence between a collectivity and a discursive field aimed at its (re)creation.

Mass migration is one possible source of such disruption. From the perspective of the host society, adjustment in this case normally takes the form of the immigrants' assimilation, through internalization of the dominant discourse of that society. In other cases, immigrants retain more or less significant elements of their previous identity by mixing discourses of both their former and current societies. However, leaders of an immigrant group may also attempt to build a collective identity of its own, by means of discourses drawing primarily from resources of the pre-immigration society. They may even assert the priority of this identity among the group members, thus challenging their belonging to the host society. This is more probable in cases where new settlers are isolated from the rest of society. Refugee camps are a pertinent example of such a situation.

This chapter examines a rather special case wherein a migrant community acted as a breeding ground for the (trans)formation of an ethnic and national identity. It seeks to analyse the discursive construction of a specific émigré identity among Ukrainian Displaced Persons (DPs) in the Western occupation zones of Germany and Austria during the early post-World War II period. Although Ukrainians were located in a number of camps, quite isolated not only from the respective host societies but also from each other, discourses operating both within a camp and throughout the entire Western-occupied territory aimed at uniting all Ukrainian DPs into a larger community. It was designed as a 'political emigration' closely connected with Ukraine and its struggle against the Soviet regime. Referring to the DPs, scholars have noted 'the unprecedented integration of Ukrainians of different social backgrounds, regions, and religious persuasions into one nationality-conscious community' and pointed to a number of factors (both working during the camp period and earlier in Ukraine) which contributed to 'a heightened sense of national identity and unity' in this community.[2] However, until now, the discursive channels through which this feeling was created have not been studied. Based on a detailed examination of a selection of newspapers published by and for Ukrainian DPs, this chapter analyses how media discourse contributed to the construction of the community. It is argued that, in the end, media discourse failed to uphold the alleged unity of the community in the face of confrontations between political camps and the subsequent dispersal of the community to many countries of the world.[3]

Ukrainians in DP Camps

Numbering about two million persons, Ukrainians were one of the most numerous ethnic groups among the Displaced Persons in Germany and

Austria.[4] Among them were former forced labourers, prisoners of war and political prisoners, as well as people who had fled their homes due to the westward advance of the Red Army (the last group ranging from victims of Soviet repression to Nazi collaborators). An overwhelming majority of Ukrainians who found themselves in zones occupied by the Western Allies were quickly returned to the USSR, in many cases against their will, as had been agreed upon at the Yalta conference in February 1945.[5] However, roughly 200,000 persons escaped repatriation,[6] primarily those from the western Ukrainian region of Galicia; these individuals had not been Soviet citizens until 1939 and, hence, were exempted from forcible repatriation by the Western Allies. Prior to their resettlement in 1947-52 to North and South America, Australia and a number of European countries,[7] they spent several years in hundreds of camps established throughout Germany and Austria by the United Nations special agencies in charge of the DPs.[8]

Notwithstanding inadequate housing conditions, material shortages and serious psychological problems (of which fear of repatriation and uncertainty about the future were the most salient), the camp constituted a sheltering environment for its inhabitants. Not only were all of them guaranteed food and a roof over their heads, but lack of jobs within the camp or elsewhere gave the DPs plenty of free time.[9] Although Ukrainians were initially not treated as a separate nationality by the Western Allies (as no Ukrainian state had existed), they were allowed to establish a number of ethnically homogeneous camps, primarily in the American zone of Germany, where a majority of all Ukrainian non-returnees found themselves after the war.[10] These two factors, together with the demographic and social composition of the Ukrainian DPs (most of them were rather young and a relatively high percentage were professionals),[11] made it possible for the camps to become centres of social, cultural and political activity. There emerged a viable network of institutions and associations, which included elected self-government bodies, churches, schools, newspapers, as well as a number of cultural, professional and other voluntary groupings. A dozen Ukrainian political parties were revived or newly formed in the Western-occupied territory which structured the power relations in the camps (the stronger of the parties took part in the elections of camp administrations) and contributed to their becoming something akin to mini-states.[12]

While the Galicians used the favourable conditions of the camps to preserve traditions of social and political organization they had developed under the relatively liberal rule of the Austro-Hungarian empire – and retained under a much tougher, but still tolerant, Polish interwar regime[13] - many refugees from Soviet Ukraine engaged in civil society activities for

Source: Stebelsky, 'Ukrainian Population Migration after World War II', p. 38.

the first time in their lives.[14] Moreover, the very opportunity for Ukrainians from different regions, classes and denominations to get a good knowledge of, and a proximity to, each other in free exchange of ideas and common everyday experience had no large-scale precedent in Ukrainian history.[15] As Markus asserts: 'For the first time, an idea of a united Ukrainian society ... in a limited space and time, materialized'.[16] Since this took place under relatively liberal conditions, Ukrainians could not only preserve and strengthen their ethnic identity, but also acquire an experience of participation in democratic procedures.

Rather than many mini-states confined within the camp walls, however, leaders of the community aimed at creating one 'state within a state'[17] which would unite all Ukrainian DPs and serve as a substitute for the Ukrainian state in their home country. Effective self-organization was a precondition for resolute opposition to the threat of forced repatriation and for effective (in both an economic and an ethnocultural sense) resettlement of the DPs. Organization was also necessary for arranging their temporary life in Germany and Austria and defending their group interests vis-à-vis the military government, the UN agencies in charge of the refugees and the authorities of the host countries. Last but by no means least, the community had to be united in order to succeed in doing what its leaders and many rank-and-file members believed to be both the strongest desire and the highest duty of the 'émigrés': preserving their Ukrainian identity and contributing to the liberation of their homeland from Russian communist oppression which would allow them to return.

A number of institutions and their respective discourses contributed to the 'imagining' of a Ukrainian émigré community. School children from different Ukrainian regions and denominations were brought together and socialized, through curricular and extracurricular education with a strong nationalist component,[18] not only into the linguistically and culturally kindred environment of a camp, but also into a nation of which the emigration was considered an integral part. The Greek Catholic (Uniate) Church continued to play the traditional role of the national church for its believers from Galicia.[19] Meanwhile, the Ukrainian Autocephalous Orthodox Church (UAOC) in a sense taught refugees from pre-1939 Soviet territories to be both Orthodox and Ukrainian,[20] after more than a decade of militant atheism and increasing Russification had left a heavy imprint on Soviet citizens.[21] Both churches 'made the inculcation of irredentist ideals part of their programme' – as did the schools, youth organizations and many camp and supra-camp associations.[22]

As early as autumn 1945, the delegates of the spontaneously created camp administrations and relief committees established a four-level framework for the Ukrainian refugee community in Germany, with local and regional representative bodies subordinated to a single centre. This framework, known as the Central Representation of the Ukrainian Emigration (*Tsentral'ne Predstavnytstvo Ukrains'koi Emigratsii*) was originally conceived as a non-political relief organization. Later, however, an attempt was made to transform its popularly elected central council into a kind of parliament which would appoint an executive body to govern the refugee community that was thus given a semblance of 'a statelike organization or quasi-polity'.[23] Even more ambitious were the political parties in presenting themselves not as organizations of refugees, but rather as exile parties working for the whole Ukrainian nation and mobilizing its members in all the Western world (including labour emigrants from previous decades). In summer 1948, the parties established an alternative, purely political representative body, the Ukrainian National Council which was declared an exile legislature of the Ukrainian People's Republic (*Ukrainis'ka Narodna Respublika*, UNR) – the state which had been proclaimed in late 1917 and ultimately defeated by the Bolsheviks three years later.

The DP Press

Media discourse played an important role in this process of 'nation-' and 'state-building'. Not only did it enhance the effectiveness of many other discourses (by facilitating their reception by a respective target audience and beyond), it also provided a forum for Ukrainians with very different economic backgrounds and political cultures to discuss the past, present, and future of Ukraine and the prospects of the DP community. There emerged a dense network of more than 300 periodicals (two-thirds of which were published in the American zone of Germany) which were mostly run either by camp councils or by various organizations (student, scout, religious, professional associations, political parties, etc.). Many of the latter circulated in the entire Western-occupied territory. While most were short-lived, low-circulation and not really periodical, there was a small group of newspapers in the proper sense of the word that appeared weekly or biweekly for three to five years (a few of them even longer) and were read not only in all Western zones, but also in other European countries and even overseas. When, after an initial phase of legal uncertainty, the American military authorities and the United Nations Relief and Rehabilitation Administration (UNRRA) introduced licensing of the DP press in early 1947, it was mostly these stable and popular newspapers that were allowed to continue publishing (though many others survived as well) and even given the right to a free paper ration. With this assistance and a thirst of the DP masses for information and printed matter in their mother tongue, the licensed newspapers could successfully appear in what amounted in some cases to 15,000 copies. While the German currency reform of 1948 severely undermined the DPs' purchasing power, the final blow to the Ukrainian press was delivered by the dispersal of their former audience around the globe in the following years.[24]

Journalists were keenly aware of their important role in constructing an 'imagined community' of Ukrainian DPs. Not only were their newspapers meant to inform the refugees of news from Ukraine, the world and the camps; they were also to give them, in their current difficult situation, 'Ukrainian reading, information, and consolation'.[25] As one of the editors wrote in the first issue of his newspaper, the task was to unite 'with the Ukrainian word, all Ukrainian forced settlers who are dispersed in small groups across the American occupation zone of Germany, into one community'.[26] He and his colleagues repeatedly argued that the Ukrainian press – and the emigration in general – might not 'contain itself within the narrow limits of camp life', but was obliged to focus on more important problems of Ukraine and to present its cause to the world.[27] Being convinced of the newspapers' role in forming (not just reflecting) public opinion, the journalists aimed in particular at familiarizing Ukrainian refugees from different regions and social groups with each other, by 'underlining everything that unites us as a political and cultural community and denouncing all ruining and disuniting manifestations'.[28] While defending the DPs' rights, the press also wanted to remind them of their duties, which it viewed as those of political émigrés.[29]

Although mostly influenced by political groups competing with each other for the DPs' support, the newspapers almost unanimously presented the refugee community as 'the political emigration' which served as an external representative of 'struggling Ukraine'. At the same time, the media discourse became the primary site of the propagandist competition among the political groups, which undermined the persuasiveness of such a presentation.

'The Political Emigration'

To an extent, the presentation of the Ukrainian DPs was determined by their current conditions, namely living on a territory occupied by the Western democratic powers which sought to eradicate the consequences of

Nazi totalitarianism, as well as the threat of forcible repatriation to the USSR. From the very beginning, newspapers with various political and ideological preferences appraised the democratic achievements of the Western societies and declared their own devotion to the idea of democracy as well as hostility to any kind of totalitarianism and dictatorship. These declarations were extended to the entire Ukrainian people who, according to this line of argument, had old democratic traditions and strongly aspired to democracy and freedom after having experienced totalitarian systems 'on their own body'.[30] Accordingly, accusations of collaboration with the Nazis on the part of Ukrainians in general and the DPs in particular were vehemently rebuffed.

Overt criticism of the USSR as a totalitarian state was initially limited by the occupation authorities' prohibition of any activities which could 'disrupt unity among the Allies'.[31] In particular, anti-repatriation propaganda was forbidden.[32] However, as the relations between the Western Allies and the USSR evolved toward the Cold War and the former displayed increasing reluctance to forcibly transfer resistant refugees to the latter, the DPs began to attack the Soviet regime vehemently. They sharply contrasted the policies of the two camps, blamed Moscow for the absence of a stable peace in the world, and urged the West to take resolute measures to liberate the nations 'enslaved' by the Communist regime and stop its further 'aggression'. Although some authors argued that this could be done by active diplomatic pressure and increasing resistance by those nations themselves,[33] more often it was clear that nothing less than war was called for, which would, moreover, have to include the use of the atomic bomb.[34]

On the whole, othering was an important element in the discursive construction of the Ukrainian DP community and the nation it was part of. Positioning both of them in the democratic camp opposing the totalitarian one presupposed unequivocal separation from those forces portrayed as belonging to the latter. Not only was the resolute struggle of the Ukrainian people against the Nazis described; additionally, the Germans were often presented as a people which had traditionally displayed uncritical obedience to their leaders and aggression against other peoples; hence they readily supported the Hitler regime and helped commit its crimes.[35] This obedience and aggression that the Germans allegedly shared with the Russians doomed both peoples to suffer under dictatorial regimes and made their neighbourhood dangerous for peoples of Central and Eastern Europe. The latter, therefore, had to join efforts in defending themselves.[36] For Ukrainians, according to the DP press, the Russians were the main danger and hence the primary 'other' to contrast themselves with.[37] Although the enemy of the Ukrainians was mostly defined as the Russian imperial regime, rather than the Russian people, DP authors repeatedly stressed that the imperial idea was not that of a group only, but rather

> a product and property of the whole Russian people, of all their social strata and classes throughout their entire history. Russian imperialism and messianism are historical categories and an immanent feature of a Russian individual, regardless of [his or] her social position, conviction, and current pro- or anti-regime attitude.[38]

Accordingly, the current policy of the Moscow regime was viewed as not only communist, but also Russian, continuing the expansionist and assimilationist strivings of Tsarism. Further proof of the Russians' immanent aggressive inclinations was the insistence of the Soviet regime's émigré opponents on preserving the empire after a future overthrow of Bolshevism.[39]

In view of these inclinations, it was presented as a matter of survival for the Ukrainian people to do their best to separate and defend themselves from the Russians, something they had allegedly been doing for centuries. The armed struggle of 1917-20 was celebrated as a crucial experience which had helped overcome the consequences of centuries-long slavery for the Ukrainian consciousness and transformed an amorphous mass into a nation mature enough to lay claims to sovereignty ever afterwards. As was argued, the blood of Ukrainian fighters against Russian Bolshevik aggressors 'finally drew a limit and broke those artificial spiritual ties that had still connected us with Russia'.[40] The cult of heroes and martyrs of the struggle for independence played an important role in attempts to unite and mobilize the DPs from all parts of Ukraine as alleged successors of that struggle. That meant, in particular, implanting the independence orientation in former Soviet citizens whose Ukrainian identity was far from unequivocally prevailing over a broader Soviet/all-Russian identity (despite it being stimulated by the armed struggle and the ensuing recognition by the Soviet regime of a separate Ukrainian nation, institutionalized in its would-be sovereign republic).[41] Attempts of some Russian émigré authors at reanimating the pre-revolution concept of the united Russian people, which included (eastern) Ukrainians, were rejected as the 'ravings of madmen'.[42] Instead, the following version of relations between the two peoples was presented as common sense knowledge in order to keep the line once drawn:

> The history of Ukrainian-Russian relations knows not a single serene moment but only the irreconcilable struggle for life and death which started as early as 1169 when Prince Andrei Bogoliubsky of Suzdal ruined Kyiv

> because of his hatred of 'the mother of Rus' cities'. ... A sea of innocent Ukrainian blood lies between Ukraine and Russia, and there is no force capable of reconciling the Ukrainian and Russian peoples. For only a rout of the Russian empire and its complete liquidation can be a guarantee of the Ukrainian people's free and independent existence.[43]

The concept of political emigration completed this presentation. All the Ukrainian DPs, regardless of the actual reasons for which they found themselves abroad and for which they refused to return home,[44] were from the very beginning declared political émigrés and placed within a tradition begun by Cossack Hetman Ivan Mazepa and his collaborators, who had fled abroad after being defeated by the Muscovite army in the battle of Poltava in 1709.[45] While admitting that a considerable part of this unprecedented number of refugees had still to be made 'nationally conscious', politicians and professionals from Galicia and intellectuals from eastern Ukraine projected their own voluntary escape in face of the returning Soviets to forcibly deported peasants and workers. They were all included in

> the political emigration which left the homeland not for personal business, not in search of adventures or better living circumstances, not because of difficult life in *kolkhozes*, but in order to continue serving the cause of its people abroad until the time of a free and joyful return home, to the fatherland.[46]

By denying personal reasons for which people refused to return sooner, this discourse, paradoxically enough, presented the mass exodus of Ukrainians from their motherland not as evidence of a national disaster, but rather of national resistance against the oppressing regime, 'an indicator of awakened national and political consciousness of the enslaved people'.[47] Even authors who pointed to the fact that the exodus would have tragic consequences for Ukraine, expressed hope that faithfully serving the nation could transform the tragedy of emigration into a 'grand triumph of the common cause'.[48]

Therefore, the honorary title of 'émigré' imposed rather severe constraints and obligations on the DPs' way of life. Both within and outside the camp, he or she dared not stain the name of a Ukrainian and the idea allegedly served. That entailed not only high levels of morale, but also the duty to use contacts with foreigners for informing them of Ukraine and its 'liberation struggle'.[49] In particular, the émigré propaganda was to keep drawing the attention of the West to the imminent threat posed by the USSR and its Communist 'fifth columns' around the world, as well as to a neglected force which could be used in overcoming that threat, namely 'the liberation movements of the enslaved nations'.[50] Naturally, fulfilling this mission of the 'external representation' of the Ukrainian nation's liberation struggle would have been impossible without close ties with the motherland, from which the emigration hence should not dare to 'move far away neither physically nor spiritually' and to whose demands they had to subordinate their lives and activities.[51]

The internal consolidation of the émigré community was unanimously presented as a precondition for both the external representation of Ukraine and for keeping in touch with its struggle. By educational and cultural efforts, every DP should be made conscious of his or her belonging to the community and of its sacred mission. Individual egoism and regional particularism had to be contained in favour of collective all-Ukrainian values.[52] Furthermore, social self-organization on both camp and supra-camp levels was seen as organizational capital, which might help not only the DPs themselves, but also their motherland when the time came to invest it there. Besides, such proof of the Ukrainian nation's maturity for independent democratic existence would, it was argued, facilitate its being taken into account by the Western powers in their plans for a future political order in Eastern Europe.[53] Although initial hopes for a 'defensive front of world democracy against Bolshevik totalitarianism' with participation of 'the enslaved peoples' themselves[54] soon disappeared, calls for internal unity became even more persistent. After all, it was the only one of its alleged tasks that 'the emigration' was able to fulfil by its own efforts.[55]

Split in the Name of Unity

It was here, however, that the Ukrainian DP community met with its most perceptible failure, which, ironically, the unity-oriented newspapers significantly contributed to. A controversy over the consolidation principles soon turned into a real propagandist war between two political camps which split the media discourse, as none of major newspapers remained open to supporters of both of the opposing positions. Moreover, mutual othering seriously undermined the legitimacy of the unified narrative by questioning some of its premises, namely ideas of Ukrainians' immanent hostility to totalitarianism in general and Nazism in particular, of their maturity for independence and democracy, of Ukraine's liberation struggle as the primary factor in achieving those goals and, finally, of the important supporting role which 'external representation' was to play.

The two camps, often referred to as 'nationalist' and 'democratic', represented two different trends in Ukrainian political and intellectual history. The former got its name from one of the two rival factions of the Organization of Ukrainian Nationalists (OUN) which had emerged in the late 1920s as an integral nationalist force renouncing the traditional legal methods of Ukrainian parties in favour of a clandestine (often terrorist) struggle against foreign rule. In the 1930s the OUN had become the dominant political force in Galicia. Although weakened by an internal split on the eve of the Nazi occupation of Ukraine, it managed to retain its underground structure and expand its activities to central and eastern Ukraine, while the legal Galician parties were immediately dissolved by the Soviets in September 1939. The stronger and more active of the two factions, the OUN-B (or Banderites, after the name of their leader, Stepan Bandera), had originally hoped to be able to profit from the advance of Nazi Germany and made a failed attempt, in the first days of the German occupation, to proclaim Ukrainian independence. After the Nazis established a brutal occupation regime in Ukraine and resorted to severe repression of nationalist activities, the Banderites took the lead in organizing mass armed resistance. In particular, in 1942, they organized a Ukrainian Insurgent Army (*Ukrains'ka Povstans'ka Armiia*, UPA) which waged guerrilla warfare against the Germans and, between 1944 and the early 1950s, against Soviet and Polish troops on the Ukrainian-populated territories divided between the respective states. With a majority of the Ukrainian DPs coming from nationalist-sympathetic Galicia and many experienced activists of the organization on Western-controlled territory, the OUN-B appeared to be the strongest political force in the camps, and from the very beginning strove to dominate the social and political life of the community.[56]

It was opposed, on the one hand, by a rival nationalist faction, the OUN-M (led by Andrii Melnyk), and on the other, by a plethora of tiny, mostly socialist or social-democrat parties claiming to be successors of organizations which had existed in the Ukrainian People's Republic or interwar Galicia, as well as the Ukrainian Revolutionary Democratic Party, newly established by refugees from Soviet Ukraine.[57] The main discursive competition arose between the OUN-B and the latter group of leftist parties, which presented themselves as truly democratic. The central issue was the self-organization and political consolidation of the DP community, with each of the competing parties advocating principles which would give it more power over camp and supra-camp bodies and more authority of Ukraine's representative. The overwhelming strength and monopolistic aspirations of the OUN-B were perceived by the other parties as a threat to their role and very existence. The threat compelled them to join forces, regardless of their ideological and political orientations. Accordingly, the political process and the propagandist competition between its subjects increasingly turned into a confrontation between the two camps.[58]

In a sense, the 'democratic' forces fell victim to their calls for self-organization of the Ukrainian DPs and insistence on a multiparty system as a precondition of democracy. The election of camp councils was initially greeted as a 'school of democracy' for people who had until recently lived under a totalitarian regime.[59] However, as soon as it became clear that the OUN-B was capable of gaining a majority of votes in most camps and thus able to control their councils and administrations, the losers began to question the relevance of party participation in elections to non-political bodies which were, moreover, to exist during a transitory period only. Besides, they demanded that elected officials be obliged to serve their electorate, instead of dominating it in a totalitarian manner. The presence of the latter pattern in the Ukrainian DPs' thinking was explained by their having been influenced by totalitarian regimes and ideologies (not only those of the USSR, but also, or rather first of all, of semi-fascist interwar Poland and the OUN with its principle of authoritarian leadership).[60]

References to totalitarian influences on Ukrainian civic and political culture clearly contradicted the thesis of democratic maturity of the Ukrainian people. Indeed, this thesis was increasingly questioned in the anti-Banderite discourse, as the OUN-B put more camps under its control and demonstrated its understanding of democracy as unrestricted power of elected bodies and of a party supported by a majority.[61] From autumn 1946 some Banderite-controlled administrations tried to censor the camp newspapers and remove editors who espoused leftist ideas and favoured publications reflecting their ideological interests.[62] A series of violent attacks on journalists and distributors of the 'democratic' newspapers and other activists occurred in various camps, and, as neither administrations nor periodicals of the OUN-B clearly distanced themselves, their opponents held that party responsible.[63] These events contributed to a sharp reaction of the 'democratic' press, which now overtly confronted the 'nationalist' camp and began to revise basic ideas of the formerly common discourse.

First of all, they contrasted values of democracy with those of unity and self-organization and gave clear preference to the former. Contrary to the demands of their Banderite opponents, the newspapers of the 'democratic' camp no longer kept silent about criminal activities in the Ukrainian camps. As they argued, rather than the publication of these deeds, silence about them would discredit the entire community.[64]

Secondly, the 'democratic' periodicals questioned the role of the self-organization structures of the DPs as democratic authorities and incipient bodies of an independent Ukrainian state. They came to deny any legitimacy to camp administrations dominated by the OUN-B, arguing that not only had the party achieved an electoral majority through use of threats and manipulations, but that it also exercised power by means of intimidation which had nothing to do with democracy.[65] The anti-Banderite press called such regime a 'police state' and presented it as the leading edge of an ideal outcome envisaged by the OUN-B for a future Ukraine.[66] Any dictatorship, it was claimed, meant national death for the Ukrainian people, and the Banderites were thus portrayed as a mortal enemy of the people which had to be excluded from the legitimate public discourse. The OUN-B was furthermore denounced as an analogue of the Nazi and Bolshevik parties and even as an ally of the former. Contrary to the earlier story of unanimous Ukrainian hostility and resistance to German totalitarianism, the 'democratic' press increasingly presented the OUN-B as an active collaborator with the Nazis. The above-mentioned attempt at establishing an independent Ukrainian state under German auspices was discredited as an attempt to 'seize power over the Ukrainian people with Hitler's assistance'. Even the leading role of the OUN-B in the guerrilla movement was questioned.[67] Finally, those presenting themselves as true democrats denied any democratic evolution of the Banderite party arguing that its apparent recognition of democratic principles was but an opportunistic adjustment to the conditions of the Western occupation.[68] Their call for eliminating threats to democracy by banning, alongside the Nazi party, all other totalitarian organizations[69] implied, therefore, not only Communist 'fifth columns' of the USSR, but also the Ukrainian 'totalitarianists'.

The anti-Banderites were weaker and hence not capable of gaining their ends by political or administrative means. Thus, they employed aggressive rhetoric in order to influence the opinions of the DPs and the foreign authorities. The OUN-B, on the other hand, seemed to attach less importance to discrediting their opponents and more to retaining the legitimacy of the unified nationalist narrative. Rather than drawing attention to imminent threats, it preferred to present a picture of impressive achievements of both the nation and its leading organization. Although not averse to characterizing the socialist parties as Moscow's ideological allies or even agents,[70] the Banderites mostly portrayed their opponents as ridiculous do-nothings – outdated émigré pretenders bearing no relation to the current situation in Ukraine. The real threat was Bolshevism whose overcoming was a precondition for achieving the highest goal of the

Ukrainian people, namely, the independent state which they allegedly had been fighting for under the leadership of the OUN-B.

Although they recognized the value of a democratic system in principle, the integral nationalists believed it to be 'ideal for those people who have their own state standing on guard of their tasks', but not in the current Ukrainian situation where 'a ruthless struggle is being waged for obtaining elementary human rights which we as a nation are deprived of. This struggle has required our sacrifices and rigid discipline, a full consolidation of all spiritual and physical forces of our emigration'.[71] The socialist parties were denounced exactly on the ground that, in the crucial months of 1917, they had allegedly preferred the idea of socialist internationalism (a masked form of imperialism on the part of other nations, first of all the Russians) to the imperative of state-building. This was made clear by their failing to organize a national army and even ordering demobilization of existing military units.[72] This demobilization, it was argued, had caused a failure of the independent state and the ensuing suffering of the Ukrainian people under the Bolshevism. Since then, the lead in the 'liberation struggle' had been assumed by nationalism, in whose tradition the Banderite discourse tried to incorporate all manifestations of Ukrainian resistance. In particular, the alleged recognition by the Ukrainian Insurgent Army of the leadership of the OUN-B and its non-party creature, the Supreme Ukrainian Liberation Council (*Ukrains'ka Holovna Vyzvol'na Rada*, established in July 1944 in Ukraine), was presented as a clear guide for the DP community.[73]

Initially, limited information from behind the Iron Curtain gave little proof of the Banderite role in Ukraine's resistance and even of the resistance itself. While newspapers of the OUN-B justified an emphasis on armed struggle in the DP discourses by arguing that it was an 'invaluable capital without which we are nothing but a cluster of homeless refugees',[74] their opponents disclaimed the 'fantastic image of a general uprising' as the Banderites' indecent exploitation of the refugees' nostalgia and longing for the soonest possible return to Ukraine.[75] Under these circumstances, the unexpected appearance in autumn 1947 of UPA units in West Germany presented an opportunity for the OUN-B to substantiate its leadership in the resistance movement, as the newcomers declared themselves to be Banderites. Moreover, their astonishing march drew the attention of the Western media, thus providing a long-desired opportunity to inform the world about the struggle in Ukraine. The Banderite newspapers called upon the emigrants to take this opportunity by a concerted propagandist action which would transform a journalistic sensation into a change in the Western thinking.[76] Accordingly, they portrayed the westward march of the UPA combatants as a 'manifestation of Ukrainian force', and evidence that

'Ukraine is struggling, Ukraine is not surrendering'.[77] Simultaneously, they tried to counter the claim that the guerrilla army was being wiped out of Ukraine and adjoining Ukrainian-populated territories by common effort of the Soviet, Polish and Czechoslovak troops. On the contrary, it was argued that the march – which was allegedly not a retreat but a directed relocation – demonstrated a failure of the campaign intended to destroy the UPA.[78]

No wonder that the 'democratic' camp strongly objected to this attempt of the OUN-B to use the retreat of insurgent units for its political gains and to 'draw out new funds for their irresponsible work among the emigration by means of demagogic propaganda and threats'. While asserting that 'the Ukrainian liberation movement is not the matter of one party, but of the whole Ukrainian people',[79] the anti-Banderite press, at the same time, did not hesitate to reveal that movement was doomed and hence

> the Ukrainian people, as well as other nations enslaved by the Russian Bolshevik imperialism, are almost defenceless. Exhausted by the world war, terror of the German Nazis, and incessant extermination during many years of the Bolshevik rule, our people cannot overthrow the inhuman tyranny, even if they stand to the last man against the oppressors. Whoever takes pleasure in hopes for overcoming the enemy by the insurgent force, demonstrates a lack of understanding of the circumstances. Would have the Ukrainian insurgents retreated from the Carpathians as far as the western zones of Germany, had they had hopes for a success of further struggle?[80]

Anti-Banderite authors argued that cherishing hopes for liberation by means of an armed uprising was for the benefit of the Soviet regime which would be interested in provoking such an uprising in order to further decimate the Ukrainian people. They believed that the fate of Ukraine could not be settled independently of international circumstances.[81]

Given the opposing polarity of the two discourses, one may wonder how the consolidation of the 'emigration' could be hoped for at all. For a long time, each of the camps bluntly rejected what the other camp proposed: The 'democrats' called for equal representation of all parties in a consolidated body,[82] which would enhance the standing and power of the tiny socialist groups. In contrast, the OUN-B suggested a 'coalition government' formed on a proportional basis in accordance with the perceived strength of the respective groups.[83] It was thus to be a body where the strongest party would exercise power in the name of many small ones. As it became obvious that the 'democratic' parties would not hesitate to proclaim consolidation without the Banderites, the latter preferred not to be left aside. They agreed to enter the newly established Ukrainian National Council which was to play the role of a legislative body in a reorganized 'exile state centre of the UNR'. But after their demands were rejected at a founding session in July 1948, they decided to form an 'opposition' within the council and not to participate in the executive.[84] Very soon, the OUN-B came to criticize the ineffectiveness of the executive and, unable to get it changed, lost interest in this 'state-building' play. In April 1950, the party withdrew from the council.[85]

This impressive manifestation of the disunity of the 'political emigration' was preceded by a no less perceptible split of the Central Representation of the Ukrainian Emigration, when the anti-Banderites who did not want to tolerate the domination of the OUN-B in October 1949 established an alternative relief organization, the Association of Ukrainians in Germany.[86] The failure of the consolidation effort was all the more obvious as the established centre achieved no impressive results in representing the Ukrainian cause to the world, which would have demonstrated its importance to the refugees. But then, most of the refugees who had been waiting for a solution to their fate for several years (to which the representation might have contributed) were on their way to countries of new settlement by that time.

Dispersal

As the media discourse focused on the 'liberation struggle' in Ukraine and the DPs' participation therein, the problem of their resettlement to other countries in Europe and overseas had been relegated to a somewhat marginal position in their prescribed structure of concerns. Although of utmost importance for the refugees' sheer survival, it was to be subordinated to serving the nation by fulfilling higher tasks of the emigration.

To the extent that hopes for an immediate return to Ukraine as a result of a war between the Western powers and the USSR were dismissed as naïve, it was from the very beginning of the DP era quite clear that resettlement was inevitable. Both a realistic assessment of the economic situation in Germany and the above-mentioned othering of its people as hostile to the refugees implied that the latter would have to wait for the desired return home somewhere else.[87] Since it was not known for several years what countries would be willing to accept them, the DPs had enough time to think of preferred destinations. Alongside material considerations, like the possibility of finding decent, well-paid jobs, or a climate and way of life that would not differ too much from that in Ukraine, other factors were discussed which could be favourable for preserving national identity and serving the homeland. In view of a possible return to Ukraine, some authors presented Europe as a preferable place since 'our people do not want to go too far away from the homeland'.[88] However, the possibility of establishing a relatively compact settlement, which would allow the immigrants to preserve their identity in a foreign environment until time came to return home, emerged as the most important factor under consideration. Under such a scenario, the émigré community would be able to materially support its intelligentsia, who in turn would not only help retain the national consciousness of the masses, but also create valuable scholarly and cultural works – one of the tasks which the emigration had to fulfil as long as the oppressing regime prevented the Ukrainian people from doing that in their own country.[89]

As time passed, the difficulties and uncertainties of camp life made the resettlement problem more pressing for the DPs, and lack of a positive solution on the part of the Western powers or the UN compelled them to try to advance their own efforts. The most outspoken and naïve proposal came in the autumn 1946 from a prominent journalist of the 'nationalist' camp who called for an organized action aimed at transferring the whole Ukrainian DP mass to a rural region in a vast country like Canada or Argentina, where they would soon transform the allotted land into a 'flourishing colony'.[90] The suggested petition to the respective government and the UN with many thousands of signatures was never launched, but a special body established in early 1947, the Supreme Ukrainian Resettlement Council, defined compact resettlement as a priority.[91]

Other authors also stressed the importance of the DPs' own efforts, but paid particular attention to the responsibilities of individuals. First of all, it was argued, the refugees should prepare themselves for life and work in a new country by learning its language and acquiring a skill useful for future employment.[92] Moreover, since only 'people of energy, of great professional knowledge, persistent, with permanent aspiration to new achievements' would succeed in the countries of destination, the DP education should be oriented toward these values. In order to reconcile this new pragmatic priority with older imperatives of the 'political emigration' discourse, another Banderite author argued that an 'economically unsecured emigration will not fulfil those tasks which it must fulfil'.[93]

It soon became clear that no country was willing to provide for large-scale compact settlement of the Ukrainian community and even the most democratic and civilized states were looking primarily for young single males to be used as cheap unskilled labour force. Moreover, those eligible took every opportunity to flee the uncertainty and poverty of the camps in pursuit of stability and well-being, even if that meant hard work under terrible conditions and sometimes ended with frustration or even return to Germany.[94] As early as summer 1947, the resettlement council gave up its orientation toward compact resettlement in what was seen as an adjustment to the realities.[95] A year later, when the Displaced Persons Act passed by the US Congress in June 1948 announced the beginning of large-scale resettlement, Ukrainian refugees were eager to start new lives as soon as possible and seemed to prefer not to stay in Europe, which they considered as being vulnerable in case of a war.

The same author, Roman Ilnytzkyj, who had called for people of energy, wrote of a radical change in the attitudes of the Ukrainian DPs, marked by the renunciation of sentimentalism and dreaminess in favour of resoluteness and realism. For many, however, that also meant preferring individual needs to communal and national goals. Given the assimilation-oriented immigration policies of the host states, this priority posed a threat for the very existence of the Ukrainian emigration. Ilnytzkyj did not want to 'agree with the opinion that with the disbanding of the camps we are also untying those knots that have been uniting us in an integral body which was called the political emigration'.[96] He therefore prescribed uniting the dispersed Ukrainians with the press and books in their mother tongue and called for retaining the DPs' major periodicals as global Ukrainian press organs.[97] As the editor of one of them, he took part in an attempt to establish such an organ that however failed very soon.[98]

Conclusion

The attempt to inscribe a specific émigré identity onto the Ukrainian refugees and thus to unite them into 'one nationality-conscious community' was facilitated by a number of factors, including the virtual isolation of the Ukrainians in the camps, a guaranteed material minimum which for some time freed the DPs from struggle for physical survival, and the presence of a large number of people espousing the common political idea of Ukrainian independence. The discursive construction of unity was, however, impeded by a competition between two political camps drawing on different ideological traditions and having mutually incompatible strategies of asserting their political role among the refugees. By aiming delegitimizing narratives against one another, they undermined some important premises of the common discourse of 'the political emigration', thus significantly diminishing its persuasiveness. A final blow was delivered by the resettlement, which relegated to an uncertain future the emigrants' return to

Ukraine and made hardly possible their participation in any collective acts in the name of the national cause.

Although it did not succeed in introducing a political émigré identity as a key determinant of the (former) refugees' consciousness, or in establishing viable forms of co-ordinated activities among Ukrainians worldwide, the 'imagining' effort was by no means a complete failure. On the one hand, the camp experience significantly strengthened or, for many DPs, created a sense of belonging to the (dispersed) Ukrainian nation. On the other hand, a momentum developed during that period exerted a considerable influence on Ukrainian institution building in the DPs' new host countries. Not only the nationalist sentiments and organizational skills of the new settlers, but also the transfer of many cultural and political institutions established in the camps, facilitated an intensification and 'modernization' of the community life in the host countries, where Ukrainians had already been present for decades.[99] New people and institutions contributed to the preservation and reproduction of the immigrants' cultural distinctiveness and relatively strong attachment to Ukraine during the following decades. The statelessness of the country which many continued to view as their homeland added an émigré element to the identity of diaspora Ukrainians. However, with the passage of time they became firmly rooted in their respective countries of residence, as evinced by the fact that very few 'returned' to Ukraine after the break-up of the USSR and the proclamation of Ukrainian independence.

Notes

The research for this chapter was made possible by a grant from the Michael and Daria Kowalsky Endowment Fund and a fellowship from the John Kolasky Memorial Endowment Fund, both administered by the Canadian Institute of Ukrainian Studies, University of Alberta, Edmonton, Canada. I am also grateful to Marta Dyczok, Rainer Ohliger and Myroslav Yurkevich for their help with getting access to relevant literature, as well as to Karen Schönwälder and Triadafilos Triadafilopoulos for their suggestions on earlier drafts of this text.

1 Lincoln, *Discourse and the Construction of Society*, pp. 3-11.

2 Zielyk, 'The DP Camp as a Social System' (quotes on pp. 464, 467); Isajiw, 'Community, Class, and Social Mobility'.

3 The analysis focuses on two newspapers, 'Chas' and 'Nashe Zhyttia', which were close to the nationalist and socialist camps respectively. The former was published in a Ukrainian camp in Augsburg from September 1945 to March 1948; the latter appeared outside the camp walls in Fürth, near Nürnberg, from October 1945 to July 1949 (in both cases, all issues were examined). These newspapers were selected not only because they actively propagated the positions of two main political camps, but also as popular periodicals which played an important role in the processes under consideration. For the

current location of the press and other sources for research on the Ukrainian DPs, see: Boshyk and Balan, *Political Refugees and 'Displaced Persons'*.

4 By Displaced Persons, I mean all those who had to leave their places of residence because of the war, including individuals who voluntarily left because of the fear of persecution. Not all of them, however, were qualified as such (hence eligible to material aid) by the UN agencies in charge of the DPs. On changing definitions, see: Dyczok, *The Grand Alliance and Ukrainian Refugees*, chs. 2, 4. Some authors prefer to use the term 'refugees' in the broader sense, while others keep it for the non-returnees only. In this chapter, both terms are used interchangeably.

5 Stebelsky, 'Ukrainian Population Migration after World War II', pp. 21-22; Isajiw and Palij, 'Refugees and the DP Problem in Postwar Europe'; Dyczok, *The Grand Alliance*, chs. 2 and 3; Boshyk, 'Repatriation'.

6 Estimates vary considerably. For details see: Stebelsky, 'Ukrainian Population', pp. 22-28, 39-51.

7 Stebelsky, 'Ukrainian Population', pp. 28-37, 52-60.

8 Actually, a considerable part of the Ukrainian refugees lived in private dwellings, many of them choosing to stay outside the camps because of the fear of forced repatriation.

9 Zielyk, 'The DP Camp', p. 463.

10 Kubijovyč, 'Z demohrafichnykh problem ukrainskoi emigratsii', p. 17. On the attitudes of the Western powers toward Ukrainians and their eventual recognition as a separate group, see: Dyczok, *The Grand Alliance*, chs. 3 to 6.

11 Isajiw and Palij, 'Refugees and the DP Problem', p. xx.

12 For analyses of various fields of the Ukrainian DPs' activities, see several essays in Isajiw, Boshyk and Senkus, *The Refugee Experience*.

13 Galicia belonged to the Habsburg Empire from 1772 to 1918 and to Poland between the two wars. On the development of the Ukrainian movement in the region, see: Rudnytsky, 'The Ukrainians in Galicia under Austrian Rule'.

14 The primary source of information about the identities of eastern and central Ukrainians is the data of the Harvard Project on the Soviet Social System. In 1950-51, interviews were conducted and questionnaires administered to thousands of the DPs from pre-1939 Soviet territories. Ukrainians were featured in that project, at least as far as the nationality problem is concerned. Inkeles and Bauer, *The Soviet Citizen*, p. 340.

15 Zielyk, 'The DP Camp', pp. 467-468.

16 Markus, 'Political Parties in the DP Camps', p. 115.

17 Ibid.

18 Markus, 'Education in the DP Camps', pp. 192, 193, 200.

19 Rudnytsky, 'The Ukrainians in Galicia under Austrian Rule', p. 317. On the activities of the church in post-war Germany, see: Baran, 'The Ukrainian Catholic Church'.

20 The UAOC was established in the early 1920s as a national church with services in Ukrainian, rather than Church Slavonic, banned by the Stalin regime ten years later and then revived for a short period of the Nazi occupation. On the DP period of its history, see: Bociurkiw, 'The Ukrainian Autocephalous Orthodox Church in West Germany'. The church competed for Ukrainian believers with the Russian Orthodox Church, which had established its monopoly in the religious life of Ukraine during the 1930s after the UAOC had been forbidden. The believers of the 'Russian' church who did not fit the featured presentation of the Ukrainian DP community were discursively excluded from it, as periodicals kept silent about them, while paying much attention to activities of the two 'national' churches.

21 The Harvard Project revealed that the former Soviet citizens, while rejecting the Soviet regime and 'Communism', accepted many of the institutional features of the Soviet society and retained some basic Marxist notions. Bauer, Inkeles and Kluckhohn, *How*

the Soviet System Works, p. 34. Furthermore, the project data arguably indicated that 'the nationality problem is not very salient for Ukrainians'. Inkeles and Bauer, *The Soviet Citizen*, p. 352.

22 Zielyk, 'The DP Camp', p. 468.

23 Ciuciura, 'Common Organizational Efforts', p. 102.

24 Ilnytzkyj, 'A Survey of Ukrainian Camp Periodicals'. A few papers managed to survive, however, and were published in Germany for years afterwards, with their readers in many countries of the world.

25 *Nashe zhyttia*, 5 September 1945, 11 February 1947 (quote).

26 *Chas*, 1 October 1945.

27 *Chas*, 31 August 1947.

28 *Nashe zhyttia*, 14 November 1945; *Chas*, 5 October 1946 (quote).

29 *Nashe zhyttia*, 19 December 1945.

30 *Nashe zhyttia*, 23 January 1946 (Appendix).

31 Such a prohibition was included in a circular on the DP publications issued in February 1947 in the American zone. In the same vein, the UNRRA officials often insisted that journalists of the camp press 'stay away from all politics'. Ilnytzkyj, 'A Survey', pp. 274-275.

32 Dyczok, *The Grand Alliance*, chs. 3, 4.

33 *Nashe zhyttia*, 16 March 1946.

34 *Nashe zhyttia*, 6, 20 March 1946. In the Harvard Project, Ukrainians, asked if they would favour dropping an atom bomb on Moscow, revealed a much higher support for the idea than the Russian DPs. The authors of the survey explained the difference by Ukrainian opposition not only to the regime, but also to the empire (they suggested that nationalist sentiment was partly a result of the DP newspapers' propaganda). Inkeles and Bauer, *The Soviet Citizen*, pp. 353, 371.

35 *Chas*, 28 September 1946; *Nashe zhyttia*, 23 March 1946.

36 *Nashe zhyttia*, 5 May 1947.

37 In this, the DP discourses inherited a strong nationalist tradition. In particular, Russia's animosity to Ukraine was featured in the influential interwar writings by Dmytro Dontsov: Motyl, *The Turn to the Right*, ch. 6. Anti-Russianness was to supersede the prejudices against Poles, Jews and other groups, which were deep-rooted in some regional or social groups of the Ukrainian people, and thus unite them for the common struggle against a 'true' enemy. In particular, the Poles, a centuries-long antagonist of the Ukrainians and the primary 'other' of the Galicians until as late as 1939, were propagated by the DP press as an important partner in a future union of the countries situated between Black and Baltic Seas, which would defend them against the Russian and German 'imperialisms'. *Nashe zhyttia*, 16 June 1947; *Chas*, 27 June 1948.

38 *Chas*, 30 May 1948.

39 *Chas*, 15, 29 February 1948.

40 *Chas*, 26 January 1947.

41 On the Bolshevik policy of promoting Ukrainian nation-building which was adopted in order to establish an effective control over the region where the independence struggle had raised national consciousness, but largely abandoned in the early 1930s, see: Mace, *Communism and the Dilemmas of National Liberation*, chs. 2, 7.

42 *Chas*, 27 July 1947.

43 *Chas*, 23 November 1947.

44 Of the pre-1939 Soviet citizens of all nationalities interviewed in the Harvard Project, only about 40 per cent claimed to have fled their country voluntarily. The authors estimated that from two-thirds to three-fourths of the respondents 'would have returned to their homeland if it were not for the fear of the suspicion and ill treatment with which

returnees were being greeted in the Soviet Union'. Bauer, Inkeles and Kluckhohn, *How the Soviet System Works*, p. 10.

45 On these and following Ukrainian refugees/émigrés, see: Subtelny, 'Ukrainian Political Refugees'.

46 *Chas*, 17 February 1946. In fact, opposition to the kolkhoz system was one of the main reasons why peasant DPs did not want to return to the USSR; at least they disliked it much more strongly than the nationality policy. Inkeles and Bauer, *The Soviet Citizen*, p. 352.

47 *Nashe zhyttia*, 2 February 1946 (Appendix).

48 *Chas*, 16 February, 9 March 1947 (quote).

49 *Chas*, 13 April, 4 May 1946.

50 *Chas*, 26 October 1947.

51 *Chas*, 4 May 1946.

52 *Nashe zhyttia*, 2 February 1946 (Appendix), 19 October 1945.

53 *Nashe zhyttia*, 27 July 1946 (Appendix); *Chas*, 16 February 1947.

54 *Nashe zhyttia*, 27 July 1946, 10 November 1947 (quote).

55 *Nashe zhyttia*, 1 January 1948.

56 For a brief survey of the OUN history and an analysis of its factions' positions regarding the consolidation problem, see: Yurkevich, 'Ukrainian Nationalists'. For a detailed discussion of the OUN beginnings and its activities during the war, see: Motyl, *The Turn to the Right*; Armstrong, *Ukrainian Nationalism*.

57 On the party system of the DP community, see: Markus, 'Political Parties'.

58 Ibid., p. 114.

59 *Nashe zhyttia*, 27 April 1946.

60 *Nashe zhyttia*, 15 May, 10 August 1946.

61 For an overt presentation of this view, see: *Ukrains'ka trybuna*, 13 February 1947.

62 Perhaps the most famous such attempt took place in Augsburg with the newspaper *Nashe zhyttia*. See: *Nashe zhyttia*, 18 September 1946; *Ukrains'ka Dumka*, 27 September 1946.

63 *Nashe zhyttia*, 12 May, 13 October 1947.

64 *Nashe zhyttia*, 13 October 1947. They even refused to comply with the demand of the Central Representation of the Ukrainian Emigration that publications about criminal incidents in the camps were not allowed until examination of their causes by a communal court. *Nashe zhyttia*, 2 June 1947.

65 *Nashe zhyttia*, 18 March, 8 September 1947.

66 *Nashe zhyttia*, 14 January 1948.

67 *Nashe zhyttia*, 13 October 1947, 18 January 1948 (quote). On the controversial (and not yet thoroughly investigated) circumstances of the proclamation of independence and the role of the OUN-B in the emergence of the UPA, see: Armstrong, *Ukrainian nationalism*, chs 4, 6; Hrytsak, *Narys istorii Ukrainy*, pp. 224-225, 244-247.

68 *Nashe zhyttia*, 18 January 1948; 13 October 1947.

69 *Nashe zhyttia*, 13 April 1947.

70 *Chas*, 21 and 28 December 1947.

71 *Nashe zhyttia*, 8 June 1946 (Appendix).

72 *Chas*, 30 March 1947. On the socialist leadership of the UNR and its policies in 1917, see: Kamenetsky, 'Hrushevskyi and the Central Rada'; Hrytsak, *Narys istorii*, pp. 111-125.

73 *Chas*, 10 November, 15 December 1946.

74 *Chas*, 1 December 1946.

75 *Nashe zhyttia*, 1 January 1947.

76 *Chas*, 5 and 26 October 1947.

[77] *Chas*, 28 September 1947, 28 October 1948.
[78] *Chas*, 21 September 1947.
[79] *Nashe zhyttia*, 6 October 1947.
[80] *Nashe zhyttia*, 7 January 1948.
[81] *Nashe zhyttia*, 1 February 1948.
[82] *Nashe zhyttia*, 20 August 1947.
[83] *Chas*, 9 February 1947.
[84] *Chas*, 8 August 1948.
[85] Yurkevich, 'Ukrainian Nationalists', p. 137.
[86] Ciuciura, 'Common Organizational Efforts', pp. 102-103.
[87] *Ukrains'ka dumka*, 6 October 1946; *Nashe zhyttia*, 26 May 1947, 7 January 1948.
[88] *Chas*, 19 January 1947.
[89] *Nashe zhyttia*, 12 June, 27 July 1946.
[90] *Ukrains'ka dumka*, 6 October 1946.
[91] *Chas*, 16 February 1947.
[92] *Nashe zhyttia*, 27 October 1947.
[93] *Chas*, Christmas [7 January] 1947.
[94] Stebelsky, 'Ukrainian Population', pp. 30-31.
[95] *Chas*, 13 July 1947.
[96] *Chas*, 12 September 1948.
[97] *Chas*, 19 September 1948.
[98] Ilnytzkyij, 'A Survey', p. 288.
[99] At the same time, the continuing feud between the political groupings and the former DPs' identification first of all with Ukraine, rather than with the new host countries, alienated parts of existing Ukrainian communities from the newcomers, in some cases producing 'two rather distinct Ukrainian constituencies'. For a Canadian story, see: Luciuk, *Searching for Place*, ch. 8 (quote on p. 223). Cf. also Wyman, *DP*, p. 206.

References

Armstrong, John, *Ukrainian Nationalism*, third ed., Englewood, Co., 1990.

Baran, Alexander, 'The Ukrainian Catholic Church', in: Wsevolod W. Isajiw, Yury Boshyk and Roman Senkus (eds), *The Refugee Experience. Ukrainian Displaced Persons after World War II*, Edmonton, 1992, pp. 147-157.

Bauer, Raymond A., Alex Inkeles and Clyde Kluckhohn, *How the Soviet System Works. Cultural, Psychological, and Social Themes*, Cambridge, MA, 1956.

Bociurkiw, Bohdan R., 'The Ukrainian Autocephalous Orthodox Church in West Germany, 1945-50', in: Wsevolod W. Isajiw, Yury Boshyk and Roman Senkus (eds), *The Refugee Experience*, Edmonton, 1992, pp. 158-181.

Boshyk, Yuri and Boris Balan, *Political Refugees and 'Displaced Persons', 1945-1954. A Selected Bibliography and Guide to Research with Special Reference to Ukrainians*, Edmonton, 1982.

Boshyk, Yury, 'Repatriation. Ukrainian DPs and Political Refugees in Germany and Austria, 1945-48', in: Isajiw, Boshyk and Senkus (eds), *The Refugee Experience*, pp. 360-382.

Ciuciura, Theodore B., 'Common Organizational Efforts, 1945-52. Structure and People', in: Wsevolod W. Isajiw, Yury Boshyk and Roman Senkus (eds), *The Refugee Experience*, pp. 90-108.

Dyczok, Marta, *The Grand Alliance and Ukrainian Refugees*, Houndmills, 2000.

Hrytsak, Yaroslav, *Narys istorii Ukrainy. Formuvannia modernoi ukrains'koi natsii XIX-XX stolittia*, Kiev, 1996.
Ilnytzkyj, Roman, 'A Survey of Ukrainian Camp Periodicals, 1945-50', in: Wsevolod W. Isajiw, Yury Boshyk and Roman Senkus (eds), *The Refugee Experience*, pp. 271-291.
Inkeles, Alex and Raymond A. Bauer, *The Soviet Citizen. Daily Life in a Totalitarian System*, Cambridge, Mass., 1959.
Isajiw, Wsevolod W., 'Community, Class, and Social Mobility as Dynamic Factors in the DP Experience', in: Wsevolod W. Isajiw, Yury Boshyk and Roman Senkus (eds), *The Refugee Experience*, pp. 471-479.
Isajiw, Wsevolod W. and Michael Palij, 'Refugees and the DP Problem in Postwar Europe', in: Wsevolod W. Isajiw, Yury Boshyk and Roman Senkus (eds), *The Refugee Experience*, pp. xv-xxiv.
Isajiw, Wsevolod W., Yury Boshyk and Roman Senkus (eds), *The Refugee Experience. Ukrainian Displaced Persons after World War II*, Edmonton, 1992.
Kamenetsky, Ihor, 'Hrushevskyi and the Central Rada', in: Taras Hunczak (ed.), *The Ukraine, 1917-1921. A Study in Revolution*, Cambridge, MA, 1977, pp. 33-60.
Kubijovyč, Volodymyr, 'Z demohrafichnykh problem ukrainskoi emigratsii (Na prykladi taboriv u Mittenval'di)', *Sioihochasne i mynule* 1-2 (1949): pp. 14-27.
Lincoln, Bruce, *Discourse and the Construction of Society. Comparative Studies of Myth, Ritual, and Classification*, New York, 1989.
Luciuk, Lubomyr Y., *Searching for Place. Ukrainian Displaced Persons, Canada, and the Migration of Memory*, Toronto, 2000.
Mace, James E., *Communism and the Dilemmas of National Liberation. National Communism in Soviet Ukraine 1918-1933*, Cambridge, MA, 1983.
Markus, Daria, 'Education in the DP Camps', in: Wsevolod W. Isajiw, Yury Boshyk and Roman Senkus (eds), *The Refugee Experience*, pp. 185-200.
Markus, Vasyl, 'Political Parties in the DP Camps', in: Wsevolod W. Isajiw, Yury Boshyk and Roman Senkus (eds), *The Refugee Experience*, pp. 111-124.
Motyl, Alexander J., *The Turn to the Right. The Ideological Origins and Development of Ukrainian Nationalism, 1919-1929*, Boulder, 1980.
Rudnytsky, Ivan L., 'The Ukrainians in Galicia under Austrian Rule', in: Ivan L. Rudnytsky, *Essays in Modern Ukrainian History*, Edmonton, 1987, pp. 315-352.
Stebelsky, Ihor, 'Ukrainian Population Migration after World War II', in: Wsevolod W. Isajiw, Yury Boshyk and Roman Senkus (eds), *The Refugee Experience*, pp. 21-66.
Subtelny, Orest, 'Ukrainian Political Refugees. An Historical Overview', in: Wsevolod W. Isajiw, Yury Boshyk and Roman Senkus (eds), *The Refugee Experience*, pp. 3-20.
Wyman, Mark, *DP: Europe's Displaced Persons, 1945-1951*, Philadelphia, 1989.
Yurkevich, Myroslav, 'Ukrainian Nationalists and DP Politics', in: Wsevolod W. Isajiw, Yury Boshyk and Roman Senkus (eds), *The Refugee Experience*, pp. 125-143.
Zielyk, Ihor V., 'The DP Camp as a Social System', in: Wsevolod W. Isajiw, Yury Boshyk and Roman Senkus (eds), *The Refugee Experience*, pp. 461-470.

Chapter 12

The Impact of Distorted Memory: Historical Narratives and Expellee Integration in West Germany, 1945-1970

Pertti Ahonen

Among the many cruelties that darken the history of twentieth-century Europe, mass expulsions of ethnic groups occupy a prominent position. The precedent set by such events as Turkish deportations of Armenians during World War I and the forcible Greco-Turkish and Greco-Bulgarian population transfers of the 1920s found application on numerous subsequent occasions, particularly during and shortly after the Second World War. As a result, at least some 50 million Europeans were forcibly uprooted from their homes in the course of the last century.[1] Many millions lost their lives in the process, and those who survived the ordeal typically bore lasting scars, emotional and often also physical, from the violence and turmoil they had witnessed. To make matters worse, the tribulations of the forced migrants did not conclude with the end of the expulsions themselves. The next challenge for the typically impoverished and demoralised expellees was to adjust to the societies in which they had found refuge. Their integration thus became an urgent task, not only for the newcomers themselves but also for the polities which had received them, as the potentially destabilizing effects of discontented expellee populations soon scared policy-makers and other leaders into action.

Given the magnitude of these challenges – which have retained a good deal of contemporary urgency in view of the migrations, forced and otherwise, that have continued to sweep across the continent – it is no surprise that the problems of expellee integration in twentieth century Europe have begun to attract increasing attention from historians and social scientists. The social, economic and political processes involved have been studied in some depth – at least within individual countries – with a range of different approaches, particularly since the end of the Cold War helped to open up new sources and fresh interpretive paradigms. But several important questions still remain largely unanswered, including those having to do with the key ways in which the actions of the expellees affected their own integration.

Admittedly, the expellees have always been extremely central figures in the literature that ultimately revolves around them. But many existing studies have viewed them in one of two ways: either as large collective units within a framework of broad structural changes in society, or – to a lesser degree – as individuals or small groups in specific localities, analyzed in a biographically-oriented perspective that focuses largely on the reconstruction of individual experiences.[2] Although valuable regional and other studies have recently helped to fuse together elements of both approaches, an important intermediate dimension has nevertheless remained largely unexplored: that of collective action carried out by the expellees themselves through organized pressure groups and other similar institutions in an effort to exert direct influence on the political, social and economic systems within which they found themselves.[3]

To be fair, there are good reasons for the rarity or downright absence of these types of analyses in many national contexts. The countries of the former Eastern bloc, for example, generally suppressed any overt collective action by their resident expellee populations, preferring instead to accentuate the supposedly stunning successes of governmental integration policies.[4] Other nations, such as Finland and Greece, allowed expellee organizations to form but restrained their public activities, at least in particularly sensitive policy areas. By contrast, one European country in particular stood out in its pronounced toleration, even encouragement, of vocal collective action by expellees: West Germany. Although the occupation powers had initially placed tight restrictions on the formation of any expellee organizations, these were soon lifted in the western zones, and as a result a panoply of groups purporting to represent the collective interests of the German expellees emerged in what became the Federal Republic. They included a complicated network of pressure groups as well as a short-lived political party, which scored a string of striking electoral triumphs in the early 1950s and even held seats in the federal cabinet around the middle of the decade.[5] From the late 1940s on, expellee organizations were thus a notable presence in the Federal Republic: a highly active and visible force whose strident demands seemed to hold considerable sway in the political system.

Despite their public prominence, however, the organizations have received little scholarly attention even in the West German context. During much of the Cold War era, most relevant publications concentrated on polemics. Leftist critics launched angry broadsides against the organizations, tarring them with the brush of chauvinism and reaction, while pro-expellee circles eulogized the same groups as champions of justice and self-determination.[6] Dispassionate scholarly analyses were very few, and although some progress has been made more recently, particularly with the appearance of several solid regional studies, many questions about the organizations, their activities, and their broader societal impact remain unanswered.[7]

This chapter attempts to highlight one particular way in which the activities of the expellee organizations affected the general development of West German society between the 1940s and the end of the 1960s. It analyses the public portrayal of the expulsions promulgated by the West German expellee lobby and explores the impact of this discussion on the integration of the expellees into West German society.[8] The article consists of four parts. The first lays out a general framework for the argument through some observations about the broader West German public discourse on that problematic segment of the national past within which the expulsions were embedded: the Nazi period. The second section goes on to examine a specific segment of this general discourse: the public portrayal of the expulsions, including their antecedents and consequences, provided by the leaders of the organized expellee movement in the two and a half decades following the end of the Second World War. The analysis draws upon the two pressure groups that claimed to represent the numerically largest and in many ways politically most significant expellee populations – the Homeland Societies of the Silesians and the Sudeten Germans (the *Landsmannschaft Schlesien* and the *Sudetendeutsche Landsmannschaft*, respectively). The third section discusses the broader effects of the expellee lobby's public rhetoric, primarily on integration within the expellee sector but, by extension, also on all of West Germany, nearly 20 per cent of whose total population consisted of expellees during the first two post-war decades. The fourth segment is a brief conclusion that reiterates the key arguments and offers some reflections on the transferability of the lessons of the German case to other contexts.

The Uses of Memory: West Germany, the Third Reich and the Rhetoric of Victimization

The public representation of the experience of the Second World War in post-1945 Europe has come under close scholarly scrutiny in recent years. A steady stream of monographs and articles has explored the ways in which Europeans remembered and portrayed the war and the events surrounding it. Because Germany and the Germans stood at the centre of most of the wartime horrors – from the planning and unleashing of the conflagration to the barbarism practised on the Eastern front to the systematic annihilation of European Jewry – Germany, and particularly the Federal Republic, the larger and more powerful of the two states created from the ruins of the Reich, has received the most attention in this literature. At the risk of some oversimplification, one could claim that the growing stacks of publications on West German public memory of both the war and the Third Reich fall into two broad interpretative categories. Until recently, the dominant view was that West Germans had suppressed nearly all memories of the Nazi period during the first decade and a half after the Second World War. According to this interpretation, the 1950s in particular were characterized by deliberate repression and forgetting, and the silence was not broken until the 1960s, when a new, self-critical examination of the recent past replaced the earlier outlook.[9]

In recent years, several scholars have taken issue with this rather simplistic analysis and provided a more nuanced portrayal of historical memory in the Federal Republic. Among the key findings of this recent literature has been that public memory of the Third Reich and the crimes and catastrophes associated with it was very much present in the Federal Republic, even before the 1960s – but in a selective and often instrumentalized form. Although West Germans frequently acknowledged that crimes had indeed been committed 'in the name of the German people', they typically downplayed both the complicity of ordinary Germans in these events and the suffering of the victims, thus relativizing the enormity of the recent past and promoting what Norbert Frei has recently called German 'self-rehabilitation'.[10]

In these attempts at relativization and rehabilitation, portrayals of a certain kind of victimhood played a key role – a victimhood not of those tormented and killed by Germans but of Germans victimized by others, especially during the final phases and the immediate aftermath of the war. As Robert G. Moeller has shown in his recent, pioneering work on this topic, the fate of two victim groups in particular dominated West German public discourse during the 1940s and the 1950s: that of the approximately three million German soldiers who had endured Soviet captivity and of the roughly 15 million German expellees forcibly uprooted from their former homes in Eastern and East-Central Europe. According to Moeller, the stories of suffering promulgated by these two groups quickly became the key component of broader 'rhetorics of victimization' that enjoyed wide currency in the early Federal Republic.[11] Focused on German suffering and its comparability to that of the victims of German crimes, these rhetorics enabled West Germans to address the Nazi past while evading questions of collective responsibility and to suggest that the German people, too, had ultimately been victims of Hitler and his psychopathic henchmen. Through this type of discourse, Moeller further argues, citizens of the Federal Republic developed a strong integrative myth of suffering and hardship that functioned as a key source of collective identity and legitimacy for the new state.

Moeller's analysis is highly persuasive, and he succeeds admirably in linking the expellee issue to broader societal developments in the Federal Republic. But his work, too, ultimately downplays the significance of the collective action carried out by the expellees themselves. His analysis of the transmission mechanisms through which accounts of German suffering came to permeate West Germany's public consciousness in the 1950s concentrates on four fields: social policy debates, historical scholarship, the popular press and the cinema. By contrast, the rhetorical exploits of the expellee organizations receive only passing attention, although much of the imagery that was subsequently promulgated to the West German public through the types of channels described by Moeller first emerged from within the organized expellee movement. The historical narrative employed by the expellee lobby also had its own quirks and singularities which set it apart from that prevalent in society at large, not only in the early phases of the Federal Republic but in later years as well, which, in turn, was to have significant effects within the expellee sector. A closer look at the expellee organizations and the rhetoric employed by them therefore becomes imperative.

The Historical Narrative of the Expellee Lobby

The expellee lobby cut a powerful public figure in the early Federal Republic, particularly in the 1950s but also in the following decade. The various organizations claimed a combined membership of at least two million throughout this period, and the Sudeten and Silesian Homeland Societies made the greatest contributions to that total. The *Sudetendeutsche Landsmannschaft* managed to recruit some 350,000 members from among the nearly two million Sudeten Germans resident in the Federal Republic, while its Silesian counterpart boasted a total membership of about 300,000, roughly one out of five Silesians in the country.[12] Both organizations also knew how to translate their numerical strength into public prominence. They held massive political rallies that consistently drew hundreds of thousands of participants and received extensive coverage in the national media. They also promulgated their views through their own newspapers, several of which had a circulation in the high tens of thousands, as well as through a range of other publications, such as various books and pamphlets tailor-made to highlight the organizations' political narrative.[13]

The narrative typically began with an account of the expulsions, rooted in a broader historical context. But that context did not revolve around the most obvious antecedent of the expulsions – the Third Reich and its crimes. To be sure, the transgressions of the Nazi period were often present in the expellee lobby's public discourse, but only peripherally. The standard rhetorical gambit was first to condemn any 'violent acts' committed by the Nazis, without going into details, and then to relativize that stance with two qualifiers.[14] The organizations typically stressed that the expellees themselves had exerted 'no influence' on the small clique of Nazis who allegedly bore responsibility for the Third Reich's wrongful deeds and that their condemnation extended not only to Nazi crimes but also to those of 'all totalitarian regimes in the world', including, of course, West Germany's Cold War nemesis, the Soviet Union.[15]

This brief and cautious distancing from Nazi crimes was usually followed by an in-depth discussion of another, longer-term historical trajectory, which the organizations viewed as the proper framework for understanding the expulsions. The narrative began with a vision of an idyllic, harmonious *Gemeinschaft* that had purportedly characterized the relations between Germans and Slavs throughout East-Central Europe in previous centuries. To be sure, the Germans had been the dominant party in the relationship; they had 'cleared the forests, established cities, villages, mines and factories, built cultural monuments, and created the basis of a thriving trading system'.[16] But both partners had accepted their assigned roles and flourished – until the arrival of petty nationalisms in the late nineteenth century had poisoned the atmosphere and turned the Slavs against their benefactors. According to the expellee activists, the irrational anti-German resentments thus created had come to a head in the post-World War I peace settlement, a disastrous *Diktat* to which 'all the misfortunes that subsequently befell Europe, including the Second World War', could be traced.[17] The vindictive humiliation of the German Reich, combined with the 'senseless dismemberment' of Austria-Hungary, had destroyed the stability of the European state system and led to a number of grave injustices, including the unfair relegation of large numbers of ethnic Germans to a minority status in newly established East European states.[18]

This aspect of the post-World War I settlement received particularly strong condemnation from the Sudeten-Germans, for whom the peace treaties had brought a sudden demotion in status from a privileged Germanic community within Austria-Hungary to a mere national minority in inter-war Czechoslovakia. Time after time, Sudeten German leaders denounced the way in which they had been 'forced' into Czechoslovakia 'against their will' and then systematically oppressed for two decades by a vengeful Czech elite imbued with an ideology of 'pan-Slavic imperialism'.[19] Against this background of subjugation, the notorious Munich Agreement of 1938 – through which Hitler had forcibly annexed the Sudetenland to the Reich – waxed into a landmark of 'reason and justice' in the standard Sudeten-German narrative. [20] Activists greeted the treaty as a long overdue revision of the post-World War I peace settlement which, in keeping with the principle of self-determination, had granted them 'liberation from foreign rule and union with our blood brothers [*Stammesgenossen*] in Germany'.[21] At the same time, however, the activists distinguished sharply between the just cause of self-determination inherent in the Munich Accord and the subsequent policies of the Nazi regime, with which the Sudeten Germans in their view had nothing to do.[22] Ultimately, this narrative thus presented the Sudeten Germans – and, by extension, other Germans of the East – as victims who had undergone decades of torment in the hands of overzealous Slav nationalists only to become innocent pawns of scheming Nazis.

The story of German hardship and suffering reached its culmination in the expulsions at the end of the Second World War. According to the expellee activists, this cataclysm became possible when the Western Allies decided to turn their military offensive against Nazism into an immoral 'crusade against the German people', a decision influenced by Soviet and East European Communists and other evil forces.[23] The result was a vast iniquity which expellee leaders never tired of denouncing in the strongest possible terms. In their public discourse, the expulsions constituted not only a 'crime against humanity and a violation of the basic ethical principles of our civilization'.[24] Because of their indiscriminate brutality and sweeping scope, they amounted to something much worse: 'the greatest collective crime in history' which could 'not be justified with reference to the transgressions of the Hitler regime' and which endowed the expellees with a victim status comparable to that of Jewish survivors of the Holocaust.[25]

As compensation for the crimes committed against them, the expellee organizations demanded massive revisions of the post-World War II status quo, chief among them the reincorporation into Germany of the territories that in the aftermath of the expulsions had passed from the Reich to Poland, Czechoslovakia and the Soviet Union. Such revisions, they claimed, would not promote backward-looking nationalistic interests. By righting past wrongs, they would rather help to restore 'morals, ethics, justice and political reason' to their proper place in the international order and thus boost transnational cooperation throughout Europe and the rest of the world.[26] In the myopic expellee vision of the late 1940s and the 1950s, German gain was thus seemingly identical with the greatest good of all.

Remarkably, the expellee lobby's main arguments remained essentially unchanged even in the 1960s. The discourse of German victimization, with its one-sided reading of many key events of the recent past, continued unabated. A resolution adopted by the Silesian Homeland Society in the autumn of 1962, for example, labelled the post-war territorial status quo in Central Europe the unjust result of 'Communist imperialism' while downplaying Nazi Germany's heavy contributions to that outcome.[27] Continuity was equally evident in the expellee activists' repeated calls for major revisions of that post-war order, couched in grandiose moral and legal terms. According to a pronouncement issued by the top leader of the Sudeten German Homeland Society in the spring of 1964, the road to 'reconciliation among the peoples' of Europe ran through 'justice for all', which would be ideally served by 'the return of the Sudeten German homeland to the Sudeten German people'.[28] Also unaltered was the persistent effort to relativize German crimes of the Nazi era by comparing them to exaggerated accounts of the atrocities inflicted upon Germans during the expulsions. Thus the Sudeten-German Homeland Society proclaimed as late as 1968 that although 'thousands of Czechs and Slovaks' had fallen victim to 'National Socialist terror between 1939 and 1945', a much larger number of Sudeten-Germans – 241,000 in all – had perished as a result of the subsequent expulsions.[29] Even in the rapidly changing social and political climate of the 1960s, the expellee organizations thus remained true to the tendentious historical narrative with which they had operated since the early post-war years.

The Impact of Distorted Memory: On the Effects of the Expellee Lobby's Narrative

On balance, the expellee lobby's depiction of the expulsions was highly distorted. It lacked both a sense of proportion about the main forces that had propelled Europe's tragic recent past and a critical perspective vis-à-vis the pivotal role that Germany and the Germans had played in these developments. The narrative perpetuated old stereotypes about the Germans and their eastern neighbours systematically downplayed the complicity of the German people in the crimes of the Nazi era and used exaggerated accounts of German suffering to justify dubious historical comparisons on the one hand, and raw post-war revisionism, on the other. Given these realities, an evaluation of the broader effects of this rhetoric must begin by acknowledging that the distorted public memory which the expellee discourse helped to promote had several consequences for West Germany which, at least from today's vantage point, can only be regarded as negative. The costs began to add up as soon as slightly expurgated versions of the expellee lobby's standard narrative began to permeate West German society and to gain widespread acceptance as a part of broader rhetorics of victimization. By the late 1940s and early 1950s, many elements of that narrative had become embedded in broader public discussions led by mainstream politicians, publicists, artists and other figures. While filtering out particularly tendentious elements of the expellee story – such as the glowing appraisals of the Munich Agreement provided by some Sudeten German activists – these discussions typically highlighted German suffering, often with the use of graphic examples drawn from expellee experiences, while referring to German crimes and their victims only in broad, abstract terms.

The selective public memory thereby created fostered a general atmosphere in which difficult questions about individual responsibility and state-society relations during the Third Reich were long dodged. In the words of Michael L. Hughes, the situation was 'tailor-made for masking moral agency', for suppressing investigations of German guilt for Nazi transgressions.[30] As a consequence, the cause of justice suffered severely, as West German courts took little legal action against perpetrators of crimes against humanity until the 1960s, and Adenauer's government, at least initially, invested much more effort in securing the release of convicted German war criminals from foreign jails than in tracking down unpunished mass murderers at home.[31]

In addition, the expellee activists' tendency to airbrush the bulk of the Second World War out of their historical narrative helped to postpone a full reckoning with the fact that Germany had planned, launched and lost the war – and was therefore destined to pay a heavy territorial price for it. As I have argued elsewhere, this problem grew particularly severe because the expellee lobby's calls for border revisions in the East became instrumentalized in West German domestic politics early on. Although aware that the pursuit of reannexations east of the GDR was neither possible nor desirable, Bonn's governmental and party elites carefully cultivated the impression of a far-reaching congruence of interests between themselves and the expellee movement on these issues, primarily because of electoral calculations and the expellee lobby's usefulness for the Adenauer government's broader policy agenda. As a result, West Germany's political leaders soon found themselves trapped in seemingly revanchist Eastern policy stances which caused growing problems for the country's foreign and reunification policies but which the political leadership was loath to readjust until the late 1960s, largely for fear of electoral retribution from the millions of expellee voters whose interests and demands the expellee organizations were assumed to represent.[32]

Despite these and other problems, the distorted historical narrative promulgated by the expellee organizations also had significant positive effects, at least within the expellee sector. Most notably, it facilitated the peaceful integration of the expellee multitudes into West German society in two distinct temporal contexts. First, during the early post-war period, at a time when millions of impoverished, demoralised and homesick expellees eked out a very precarious existence in West Germany, typically facing prejudice and discrimination from the native population at every turn, the expellee lobby's peculiar public rhetoric arguably provided important psychological succour for the uprooted newcomers. To be sure, the oft-repeated claims regarding the traditional superiority of Germans over Slavs and the continued pre-eminence of Germans – and particularly the expellees – as guardians of justice and other virtues had a deeply offensive ring in view of the moral record of the Third Reich. But arguably these sentiments also helped average expellees maintain a sense of self-worth amidst their threadbare existence on the bottom rung of the Federal Republic's social ladder.

The prospect of an eventual return to the old homelands, fostered by the expellee leadership's revisionist proclamations, was another source of hope and motivation for large numbers of West German expellees. In a statement typical of the late 1940s, a Silesian woman gave apt expression to the strength and inspiration which this vision of a better future could provide. 'One day we'll return to our own land', she assured an interviewer. 'We all firmly believe that. Until then we don't let ourselves get down-hearted – there's no point in that...'.[33] Similar beliefs were also rife among the Sudeten Germans, particularly those of older generations, many of whom were apparently 'fully convinced' that after 'a certain amount of time we will get to go home again'.[34] Although economic growth and specific governmental policies provided the basic material framework for expellee integration in the early Federal Republic, psychological dimensions were also significant to the process through which the vast majority of the expellees ultimately proved resistant to what many contemporary observers had dreaded: a large-scale political radicalization.[35]

Many of the offensive distortions propagated through organized expellee discourse could – and should – undoubtedly have been avoided, even in the early post-war period. The West German political elite, in particular, could have been expected to show greater courage in gradually standing up to the expellee lobby, at least on issues where nearly all responsible politicians disagreed with the expellees by the mid 1950s at the latest, chief among them the desirability of pursuing territorial revisions in Eastern Europe. Such an approach would have promoted a less taboo-ridden political atmosphere at home and brought long-term foreign policy benefits by facilitating a reconciliation with Eastern Europe.

But a fully accurate public narrative of the darkness of the Nazi past and of the grim political realities of the post-war era might well have overburdened not only the expellees but also the fragile democracy then taking root in West Germany.[36] To take just one example, an open discussion of the high level of support which the Nazi regime had enjoyed among many expellees, particularly in such contested border areas as the Sudetenland, would have made it easier for the long-term residents of western Germany to do what many of them had begun to do in the early post-war years in any case: use the expellees as scapegoats on whom the guilt for the Nazi period and its transgression could be projected. This development would have further deepened the chasm separating the newcomers from the long-term residents of western Germany, which, in turn, would have hampered expellee integration and facilitated the emergence of resentful, possibly anti-democratic groups, much as in Weimar times. Despite its many infelicities, the elision of painful truths in the expellee narrative arguably helped to prevent such dangers in the early post-war years.

The second period during which the expellee lobby's distorted public narrative of the recent past proved to be a blessing in disguise for both expellee integration and the broader good of the Federal Republic was, paradoxically, the latter half of the 1960s. By this time, the tenor of mainstream West German public discussions of the Nazi period and its legacies had changed dramatically. Thanks in large part to broad generational and social changes, large segments of the population – including most leading journalists and other so-called opinion-makers – were increasingly willing to face many troubling aspects of their nation's past. The nature of Nationalist Socialist rule came under growing scrutiny, with an increasing preparedness, especially among the younger generation, to acknowledge that the regime had acted not only in 'the name of the German people' but with the support of much of the population and the active involvement of numerous ordinary Germans.[37]

As a part of this broader general development, the long-standing West German tendency to dwell on the expulsions and their horrors at the expense of Nazi crimes drew intensifying public criticism, as did the continued salience of revisionist Eastern policy doctrines in much of the country's public oratory. In 1964, for example, a controversial television documentary made by one of the country's leading journalists exhorted Germans to 'accept the facts, even the painful ones' about the territories which the Reich had ceded to Poland after the war.[38] About a year later a starkly worded public memorandum by a sub-organ of the Protestant Church denounced the 'self-righteousness' characteristic of 'rigid and one-sided' revisionist claims rooted in presumed German 'rights' and exhorted Bonn to adjust to the advance of detente by committing itself to a policy of 'reconciliation with [its] eastern neighbours'.[39]

As these kinds of messages and the accompanying public debates began to make an impact on the West German public in the course of the 1960s, the resulting attitudinal changes soon extended to the expellee sector as well. By the end of the decade, a clear majority of West Germany's expellees were reasonably well economically and socially integrated and increasingly willing to adjust to the changing times.[40] In late 1969, for example, only 29 per cent of them still expressed interest in returning to their old homelands, should they again become German, while 62 per cent acknowledged that post-war Polish residents of the former German territories had acquired an inalienable right to a permanent domicile there.[41] However, as indicated above, the expellee organizations still refused to budge from their traditional stances. In the face of rising public challenges to their established doctrines, they instead added increasingly radical-sounding accents to their rhetorical repertoire, typically attacking journalists, politicians and other critics with derogatory epithets reminiscent of the destructively polarized debates of the Weimar era. The ominous-sounding term *Verzichtspolitiker* (abandonment politician) gained particular notoriety as a pejorative employed by expellee activists to denounce politicians deemed unfriendly to their revisionist cause, and one prominent Silesian activist even demanded 'prison sentences' to those who publicly advocated the 'abandonment [*Verzicht*] of pieces of German soil'.[42]

Through their inability to adjust to the social, political, and attitudinal changes of the 1960s, the expellee activists again made a positive contribution to both expellee integration and broader social stability in West Germany, albeit in a paradoxical fashion: by alienating the majority of the people whom they purported to represent. After having proclaimed for years that a recognition by Bonn of the territorial status quo in Eastern Europe – an issue symbolic of a broader willingness to accept German responsibility for the Second World War – would provoke massive expellee protests and risk large-scale political radicalization, expellee leaders were now forced to recognize that the bulk of their supposed followers refused to conform to such stereotypes. Far from rushing to the barricades to demand continued hard-line policies, a growing number of expellees explicitly rejected the popular legitimacy of their self-proclaimed representatives, publicly accusing the activists of 'fanaticism' and 'dangerous illusions'.[43] Many others backed away from the expellee movement with less fanfare. This trend was evident within the organizations by the mid-1960s at the latest. By that time, ranking Silesian leaders admitted in private that 'the mass of the Silesians [did] not belong or no longer belong[ed] to the Homeland Society' and that the level of interest among youth in particular was 'minimal'.[44] Internal Sudeten German records told a very similar story, and the general picture within the expellee lobby was one of steady shrinkage, funnelled around a hard core of ageing and increasingly embittered devotees.[45] The broader impact of these developments became clear as Willy Brandt's Social-Liberal coalition began to implement its new *Ostpolitik* from 1969 on. Although expellee activists continued to protest vociferously, most of the public supported the government's Eastern policy, and political radicalism remained confined to small fringe groups, even among the expellees.

Conclusion

Some two and a half decades after the war's end, the Federal Republic was thus becoming increasingly ready to face the Nazi era and its harsh legacies, both externally – through a foreign policy that broke with past taboos – and internally – through an increasingly open and critical public dialogue about the recent past. The integration of the expellees, the largest and best organized group of Germans severely victimized by the war, was of crucial significance to this process, and the relative success of integration, in turn, owed a good deal to the distorted historical narrative promulgated by the expellee lobby. During the late 1940s and 1950s, this narrative matched the psychological needs of the majority of the expellees, helping them to endure a difficult transitional period. By the late 1960s, the same rhetoric served to alienate the bulk of the expellees, many of whom were by then increasingly secure in material terms and no longer interested in backward-looking rhetorics and revisionist dreams. In different ways, distorted public memory thus acted as a brake on potential threats to West Germany's young democracy in both periods.

Problems similar to those faced by the Federal Republic in the integration of its expellees have also plagued a number of other societies since then – and continue to do so today. Various victims of 'ethnic cleansings', to use present-day parlance, still need to find their bearings in new social settings after highly traumatic experiences. The question therefore arises as to whether the West German case could be seen as a model for other transitional societies and whether similarly distorted public discussions of recent crises could produce comparably positive outcomes elsewhere. In answering such questions, great caution seems necessary. Deliberately distorted public narratives of violent conflicts are inherently dangerous projects that can result in many unintended consequences, even in the absence of evil intentions. Ethnic animosities and irredentist desires are forces that should not be toyed with. In addition, the case of post-1945 Germany was in many ways unique. The presence of the Allied occupiers as a benevolent force ready to crack down on anti-democratic excesses acted as a strong moderating influence on all political extremists. Furthermore, the so-called economic miracle, an absolutely crucial event for the success of expellee integration, resulted from a fortuitous confluence of happy factors and circumstances extremely unlikely to be repeated elsewhere. What worked in the Federal Republic of the 1950s and 1960s is therefore very unlikely to be transferable to other temporal and geographical contexts, and the rhetorical practices of the German expellee activists should not be seen as a general model for similar lobbyists elsewhere.

Notes

I wish to thank Tony Judt, Gabriella Etmektsoglou, Bess Rothenberg, Hugh Wilford, Timothy Baycroft, Christof Morrissey, as well as the editors of this volume and the other participants of the Network Migration in Europe conference, for their helpful comments on earlier drafts of this paper.

1 For general perspectives on this aspect of the twentieth century, see Naimark, *Fires of Hatred*, as well as the following two works, both of them by now somewhat dated: Marrus, *The Unwanted* and Nuscheler, 'Das Jahrhundert der Flüchtlinge'.

2 For two prominent examples of each of these two general approaches in the context of post-war Germany, probably the most intensely studied geographical region in the field of expellee integration, see (for the first approach) Lüttinger, *Integration der Vertriebenen* and Frantzioch, *Die Vertriebenen* and (for the second approach) Lehmann, *Im Fremden ungewollt zuhaus* and Plato, 'Fremde Heimat'. For similar examples about Greece, see (for the first approach) Pentzopoulos, *The Balkan Exchange of Minorities* and (for the second approach) Hirschon, *Heirs of the Greek Catastrophe* and Salamone, *In the Shadow of the Holy Mountain*.

3 Examples of strong regional work in the German context include Messerschmidt, *Aufnahme und Integration der Vertriebenen und Flüchtlinge in Hessen, 1945-1950*; Schraut, *Die Flüchtlingsaufnahme in Württemberg-Baden, 1945-1949*; and Beer, *Zur Integration der Flüchtlinge und Vertriebenen im deutschen Südwesten nach 1945*.

4 For an excellent comparative study that highlights the situation in the East bloc, see Ther, *Deutsche und polnische Vertriebene*.

5 The party was the *Bund der Heimatvertriebenen und Entrechteten* (BHE). On it, see Neumann, *Block der Heimatvertriebenen* and Stöss, 'Der Gesamtdeutsche Block'. The

most accessible English-language overview of the various organizations is Schoenberg, *Germans from the East*, chapter 4.

6 For polemical attacks against the expellee organizations, see, for example, the various works of Georg Herde, including 'Die Rolle der Landsmannschaften'; as well as Herde and Stolze, *Die Sudetendeutsche Landsmannschaft*. Pro-expellee polemics include Kuhn, *Nicht Rache*.

7 The best older scholarly work is Mühlen et al., 'Vertriebenenverbände und deutsch-polnische Beziehungen'. Newer regional studies include Steinert, *Vertriebenenverbände in Nordrhein-Westfalen*; Grebing, *Flüchtlinge und Parteien in Niedersachsen*; and Bauer, *Flüchtlinge und Flüchtlingspolitik in Bayern*.

8 Fruitful and interesting discussions have taken place in recent years about the terms to be used in the study of integration processes, whereby the definition of concepts such as 'integration', 'assimilation' and 'acculturation' has come under close scrutiny. Because of space limitations, I will sidestep these issues here. For the purposes of this brief paper, the word 'integration' will be used as a general term for the long-term process through which expellees rebuild their material existence and adjust to the political, social and cultural conditions in their new environments.

9 Prominent proponents of this interpretation include Mitscherlich and Mitscherlich, *Die Unfähigkeit zu trauern*; and Benz, 'Nachkriegsgesellschaft und Nationalsozialismus'.

10 For examples of these kinds of viewpoints, see Moeller, *War Stories*; Moeller, 'War Stories'; Frei, *Vergangenheitspolitik*; and, with a somewhat different accent, Herf, *Divided Memory*. For the quotation by Frei, see p. 402 of his book.

11 For the quotation, see Moeller, 'War Stories', p. 1013. Moeller develops his points more extensively in his new book, also entitled *War Stories*. For similar, persuasive arguments, see Hughes, 'Through No Fault'; and Münz and Ohliger, 'Vergessene Deutsche'.

12 On the membership figures, see Schoenberg, *Germans from the East*, p. 317 and pp. 94-95.

13 On these points, see ibid., esp. chapter 4 and Gaida, *Die offiziellen Organe*.

14 See, for example, the September 1952 pamphlet 'Die Tschechoslowakische Frage', published by the Sudeten-German Homeland Society and available in Sudetendeutsches Archiv (SDA): NL Lodgman, XII/1.

15 For the second quotation, see ibid. For the first, see Rudolf Lodgman von Auen's speech at the 1955 annual rally of the Sudeten-German Homeland Society, as quoted in 'Überwältigendes Treuebekenntnis zu Volk und Heimat', *Sudetendeutsche Zeitung*, 4 June 1955. See also the Silesian Homeland Society's memorandum 'Erwägung zu dem deutsch-polnischen Verhältnis', Bundesarchiv Koblenz (BAK): B136/6791.

16 For the quotation, see the September 1952 pamphlet 'Die Tschechoslowakische Frage', published by the Sudeten-German Homeland Society and available in SDA: NL Lodgman, XII/1. See also the 12 June 1949, resolution of the Schlesien-Verein München, in: Landsmannschaft Schlesien, *40 Jahre Landsmannschaft Schlesien*, pp. 7-9.

17 For the quotation, see Rudolf Lodgman von Auen's March 1959 essay 'Der 4. März 1919 als Menetekel', SDA: NL Lodgman, VIII/1:1.

18 For the quotation, see Schütz, 'München – eine offene Frage', p. 80.

19 For the two quotations, see, respectively, ibid., p. 82; and Rudolf Lodgman von Auen's address at the 1952 annual rally of the Sudeten-German Homeland Society, in: Simon, *Rudolf Lodgman von Auen: Reden und Aufsätze*, p. 110.

20 For the quotation, see 'Die Lunte hing am Pulverfass', *Sudetendeutsche Zeitung*, 29 September 1951.

21 See Rudolf Lodgman von Auen's address at the 1955 annual rally of the Sudeten-German Homeland Society, as cited in 'Überwältigendes Treuebekenntnis zu Volk und Heimat', *Sudetendeutsche Zeitung*, 4 June 1955.

[22] See, for example, ibid., as well as the September 1952 pamphlet 'Die Tschechoslowakische Frage'.

[23] See Rudolf Lodgman von Auen's 16 October 1952 address at an expellee event in Berlin, reprinted in Simon (ed.), *Rudolf Lodgman von Auen*, p. 115.

[24] See the September 1952 pamphlet 'Die Tschechoslowakische Frage'.

[25] For the quotes, see Walter Rinke in a 18 July 1954 address at a Silesian rally, reprinted in *Bulletin des Presse- und Informationsamtes der Bundesregierung*, 21 July 1954, p. 1203. For an explicit attempt to equate the fate of the German expellees with that of Jewish Holocaust victims, see Rudolf Lodgman von Auen at the *Hauptversammlung* of the *Sudetendeutsche Landsmannschaft*, 21 September 1954, SDA: NL Lodgman, I/0/2:5, 18-19.

[26] See the September 1952 pamphlet 'Die Tschechoslowakische Frage'.

[27] Resolution of the Bundesdelegiertenversammlung of the *Landsmannschaft Schlesien*, 30 September 1962, attached to a letter dated 4 October 1962 from the Landsmannschaft to Erich Mende, Archiv des deutschen Liberalismus (ADL): A31-160.

[28] Address by Hans Seebohm at the Sudetendeutscher Tag in Nuremberg, 17 May 1964, SDA: NL Seebohm/46, p. 14 of the typed manuscript.

[29] See the organization's 3 October 1968 press release 'Stellungnahme des Bundesvorstandes der Sudetendeutschen Landsmannschaft und des Präsidiums des Sudetendeutschen Rates zur 30jährigen Wiederkehr der Unterzeichnung des Münchner Abkommens', SDA: NL Becher, 365.

[30] Hughes, 'Through No Fault of Our Own', p. 209. See also Moeller, *War Stories*.

[31] The best account of these problems in the early Federal Republic is Frei, *Vergangenheitspolitik*.

[32] On these problems in the Adenauer years, see my article 'Domestic Constraints on West German Ostpolitik' and my dissertation *The Expellee Organizations and West German Ostpolitik*.

[33] See Schulze, 'Growing Discontent', p. 65.

[34] Oral history interview with a Sudeten German expellee, cited in Volbrachtova, 'Distinktions- und Integrationsschwierigkeiten der Sudetendeutschen', p. 66.

[35] On the social policy and economic aspects of integration, see Hughes, *Shouldering the Burdens*; and Lüttinger, *Integration*; as well as Holtmann, 'Flüchtlinge in den 50er Jahren'.

[36] For interesting – although in my opinion exaggerated – general arguments along these lines, see Lübbe, 'Nationalsozialismus im politischen Bewusstsein', pp. 329-349, esp. 333-336.

[37] On the changing social context of the 1960s, see, most recently, Schildt et al., *Dynamische Zeiten*.

[38] The documentary, entitled 'Deutschlands Osten – Polens Westen' and made by Hans-Jakob Stehle, aired in the Hessischer Rundfunk on 2 October 1964. A complete text of the programme can be found in Archiv der Landsmannschaft der Oberschlesier (ALdO): Presse, Rundfunk, Fernsehen, 1961-30 November 1964. The quotation is from p. 19.

[39] The memorandum, 'Die Lage der Vertriebenen und das Verhältnis des deutschen Volkes zu seinen östlichen Nachbarn', was authored by the *Kammer für öffentliche Verantwortung*, a suborgan of the Protestant Church that specialized in commenting on societal problems. For the quotations, see *Dokumente zur Deutschlandpolitik* IV/11/2, p. 896.

[40] Although the conditions of most West German expellees had improved greatly since the end of the war, problems still remained, particularly for older people, and the integration process as a whole was to continue well beyond the end of the 1960s. See Lüttinger, *Integration der Vertriebenen*.

41 For these poll results, provided by the Institut für Demoskopie in Allensbach, see Noelle and Neumann, *Jahrbuch der öffentlichen Meinung, 1968-1973*, pp. 526 and 527, respectively.

42 For a detailed report on the latter statement, made by Erich Schellhaus on 30 June 1962, see 'Gefängnis für Verzichtpolitiker?', *Süddeutsche Zeitung*, 3 July 1962. See also the radio commentaries by Peter Coulmas, 'Gefängnis für Verzichtpolitiker?' (2 July 1962) and Manfred Jenke, 'Wir sprechen zur Zone' (4 July 1962) as well as Schellhaus's radio response of 21 July 1962. All three manuscripts are in ACDP: I-378-005 (NL Schellhaus).

43 The quotations are from letters from rank-and-file expellees received by the weekly *Die Zeit*. See 'Sprechen nicht für uns', *Die Zeit*, 29 May 1964.

44 Walter Rinke to Willi Rasner, 23 November 1964, Archiv für Christlich-Demokratische Politik (ACDP): I-294-076/2 (NL Gradl).

45 On the Sudeten Germans, see, for example, the membership data of 31 December 1965 available in SDA: NL Becher, 227.

Archival Sources

Archiv der Landsmannschaft der Oberschlesier, Ratingen (AldO)
  Presse, Rundfunk, Fernsehen 1961-30.11.1964
Archiv des deutschen Liberalismus, Gummersbach (ADL)
  Nachlass Erich Mende (A 31)
Archiv für Christlich-Demokratische Politik, Sankt Augustin (ACDP)
  Nachlass Johann Baptist Gradl (I-294)
  Nachlass Erich Schellhaus (I-378)
Bundesarchiv, Koblenz (BAK)
  Bundeskanzleramt (B 136)
Sudetendeutsches Archiv, Munich (SDA)
  Nachlass Rudolf Lodgman von Auen
  Nachlass Hans Christoph Seebohm
  Nachlass Walter Becher

References

Ahonen, Pertti, 'Domestic Constraints on West German Ostpolitik: The Role of the Expellee Organizations in the Adenauer Era', *Central European History* 31 (1998): pp. 31-64.

Ahonen, Pertti, *The Expellee Organizations and West German Ostpolitik, 1949-1969*, PhD, Yale University, 1999.

Bauer, Franz J., *Flüchtlinge und Flüchtlingspolitik in Bayern 1945 bis 1950*, Stuttgart, 1982.

Beer, Matthias (ed.), *Zur Integration der Flüchtlinge und Vertriebenen im deutschen Südwesten nach 1945. Bestandsaufnahme und Perspektiven der Forschung*, Sigmaringen, 1994.

Benz, Wolfgang, 'Nachkriegsgesellschaft und Nationalsozialismus. Erinnerung, Amnesie, Abwehr', *Dachauer Hefte* 6 (1990): pp. 12-24.

Frantzioch, Marion, *Die Vertriebenen. Hemmnisse, Antriebskräfte und Wege ihrer Integration in der Bundesrepublik Deutschland*, Berlin, 1987.

Frei, Norbert, *Vergangenheitspolitik: Die Anfänge der Bundesrepublik und die NS-Vergangenheit*, Munich, 1996.

Gaida, Hans-Jürgen, *Die offiziellen Organe der ostdeutschen Landsmannschaften*, Berlin, 1973.

Grebing, Helga, *Flüchtlinge und Parteien in Niedersachsen. Eine Untersuchung der politischen Meinungs- und Willensbildungsprozesse während der ersten Nachkriegszeit, 1945-1952/53*, Hannover, 1990.

Herde, Georg, 'Die Rolle der Landsmannschaften im politischen Leben der Bundesrepublik Deutschland', *Blätter für deutsche und internationale Politik* 11 (1966): pp. 1136-1149.

Herde, Georg and Alexa Stolze, *Die Sudetendeutsche Landsmannschaft: Geschichte, Personen, Hintergründe. Eine kritische Bestandsaufnahme*, Cologne, 1987.

Herf, Jeffrey, *Divided Memory: The Nazi Past in the Two Germanys*, Cambridge, MA, 1997.

Hirschon, Renée, *Heirs of the Greek Catastrophe: The Social Life of Asia Minor Refugees in Piraeus*, Oxford, 1989.

Holtmann, Everhard, 'Flüchtlinge in den 50er Jahren. Aspekte ihrer gesellschaftlichen und politischen Integration', in: Axel Schildt and Arnold Sywottek (eds), *Modernisierung im Wiederaufbau: Die westdeutsche Gesellschaft in den 50er Jahren*, Bonn, 1993, pp. 349-361.

Hughes, Michael L., *Shouldering the Burdens of Defeat: West Germany and the Reconstruction of Social Justice*, Chapel Hill, NC, 1999.

Hughes, Michael L., '"Through No Fault of Our Own": West Germans Remember Their War Losses', *German History* 18 (2000): pp. 193-213.

Kuhn, Ekkehard, *Nicht Rache, nicht Vergeltung. Die deutschen Vertriebenen*, Munich, 1987.

Landsmannschaft Schlesien (ed.), *40 Jahre Landsmannschaft Schlesien: Eine Dokumentation*, Königswinter, 1989.

Lehmann, Albrecht, *Im Fremden ungewollt zuhaus. Flüchtlinge und Vertriebene in Westdeutschland, 1945-1990*, Munich, 1993.

Lübbe, Hermann, 'Nationalsozialismus im politischen Bewusstsein der Gegenwart', in: Martin Broszat et al. (eds), *Deutschlands Weg in die Diktatur: Internationale Konferenz zur nationalsozialistischen Machtübernahme*, Berlin, 1983, pp. 329-349.

Lüttinger, Paul, *Integration der Vertriebenen. Eine empirische Analyse*, Frankfurt, 1989.

Marrus, Michael R., *The Unwanted: European Refugees in the Twentieth Century*, Oxford and New York, 1985.

Messerschmidt, Rolf, *Aufnahme und Integration der Vertriebenen und Flüchtlinge in Hessen, 1945-1950. Zur Geschichte der hessischen Flüchtlingsverwaltung*, Wiesbaden, 1994.

Mitscherlich, Alexander and Margarete Mitscherlich, *Die Unfähigkeit zu trauern. Grundlagen kollektiven Verhaltens*, Munich, 1967.

Moeller, Robert G., 'War Stories: The Search for a Usable Past in the Federal Republic of Germany', *American Historical Review* 101 (1996): pp. 1008-1048.

Moeller, Robert G., *War Stories: The Search for a Usable Past in the Federal Republic of Germany*, Berkeley and Los Angeles, 2001.

Mühlen, Patrik von zur, Barbara Müller and Karl Schmitz, 'Vertriebenenverbände und deutsch-polnische Beziehungen nach 1945', in: Carl Christoph Schweitzer and Hubert Feger (eds), *Das deutsch-polnische Konfliktverhältnis seit dem Zweiten Weltkrieg*, Boppard am Rhein, 1975, pp. 96-161.

Münz, Rainer and Rainer Ohliger, 'Vergessene Deutsche – Erinnerte Deutsche: Flüchtlinge, Vertriebene, Aussiedler', *Transit: Europäische Revue* 15 (1998): pp. 141-157.

Naimark, Norman M., *Fires of Hatred. Ethnic Cleansing in Twentieth-Century Europe*, Cambridge, MA, 2001.

Neumann, Franz, *Der Block der Heimatvertriebenen und Entrechteten: Ein Beitrag zur Geschichte und Struktur einer politischen Interessenpartei*, Meisenheim, 1968.

Noelle, Elisabeth and Erich P. Neumann (eds), *Jahrbuch der öffentlichen Meinung, 1968-1973*, Allensbach, 1974.

Nuscheler, Franz, 'Das Jahrhundert der Flüchtlinge', in: Rainer Schulze, Doris Brelie-Lewien and Helga Grebing (eds), *Flüchtlinge und Vertriebene in der westdeutschen Nachkriegsgeschichte. Bilanzierung der Forschung und Perspektive für die künftige Forschungsarbeit*, Hildesheim, 1987, pp. 6-23.

Pentzopoulos, Dimitri, *The Balkan Exchange of Minorities and Its Impact Upon Greece*, Paris and The Hague, 1962.

Plato, Alexander von, 'Fremde Heimat. Zur Integration von Flüchtlingen und Einheimischen in die neue Zeit', in: Alexander von Plato and Lutz Niethammer (eds), '*Wir kriegen jetzt andere Zeiten'. Auf der Suche nach der Erfahrung des Volkes in nachfaschistischen Ländern. Lebensgeschichte und Sozialkultur im Ruhrgebiet*, Berlin and Bonn, 1985, pp. 172-219.

Salamone, Stephen, *In the Shadow of the Holy Mountain: The Genesis of a Rural Greek Community and Its Refugee Heritage*, New York, 1987.

Schildt, Axel, Detlef Siegfried and Christian Lammers (eds), *Dynamische Zeiten. Die 60er Jahre in den beiden deutschen Gesellschaften*, Hamburg, 2000.

Schoenberg, Hans W., *Germans from the East. A Study of Their Migration, Resettlement and Subsequent Group History since 1945*, The Hague, 1970.

Schraut, Sylvia, *Die Flüchtlingsaufnahme in Württemberg-Baden, 1945-1949. Amerikanische Besatzungsziele und demokratischer Wiederaufbau im Konflikt*, Munich, 1995.

Schulze, Rainer, 'Growing Discontent: Relations Between Native and Refugee Populations in a Rural District in Western Germany after the Second World War', in: Robert G. Moeller (ed.), *West Germany under Construction: Politics, Society, and Culture in the Adenauer Era*, Ann Arbor, MI, 1997, pp. 53-72.

Schütz, Hans, 'München – eine offene Frage', Schriftenreihe der Ackermann-Gemeinde, no. 12, 1958.

Simon, Albert Karl (ed.), *Rudolf Lodgman von Auen: Reden und Aufsätze*, Munich, n. d.

Steinert, Johannes-Dieter, *Vertriebenenverbände in Nordrhein-Westfalen, 1945-1954*, Düsseldorf, 1986.

Stöss, Richard, 'Der Gesamtdeutsche Block/BHE', in: Richard Stöss (ed.), *Parteien-Handbuch*, vol. I, Opladen, 1984, pp. 1424-1459.

Ther, Philipp, *Deutsche und polnische Vertriebene. Gesellschaft und Vertriebenenpolitik in der SBZ/DDR und in Polen 1945-1956*, Göttingen, 1998.

Volbrachtova, Libuse, 'Distinktions- und Integrationsschwierigkeiten der Sudetendeutschen beim Einlebensprozess', in: Sylvia Schraut and Thomas Grosser (eds), *Die Flüchtlingsfrage in der deutschen Nachkriegsgeschichte*, Mannheim, 1996, pp. 55-73.

Chapter 13

Do National Narratives Matter? Identity Formation among Portuguese Migrants in France and Germany

Andrea Klimt

In discussions of citizenship law and models of national membership, Germany and France have often been contrasted as representing opposite ends of the spectrum with profoundly different and historically entrenched traditions of national belonging.[1] The German system is traditionally cited as typifying the 'ethnic nation' where membership is defined along principles of descent and notions of inherent and homogeneous 'Germanness'. France, on the other hand, is thought to exemplify the 'civic nation' where membership is based on shared political allegiance and acquired cultural knowledge. Newcomers to Germany without provable connections to German bloodlines have by and large remained perpetual outsiders, regardless of their degree of cultural fluency or length of residence in Germany, whereas new arrivals in France have encountered fairly permeable borders and at least legally been incorporated into the nation. Becoming 'French' has long been an encouraged and expected transformation; becoming 'German' has until very recently been a logistically formidable process and ideologically difficult to imagine.[2]

Most comparative analyses of national belonging in France and Germany, as well as in other European states, draw primarily on the laws, political debates, and government policies around citizenship to fashion arguments about underlying models and historical trends in membership criteria. The impact of citizenship laws on residents in any particular polity is largely measured through naturalization figures and aggregate data on transnational movement. Evidence as to how legal frames of belonging shaped the lives and identities of actual people is often missing. The comparisons of citizenship law and ideologies of national membership have developed extremely useful frameworks and provocative insights, but, as this chapter argues, an in-depth understanding of the lived experiences of national belonging is a missing – and absolutely necessary – piece of the puzzle.

An ethnographic exploration of the ways in which different groups of people negotiate national boundaries, categories, and spaces will help ground discussions of future and possible alternative models of belonging in the priorities and concerns of actual people. Discussions of national belonging often ponder such questions as why recent reforms in German citizenship law have failed to elicit higher naturalization rates among one-time 'guestworkers', or what French citizenship actually means to recently naturalized migrants who opt for dual citizenship.[3] The pervasive reliance on macro-level data and the perspectives of political elites often leads to answers that miss the ways in which one-time migrants and their families construct their own meanings of home and belonging and have come to arrange their lives *across*, rather than within national spaces and categories. As Glick-Schiller, Basch and Blanc have pointed out, the consequence of not paying attention to how people actually organize and conceptualize their allegiances is that 'a concept of "transnationalism" has not developed in Europe that would allow students of migration and policy makers to respond to the fact that immigrants live their lives across national borders and respond to the constraints and demands of two or more states'.[4]

The aim of this inquiry is to compare French and German frames of national belonging – but from the bottom up. That is, how do relative newcomers to these two polities conceptualize who they are and where they 'belong'? Specifically, how have one-time 'guestworkers' and their descendents in France and Germany made sense of the hegemonic narratives and legal codes governing national belonging? And even more specifically, how has a particular national group, namely the Portuguese in France and Germany, constructed their identities and notions of home and organized their lives and communities within these two rather different contexts? How do Portuguese of various generations feel about becoming 'French' or 'German' or about staying 'Portuguese'? What decisions have they made regarding citizenship and legal forms of belonging? How do the forms of engagement with German society compare to those with French society? Have these two populations established similar forms of interconnectedness between their lives in France or Germany and their communities of origin? Reflections will focus on what we might learn from an ethnographic exploration of the complex and continually shifting interplay of the hegemonic narratives of belonging in France and Germany and the identity trajectories of their respective Portuguese populations.

The comparison between the Portuguese in France and Germany is based on key similarities in the history of Portuguese emigration to these two destinations. The migration to both countries is part of the same exodus to industrialized centres of Western Europe that occurred during the 1960s and 1970s. Migrants came from the same rural areas in Portugal and stem from approximately the same social backgrounds. Most importantly, migrants to both France and West Germany all left with the intention of returning to Portugal as soon as they had succeeded in financing a better life 'at home'. Going abroad was broadly conceived by participants in this migratory wave as a temporary sojourn and not as a permanent departure.[5] An important difference between the two populations is that the flow to France was significantly larger than to West Germany. Portuguese emigration to France has been estimated to total about one million, the current population in Germany is approximately 130,000.[6] State control over the influx of migrants was also markedly more stringent in Germany than in France. These differences will be considered at length in the following comparison of these two Portuguese populations.

As ideas and rules about national belonging obviously change over time, a central dimension in this analysis will be a diachronic consideration of how over the last several decades, Portuguese migrants and their descendents have negotiated the shifting – and some say, converging – forms of national belonging in France and Germany. The increasingly multicultural reality of the resident population in Germany has provoked heated arguments about who can and cannot be 'German' and citizenship law has moved – albeit very slowly and only against great resistance – towards a more flexible and permeable definition of national membership. The tremendous influx of immigrants into France has also provoked intense debate about who can and cannot be 'French' and created political pressure to shift citizenship law towards increased exclusivity. The movements in these definitions of national belonging are an important part of the following story.

Other relevant frames of belonging for the Portuguese in both France and Germany – namely, those of Europe and of Portugal – are also in flux. The emergent ideological and logistical importance of 'being European' is providing new options to Portuguese migrants and their descendents for negotiating national boundaries and spaces. The increasingly deterritorialized conceptualization of the Portuguese nation is also an extremely important factor, as it is becoming easier to officially remain 'Portuguese' even while residing long periods, or even permanently, outside the geographic bounds of the nation. The changing dynamics between being 'French', 'Portuguese', and 'European', and those between being 'German', 'Portuguese', and 'European' thus also constitute central themes in this exploration of identity formation.

This comparison is based on very different sources. The insights on the German situation emerge from my own long-term fieldwork in Hamburg, where I have been working with Portuguese families since 1984.[7] The material on the Portuguese in France is drawn from the work of other social scientists who sometimes did and sometimes did not ask the questions I am exploring in this chapter. The account of the dynamics in Germany thus obviously goes into greater depth and offers richer ethnographic detail. My understanding of the French situation is by necessity an analysis of multiple analyses and as a result contains gaps and unanswered questions. My hope is that despite the unevenness of the accounts, the comparison between these two national contexts will provide insights into the process of identity formation among minority populations. An analogous aim is to encourage comparative ethnographic collaborations in this area. Understandably enough, most of the comparative work to date has relied on quantitative and aggregate data, as qualitative research, with its emphasis on interpretation, context specificity, and long-term personal relationships, is certainly much harder to coordinate. The following analysis will hopefully make the benefits of such collaboration readily apparent.

The Portuguese in Germany

The Portuguese in Germany were, along with other southern European, Turkish, and Yugoslav migrants, first recruited to work in West Germany and other points in Western Europe in the mid-1960s and early 1970s to meet the growing demand for cheap and accommodating labour. The influx to Germany was centrally organized and tightly controlled. Recruitment centres in major Portuguese cities funneled workers to particular jobs in Germany and migrants were generally not able to follow family or fellow villagers to their destinations abroad. West German law carefully regulated migrants' movements and only spouses of migrants and their underage children were legally allowed to enter the country. Residence permits were time-limited and linked to employment and leaving West Germany, especially after the 1973 recruitment stop, for more than three months meant forfeiting the possibility of reentry. Consequently, migrants came to West Germany from many different regions of Portugal and did not establish any significant patterns of chain migration. Although some individuals successfully circumvented state regulations and were able to facilitate the recruitment of kin, or change residence and employment after their arrival, the concentrations of Portuguese in Germany were not tied to particular sending communities and did not reconstitute extended family or village connections in the migratory context. The Portuguese population in Hamburg where I did my fieldwork, for example, consisted of people from every region in Portugal, and migrant families, often the only ones from their village or town to have left for Hamburg, or even for Germany, tended to consist only of working parents and underage children.

Most everyone expected this migration to be temporary and circular. The Portuguese who went to Germany during this time planned to work abroad for a few years in order to build a better future for themselves and their children in Portugal. But as the well-known story goes, the few years stretched into what is now over three decades and the temporary 'guests' have become long-term established residents. Contrary to the initial expectations of both Germans and Portuguese, many migrants consolidated their families in Germany and by the time of my initial fieldwork in 1984-85, the population had evolved into one consisting primarily of young couples and their children. An increasingly institutionalized and visible community life also developed over the 1970s and 1980s, even though the population in Germany, totalling about 77,000 in 1984, made up only a scant three per cent of the total 'guestworker' population. Given their small number, the lack of concentration of the population in any one area of the city, and the relative absence of ethnic businesses, the Portuguese were largely invisible to most Germans.[8] Even in Hamburg where the Portuguese totalled about 6,000 or approximately six per cent of the non-German population, their presence was, outside of a few popular fish restaurants, not readily apparent to most people outside the migrant community.

None of the Portuguese migrants I interviewed in the mid-1980s had any intention of settling permanently in Germany or acquiring German citizenship despite their increasing entanglement with German society. Among the people I worked with during that time, everyone, without exception, adamantly maintained a commitment to returning 'home' to Portugal and actively defined their presence in Germany as ephemeral, even though most of them had already been abroad between 10 and 15 years. Their sense of self was firmly linked to an anticipated return and their resources and ambitions were all aimed at creating the perfect 'home' in Portugal.[9] During this time, construction sites and grand, if half-finished, houses dotted the Portuguese countryside – the concrete markers of the absentee owners' firm intention to return.

Arranging their dreamed-of future in Portugal turned out, however, to be much more difficult than many migrants had anticipated. Life in Germany was expensive, salaries did not stretch as far as they had expected, and new projects, such as the education of their children, continued to keep them in Germany. Remaining in Germany was, however, always cast as a postponement, never as a change of heart. Annual trips home, nostalgic stories of village life, photos of the dream home in Portugal on the coffee table in Hamburg, and a studied lack of investment in life in Germany served as markers to themselves and everyone else of the steadfastness of their commitment to a future in their Portuguese homeland. By the mid-1980s, the first generation of Portuguese migrants had spent the better part of their adult lives away from 'home' and the next generation had grown up abroad and was often more culturally fluent in Germany than 'at home' in Portugal. Yet all of them during this period, regardless of generation or degree of comfort in Germany, planned to eventually return and permanent settlement in Germany did not enter into any migrant's serious considerations.

By the 1990s, the consensus among social scientists and more left-leaning German politicians was that the migrant population had over time become *de facto* permanent residents. After almost three decades, many argued, non-German residents were firmly entrenched in German society and no longer had realistic options for making a life in their home societies. The oft-heard conclusion was that 'even though many [migrants] have the goal to return sometime, this goal becomes increasingly unlikely the longer they stay in Germany. For many of the families who have established themselves here, there are no possibilities left in the country of origin'.[10] Any asserted commitment to return was dismissed as myth, unrealistic dream, or misguided illusion and the term *Heimkehrillusion*, or 'illusion of returning home', was quite prominent in German sociological literature and political position papers.

While this argument was politically quite important in pushing the state to acknowledge and take responsibility for Germany's multicultural reality, permanent settlement in Germany and the disappearance of options in Portugal did not accurately reflect the prevalent trajectory among Portuguese migrants and their newly adult children. The hopes of most of the first generation of Portuguese migrants I interviewed again on repeated visits in the 1990s, *still* focused on returning 'home' and on ensuring their economic survival in Portugal – and not on settling permanently in Germany. The timing of their planned departure from Germany had, however, shifted from earlier envisioned trajectories and first-generation migrants, most of whom were in their fifties, were planning to return only after they became eligible for their German pensions. As one woman told me, 'I've stood it so long, I might as well wait a few more years'. Many were also being forced into early retirement as the wide-spread trend of automating industrial production had led to the laying off of many older migrants. In any case, the migrants of this generation were carefully calculating their financial futures before realizing their return, as the cost of living in Portugal had risen substantially and accumulated savings were no longer adequate for retirement.

The intentions of the second generation in Hamburg were for obvious reasons much more complicated and conflicted. Many second-generation Portuguese had grown up with strong parental expectations that they too would eventually return to Portugal. Now that they were adults and beginning to establish families of their own, they were faced with actually making the decision for themselves as to where to situate their lives and anchor their identities. Many of this generation were experimenting with arenas of belonging and finding creative ways to avoid making a definitive choice between national spaces.

Most second-generation Portuguese in the population I worked with rejected the idea of integrating themselves permanently into German society. While most were fluent in German, had successfully established a career track, and developed a social niche in Hamburg, they had no interest in making a permanent commitment to Germany. They rejected this possibility even though most had many more friends and connections in Hamburg, where they had grown up, than in Portugal, which they primarily had known as vacation visitors. In conversations with young adults during my last visit in 1997, it became apparent that the possibility of acquiring German citizenship still held little appeal and most continued to consider 'becoming German' a distasteful prospect. Despite the easier access to German citizenship, most felt that Germans would, regardless of the colour of their passport, continue to regard them as foreigners. As the acquisition of German citizenship required the relinquishing of Portuguese citizenship, most Portuguese also considered changing nationality akin to treason and indicative of a lack of self-respect. Despite significant liberalizations in German citizenship law, the naturalization rate in 1997 was still at a very low 1.13 per cent of the total foreign resident population.[11] The Portuguese had still lower naturalization rates than the lowest rate noted in official reports, that of Greeks at 0.1 per cent of the resident population. Most Portuguese migrants and their descendents expected Portugal to continue being the state through which they received the benefits of national membership and even the most politically active of this generation were primarily concerned with engaging Portuguese politics and encouraging the Portuguese state to tend to its deterritorialized population, than with participating in German politics and arguing for a recognized place within the German polity. The rhetorical commitment to return was central in their assertions of continued Portugueseness even though when and exactly under what circumstances they would actually leave Germany usually remained quite vague. 'When I've finished my apprenticeship', 'after I've got my degree', or, in words reminiscent of people in their parents' generation, 'after we've finished building our house in Portugal' – were all frequently heard refrains from second-generation Portuguese.

A common way in the 1990s for second-generation Portuguese to organize their lives across national arenas was to maintain what some referred to as 'geographic flexibility'. They, like their parents, aspired to social mobility but did so in different ways. Whereas their parents envisioned becoming members of the bourgeoisie in their natal villages, many of the second-generation imagined using their German education to find good jobs in urban Portugal. One father who described his daughter as tied to the cultures of two countries, explained how her choice of career kept her 'geographic options' open. She was planning to become a math teacher rather than a social worker, because math was the same thing in Portugal and in Germany, whereas social work was tied to nationally specific programmes and laws. Another way to realize this 'geographic flexibility' was for second-generation Portuguese to acquire positions in either Portuguese firms doing business in Germany or in German firms with subsidiaries or plants in Portugal. One young couple I knew, for example, had accepted a three-year contract with a German company to work in their Lisbon office because they wanted to 'try out' what it was like to actually live in Portugal. Others' decisions of how to balance the Portuguese and German arenas of their lives were shaped primarily by family contingencies. One young woman who had already returned to Portugal to marry a man near her parents' village, had returned again to Germany after the birth of her second child. Her parents were still in Germany and she needed her mother's help with childcare and her husband wanted to find a higher paying job than he was able to secure in Portugal.[12]

Even the few people I knew who admitted to wanting to stay in Germany kept open the possibility of someday returning to Portugal. Some said they would eventually go to work in Portugal 'to see what it was like', while others were more pragmatic and said that if things did not turn out in Germany the way they hoped, they could always return to Portugal. As one young woman explained to me, for example, if she did not get into the University of Hamburg she could always go to the University of Coimbra. The small number of Portuguese of this generation who had definitively relinquished the idea of a permanent return were, by and large, married to non-Portuguese. Their version of 'geographic flexibility' was to continue the tradition of annual vacations in Portugal – but to locate their permanent 'homes' in Germany.

The question of 'identity' remained a conundrum for many second and third generation Portuguese and when asked directly, it often produced discomfort and confusion. As the following, rather meandering, comment by a young Portuguese born in Hamburg illustrates, the construction of belonging is an on-going and rather doubt-ridden process:

> Well, I certainly don't feel German. ... In first place, I feel as ... as ... yes, I am Hamburger. In second place, no, ah, parallel to being Hamburger, I'm Portuguese. I know – I'm Portuguese. But if someone asked me 'Where do you come from?' I wouldn't say 'I come from Lisbon or Guarda'. I would say, 'I come from Hamburg'. And that would settle the matter. So, I feel myself to be a Hamburger, I feel myself to be Portuguese, and as a kind of overarching feeling I have something like Europe. I feel I belong to Portugal, but not so much that I would go to war for the Portuguese. So, I guess in the extreme situation, I'm not Portuguese... Yes, that's so. So that is a statelessness... Well statelessness is wrong. I have, well, legally I'm naturally according to my passport, I'm Portuguese. So, according to that I know, aha, 'You are Portuguese'. ... Nowhere in the world would I say, 'I am German'. I would just always say 'I'm a Hamburger', or I would say, 'I'm a European'. Ah,... European is also kind of stupid....[13]

Nothing for this generation quite fits all the time. Being 'Portuguese' was certainly affectively relevant, but did not cover extreme commitments such as going to war or the daily reality of living in Germany. Being 'German' in any case was tainted and undesirable. As another young member of the second generation who culturally and physically could have easily 'passed' as German, told me, she would never get a German passport because, 'If somebody like Hitler ever comes again, I want to be sure I can leave quickly'. Being 'European' mitigated the pressure to reconcile geographic residence and national membership, but was at times too distant and abstract a concept. More localized city or regional identities, such as 'Hamburger' reflected daily life and could be distinguished from the negativity of 'Germanness', but in some instances was too circumscribed and local.

To emphasize their continued rejection of permanence in Germany is not to say the Portuguese refrained from establishing themselves in Germany. People certainly had full lives in Germany. In Hamburg, Portuguese community associations were numerous and active and people lived fairly comfortably, had friends, and engaged in leisure activities. Young people got married, had families, made friends, pursued careers, had fun, etc. But many aspects of their lives spanned the borders of Germany and Portugal and did not fit neatly inside of one or the other national space. Through annual vacations in the natal village, almost daily communication via phone, frequent visits back and forth, exchange of video recordings of daily life, etc., the Portuguese in Germany continually maintained and created connections between the multiple sites of their lives. The significantly improved and more affordable modes of transportation and communication have, as is the case for many groups of migrants around the globe, made it progressively easier for the Portuguese in Germany and France to maintain connections across geographical distance.[14]

Negotiating the options in both national spaces was how the Portuguese made the best of their vulnerable position in both national economies. Over the years the periodic recessions and retrenchments of the German economy have undermined the ability of the Portuguese to get and keep well paying jobs. Recent trends in Germany to automate production and downsize the labour force had hit older Portuguese workers especially hard and created a much more competitive job market for younger workers. Keeping their options open in Portugal was thus a necessary balance to the uncertainties of the German labour market, whether it was through negotiating an early retirement, opening a family business at 'home', or finding a job in Portugal's service and professional sector. Life in Portugal had, on the other hand, become increasingly expensive and savings earned in Germany no longer guaranteed economic security in Portugal. The availability of well-paying white-collar jobs had also not kept pace with the rise in cost of living and especially members of the second generation could not be certain of getting the kinds of jobs in Portugal that they had been trained to do in Germany. Maintaining a transnational way of life was thus a way for the Portuguese in Germany to hedge their bets and increase their chances of being able to make a decent living.

While many aspects of life were transnational, primary allegiance and final commitment were still firmly linked to 'being Portuguese'. What the Portuguese in Germany generally did not do, for example, was to buy family homes or get buried in Germany. None of the people I knew declared Germany to be their primary home, identified with 'being German', or elected to take on German citizenship. Whether or not the return 'home' was a realistic option, it had remained a central theme in how the Portuguese in Germany organized their lives and defined their sense of self.

German Frames of National Belonging

Hegemonic definitions of Germanness have made it very difficult for Portuguese migrants to imagine becoming part of the German nation. During the first two decades after the initial arrival of the 'guestworkers', descent remained the ideological and legally encoded underpinning of German national belonging.[15] 'Being' German was defined as an innate and inherited quality and ethnic non-Germans understood they could never really 'become' German. Many migrants explained that even the acquisition of German citizenship would never change their status as perpetual foreigners.[16] Political debate focused on 'foreigners' and never on 'immigrants' and while there was increasing discussion about the need to 'integrate' non-Germans and recognize the *de facto* multiculturalism of German society over the 1970s and 1980s, even the most progressive arguments stopped short of pushing for the full incorporation of cultural difference into the German polity.[17] The voices from the left that argued for the equitable incorporation of long-term foreign residents into German society continued to designate ethnic non-Germans, regardless of citizenship or fluency in German culture, as distinct and different from 'real' Germans. The term frequently used in the 1980s of *ausländische Mitbürger*, or 'foreign co-citizens', for example, was meant to designate inclusion, but ironically enough illustrated the ideological impermeability of Germanness.[18] Government policy during this period aimed to maintain the temporary and liminal status of migrant workers and steadfastly refused to acknowledge Germany's transformation into an 'immigration country'. German citizenship was difficult and expensive to acquire, there were no provisions for the acquisition of citizenship for those born within Germany, and criteria included, among other things, a 15 year residency period and a 'positive attitude toward German culture'.[19] Although efforts were made in 1977 to clarify the guidelines for citizenship, 'only those who had attained a very high degree of cultural integration could hope to be successful in their applications'.[20] Naturalization rates during this period were extremely low and by 1985 were still under 3 per cent of the resident foreigner population.[21] There were some attempts to regularize the status of long-term 'guestworkers', but legal measures were primarily intended to restrict entry and encourage permanent repatriation.[22] During the mid-1980s, for example, policies aggressively encouraged migrant repatriation through offers of cash pay-outs of pension contributions for those Portuguese (and Turkish) migrants who agreed to permanently leave Germany. About a quarter of the Portuguese population did in fact take advantage of this programme and left for Portugal during this time.[23] For those who stayed the message was quite clear that national membership was reserved for those born German.

By the 1990s, Germany's definitions of national membership had finally, after intense political debate, begun to open up and move away from exclusively ethnocultural parameters.[24] Revisions in German citizenship law introduced in 1990 made naturalization significantly easier for second and third generation descendents of the original 'guestworkers' as well as for older immigrants with at least 15 years residence. Administrative charges were reduced and further amendments in 1993 reduced the residency requirement to eight years, removed 'the need to positively demonstrate a deep loyal attachment to "German culture"', and permanently established naturalization as a right that, given fulfillment of listed criteria, could not be refused.[25] Recent amendments in 1999 introduced for the first time principles of *ius soli* and represent 'a seismic shift in German citizenship law and a firm change of direction away from its previous ethnocultural emphasis'.[26] For the first time, children born in Germany of non-German parents will automatically receive German citizenship if at least one parent fulfills certain residency requirements. Children of resident foreigners with dual citizenship are required to choose a single nationality by the age of 23 and to relinquish their other citizenship in order to retain their German citizenship.[27]

Dual citizenship is allowed in exceptional cases and estimates of naturalizations that tolerate dual citizenship are over 20 per cent.[28] Some scholars, however, note that the 'very fact that dual citizenships remain formally rejected raises perhaps the strongest doubt ... over the capability of the new provisions to deliver results in terms of higher naturalization rates'.[29] It is still too soon to assess the impact of the 1999 revisions in German citizenship law, but to date most Portuguese resident foreigners considered relinquishing their Portuguese citizenship too high a price to pay for official membership in the German polity.

The Portuguese in France

Much like their compatriots who left for Germany, the Portuguese who went to France in the 1960s and 1970s went with the intention of returning to Portugal as soon as possible. Like the migrants in Germany, they were impoverished peasants primarily from rural regions of Portugal who hoped to finance social mobility and a better life 'back home' through several years of work abroad. France was the primary destination for Portuguese migrants during this time, with approximately 760,000 having arrived in French urban centres by 1982. By 1990, there were officially 645,578 Portuguese migrants in France, making them the largest single group of new arrivals in the country.[30] Governmental control of this influx, both on the Portuguese and French side, was very weak and a particular characteristic of this migratory wave was its extremely high rate of illegality.

Clandestine entries are estimated at about 50 per cent and included large numbers of political exilees and people avoiding the military draft during Portugal's colonial wars.[31] Because of the lack of state control, migrants tended to follow and depend upon family, friends, and village acquaintances and were not, as was the case in Germany, recruited and screened by official employment agencies for pre-arranged jobs. The Portuguese population in France thus tended to be geographically extremely concentrated, with about 45.5 per cent of the Portuguese living in the region of Île-de-France, especially in Paris and the surrounding poorer neighborhoods. The large migrant communities were tightly linked to particular sending communities in Portugal and built around social connections that had already been established in Portugal. Because of the high rate of illegal entry, the Portuguese in France also tended to be less skilled and have less education than those who went to Germany and other destinations in Western Europe.[32]

The first generation of Portuguese migrants in France, much like their compatriots in Germany, focused their energies on creating the dream home in Portugal, both as the practical anchor for their future and strong symbolic assertion of their continued commitment to return 'home'. Annual vacations in natal villages, patterns of substantial remittances, and frequent communication with friends and family in Portugal became, as it did for compatriots in Germany, a regular part of life for migrants in France. Family and community interaction spanned national spaces and the now almost four decades in France have definitely not led to the disappearance of connections with Portugal.[33] Researchers have emphasized the double affiliation and transnational way of life of most Portuguese in France.[34] Return visits, some estimate, are more frequent than during the early stages of this migratory wave, connections with family in Portugal are actively maintained, and the preferred site of marriages and funerals is still in Portugal. 'Families are habituated to living in two countries: they come and they go'.[35] The commitment to return has evolved into a transnational web of connections and identities that permit them to 'maintain ties with both countries and profit from what is favourable in both contexts'.[36]

The Portuguese in France have, however, established a different kind of balance between the multiple arenas of their lives than have their compatriots in Germany. 'Luso-French', as they are widely referred to, are bi-national and bi-cultural and most observers concur that the Portuguese are moving towards permanent settlement in France. Just the use of the term 'Luso-French' highlights the complete absence of an equivalent term on the German scene. Second and third generation descendents, as many social scientists observe, 'love Portugal, but it's in France that they live and it's there they have strong roots'.[37] 'Portugal is the country of vacations where the young enjoy good times in a warm atmosphere, ... But the possibility of living there that had been constantly evoked by their parents, is waning over the last several years'.[38] Portugal, for many, is an important symbolic space, a place where affective relationships and a sense of self are renewed and some Luso-French pursue strategies of 'geographic flexibility' similar to their compatriots in Germany. But the majority of the Portuguese in France, especially amongst the young, are not committed to a concrete project of return.[39] Citing current underdevelopment in Portugal, especially compared to the relative economic prosperity and higher standard of living in France, the majority of young Luso-descendents assert their desire to stay in France.[40] Reservations about permanent return were also social and cultural in nature as French and Portuguese ways of life intertwined in immigrant families. Women, for example, tended to regard a permanent return to Portugal much less favourably than did men because of the traditional gender roles still prevalent in Portugal.[41] In contrast to the trends in Germany, the house in Portugal that was constructed as the future family home has been transformed into a summer vacation house and it was becoming more commonplace for the Portuguese to buy homes and invest in family businesses in France.[42] Although the older generation was reluctant to admit they might not return 'home', the younger generation did not invest the house in Portugal with the same associations of rootedness.[43] In contrast to the continued rhetoric of return prevalent in Germany, the primary site of settlement, especially for subsequent generations of young Portuguese has definitely become France.

French Frames of National Belonging

The options for national membership in France and Germany are quite different and have led to notably different choices among migrant populations. In France, the acquisition of French citizenship is encouraged and in many ways expected. All individuals born in France of foreign parents and who have continued to live there, automatically acquire French citizenship when they turn 18 unless they express the wish to not do so.[44] The acquisition of citizenship for foreign-born residents is also relatively easy. French law encourages and facilitates the legalization of undocumented residents which resulted in the legalization of over 100,000 Portuguese between 1974 and 1982.[45] As of 1982, it became possible to have dual citizenship as Portugal changed its legal code to allow emigrants to retain their Portuguese citizenship even if they acquired the citizenship of their country of residence. Estimates are that over half of Luso-descendents in France opt for dual citizenship.[46] As one young woman explained, if acquiring French citizenship entailed giving up her Portuguese citizenship, she would opt for staying Portuguese 'because it's logical and I love my village and my house for vacations. I wouldn't want to hear, "You aren't Portuguese any more because you're French"'.[47] The Portuguese are second only to Moroccans in naturalization rates, with 52,280 Portuguese taking on French citizenship in 1990, 68,300 in 1982, and 35,700 in 1975.[48] Even before dual citizenship was an option, large numbers of Portuguese were choosing to take on French citizenship and the numbers of Portuguese who opted for French citizenship was larger than those who acquired French citizenship automatically. Although motive is always hard to infer, these choices seem to indicate migrants' desire to make a long-term commitment to living in France and participating in French society.[49] Although naturalization did not, as one researcher noted, cause people to become less connected with their ethnic community in France, renounce relations with Portugal, or automatically lead to greater degrees of social integration or political participation in France, legally at least, a large portion of Portuguese migrants and their descendents are officially French and benefited from the protections of citizenship.[50] They did not have to worry about whether changes in the political atmosphere would lead to changes in their right to remain in France. The contrast with Germany, where dual citizenship is usually not accepted and where hardly any of the Portuguese, regardless of generation, have opted for German citizenship, is striking.

Identification with 'being French' also follows markedly different trends from how Portuguese migrants felt about 'being German'. Studies repeatedly document the bi-cultural identities of Luso-descendents in France. Although it was sometimes difficult to discern from the various accounts, being French, in conjunction with being Portuguese, was simply a way for Luso-descendents to describe the intertwined realities of their lives. One researcher noted that children who had difficulty choosing between French and Portuguese identities, did not feel completely or exclusively French or Portuguese, and most frequently chose both.[51] Despite the strongly assimilationist model prevalent in France that explicitly did not nurture multicultural images of the nation, Portuguese immigrants who have grown up and come of age in France assert their affinities to *both* cultures.[52] Ambivalence noted among young Luso-French about being Portuguese was primarily due to its associations with lower class status and lack of education. It was not that they did not want to be seen as Portuguese, but they did not want to be seen as children of working class immigrants and tried to find more middle-class ways of being 'Portuguese'.[53]

In contrast to the attitudes of Luso-descendents in Germany towards 'Germanness', 'Frenchness' was not a tainted or disdained identity and researchers found that Portuguese migrants, unlike ex-colonial subjects, did not talk of France or of being French in a negative manner.[54] They considered themselves to be more favourably regarded by the French than other immigrant groups and less subject to xenophobia and racism. I could find no cases that communicated as much discomfort with 'being French' as the young man in Hamburg who so adamantly rejected the label of German. One social scientist noted that 'as there aren't major conflicts with French society, they are able to live their mixed identity without ruptures or obvious contradictions'.[55] Most young Luso descendents in France asserted their commitment to a continued Portugueseness, but did not perceive that that identity contradicted the possibility of their being 'French' as well.

Much has been made of the ideology of return among all the Portuguese who left for Western Europe. Amongst those in France, there is evidence that it is beginning to wane, especially among the second and third generations of Luso-descendents, who were developing ways of negotiating the possibilities available in both national spheres rather than assuming they must make a permanent and mutually exclusive commitment. But Luso-descendents in France declared permanent return a distant and unrealistic option and asserted France as their primary home to a much greater extent than did their peers in Germany. Relinquishing or at least being much less engaged with the commitment to return did not seem to threaten claims to a continued 'Portugueseness' among Luso-descendents in France. Second-generation Portuguese in Germany, on the other hand, continued to give primacy to the ultimate return to Portugal, even if the plans around that eventuality often remained quite vague. Portugal was still the ultimate home and crucial to their assertions of 'Portugueseness' and life in Germany remained framed as temporary and conditional.

European Contexts

Notions of 'Europe' did not enter into most people's sense of belonging or shape the ways they inhabited transnational spaces during the 1970s and 1980s. Although Portugal was officially accepted into the European Community in 1986, the changes that would most impact the Portuguese in Germany or France, such as the free movement across inter-European borders and the coordination of social benefits, did not come into effect until 1992. Before then, being 'European' was, for most migrants, an irrelevant concept. When Portuguese migrants did speculate on how this as yet unfamiliar entity would affect their lives, it was with trepidation. In Germany, their main fear was that Europe-wide coordination of social benefits would limit their ability to trade pension contributions into available cash. The possibility of a less oppositional stance between European national spaces was too remote a scenario to even imagine. Everything in the migrants' experience to date made clear that once they had left for home there would be no going back. The decision to return to Portugal was thus weighed very carefully and frequently postponed in order to better secure the future they envisioned for themselves and their children.

With Portugal's full incorporation into the European Union in 1992, however, new ways opened up for Portuguese migrants to configure their identities and arrange their families and communities across national spaces. Some analysts argue that this cycle of migration is qualitatively different than that of earlier periods because of the politically different conditions in which it is taking place.[56] As 'Europeans', Portuguese migrants are now able to move with relative freedom across national borders, which previously had been tightly regulated. The numbers of Portuguese in Germany increased significantly from 77,000 in 1985 to over 133,000 in 1998, as many people who had returned to Portugal in earlier years, as well as many first time migrants, took advantage of the open borders. Changes in migration to France are more difficult to ascertain, as border crossings are not regulated and the Portuguese who acquired French citizenship are no longer counted as Portuguese. Access to social benefits is also becoming increasingly standardized across the EU. Of special interest to the Portuguese is that their pensions include contributions made from anywhere in Europe and can be received regardless of place of residence. They are also able to vote for the European Parliament, although for most Portuguese migrants this mode of political representation seemed rather remote.

The increasing reality of 'Europe' has mitigated the rigid divide between staying abroad and returning to Portugal, reduced the pressure to definitively decide between national spaces, and greatly facilitated the ability of Portuguese migrants and their descendents to maintain and intensify their transnational way of life. Staying and returning are no longer such irreversible or mutually exclusive decisions and it was becoming possible for migrants to organize their lives more fluidly across national spaces and integrate the multiple localities of their identities and communities. 'Being European' has also given the Portuguese of all generations a new way to diffuse the tension between their continued stay abroad and their commitment to staying 'Portuguese' and it is becoming increasingly commonplace for 'Europeans' to live in one national space while 'belonging' to another. The Portuguese can remain in Germany, France, or any other EU country without calling their commitment to being Portuguese into question.

Becoming officially European has had a much greater impact on the Portuguese in Germany than those residing in France. In Germany, the rights associated with European citizenship have opened up previously unavailable options and greatly facilitated the navigation of transnational spaces. As 'Europeans', they can continue to live and work, cross international borders at will, and receive social benefits – all without the benefits of German citizenship. What they cannot do as Portuguese Europeans in Germany is participate in national level politics or gain official representation within the polity. Their Europeanness, while making transnational life easier to realize has, ironically enough, also reduced the pressure to resolve their political disenfranchisement within Germany. For the Portuguese in France, however, the access to dual citizenship has long made transnational ways of life relatively easy to realize. As citizens of both France and Portugal, migrants and their descendents did not have restrictions placed on their ability to cross national borders, secure work in either national space, or reunite their families. They also had access to the political process in both countries and could appeal as citizens to both nations. Becoming 'European' was thus in many ways redundant and did not open up dramatically new possibilities for the Portuguese in France.

Shared Contexts: Portugal

The circularity of the migrants' journey to countries in Western Europe was actively nurtured by various sectors of Portuguese society. The borders migrants had to negotiate in leaving and returning to Portugal have long been ideologically and physically quite porous and leaving one's homeland in search of a better life is a very familiar trajectory for most people in Portugal.[57] About one third of Portugal's nine million people live outside the national borders in various corners of the globe and migrant remittances constitute a significant portion of the national economy.[58] After the loss of its colonies in 1975, Portugal 'began to incorporate the Portuguese immigrants spread across the world in the imagining of an (unbounded) nation based on population rather than territory'.[59] Leaving with the intent to return and maintaining an allegiance to Portugal while residing for long periods of time outside the country have been actively encouraged by both state and private institutions in Portugal. Portuguese banks, for example, facilitate the transfer of remittances and offer special interest rates to migrants. The Portuguese Catholic Church actively cultivated migrant congregations abroad and in Hamburg for example, the Portuguese priest nurtured and frequently underscored the commitment of his flock to returning 'home'. The state supported Portuguese language schools and training programmes for migrant children in order to encourage a continued sense of Portugueseness and to facilitate their return to Portugal. Migrants are also encouraged to participate in Portuguese elections, have representation as migrants in the Portuguese political process, and are allowed to hold dual citizenship. For the Portuguese in Germany and France, it was thus not odd or idiosyncratic to imagine being part of the Portuguese nation even after decades of not residing on Portuguese soil. The increasing deterritorialization of Portugueseness thus dovetails with the increasing relevance of being officially European. Together these developments loosen the connection between geographic residence and national belonging and enable migrants and their descendents to continue thinking of themselves as 'Portuguese' while establishing their families and communities in countries other than Portugal.

Divergent Trajectories

The Portuguese populations in France and Germany have developed families, communities, and personal trajectories that span national spaces. Several shared dynamics have facilitated the transnational way of life they have developed over the past four decades including the increasing relevance of 'being European', the emerging transnational definitions of 'Portugueseness', and the growing ease of communication and travel across time and space. The ways in which these migrant populations have negotiated the frames of national belonging have, however, clearly diverged.

Differences in citizenship law and controversies about the nature of membership in the national polity have clearly contributed to the divergence in how the Portuguese in France and Germany balance the multiple arenas of their lives. A German passport would not, at least in the minds of most Portuguese migrants, have fully legitimized their membership in the German nation. In their rejection of what they understood they could not have anyway, migrants adamantly asserted their commitment to staying Portuguese and eventually returning 'home' and frequently invoked the tainted and indelible memories of Germany's xenophobic past to underscore their disinterest in German citizenship. Many analysts of the French situation have focused on the continued insularity of Portuguese ethnic enclaves and lack of integration with the 'real' French, but the fact remains that being legally 'French' has provided an identity and legitimate place for the Portuguese within French society. The readily available legal option of staying 'Portuguese' has certainly helped make the process of becoming 'French' more appealing to people already entrenched in a transnational way of life. The possibility of continuing to officially remain 'Portuguese', has also made it easier for Luso-French to resist assimilationist expectations and assert their own more multicultural understandings of 'being French'.

Differences in the migration patterns of Portuguese to France and Germany and the resulting nature of the migrant communities have also helped shape these populations' divergent trajectories. In Germany, the small Portuguese communities do not offer a visible and all-encompassing environment complete with ethnic businesses, institutions, or social networks with extended kin and fellow villagers, whereas in France, the Portuguese migrant communities are large, institutionally complete, and include relationships already established in Portugal. The consequences are several. The small size of the Portuguese communities and their scattered location across different regions of Germany meant that 'broker' positions – such as teaching, social work and political organizing – that might have been open to the bi-cultural and better educated second and third generations of Portuguese, were much fewer and more difficult to realize in Germany than in France. Similarly, options for opening ethnic businesses were more constrained in Germany. Since leaving Germany was an irrevocable decision before the era of more open European borders, return was of necessity conceptualized as a permanent move. For Portuguese migrant families in France, patterns of chain migration that reunited extended families and the permeability of the border between France and Portugal meant that permanent return did not become established as the only way to meet familial obligations.

The well-established transnational way of life of the Portuguese in both France and Germany clearly shows that families, communities and individual trajectories can be anchored in multiple arenas. Neither population is on their way to making a single national space coincide with the actual spaces in which they live their lives. In France, the option of dual citizenship along with ready legal incorporation of newcomers have served as means of reconciling the complexities of geographic residence with those of national allegiance. Germany, on the other hand, is attempting to incorporate its newcomers through mutually exclusive definitions of membership. It remains to be seen as to whether future forms of national belonging will help ensure that people whose lives span national borders will not be relegated to perpetual marginality and disenfranchisement.

Notes

1 Brubaker, *Citizenship and Nationhood in France and Germany.*

2 Green, 'Beyond Ethnoculturalism?'; Hagedorn, 'Falling Borders'.

3 Hagedorn, 'Falling Borders'.

4 Glick-Schiller, Basch and Szanton Blanc, 'From Immigrant to Transmigrant', p. 85.

5 Brettell, 'The Emigrant, the Nation, and the State in Nineteenth and Twentieth Century Portugal'; Klimt, 'Temporary' and 'Permanent' Lives; Klimt, 'Home and Belonging'.

6 Baganha, 'Migrações internacionais de e para Portugal'; Klimt, 'Home and Belonging'. Given the high rate of illegality, it is very difficult to get precise figures on Portuguese emigration to France.

7 I conducted fieldwork in Hamburg, Germany for two years in 1984/85 and follow-up research in 1992 and 1997. Research was funded through a Fulbright dissertation grant and a research grant from the Center for Portuguese Studies and Culture at the University of Massachusetts, Dartmouth.

8 Prior to Portugal's acquisition of full membership in the European Community in 1992, restrictions on foreign ownership made it difficult for migrants to own and operate businesses in Germany.

9 Klimt, 'Returning Home'; Klimt, *'Temporary' and 'Permanent' Lives.*

10 Institut für Zukunftsforschung, *Ausländer oder Deutsche*, p. 15.

11 Federal Government's Commissioner for Foreigners' Issues, *Facts and Figures.*

12 Most Portuguese people did not register their return with the German authorities in case they wanted to come back at a later date. The population figures, which are based on residence records, are thus somewhat inflated.

13 Heuer, 'Saudades Am Tor Zur Welt', p. 140.

14 Foner, 'What's New About Transnationalism'; Goldring, 'Power and Status in Transnational Social Spaces'; Mountz and Wright, 'Daily Life in the Transnational Migrant Community of San Agustin'.

15 Brubaker, *Citizenship and Nationhood in France and Germany*; Fijalkowski, 'Incorporating Immigrants and Expanding Citizenship'.

16 White, 'Turks in the New Germany'.

17 Dittgen, 'Volk Nation or Nation of Immigrants?'; Kvistad, 'Membership without Politics?'.

18 Mandel, 'Turkish Headscarves and the "Foreigner Problem"'; White, 'Turks in the New Germany'.

19 Kvistad, 'Membership without Politics?', p. 150. Prior to the reforms of the 1990s, naturalization criteria also included: 'adequate accommodations; a good reputation; the capability to make a living for self and dependents without reliance on welfare; spoken and written German-language fluency; a "voluntary attachment" to Germany; a basic knowledge of Germany's political and social structures; no criminal record; and a positive commitment to the Federal Republic's "free democratic basic order"', ibid. Whether a particular person met these criteria was subject to the discretion of local bureaucrats and there was considerable regional variation in how they were applied.

[20] Green, 'Beyond Ethnoculturalism?', p. 106.

[21] Federal Commissioner for Foreigners' Affairs, *Facts and Figures.*

[22] Barbieri, *Ethics of Citizenship: Immigration and Group Rights in Germany.*

[23] The Portuguese population in Germany dropped from 99,500 in 1983 to 77,000 in 1985 largely as a result of this incentive package.

[24] Green, 'Beyond Ethnoculturalism?'; Hagedorn, 'Falling Borders: Liberal Trends in German Citizenship Politics'; Marshall, 'Turkish Headscarves and the "Foreigner Problem"'.

[25] Green, 'Beyond Ethnoculturalism?', p. 151; Kvistad, 'Membership without Politics?'.

[26] Green, 'Beyond Ethnoculturalism?', p. 114.

[27] Ibid.

[28] Federal Commissioner for Foreigners' Affairs, *Facts and Figures*. Dual citizenship was usually granted to people who could not obtain an official release from their prior nationality, which led to very different rates among different nationalities.

[29] Green, 'Beyond Ethnoculturalism?', p. 117.

[30] Population figures have gone down slightly, but this may be misleading as census figures do not include those Portuguese who have acquired French citizenship or who hold dual citizenship.

[31] Carreira and Tomé, *Portugais et Luso-français*. Some estimates of the numbers escaping the Portuguese military draft are as high as 180,000. The people in this group did not have the same ambitions to return to Portugal as they could not return until after the Salazar's regime fell. They tended to integrate much more quickly into French society, have higher rates of intermarriage, and be more active and left-leaning in their politics. The presence of this group gave the Portuguese community a different quality than the other migrant communities in Europe.

[32] See Barre, *Jeunes d'origine portugaise en association*; Carreira and Tomé, *Portugais et Luso-français*; Koven, *French-Portuguese Bilingual's Enactments of Self in Two Languages*; Leandro, *Au-delà des apparences*; Schor, *Histoire de l'immigration en France*; and Tribalat, *Histoire de L'immigration en France*; for analyses of Portuguese immigrant communities in France and French immigration policies.

[33] Carreira and Tomé, *Portugais et Luso-français*; Leandro, *Au-delà des apparences*.

[34] Leandro, *Au-delà des apparences*, p. 323.

[35] Carreira and Tomé, *Portugais et Luso-français,* p. 97.

[36] Ibid., p. 97.

[37] Ibid., p. 90.

[38] Cunha, *Portugais de France*, p. 64.

[39] Carreira and Tomé, *Portugais et Luso-français*, p. 23.

[40] Leandro, *Au-delà des apparences*, p. 286.

[41] Carreira and Tomé, *Portugais et Luso-français*, p. 103.

[42] Leandro, *Au-Delà des apparences*, p. 323. After 1980, the Portuguese government allowed migrants to have accounts in Portuguese banks in the currency of the country where they were working and to transfer back the money in the same currency. The intent was to stimulate the sending of remittances to Portugal. In fact, it made it easier to use savings in Portugal for purchases of homes or start up of a small business in France easier and the Portuguese invested more and more in the improvement of their lives in France.

[43] Carreira and Tomé, *Portugais et Luso-français*, p. 107.

[44] Leandro, *Au-delà des apparences*, p. 37.

[45] Ibid., p. 39.

[46] Ibid., p. 291.

[47] Tomé and Carreira, *Portugais et Luso-français*, p. 56.

48 Carreira and Tomé, *Portugais et Luso-français*, p. 86.
49 Leandro, *Au-delà des apparences*, p. 38.
50 Ibid., p. 291.
51 In an interview, 91 per cent responded yes to the question 'I am French and Portuguese'; 64 per cent responded yes to 'I am French'; and 95 per cent responded yes to 'I am Portuguese', Carreira and Tomé, *Portugais et Luso-français*.
52 Bleich, 'Re-Imagined Communities?'.
53 Koven, *French-Portuguese Bilingual's Enactments of Self in Two Languages*.
54 Carreira and Tomé, *Portugais et Luso-français*, p. 170; Cunha, *Portugais de France*, p. 55.
55 Cunha, *Portugais de France*, p. 59.
56 Baganha, 'Migrações internacionais de e para Portugal', p. 248.
57 Brettell, 'The Emigrant, the Nation, and the State in Nineteenth and Twentieth Century Portugal'.
58 Baganha, 'Migrações internacionais de e para Portugal'.
59 Feldman-Bianco, 'Immigration, Saudade, and the Dialectics of Deterritorialization and Reterritorialization', p. 2.

References

Baganha, Maria, 'Migrações internacionais de e para Portugal. O que sabemos e para onde vamos?', *Revista Crítica de Ciências Sociais* 52/53 (1999): pp. 229-280.

Barbieri, William A. Jr., *Ethics of Citizenship: Immigration and Group Rights in Germany*, Durham, 1998.

Barre, Jorge de la, *Jeunes d'origine portugaise en association. On est Européen sans le savoir*, Paris, 1997.

Bleich, Erik, 'Re-Imagined Communities? Education Policies and National Belonging in Britain and France', in: Adrian Favell and Andrew Geddes (eds), *The Politics of Belonging. Migrants and Minorities in Contemporary Europe*, Aldershot, 1999, pp. 60-75.

Brettell, Caroline, 'The Emigrant, the Nation, and the State in Nineteenth and Twentieth Century Portugal. An Anthropological Approach', *Portuguese Studies Review* 2, 2 (1993): pp. 51-65.

Brubaker, Rogers, *Citizenship and Nationhood in France and Germany*, Cambridge, MA, 1992.

Carreira, Teresa P. and Tomé, Maria A., *Portugais et Luso-français,vol. I: Double culture et identité*, Paris, 1994.

Cunha, Maria do Céu, *Portugais de France. Essai sur une dynamique de double appartenance*, Paris, 1988.

Dittgen, Herbert, 'Volk Nation or Nation of Immigrants? The Current Debate About Immigration in Germany and the United States in Comparative Perspective', in: Jürgen Fijalkowski, Hermann Kurthen and Gert G. Wagner (eds), *Immigration, Citizenship, and the Welfare State in Germany and the United States: Welfare Policies and Immigrants' Citizenship*, Stamford, CT, 1998, pp. 107-138.

Federal Commissioner for Foreigners' Affairs, *Facts and Figures on the Situation of Foreigners in the Federal Republic of Germany,* June 1999 (http://www.einbuergerung.de/date_dat_fakt.html).

Feldman-Bianco, Bela, 'Immigration, Saudade, and the Dialectics of Deterritorialization and Reterritorialization', paper delivered at Wenner Gren Foundation, Foundation for

Anthropological Research, Symposium 117, *Transnationalism, Nation-State Building, and Culture*, Mijas, Spain, 1994.

Fijalkowski, Jürgen, 'Incorporating Immigrants and Expanding Citizenship', in: Jürgen Fijalkowski, Hermann Kurthen and Gert G. Wagner (eds), *Immigration, Citizenship, and the Welfare State in Germany and the United States. Welfare Policies and Immigrants' Citizenship*, Stamford, CT, 1998, pp. 159-174.

Foner, Nancy, 'What's New About Transnationalism. New York Immigrants Today and at the Turn of the Century', *Diaspora* 6, 3 (1997): pp. 355-375.

Glick-Schiller, Nina, Basch, Linda and Szanton Blanc, Christina, 'From Immigrant to Transmigrant: Theorizing Transnational Migration', in: Ludger Pries (ed.), *Migration and Transnational Social Spaces*, Aldershot, 1999, pp. 74-105.

Goldring, Luin, 'Power and Status in Transnational Social Spaces', in: Ludger Pries (ed.), *Migration and Transnational Social Spaces*, Aldershot, 1999, pp. 162-186.

Green, Simon, 'Beyond Ethnoculturalism? German Citizenship in the New Millenium', *German Politics* 9, 3 (2000): pp. 105-124.

Hagedorn, Heike, 'Falling Borders. Liberal Trends in German Citizenship Politics' (http://www2.smu.edu/tower/Hagedorn.html).

Heuer, Madalena Costa Leal, 'Saudades Am Tor Zur Welt. Lebenssituation und Zukunftsperspektiven junger Portugiesen in Hamburg', diploma thesis, Universität Hamburg, 1995.

Institut für Zukunftsforschung, *Ausländer oder Deutsche. Integrationsprobleme griechischer, jugoslawischer und türkischer Bevölkerungsgruppen*, Bonn, 1981.

Klimt, Andrea, '"Returning Home". Portuguese Migrant Notions of Temporariness, Permanence, and Commitment', *New German Critique* 46 (1989): pp. 47-70.

Klimt, Andrea, *'Temporary' and 'Permanent' Lives: The Construction of Identity among Portuguese Migrants in Germany*, PhD, Stanford University, 1992.

Klimt, Andrea, 'Home and Belonging: Portuguese Migrants' Musings on European Spaces', paper presented at the colloquium series 'Multicultural German', University of Austin, Texas, 1999.

Koven, Michele, *French-Portuguese Bilingual's Enactments of Self in Two Languages*, PhD, University of Chicago, 1999.

Kvistad, Gregg O., 'Membership without Politics? The Social and Political Rights of Foreigners in Germany', in: Jürgen Fijalkowski, Hermann Kurthen and Gert G. Wagner (eds), *Immigration, Citizenship, and the Welfare State in Germany and the United States: Immigrant Incorporation*, Stamford, CT, 1998, pp. 141-157.

Leandro, Maria-Engracia, *Au-delà des apparences. Les Portugais face à l'insertion sociale*, Paris, 1995.

Mandel, Ruth, 'Turkish Headscarves and the "Foreigner Problem": Constructing Difference through Emblems of Identity', *New German Critique* 46 (1989): pp. 27-46.

Marshall, Barbara, *The New Germany and Migration in Europe*, Manchester, UK, 2000.

Mountz, Alison and Wright, Richard A., 'Daily Life in the Transnational Migrant Community of San Agustin, Oaxaca, and Poiughkeepsie, New York', *Diaspora* 5, 3 (1996): pp. 403-428.

Schor, Ralph, *Histoire de l'immigration en France de la fin du XIXième siècle à nos jours*, Paris, 1996.

Tribalat, Michèle, *De l'immigration à l'assimilation. Enquête sur les populations d'origine étrangère en France*, Paris, 1996.

White, Jenny B., 'Turks in the New Germany', *American Anthropologist* 99, 4 (1997): pp. 754-769.

Chapter 14

Whatever Happened to the Albanians? Some Clues to a Twentieth-Century European Mystery

Isa Blumi

The Balkan wars of the 1990s highlighted what had been a forgotten dynamic locked behind the 'Iron Curtain' and perhaps resurrected Western Europe's own, recent memories of the diasporic consciousness. While this sudden power to see suffering at the hands of the Balkan state seemed unassailable to European citizens, Milošević's wars were not some anomaly of the post-Communist era. Rather, the wars in Bosnia, Croatia and Slovenia were but remnants of a long history of forced expulsion in Yugoslavia. However, the history of Yugoslavia's forced migration of its Albanian-speaking population in the pre-Milošević years – a history of the expulsion of hundreds of thousands of human beings – had been largely ignored in Western Europe.[1] Frustrated by this lacuna, I set about talking to surviving members of the interwar period to help shed light on this tragic episode in modern European history. It was only after I began to informally question 'Kosovo-Albanian' men who had settled in Western Europe as early as 1949 that I realized there was perhaps another significant story to tell.[2] For the few statistical abstractions that characterize past work on these expulsions, the personal side of the experience was never considered.[3]

From 1993 to 1998, I began an unsystematic survey of men in various Kosovo-Albanian communities in Western European cities in order to clarify an underlying suspicion about the fluidity of these men's memories of their forced departure from Yugoslavia. What I soon learned was that such memories had a dual purpose of narrating a 'lived' experience for the benefit of the 'one asking the questions' and constituting a present 'self' who, it turns out, was positioned with respect to current events beamed across television screens.[4] The war in Bosnia and the collective concern for the plight of the latest victims of Yugoslav policies provided the emotional and, perhaps more importantly, rhetorical conditions for individual perceptions of the 'diasporic' experience to take new form. That is, the manner in which these individuals 'chose to remember' were as much a reflection on what was 'remembered' as an attempt to link their memories to the events they were watching unfold on their television screens.

As I began to develop a better sense of what was transpiring, I changed the angle of inquiry to one that specifically probed this malleable space of memory. The new kinds of questions I asked aimed at bringing these transmuted memories to the surface in ways that rendered presumed collective and individual identities suddenly unclear. In subsequent attempts to find primary materials to develop my rather impressionistic field observations, I came to realize that these Kosovo-Albanians were nowhere to be found using certain kinds of tools while they were everywhere, once new kinds of questions were asked. Therefore, the easy answer to the question 'Where did the Albanians go?' is that they were always there. The problem lay in that they were never 'seen' by the state bureaucracies and (as the informants insisted over and over again) by Europeans themselves. The answer to the next obvious question 'Why were they never seen?' is composed of two inter-related parts: first, no one bothered to ask; second, Kosovo-Albanians never forced their 'hosts' to see them.

In seeking to understand how it is possible that perhaps tens of thousands of Kosovo-Albanians were never seen in Western Europe, it is easiest to first investigate the 'no one bothered to ask' part of the answer. Western European bureaucracies, police forces and academic circles monitoring immigration into Western Europe simply never had a category for the Kosovo-Albanian immigrants, refugees and 'guestworkers' that populated their cities. Informal discussions with immigration officials at border towns and airports verified that, since such a category did not exist at the time, there would be no way to calculate, let alone identify, immigrants who may have self-identified as Kosovo-Albanians. This was a striking revelation at a time when Western European polities and political institutions demonstrated a sharp sense of compassion for Bosnia's Muslims, and other refugees, such as Kurds and Tamils. While the shocking images of war in Bosnia sensitized Western Europeans to the evils of 'ethnic cleansing', it became clear that every one of the Kosovo-Albanian men I spoke to experienced similar brutalities in their lives; only their suffering was never acknowledged. When answering my questions about what they felt about the wars taking place in Bosnia, the tendency was to move into recollection and not speculation. Without exception, the way in which Kosovo-Albanian men understood the wars of the 1990s was through the filter of their own personal traumas. In other words, Kosovo-Albanian men born before or during the 1950s understood Bosnia through their own, often deeply repressed traumas of exile, a sensibility that took on particular vehemence in public settings where others were involved in the discussions.[5] What is also important to note, however, is that these men of various ages also began to understand anew their own experiences through the filter of the war. This dual function of memory is suggestive when attempting to better appreciate the dynamics of 'postmodern' hybrid identities and 'double consciousness' discussed by others.[6]

What is so striking about revisiting these interviews at the time of writing (2000-2002) is how different the victims of crimes against humanity were treated in the 1990s as compared to those who experienced very similar traumas in the 1950s and 1960s in Kosovo. This had a clear impact on how my informants remembered their past and constituted themselves as individuals and community. The obvious difference was the status the host society and state granted them. The Kosovo-Albanians of the 1950s and 1960s never received refugee status, which according to their slightly distorted perceptions meant any number of material inducements in terms of special housing arrangements, food stipends, help in finding work, special language classes and, most importantly of all, collective support from the general population.[7] They were simply 'Turkish workers', an unwanted association that will play heavily in this article. Not being recognized as victims of a brutal state campaign to evict them from their homes was juxtaposed, in the 1950-1970 period, with 'others' being openly embraced by Western Europeans. Western Europe actively sought to settle (and assimilate) 'refugees' from Czechoslovakia, Poland, East Germany and Hungary, a process that the mostly shunned Kosovo-Albanians noted with a sense of frustration. Clearly the Cold War dictated the type of reception other Eastern Europeans received in host societies. Yugoslavia's warm relations with the Western European nations made it diplomatically unfeasible to recognize possible grounds of granting refugee status to Kosovo's Albanians. This contrast between what was lacking in the 1950s and 1960s, as against what Bosnians were 'given' in the 1990s, was particularly important to men living in neighborhoods with recently arrived Bosnian refugees.[8]

Issues of Scope in Exile: Second-Tier Migration

Recent discussions of the 'immigrant issue' in Western Europe do not help in understanding the experience of migration in Europe's post-war period. It is necessary to theorize the institutional process that rendered the Kosovo-Albanian men and women of the 1950s and 1960s invisible to fully appreciate the changes that would take place in the 1980s, the period during which they suddenly became visible. Contrary to commonly held views concerning European migration during most of the post-war period, large numbers of immigrants from the 1950s onward were not 'Turkish' or 'Yugoslav' men and women seeking jobs. Rather, many of these men, women and their families came from a variety of ethno-linguistic backgrounds and did not associate themselves with either of these 'identities'. In addition to a need for recognizing the cultural distinctiveness of those coming to Western Europe since the 1950s, the often forgotten pretext for their arrival is of paramount importance. Not only were many of these 'Yugoslavs' and 'Turks' actually Kurdish or Albanian speakers, but in large part because they were persecuted 'minorities' in their countries of origin, they were often expelled from their homes. This meant that the overwhelming majority of Kosovo-Albanians came to Western Europe on entirely different pretexts than those with whom they were ultimately associated with in the 1950-80 period. Being a Turkish or Yugoslav 'guestworker' and being a victim of political violence were two entirely different experiences, experiences that were all but erased by the very associations attached to being 'ethnically' attached to the immediate countries of origin.

Introducing the concept of *second-tier migration* may help address this problem. The issue is how to monitor the flow of tens of thousands of individuals to Western Europe by way of intermediary, officially recognized countries of 'origin'. Since Kosovo-Albanians' immediate country of origin during the immigration process was Turkey or Yugoslavia, they were immediately categorized and subsequently treated as either Yugoslavs or Turks by the countries in which they settled. The impact of these associations with unrepresentative national identities initially led to a number of institutionalized rigidities that impacted how individuals formally interacted with their host governments. Second, the imposition of a 'false' identity created contradictory forces that simultaneously drew people closer and further apart from their 'own' identity.

How this worked in interactions with state bureaucracies may prove illuminating. Three recent informants suggested that they made some initial attempts to assert their Kosovo-Albanian identities upon arrival in the 1970s, through the opening of clubs and mosques that were separate from 'the Turks'. In their respective attempts to petition municipal governments for the right to formally establish a religious school/mosque in West Berlin, a 'cultural, sports and youth club' in Düsseldorf, and a Muslim-orientated newspaper in Zürich, they were all refused permission on grounds that their services were 'redundant'. In other words, the bureaucracies charged with the care of these 'guestworkers' did not recognize the distinctive importance of these sites of culture, identity and place. In all three cases, it was thought that these proposed institutes 'already existed' in these cities. Why these projects were 'redundancies' in the eyes of local officials was due to the fact that the individuals making the requests were categorically considered 'Turks' and 'Muslims'. Indeed, there were specifically Turkish Muslim organizations that operated social clubs in these cities, but as the point about *second-tier migration* suggests, German and Swiss authorities in the 1970s had no means of recognizing that the label 'Turk' did not apply to those self-identified Kosovo-Albanian men seeking permission.[9]

There is a need to provide some further historical background to this problem. Turkey has throughout the twentieth century served as a point of destination for much of the Balkan's Muslims largely due to the legacy of imperial-era abstractions. The demographic categories adopted by most European demographers in the nineteenth century haphazardly identified all Muslims as Turks. These all-inclusive categories carried over as an instrumental mechanism for state-builders in interwar Yugoslavia and Greece who ruled over millions of Muslim Slavs, Albanian-speakers, Turkish-speakers and Bulgarians. In the effort to homogenize Yugoslavia's and Greece's population, a number of efforts were undertaken to send Turks (i.e., Muslim Albanians, Slavs and Bulgarians) 'back' to Turkey from the 1920s onwards.[10] Non-Serb scholars have generally accepted today that Serbian administrators, in seeking to evict non-Slav inhabitants from Yugoslavia, abused the label Turk to represent all Muslims living in the Balkans.[11] The subsequent policies of colonization coalesced in the Balkans throughout the interwar and post-World War II periods around formal 'repatriation' treaties signed between Yugoslavia, Greece and the Turkish Republic.[12] According to the records of the Austro-Hungarian Empire from the First World War, a large majority of the Muslims in the Balkans were Albanian speakers. Indeed, the areas targeted by these treaties were generally not the Slavic-speaking areas of Bosnia at all, but the Albanian-speaking majorities in the highlands of Montenegro and the provinces of Kosovo and Macedonia.[13] According to Serb figures that Albanians dispute, the number of Albanians expelled to Turkey during the interwar period was over 150,000.[14] For the post-war period, Turkish government statistics suggest that another 200,000 had departed for Turkey.[15]

Recognizing this suggests that a significant demographic shift occurred in the population of Turkey itself. The legacy of these 'expulsions' or repatriations is apparent in the extensive Albanian-speaking neighbourhoods in Izmir, Ankara, Bursa and Istanbul that exist today.[16] What this means for understanding post-war immigration to Western Europe is clear when it is recognized that large numbers of, in particular, young men, never actually settled in Turkey upon arrival. Rather, now possessing 'Turkish' documentation and Turkish surnames they were often forced to adopt, many of these men and women joined the waves of Turkish migrants and 'guestworkers' who flowed into Europe during its severe labour shortages in the early 1950s and 1960s.[17]

Appreciating this factor dramatically changes how post-war European settlement can be studied. As observed from within the Albanian-speaking diaspora in Western Europe during the 1990s, this process of *second-tier migration* would have important effects on the cultural development and levels of political activism within Kosovo-Albanian communities throughout the 1950s, 1960s and 1970s. In fact, the central tension in composing this article lies in articulating a general impression gathered from discussions over some ten years with individuals who, although representing themselves as 'typical' Albanians, were, as far as their host societies were concerned, living as Turks, Yugoslavs, Italians or Greeks. The reason for such categorical uncertainty stems from how informants understood their associations with other groups – Yugoslav, Italian, Greek or Turk – and the consequences assumed to have derived from what are now claimed to have been 'false' associations.

(Re)Discovering the Personal Side of Second-Tier Migration

It is through exploring the humanity of those experiencing the effects of *second-tier migration* that we may best answer the questions raised about Kosovo-Albanians' invisibility over the years. One aspect of the humanity of this case is the experience of loss felt by many Kosovo-Albanians at the time of immigration. The impact that the initial expulsion and forced settlement in countries such as Turkey had on individual lives was clearly traumatic, as was made clear during the course of my conversations. It is interesting to note that for some of the informants who had left their temporary homes in Turkey for Western Europe in the 1950s, the sense of loss was not an overwhelmingly material one. While everyone spoke of the loss of their lifetime savings, property and material heritage, many also spoke of losing their identity as well.[18] Paradoxically, the very act of expulsion would prove to be the solidifying agent for people otherwise forced to adopt and live other identities. How individuals in these subsequently identified 'weak' communities interacted in shifting socio-economic and eventually political environments, therefore, is of central concern here.

Patterns of Settlement

Albanian-speakers reportedly settled and socialized in tight-knit units throughout Western Europe during the period in question. While initially, individual men scattered to find employment, the eventual consolidation of small niches within larger immigrant neighborhoods is an important point stressed by most members of the first generation of immigrants. It is clear from discussions about these '*mahalle i Shqiptare*' [Albanian quarters] that a universal Albanian identity was not the central criterion for patterns of settlement in these otherwise indistinguishable masses of 'immigrant ghettos'. While it took some prodding, some of the informants conceded that joining others from the same region back in the Balkans created their small groupings (*mahalle*). Simply being an Albanian did not necessarily result in joining the *mahalle* as such parameters of group loyalty did not yet have any salience. Besides raising questions about the value of even using ethnic categories to understand how people create communities, it is important to note the reluctance of my informants to admit, in the 1990s, that speaking Albanian was not enough to be welcome.[19] Why it took some prodding for what was clearly the pattern of settlement for almost all the Albanian communities created in post-war Europe probably reflects the rise of a larger 'national' consciousness in the 1980s among Albanian-speakers from Kosovo and Macedonia. In the 1950s, such sentiments were subordinate to trust and security, which only a more intimate association with those from the same village or valley could satisfy. It became clear during the course of my discussions that Kosovo's marginal status in the pre-1998 geo-strategic world meant the admitted parochialism of my older informants had to be qualified with justifications as much as possible. That the conditions in the mid-1990s back in Kosovo may have dictated the sense of shame for having failed to create a more universal community in the 1950s and 1960s suggests that selective forgetting compliments the selective remembering of my informants during the period of research.[20]

Patterns of Self-Reading

It may be helpful to think of identities constituted in bureaucratic and academic categories as precarious sociological moments, vulnerable to a variety of transformative situations contingent on both environmental and ideological factors.[21] Unfortunately, given the way 'ethnicity' operates in today's vernacular of Internet-driven scholarship and media production, one would presume that Albanians, for instance, constitute a community based on a variety of shared linguistic, physical, spiritual and social traits. Against such views, I would argue that as the processes of life are in constant flux, such a thing as one's ethnic identity is constantly open to factors that create immediate and dramatic shifts in how people are expected to see themselves and how others see them. This will be key to understanding the emotional and eventually, organizational capacity of Albanian-speaking individuals/groups who ultimately settled in Western Europe by way of intermediary states. Put differently, the exodus and eventual settlement of hundreds of thousands of Albanians during the period under consideration does not constitute a homogeneous and general experience. Rather, these are experiences that are scarred by personal memories, which are linked by common experiences of 'invisibility' that ultimately perpetuated the very factors that accounted for the 'host' society's blindness.

Often, the issue was not simply that of physically being ignored, but being seen as something my informants did not wish to be seen as. The central concern for many was that they would be identified as 'Turks', a racist-tinged term *au courant* in Europe at the time.[22] Over time, this developed into complicated ways of understanding individual and collective place and had profound structural effects on how Kosovo-Albanians projected themselves and their pasts to each other and the outside world.

Material as well as bureaucratic and cultural shifts in the lives of individuals mobilize certain combinations of their 'possibilities of identity' and allow them to fit in any situation.[23] For Kosovo-Albanians, there were seemingly few possibilities to enact their self-identified parochial but still Albanian identities. For my informants in Stockholm, Sweden, for example, the sense of being 'invisible' during the early years of their exile was particularly suggestive in light of the growing empowerment of Bosnians, Kurds and Tamils from Sri Lanka in the 1990s.

This, then, raises a question about the value such testimonials have in our study of the social aspects of the post-war period. The assertions that many of my informants made regarding their willingness to mobilize and actively 'fight' Serb genocidal policies if 'given the chance' does not bear out in the documented evidence of the time. But as much as we cannot 'know' how many (if any) Kosovo-Albanians immigrated to Western Europe in the 1950s and 1960s because demographers never bothered to count them as such, so too does the failure to find 'proof' of Kosovo-Albanian activism in Western Europe negate the statements made in 1994. Whatever the case may be about my self-described 'patriot' and 'rebel' informants, there was clearly a kind of memory that suddenly found its channel of articulation in the form of resentment and perhaps jealousy toward the more recent and 'better treated' exiles living among them.

Perhaps what was most telling in all this was the resentment expressed toward host societies, a common complaint heard throughout Europe in the early to mid-1990s. When asked to elaborate, the persistent answer pointed to a recurring sense of 'invisibility'. This invisibility can be partially retrofitted onto the perhaps unrealizable material ambitions of the early years of exile. But the fact that there was a general feeling of cynicism about what many Kosovo-Albanians believed were 'half-felt' sympathies among 'Christian Europeans' for Bosnian Muslims during the 1992-95 war suggests there was some lingering resentment that their own collective plight had not been recognized in the 1950s or in the mid-1990s. Indeed, as most locally produced media claimed at the time (1995), Kosovo had after all been 'sacrificed' in the Dayton accords, so why would Europeans 'really' care for what happened to Bosnian Muslims.[24] The result has been a powerful mix of contemporary forces working upon perhaps dormant but real self-representations of one's own existence as a foreigner in Western Europe. That many felt they had a right to be seen as much as others were being seen as victims is suggestive of how collective and personal identities operate in a generally exclusionist environment where everyone not European is an 'outsider' simply trying to gain access into 'fortress Europe'.

Assimilated Pasts: The Case of Balkan Expellees Becoming 'Yugoslavs'

These largely speculative conclusions have been reinforced upon inspecting some of the vast literature of post-war migration. As a scholarly topic, most studies on 'non-European' migrants have focused on the generic Turks. Tellingly, while scholars have recently been more sensitive toward making the distinction between Kurds and Turks more clear, it is still impossible to distinguish Kosovo-Albanians from the Yugoslavs or Turks with whom they have been identified until 1998 (the Kosovo war).[25]

How this capacity to fit and modify individual and collective claims within an established administrative context translates in Western Europe is of primary interest as it demonstrates the deeper complexities of immigrant communities in general. That Albanian-speakers caught up in *second-tier migration* did not want to be identified as Turks does not mean, of course, that they were successful. Often, the individual enacted through violence, an attempt to communicate 'our sense of powerlessness'. The demand for respect from local teenagers caused some interesting manifestations of collective 'rage' that translated into 'street battles with the Germans'. A number of informants who grew up in the 1960s and 1970s as teenagers in the German cities of Düsseldorf, Stuttgart and West Berlin spoke of fistfights that would be provoked by locals who referred to them as Turks or 'Arabs'. The anger mostly surfaced on individual levels and would sometimes lead to more permanent pathologies that became legendary among local neighbourhood groups of friends.[26] For the majority of informants however, violence did not become a daily affair. Although many said it was a secret fantasy to 'do battle with those little Nazis' (the term used to refer to German kids) their parents played a significant role in restricting potentially 'damaging' relations between 'weak, vulnerable Muslims' (i.e., Turks) and Germans.[27] In the face of a parent's demand not to be provoked by taunting German classmates, informants often said an internal dilemma between wanting to confront these provocations with fists and walking away, as their parents demanded, led to a sense of weakness and even 'self-hatred'. This sense of internally hemmed-in, and perhaps, unrealized 'rage' had been rationalized in the 1990s as a sign of 'moral superiority' and 'dignity', a reflection of the self-affirming rhetoric used by the popular political leader, Ibrahim Rugova, in Kosovo at the time. There is an interesting dynamic of perceived power in both the immigrant's life in Western Europe and those following Rugova's demands of passive resistance.

Upon being pushed about the subject, most of my informants finally submitted that the problem was not only that 'Germans were Nazis' but that Albanian-speakers themselves failed to better organize a campaign to represent themselves as Kosovo-Albanians. Many agreed that much of this was due to their parochial tendencies of settlement in Europe. But there seemed to be another issue at play. It is suggested here that much of it has to do with the variability of 'possibilities of identity' available at the time. The fact that my informants may have been identified as Turks by their neighbours, while anathema in the mid-1990s, cannot adequately explain how such 'imposed identities' were supposed to have been otherwise understood in the context of the 1950s and 1960s.

In the end, the issue seems to be as much a generational one as a structural one. Among those who settled in the 1950s and 1960s, it was the failure of their children to 'want' to preserve their heritage that was the root cause of not being visible earlier. From the perspective of my second and third generation informants, it was not an issue of 'betrayal' as their fathers and uncles suggested, but of 'social survival'. As it was generally framed, while the parents worked two jobs, saved their money and ultimately opened up small businesses such as Italian restaurants, the children had to grow up in an extremely 'competitive' social environment where ethnic labels, as already witnessed, were often used to keep people in or out of social spaces considered important to teenagers of the time. It is how the children of this first wave of Kosovo-Albanians were actively seeking to distinguish themselves from the arbitrary affixation of secondary ethnic identities that suggests a powerful gap of perception between parents and their children.

One of the most telling expressions of communal identities in the 1990s is their ability to influence how their host societies see them. In the eyes of many informants, the 'successful' communities in the 1990s held demonstrations, participated in parades, distributed literature, supported exhibitions and engaged in other 'outreach' programmes. As my informants stated themselves, in the case of Albanian communities, such efforts to reach out and to be seen were never successful. There are perhaps socio-historical factors to consider here. It must be remembered that those who were expelled before 1980 never lived in a political or cultural environment that promoted their Albanian identity. That most of those who arrived in Western Europe before 1980 were products of a society that openly persecuted and actively sought to erase non-Slav and Muslim history from the region goes a long way in explaining the organizational capacities of these dispersed groups of expellees.

Trying to Fit In

The lack of an effective medium of communication in the context of an urbanized, hyper-material world is among the most important factors that may account for the lack of enthusiasm among immigrant youths to perpetuate their 'native' traditions. The impact the mass media has on creating psychological spaces for the positive reinforcement of some images and the negative reinforcement of others is rarely considered. An immigrant community's ability to communicate with their host society through mass culture may be key to their relative success or failure. Under such conditions, it is suggested that communities can only be reinforced through positive manifestations of their place in the world order. Positive images of the immigrant community, however, are hard to come by in host societies, even under the best conditions.

In the 1950s and 1960s, there were no public access facilities as there were in the 1990s. In this period before the explosion of the Internet and cable/satellite television, therefore, the most effective way to win the sympathies of a host society was through associating with famous individuals featured in the regulated local mass media. Informants recollected how international sports stars, in particular, transcended the politics of race and ethnicity in their mixed neighbourhoods. Collective sympathies from host countries were probably most shaped by the successes of sports stars and, if individuals could make associations to that star, a new dynamic was possible. Many noted that Yugoslav sports heroes were well known in their neighbourhoods and conversations around Belgrade Red Star (a famous soccer club) often formed the basis for personal exchanges between immigrants and members of the host society. For men even today, the social spaces in which the divides of suspicion, jealousy and fear are still best traversed are found at local sports bars.

For the Kosovo-Albanian, there was (and still is) no example of such an internationally produced medium of exchange. In failing to represent oneself beyond the confines of a largely ignorant host-society's understanding of what individual Kosovo-Albanians were, there was no way for such a cluster of dispersed communities to find those needed 'new spaces of representation' that Stuart Hall has suggests are key to formulating new, temporary identities.[28]

This centreless patch of communities resulted in communal, familial and existential atomization during the 1950s to 1970s that even broke up the smaller units the first generation attempted to form. It was the individual who actively sought to control the terms in which he or she interacted with the outside world; the role of an imagined community-wide structure, even at the loosely formed village-based group, was all but negligible.

I have learned through my conversations over the years that the desired goals of these distinct, self-differentiating potential 'communities' inherently contradicted the goals and ambitions of individuals who actively abandoned efforts to challenge the injustices of their history, choosing instead to assimilate better into Western European society. The majority of those individual spores that sought alternative ways to avoid the stigmata of associations with the Turks were the children of the first generation of migrants. For many among the 1970s generation, in particular, the fact that these small communities could not break out of the stereotype of being Turkish gave little incentive for them to support their parents' efforts to maintain a 'dignified' existence as an invisible but 'alive and healthy' family. Quite the contrary, in order to break out of what in the mid-1990s translated into a Turkish identification trap that was 'racist to the core', youngsters often used 'adopted' identities that were seen as 'cleaner'.

In the case of the younger Kosovo-Albanians who were attending school in their host society during the 1970s and 1980s and caught in a bureaucratic and social limbo, the strategy of choice lay in publicly claiming a

Yugoslav identity. Many informants who were in their late teens during the 1970s accredited an important sense of certainty to being associated with a state like Yugoslavia. When asked to elaborate, many felt proud of the country at the time. As a well-known, then popular tourist destination, Yugoslavia had a certain cachet to it that could communicate a sense of immediate positive associations for those who evoked it. There are a number of reasons why being identified with a recognizable state may be advantageous in the short-term. There were clear psychological gains to be had for those who actively associated themselves with a state that produced Nobel Prize winning authors and world-class sports heroes. For many of those interviewed, the choice between feeling completely marginal due to their ambiguous and unappreciated place in the world and associated with Yugoslavia was simple.

It must be added, however, that such claims of self-identification only took place in public, and away from the scrutiny of family. Even for those who readily admitted 'feeling more Yugoslav' than 'a peasant [*katundare*] from Drenica', interactions at home were not in any way modified. The language of communication, the food eaten, the music and familial politics were all 'distinctly Kosovar' throughout this period.[29]

This suggests the presence of a parallel stream of consciousness capable of negotiating individual identity claims at a moment of notice. Such flexibility is at the heart of the theoretical literature on identity and is clearly at play in this study. One of the more helpful readings of this process has been proposed by Jean-Luc Nancy, whose approach is founded on a model of social linkages that sustain and promote particularities and shun generalized communal attributes.[30] Nancy's opposition to Habermas's limited notion of communal solidarity has been shared by others who also seek alternative ways of identifying interactive processes that do not rely on supra-natural categories such as 'ethnicity', or 'country of origin' that erase these many contingencies in an individual's life.[31] It is clear from these conversations with Kosovo-Albanians in Europe that transcendent factors such as ethnicity or nationality have no solid foundation upon which to rest within this and other communities. While one can accept the significance of individual declarations of being one thing or another in public and at home, putting them in specific temporal contexts is of primary importance. As has been suggested here, there are distinctive time lines in the history of this Albanian invisibility.

That the pain many felt had been referenced to a particular sense of 'failure' clarifies much about the mysteries surrounding the invisible Albanian. The pain associated with living as an invisible Kosovo-Albanian reflects upon the stated desire to 'retain some link' to a cultural heritage but also function within society at large. The issue of being 'unrecognized' is linked to the reportedly frustrated attempts to secure an autonomous space to speak their language, listen to their music and celebrate their heroes while also being able to make friends with members of the host society and not be excluded from the outside world. As one informant in Amsterdam stated, because one's cultural, linguistic and religious existence had to be carefully sequestered in sparsely attended 'cultural clubs' and in meetings that took place just once a week, individuals perpetually lived a 'divided life'.[32] This is clearly a central element of most of the testimonials given to me by Kosovo-Albanians of the 1950s and 1960s and reflects the parallel streams of consciousness their children experienced while claiming a public Yugoslav identity while living an Albanian one at home.

Post-Prishtina, 1981... The Battle for Albanianness

Contradictory interests and relationships with the 'homeland' took an interesting turn in the 1980s. The issue of violence back in Kosovo proved to be the catalyst that would ultimately start an inter-communal rivalry that translated into international intrigue and political violence as well as a reinvigoration of assumed forgotten public identities. The massacre of Albanian students in 1981 in Prishtina, which marked the apex of collective Kosovo-Albanian consciousness in an organized form, finally transformed Kosovo into an international issue with corresponding political consequences for those who were targeted by the Yugoslav state.[33] Aside from the several thousand Kosovo-Albanians imprisoned for long terms, thousands more fled to Western Europe to settle in what little there was of an organized Kosovo-Albanian diaspora. What is important to note is the dramatic difference between this new, now politically sophisticated generation of expellees and their largely rural and uneducated predecessors. This generation catalyzed a dramatic change in Kosovo-Albanian (and Albanian) intra-communal relations, for they had been politicized in an environment that at once enabled them to organize as Albanians (the Albanian language was now permitted in schools and used in Prishtina University) and persecuted them for such mobilization. As a result of wide-scale coverage of Yugoslavia's repression of the student protests, informants told me that, at least for the immediate 1981-82 period, European civilians began to appreciate for the first time that there were Albanians in Yugoslavia who were being murdered because of their struggle for cultural and political freedom. This created a new dynamic of community advocacy that produced new opportunities for previously invisible (and perhaps unconsidered) aspirations.

The years that followed saw a consolidation of particularistic Kosovo-Albanian identities in Germany, Switzerland and Sweden. While not the focus of this article, it should be noted that the economic networks that began to develop in Europe were largely operational only after the creation of this politically active, if not reclusive, diaspora in the 1980s. Savings that had accumulated over the years from earnings made in restaurants and small businesses opened during the course of the post-war period helped create strong economic foundations for further investment in a political identity that was now gaining more international attention with the 'resurfacing' of Serbian nationalism after 1986. The impact this had on individual communities is important. The older generation of Albanian speakers, although at the time insisting they were the 'leaders' of the newly invigorated community, were noticeably marginal as a new generation of Kosovo-Albanian refugees took on the responsibility of defining the hopes and dreams of Kosovo-Albanians to the outside world. This new generation adapted the best they could to a new geopolitical context that ultimately created the Democratic League of Kosova, a belated and unrecognized Republic of Kosova, and later the various groups that funded the war for liberation in the mid-1990s. In this dynamic of political change in Yugoslavia and Europe as a whole, the conditions for a fundamental change in how Albanian-speakers interacted in European host societies helped reshape a desire to be identified as a Kosovo-Albanian.

Conclusion

It is often assumed in academic circles that we should put the onus on states and their bureaucracies for the substantial personal traumas experienced in the modern world. This is indeed true when remembering that it was the Serb-dominated Yugoslav state that used a number of legal and extra-legal tactics to forcibly evict hundreds of thousands of Albanian-speakers from their homes. That said, every one of my informants actually placed far more blame for their individual traumas on neighbours, shopkeepers, individual policemen, co-workers, managers and classmates. This suggests that there is a need for a far more integrated study of how immigrant groups interact with local 'host' populations. As noted throughout, it was the failure to find a space as Albanians in the context of day-to-day life that was most traumatic for those involved in this study. Many actively adopted identities that they would have otherwise been reluctant to claim, simply on the grounds of wishing to avoid being invisible. The underlying message behind this twentieth-century European mystery, therefore, is not the exclusive necessity of institutionalized modifications, but also efforts to better address, on an individual-by-individual basis, the largely unarticulated frustrations of many of Europe's people. This is still clear in the beginning of the twenty-first century. The general feeling among Kosovo-Albanians in 2002 is that the Austrians, Germans, Swiss and Swedes are not 'getting better but are getting worse'. In this context there is a persistent fear of far-right revivalism, as has been manifested recently in Italy, Sweden, Denmark and Austria, which, it is feared, could result in a second period of forced migration, this time back to Kosovo.[34]

The consequences of not being able to sustain links to a homeland or have one's plight as a persecuted human recognized are significant for the individual and her relationship with the outside world. Lacking control over how the world perceives the individual, the generic migrant constantly struggles to articulate a distinctive identity that ultimately contributes to such fragmentation. The exclusivity of being 'native' has developed powerful traditions of personal and collective discursive exchanges, implicitly ostracizing individuals so tied to such imageries. It is hoped that such dynamics, such traumas and such histories can be reintroduced into narratives that study European migration, shedding light on the humanity of the experience and the responsibilities of all of us in the perpetuation of discrimination and the psychological pain that accompanies such journeys. The simple act of recognizing these journeys may help solve other as yet unimagined European mysteries.

Notes

I wish to thank the following for their assistance in accumulating information for this article in the early 1990s: Alex (New York), Bleron (Munich), Bekim (Kosovo/Frankfurt), Illiriana (Stockholm) and the late Mehmet Blumashi, who all share with me the pain and the sense of loss of exile from our beloved homeland.

1 Until Kosovo became a household name thanks to the events of 1998-99, few non-Albanians considered the expulsion of Albanians from 1920 to 1980 a subject worthy of inquiry. One flawed exception is Roux, *Les Albanais en Yougoslavie. Minorité nationale, territoire et développement*.

2 Unfortunately, a lack of insight into where women play in this phenomenon means this article has serious deletions and spaces of silence of its own. The article does not pretend to represent the experience of invisibility for the mothers, sisters, wives and daughters of the men with whom I had conversations over the years. It should be noted that this is an omission very much a part of the daily lives of my informants; women simply had little input into this process of remembering, a fact for which I am not proud.

3 Of the early work done by Albanians, the following stand out: Bajrami, *Rrethanat shoqërore*; Islami, 'La diaspora'; Islami, *Rrjedha demografike shqiptare*.

4 Swedenburg has masterfully explored this issue of memory when interviewing Palestinian refugees evicted during the 1948 Israeli-Arab war (Swedenburg, *Memories of Revolt*).

5 Many of the conversations took place in social gatherings organized by various Kosovo-Albanian communities during the period. These conversations engaged many participants at one time, perhaps influencing the answers given to specific questions.

6 Such dual function of memory would compliment the thrust of recent work on the above-mentioned themes. See for instance Moreiras, 'Hybridity and Double Consciousness'.

7 Very few scholars actually took a critical look at the human rights record of Yugoslavia, ultimately leading to a rather simplistic, rosy picture of the 'Tito' era. The exceptions are few: Amnesty International, *Yugoslavia*; Banac, *With Stalin Against Tito*.

8 In Stockholm, for instance, men who had come from Peja (Pec), a city in which many Slavs from Bosnia had settled in the 1940s, had demonstrated open resentment toward their new neighbors on grounds that they never received such attention when they first came to Sweden. Although my informants were financially secure by 1994, the fact that the Swedish government was so generous and the Swedish public so sympathetic toward Bosnians proved particularly upsetting, especially if they were 'Serbs'. Conversations held in April of 1994 with men expelled from Peja in 1954.

9 Conversations were held in Prishtina, Kosovo. March 2001.

10 For primary documents focusing on the plight of Albanians in Serbia in the interwar period see Elsie, *Kosovo in the Heart of the Powder Keg*, pp. 361-399 and Elsie, 'Convention Regulating the Emigration', pp. 425-434.

11 For a summary of events during this period, see Poulton, *The Balkans*, pp. 57-75 and Mertus, *Kosovo*, pp. 37, 286-287.

12 Ostensibly these treaties were devised to help populate Turkish Eastern provinces with non-Kurdish peoples while depopulating the Balkans of Muslims. For details on the agreement see Archives Diplomatiques de Ministère des Affaires Etrangères, série Europe, sous-série La Yugoslavie, vol. 31, and La Turquie, vol. 30, Paris.

13 For instance, by 1917, we see there are but 26,696 Turkish-speaking subjects in Habsburg-controlled Kosova, which included Mitrovica, Ipek and Prizren. These numbers are compared to the 110,815 Albanian speakers and 31,648 'Serbs' counted by Austrian officials. See Österreichisches Kriegsarchiv, NFA 1697, 26 Mai 1917, folio 6.

14 Krizman, 'Elaborat'.

15 The semi-official Turkish newspaper *Cumhuriyet* noted that between 1949-57, the height of Yugoslav Minister of the Interior, Alexander Rankovic's power, more than 200,000 inhabitants from Kosova and Macedonia migrated to Turkey (Cumhuriyet, 6 April 1957). That figure has been revised to upwards of 400,000 in recent research by Bajrami, *Shpërngulja e shqiptarëve gjatë viteve*, p. 132.

16 See the recent work by de Rapper, *Les Albanais à Istanbul*.

17 Every single one of the 1950s generation Kosovo-Albanian men spoken to (23 individuals) followed this pattern. With the exception of one, everyone has subsequently brought their extended families left behind in Turkey to join them in Western Europe.

18 In the diaries kept during the period of my interviews in Frankfurt and Zürich in 1994, no fewer than six of the seven men who had immigrated to the West in the 1950s spoke of this loss of identity. Since this time, I have specifically added this question and have found that everyone, from those expelled in the 1950s to those in the 1980s have detailed examples of their sense of lost identity.

19 I have specifically questioned the value of ethnic categories in understanding Balkan history. See Blumi, 'The Commodification of Otherness'.

20 Such tendencies to look inward ultimately proved detrimental to these communities' larger interests. For an elaboration on the issues pertaining to Kosovo's diplomatic marginality, see Blumi, 'Kosova: From the Brink'.

21 This careful inspection of the categorical truisms imposed on such communities follows the interpretive thrust set by among others, James Clifford. See his 'Travelling Cultures'.

22 Every single Albanian spoken to on the subject felt that most Europeans were 'racists' at one level or another. In fact, it is hard to find any individual immigrant of 'non-European' or Muslim origin who would not have made similar characterizations. Adding personal testimonials to this effect is not necessary but the topic is vastly understudied when compared to how much attention everyday experiences with racism have dominated scholarship in the United States. This is not something to brush aside; perceptions of animosity and discrimination are central components to the issue of invisibility. The term racist itself (*raciste* or *dallim racial*-racial discrimination) as Albanians use it has been a term imported from Yugoslavia where it was often used in the context of Albanian-Serb relations.

23 See Blumi, 'Contesting the Edges of the Ottoman Empire'.

24 Blumi, 'Kosova: From the Brink', p. 18.

25 A few examples demonstrate the complete failure to recognize this dynamic. Basgöz and Furniss, *Turkish Workers in Europe*; Abadan-Unat, *Turkish Workers*; Martin, *The Unfinished Story*.

26 Every one of my informants who had grown up in German cities recalls one or two local 'toughs' who were famous for beating up local Germans who were seen as being 'disrespectful' or feigning 'superiority'.

27 The intervention of parents is a common theme which suggests a generational gap in terms of how to confront the racism experienced every day.

28 Hall, 'Cultural Identity and Diaspora'.

29 Indeed, it is hard to find a family that does not use Albanian at home. What is even more interesting is that the children of these immigrants have retained the regional accents of their parents, suggesting little integration among Kosovo-Albanians until the 1980s.

30 Nancy, *The Inoperative Community*, p. 121.

31 Mitchell, 'Nationalism, Imperialism, Economism'; Malkki, 'Things to Come'.

32 Interview with a man from Prishtina who was working for the Dutch Railroad as an engineer in September of 1994. He had moved from Istanbul in 1965.

33 For background and description of events, see Malcolm, *Kosovo*, pp. 334-37.

34 This is a theme often brought up in the commentaries and feature stories of Kosovo-Albanian newspapers and magazines published in Europe today. In particular the monthly *Ekskluzive* and the daily European edition of *Koha Ditore*.

Archival Sources

Archives Diplomatiques de Ministère des Affaires Etrangères, Paris: série Europe, sous-série La Yugoslavie, vol. 31 and La Turquie, vol. 30.

Österreichisches Kriegsarchiv, Vienna: NFA series, no. 1697.

References

Abadan-Unat, Nermin (ed.), *Turkish Workers in Europe (1960-1975)*, Leiden, 1976.

Amnesty International, *Yugoslavia: Prisoners of Conscience*, London, 1982.

Bajrami, Hakif, *Rrethanat shoqërore dhe politike në Kosovë më 1918-1941*, Prishtina, 1981.

Bajrami, Hakif, *Shpërngulja e shqiptarëve gjatë viteve 1875-1966*, Tirana, 1990.

Banac, Ivo, *With Stalin Against Tito. Cominformist Splits in Yugoslav Communism*, Ithaca, NY, 1988.

Basgöz, Ilhan and Norman Furniss (eds), *Turkish Workers in Europe*, Bloomington, 1985.

Blumi, Isa, 'The Commodification of Otherness and the Ethnic Unit in the Balkans. How to Think About Albanians', *East European Politics and Societies* 12 (1998): pp. 527-569.

Blumi, Isa, 'Kosova: From the Brink – and Back Again', *Current History* 100, 11 (2001): pp. 15-20.

Blumi, Isa, 'Contesting the Edges of the Ottoman Empire. Rethinking Ethnic and Sectarian Boundaries in the Malësore, 1878-1912', *International Journal of Middle Eastern Studies*, [forthcoming].

Clifford, James, 'Travelling Cultures', in: Lawrence Grossber, Cary Nelson and Paula Treichler (eds), *Cultural Studies*, New York, 1992, pp. 96-112.

Elsie, Robert (ed.), *Kosovo in the Heart of the Powder Keg*, New York, 1997.

Elsie, Robert, 'Convention Regulating the Emigration of the Turkish Population [sic] from the Region of Southern Serbia in Yugoslavia (1938)', in: Robert Elsie (ed.), *Kosovo in the Heart of the Powder Keg*, New York, 1997, pp. 425-434.

Hall, Stuart, 'Cultural Identity and Diaspora', in: Jonathan Rutherford (ed.), *Identity: Community, Culture, Difference*, London, 1990, pp. 222-237.

Islami, Hivzi, 'La diaspora d'un peuple méditerranéens: le cas des Albanais', *Peuples Méditerranéens* 15, 15 (1981): pp. 73-84.

Islami, Hivzi, *Rrjedha demografike shqiptare*, Pejë, 1994.

Krizman, Bora, 'Elaborat dra Ive Andrica o Albaniji iz 1939. Godine', *Casopis za suvremenu povijest* 2 (1977): pp. 77-89.

Malcolm, Noel, *Kosovo: A Short History*, New York, 1999.

Malkki, Liisa, 'Things to Come: Internationalism and Global Solidarities in the Late 1990s', *Public Culture* 10 (1998): pp. 431-442.

Martin, Philip L., *The Unfinished Story: Turkish Labour Migration to Western Europe. With Special Reference to the Federal Republic of Germany*, Geneva, 1991.

Mertus, Julie A., *Kosovo: How Myths and Truths Started a War*, Berkeley, 1999.

Mitchell, Timothy, 'Nationalism, Imperialism, Economism: A Comment on Habermas', *Public Culture* 10 (1998): pp. 417-424.

Moreiras, Alberto, 'Hybridity and Double Consciousness', *Cultural Studies* 13 (1999): pp. 373-407.

Nancy, Jean-Luc, *The Inoperative Community*, Minneapolis, 1991.

Poulton, Hugh, *The Balkans, Minorities and States in Conflict*, London, 1991.

Rapper, Gilles de, *Les Albanais à Istanbul. Programme de recherche "Turquie - Caucase - Mer Noire"*, Les dossiers de l'IFEA: la Turquie aujourd'hui (série 3), Istanbul, 2000.

Roux, Michel, *Les Albanais en Yougoslavie. Minorité nationale, territoire et développement*, Paris, 1992.

Swedenburg, Ted, *Memories of Revolt: The 1936-1939 Rebellion and the Palestinian National Past*, Minneapolis, 1993.

Chapter 15

Recovering Memory is Regaining Dignity: Collective Memory and Migration in France

Laure Teulières

In comparison with the rest of Europe, France is an old country of immigration. France emerged as a destination for a large number of immigrants from about the middle of the nineteenth century. Contemporary understandings of immigration and immigrants developed during this period, in particular with the passage of the nationality law of 1889. Since then, immigration to France has been a continuous, enduring phenomenon. The proportion of foreigners was already roughly 7 per cent during the 1930s, when the economic crisis hit the world. After declining in subsequent years, it returned to this threshold by the mid-1970s, and has remained fairly constant since then.

Several different migration streams have shaped France's migration history: Belgians in the nineteenth century, massive movements of Italians until the 1950s, Armenian refugees following the genocide of 1915, Russians fleeing the revolution in 1917, Spanish labour migrants and republican exiles who fled after the civil war (1936-39) and the establishment of Franco's regime, Polish steel and mine workers in the interwar period, labour migrants from the Maghreb recruited during France's Thirty Glorious Years (*Trente Glorieuses*, 1945-75), the Jews of Northern Africa who came after Algerian and Moroccan independence, the Harkis and the Pieds Noirs at the end of the Algerian war in 1962, Turkish and Kurdish labour migrants since the late 1960s, South American and South-east Asian political refugees in the 1970s, and postcolonial immigrants from West and Central Africa, as well as the growing Chinese diaspora.

Considerations of collective memory and the incorporation of immigrants into it provide one way of problematizing immigration history. A thorough analysis should focus on collective attitudes, commemorative practices and public discourses linked to immigration. One needs to grasp and explain how history and the inclusion of migrants into the national historical landscape are related to the social incorporation of immigrant groups in general. Furthermore, current forms of commemoration need to be discussed and, finally, the role of immigrants within the construction and transmission of collective memory should be highlighted.

Historical Memory and the Migrant Community's Integration

Each society has its own vision of the past, particularly with regard to its national history. The manner in which immigration is perceived is connected to, among other things, general collective representations of the past. Every influx occurs within a context shaped by an eclectic mixture of various stereotypes, common ideas and interpretations. Thus, immigration and its collective representation need to be related to, and associated with, established forms and modes of commemoration in order to be grasped, understood and accepted.

This chapter takes Italian immigration to southwestern France as an example of such a representation. After the First World War, France's southwestern region was depopulated. In particular, workers were needed to cultivate agricultural holdings in the Garonne basin. After many unsuccessful efforts to lure rural migrants into this area, a migratory phenomenon of increasing scale began, which was completely new in comparison with previous cross-border movements between Spain and France. In the mid-1920s, approximately 40,000 Italians immigrated to the region within only a few years. A considerable number came with the intention of staying for good. They left Italy as an effect of overpopulation and poverty and also as a consequence of political persecution by the Fascists. Although most of them came to rent agricultural property, a minority also managed to buy it after selling holdings in Italy. Italian immigration was welcome by local authorities, agricultural interest groups, and political party leaders. It was considered to be a remedy for depopulation and the crisis in agriculture.

Mussolini tried to prevent Italian emigration from 1926 onward. However, the movement continued by way of illegal and clandestine immigration, as well as by taking detours via other French regions to the southwest. Leaving aside the years of the Second World War, immigration continued up until the 1950s. After establishing an immigrant network in southwestern France, the Italian migrants set about consolidating and stabilizing their community. At the same time, the occupational structure of the immigrants diversified as many found employment in the construction or service sectors. This allowed them to become less conspicuous (though many older people kept their Italian citizenship). At present, many claim that these Italians are 'very well integrated' and therefore constitute an immigration and integration 'success story'. However, the very notion of 'success' is ambiguous; it reveals the subjective aspect of social representation which is associated with immigration. It is more accurate to say that the Italian immigrants have succeeded in being accepted and appreciated by the French people. As such, they are looked upon favourably.

It is worth noting that historical practices of commemoration coincided with the start of immigration itself. References were made in speeches about immigration given by the republican elite of the time and other key figures, or in articles published in the regional press. By putting the current influx of migrants into a historical perspective, past and present were linked by a chain of historical precedents.

Thus, current migration streams and older or even ancient ones were interwoven. Historical episodes that could be used symbolically were emphasized to the point of exaggeration. Leading writers of the 1920s, who were particularly keen on classical culture, explained Gascony's (the Gascony region was a destination for many Italian migrants) historical bonds to Italy by referring to the Roman heritage and the impact it exercised in the ancient regions of Narbonne and Aquitaine. Moreover, commentators rediscovered the Italian priests, tradesmen and bandits who had migrated into the area during the Renaissance. These characters became symbols used to create a tradition and 'pedigree' for contemporary migrants. Commentators erected a regional Latin-Occitan pantheon, in which the more mundane history of immigration was replaced by imagined traditions of interrelations and exchanges, held together by a symbolic, largely mythical, genealogy.

One could tell in detail how this imagination worked and how it was (re)established by different actors. It helped make migration an ordinary process and may even have helped to increase acceptance. Imagined and invented traditions were also used to mark a secular proximity between native and migrant populations. For instance, during the interwar years each Italian-Catholic mission in France organized an 'annual emigrant pilgrimage' to a local shrine. With regard to the St. Mary pilgrimage to Notre Dame de Marceille (*département* Aude), an Italian missionary of the time asserted that the area's name was linked to a Roman soldier, Marcellus, who had founded a Roman colony long ago. Thus, the Italian immigrants were made to inherit the secular Roman tradition.

Memory found its highest importance for this population immediately after liberation, which followed the Allied invasion of Normandy and the end of the Nazi occupation in the summer of 1944. The disagreements and conflicts of these dark years cast their shadows for a long time. The aftermath of the Second World War did not fade away easily. Frenchmen blamed Italians for having 'stabbed them in the back' through Italy's entry into the war against France in June 1940. Rumours accused the Italian immigrants of having collaborated with the enemy during the German occupation, as well as having taken advantage of a privileged status to enrich themselves on the black market without having to experience the same ordeals as the native French. It is in this context that the Italian community had its reputation tarnished and became discredited. In the eyes of the French population, it thus had to regain legitimacy.

The immigrants managed to regain acceptance by emphasizing their indispensable economic role, their work competence and their discretion. However, other, more symbolic, approaches were also common. Certain Italian associations tried to create a different and more flattering image of their community to counter widely held negative stereotypes. Propagating an antifascist image and glorifying the blood shed by (Italian) *Résistance* fighters was one way of overcoming prejudices. This strategy was already apparent in certain clandestine leaflets produced before liberation. When a young Italian was sentenced to death in June 1944 for acts of terrorism, leaflets with the title 'He died so that France could live!' were distributed by compatriot resistance fighters.[1] The text praised this son of an immigrant, who descended from the hard-working agricultural population which had come to bring the lands of southern France back to life, until he heroically 'shed his blood in sacrifice for his adopted country'.

Commemorations were formalized in the post-war years and, as time went by, they helped to soothe the tensions of the occupation and post-liberation periods. The memory of heroes of the *Résistance* gave special meaning to commemorative practices. From the 1950s onward, some Italians organized an annual commemoration (for fallen heroes of the *Résistance*) in Toulouse as a demonstration of French-Italian friendship. In the international arena, France and Italy were already in the midst of formalizing lines of political co-operation, most notably in their participation in the creation of the European Coal and Steel Community, founded in 1951. Italian immigrants joined the procession to the war monument, commemorating Silvio Trentin's and Rosine Bet's death. The organizers celebrated the meeting as an expression of all that united Italian immigrants and Frenchmen in friendship. Those two edifying personalities epitomized an ideal symbolic pantheon. Trentin, an Italian intellectual, embodied international antifascist commitment. As a political exilee in the South around Toulouse, he provided inspiration to the French *Résistance* movement. He died while attempting to return to Italy during the partisan independence struggle there. Rosine Bet had planted a bomb in a cinema frequented by Germans and died during the course of the operation. She stood for the integrated second generation of immigrants whose commitment to the *Résistance* had been exercized entirely in France. The commemoration of the Second World War and the *Résistance* fighters showcased the different degrees of integration within the Italian immigrant community. Contemporaries employed allusions to common blood ties, shared ordeals, common fates, the solidarity of war veterans and French-Italian friendship.

Of course, this particular case has its limits. It holds true for a rather old migration cohort of European origin, based for the most part in agriculture. The context is very different for other immigrant groups, such as North Africans, who arrived more recently and have settled mainly in urban areas. In these cases, history and national memory bear a different weight and are burdened by the relationship between the centre and its former peripheral colonies – especially the Algerian war of independence. However, even if the memory at stake is different, it is no less important. What is important to note is that the impact of historical memories is influential from the very beginning of immigration processes. They always mutually mark and shape encounters between immigrants and receiving societies. Social memory plays a role in the entire realm of representation, which conditions the incorporation of immigrants.

How Does the Nation Commemorate Migration?

Immigration brings about different memories and traditions from those officially considered part of *the national history*. Understandings of the present depend considerably on what is recognized of the past. In the case of immigration, it indeed comes down to 'providing some room in the national narrative for those populations who still encounter difficulties in the process of being legitimately accepted'.[2]

Immigration has long been a disruptive factor for national consciousness in France. This is due to a combination of factors, including the influence of a Jacobin centralizing state and a unitary cultural model that tends to dismiss differences and favour common points of reference. The assimilative vocation of the country has tended to naturalize foreigners, through the granting of citizenship not only by way of kinship (*ius sanguinis*), but also by right of birthplace (*ius soli*).

Moreover, several intellectual schemes have blocked or shaped the genesis of a pluralist national identity. Since the Third Republic (1875-

1940), when the school system was expanded and standardized,[3] French people have construed their national identity in accordance with two main lines of representation and narration.[4] Most important was the notion of a more or less eternal French culture, rooted in a longstanding geographical framework, idealized and reified in the famous form of the Hexagon delimited by 'natural' borders. France's destiny has been envisioned as a nation-state marching towards unity ever since Charlemagne and the medieval dynasties. The idea of a homogeneous population, resulting from a lucky mixture of Celts, Franks and Romans, has also served as an important trope. These genealogical fictions were epitomized in the expression learned at school: 'Our ancestors, the Gauls'.

For a long time, these points of view prevented historical scholarship from stepping into the arena of immigration. For the most part, historians noted that the host country accepted and refashioned some non-native elements. The immigrants' story faded away as they became assimilated. Until the 1980s, France refused to accept that it was a society of immigrants, shaped and transformed by foreigners. It remained 'an unconscious country of immigration'.[5] It is telling that there is only one article in Pierre Nora's *Lieux de Mémoire – de la République, de la Nation et de France* dedicated to the topic 'France and the foreigners'.[6] France's national memory exhibited a blank spot, or, to put it in Gérard Noriel's words, such memories were 'magically wiped out from a history which was not very well in line with the native mythologies'.[7] Nevertheless the topic gained more and more importance in public debates. The far right, which began to invade the political scene, made it into a key part of its platform. One could argue that the lack of historical references to immigration provided a space that could easily be filled with fantasies about the present.

Since the middle of the 1980s, however, historians have made progress, initiating a first shift for a larger revision and development. A large number of scientific works were published during this period and certain titles (within the domain of immigration history) explicitly referred to the concept of memory. Trend setting works have dealt with the 'unknown Polish'[8] and, more recently, the 'seized memory' of Moroccan miners.[9] This reconquest of historiography has been analyzed in some detail.[10]

Since the 1990s, a broad readership has favourably received certain scholarly works and some have even been written for the general public. Publication activities in the historiographical domains expanded, as can be noted in the establishment of specialized historical series by the publishing houses. Examples are Autrement's *Frenchmen from Abroad, People from Here*,[11] the work *Au nom de la mémoire* ('In the name of memory'),[12] and the immigrant NGO *Génériques*, which has published a three volume archival guide on the subject.[13] Other initiatives have focussed on anchoring these issues in society, for instance by providing resources for secondary school teachers interested in covering these subjects in their classes.[14]

Indeed, these questions have begun to move the general public more than ever. The recent film 'Immigrants' Memories'[15] resonated widely. The three-part series based on life-course interviews reconstituted the history of North African immigration: 'The Fathers' focused on working life, the exploitation of labour and the solitude of immigrants in the 1950s and 1960s; 'The Mothers' was centred around the theme of family reunification in the 1970s, the memory of living conditions in the *bidonvilles* (shanty-towns) and on the alienation and disorientated feelings of immigrant wives; finally, 'The Children' brought current issues to the fore, particularly dual identities and the role of Islam in French society. The media's focus on these issues mirrors economic, political and moral concerns in France. References occur daily. The fact that Radio France broadcast a report on the Parisian Portuguese community the day before France played in the quarter-finals against Portugal in the 2000 European Football Championship is revealing.[16]

However, the question remains: what is commemorated here and which language or discursive mode dominates? Collective memories of migration are located at the crossroads of various representations. Those regarding former immigrations – which are often distorted by subsequent reconstructions and used in political and ideological controversies – interfere with those regarding the current situation, embodying public and media debates which underlie rapid cycles of change in fashion.

What can be part of the collective memory of immigrants and their integration in general? How to commemorate the long history of assimilation in France, i.e., the complete absorption and disappearance of certain immigrant groups? A popular legend holds that previous migrants were easily integrated without causing any tensions. This pops up *a posteriori* as a 'miracle' of integration, simplifying things and preventing the analysis of any sense of temporality or context.[17] These representations usually evade the hardships immigrants faced, while glorifying successful means of social integration. It is the tribute given to integration. However, it is also a way of creating invisibility and of tolerating difference, which itself is reduced to folkloristic elements of identity reserved for the private sphere. This view is very much connected with current debates. When one refers to 'the good old days of immigration', she or he implicitly suggests an unfavourable comparison with the more recent waves.

The question of migrant women also needs to be raised in this context. Women were always a part of immigration. In the 1946 census they constituted 42 per cent of foreigners and in 1990 they represented 48 per cent. Nevertheless, for a long time only the story of the (working) male was recounted. Feminist criticism of this exclusive point of view provided a whole new insight into the issue. One must recognize the practical difficulties historians faced in bringing in a gendered perspective and recovering women's history. Women rarely appear in the written sources, in public records, administrative documents or newspapers. Oral transmission predominated.[18] However, today's academic contexts and debates are more open-minded, so that thought can be given to this important dimension of immigration history. New questions and new approaches provide space for women and take into consideration the role they played. Even if immigrant women's history still needs to be written, it is now at least recognized that migration is not just men's business.

Questions concerning how immigration history's darkest episodes ought to be remembered, written about and commemorated have also been important. How might they be confronted and made publicly visible? Our era seems more capable of investigating the dark sides of the national past. Breaking with former taboos, President Chirac acknowledged the state's responsibility in the Vel-d'hiv's police action against the Jews during the occupation. It is in this context that the new immigration history needs to be seen and understood, i.e., as part of a general responsibility to do justice to victims through 'memorial duties'. While there is a long way to go in such an endeavour, first steps have been taken. It is telling that an official visit to Verdun was made on June 2000, when the Algerian President Bouteflika made a state visit to France, recognizing that a great number of Algerian soldiers died for France in the First World War.

Some groups have played a pioneering role in making those who had hitherto been forgotten visible again. One such case involved the repression of murders following a demonstration by Algerians in Paris, in October 1961. For a long time this event was blanketed with silence and testimonials were denied by public authorities. Eventually, however, the event was recovered as part of the collective memory.[19] The rediscovery started with newspaper coverage and was followed by fiction writers taking up the topic. Indeed, the story of the massacre was initially revealed to the general public through a detective story.[20] However, the main achievement was realized with the militant mobilization of second and third generation descendants of Algerian immigrants who formed the association 'In the Name of Memory' and organized a commemorative rally at the site of the 1961 events. Another symbolic act occurred in 2001, when a commemorative plaque was put near the Saint-Michel Bridge by the city council of Paris. According to an association leader, however, the most important step has yet to be taken: 'The French state [itself will] have to recognize the crime. ... Immigrant children and French citizens, we will only have our place in this country if there is equality of memory'.[21]

For the most part, immigrant and refugee groups and associations themselves have re-conquered and publicized the facts of the past. For instance, when the Federacion de Associaciones y Centros de Españoles Emigrantes en Francia (FACEEA) realized that the commemorative events marking the liberation's fiftieth anniversary did not pay appropriate attention to the republicans and *guerilleros*, the organization held a conference on the subject[22] and recorded the testimonies of eyewitnesses. The changes did not come about without turmoil and conflicts about memories. Under the title 'Argelès-sur-Mer Remembers: The Retirada, The Camp', the town of Argelès-sur-Mer, during the summer of 1999, organized 'a week [dedicated to] commemorating [the] 500,000 republicans exiled into Roussillon region in 1939'. The goal was to publicize the conditions Spanish refugees suffered under as soon as they entered French territory, including barbed-wire fencing which cordoned off accommodations on the beaches of Pyrénées-Orientales. During the week's events and discussions, a controversy about the proper means of commemorating the events emerged between different parties. Those, like the mayor, who preferred to speak of 'internment camps' were opposed by the Spaniards, who wished to use the original designation, i.e., 'concentration camps'.

Local Cultural Initiatives

Although some groups remain dissatisfied with their historical marginalization, the image of a France fertilized by immigrants' culture and history is more common of late. French society's interest in its immigrants continues to grow, partly as a result of a desire to make 'an inventory of its multiethnic heritage'.[23] Older migrations have become part of the common belief system, mainly at the local level, which is most important for making historical references. And it is not only the perception of past processes of immigrant assimilation, but also distinctive immigrant heritages which are now considered being worthy of commemoration.

However, a central national site of commemoration and national holiday has yet to be established. This is due to various reasons. For one, it would be difficult to introduce a national memorial day, since such a date is by no means obvious, given France's ongoing immigration history. Furthermore, there are only a few possible commemorative sites (*lieux de mémoire*) – like, for instance, the Toul Centre (in Lorraine) where the East European immigrants entered the country – which might be compared to Ellis Island, the famous destination of immigrants to the United States in the late nineteenth and early twentieth centuries. Unlike Ellis Island, however, nothing has remained in Toul to make it into a place for commemoration. Moreover, mainstream French society often finds it too difficult and hurtful to come to terms with these parts of its past, as was evident in the case of internment camps for foreigners during the Second World War. A plan for a museum is now being discussed. In November 2001, the French Prime Minister announced the creation of a national centre dedicated to the history of immigration in the near future.[24]

It is cities and neighbourhoods that most effectively grasp their heritage and make it visible by way of demonstrations and cultural products. Recovering immigrant history and constructing memory has become a way of reconstructing a city's past labour history or the local identity of a neighbourhood. Such projects are often financially supported by public funds such as the Ethnological Inheritance Mission (*Mission du Patrimoine ethnologique*) and the Social Action Fund (*Fonds d'Action Sociale*), among others. Moreover, various partnerships work along the same line. For instance, a project about immigrant workers in the quarries of Maine-et-Loire was implemented as an oral history initiative to collect oral testimonies of several generations of immigrants, thus linking migrant Bretons who came in the 1900s to Turkish labour migrants of the 1970s.[25] This approach and perspective is interesting in that it expresses what is generally known, i.e., that the first immigrants of the nineteenth century were Frenchmen who moved from one region to another to find work.

In other places, the city administration itself has taken up similar initiatives. For instance, the cultural department of the city of Thionville (*département* Moselle) developed a consistent action programme to 'give more social and cultural visibility to people having descended from immigrants and stress the cultural blending that stems from the intermixing of people'.[26] Since 1984, this programme has followed three stages: first, 'the time for recognition of immigration'; second, an interest in immigrants' 'cultural values'; and finally, a focus on 'cultural mixing'. Symbolic acts, exhibitions, and cultural events accompanied all three stages. Other projects have even been marketed. For example, the city council of Argenteuil in the Val d'Oise, dominated by the Communist Party, produced a compact disc box-set with songs and oral testimonies restoring the traces of popular, militant and immigrant memory throughout the twentieth century.[27]

Today's trends aim at linking immigration history to cultural events. Several means of representation (photography, concerts, cinema, drama, discussion) have recently been brought together within the partnership CIMADE. This initiative aims to 'give a different voice and image to those who had left their country behind' and to portray 'migration as a source of exchange and enrichment'.[28] However, the title of an historical exhibition presented in the renowned Hôtel des Invalides in Paris sounded rather like a declaration of principles: 'All of France' ('*Toute la France*').[29] This exhibition placed particular emphasis on immigrants' contribution to the arts, culture, cuisine and sports. Other attempts seem more original in their forms. A single, but striking example is a project supported by the cultural heritage section of the Ministry of Cultural Affairs (*Direction du Patrimoine du Ministère de la Culture*). The initiative invited children of immigrant coal-burners – all of whom are very old men today – to reconstruct in front of an audience a coal site in the forest where their immigrant parents had worked.[30] Getting as close as possible to real life, the recovery of common immigration history in this case came along with recognition of the know-how and traditions passed onto and embodied in the actors themselves, or their offspring. Historical memory of immigration was thus brought back to life in a very immediate way and shared commonly.

Finally, some twin cities have developed new forms of commemoration. If one takes again the case of Italian immigration to Southwest France, one can see that the number of French-Italian pairings has increased from the late 1980s onward. In the summer of 1999, the consular constituency at Toulouse[31] counted 65 French cities twinned with Italian ones. In most cases, former areas of immigrant origin were thus connected with areas of destination. These initiatives gave rise to events and ceremonies commemorating what immigration contributed. Bonds between two European regions were thus particularly favoured. In this light, the migrants' history and destiny seems to have anticipated the current movement of European integration.[32]

For certain cities, commemoration serves as a way of addressing their immigrant history on a local *and* European level. Some even praise it as the key element of their identity. These practices show that the memory of immigration can be made visible in a rather official and formal fashion in today's France. However, it is only possible under certain conditions. The cases noted here feature old immigration, which is no longer controversial and is generally favourably considered by the majority. Moreover, these immigrants and their descendents constitute an important constituency as a great number of them have been naturalized or have acquired French citizenship by birth.

The Migrants' Memories

As many examples have shown, the return of memory with regard to immigration is strictly dependent on the migrants' and their descendants' attitude. Sociologists have studied the family memory of migrants and have analyzed the different transmission patterns which resulted in a family history of migration.[33] The first generation is marked by emigration, i.e., the rupture between 'before' and 'after'. From the second generation on, a noticeable difference emerges between those who remain faithful to traditional family history, those who distance themselves from it and those who reshape it in their own fashion. Finally, the third generation's interest for their ancestors' migratory history depends very much on the degree of parental social success.

A new finding reveals that the internal transmission tends to be standardized. Gradually written stories have become fashionable and are passed on to close relatives. Those who write the 'novel' of their lives provide the historian with a new kind of source that calls for a specific mode of analysis. Similarly, photos and amateur home videos should be closely studied as they too serve as a means of storing the family memory. They are often passed on abroad and across borders so as to show something of one's new life to members of one's community back home.

This growing concern for family memory has helped spur a growing demand for genealogical research, which follows the same logic and expresses similar preoccupations. This movement has captured the imagination of all parts of French society and has emerged into an important market. For instance, the association *Ancêtres Italiens* ('Italian Ancestors') founded in Paris promises to reconstruct clients' family trees. In its leaflets, it claims to have established a database for Italian immigrants to France from 1820 to the late 1950s.

However, the search for memory among immigrants and their descendants has transcended the private sphere. It is particularly important that some key figures make their origin public. This was for instance the case for a former international rugby player, who is today a businessman. He discussed his social rise in the press, comparing it to his parents' situation. As immigrants from Italy, they had 'arrived in France with just a plain suitcase in hand'.[34] The successful autobiography of a Portuguese immigrant girl who became a singer[35] seems to have helped transform the 'suitcase of poverty' into a symbol for all immigrant journeys. When immigrants are interviewed, many spontaneously take up this image. Others stress the legacy of political exile. The official Internet site of Youri Djorkaeff (the football star) points out his ancestors' mother country, Armenia, and the 1915 genocide.[36] This reference to his origin may serve as a way of committing himself to this case. During the political negotiations between the Right and the far-right *Front National* which followed the regional elections in 1998, the regional president, who had just come out of the Midi-Pyrénées' regional council, declared himself to be unable to co-operate with the extreme right. He emphasized on this occasion that he was 'the son of a Venetian immigrant chased out of Italy by Mussolini'.[37]

Finally, many pieces of art and/or projects of documentation crafted by second- or third-generation immigrants are related to acts and processes of commemoration. They often declare openly their wish to regain memory for the group they stem from. The first one who articulated this for the French southwest rural immigration was a female writer, who is the daughter of an immigrant herself. By way of fiction, the author lets an old Italian man recount his memory of immigration. Reconsidering his memories, he portrays himself as defeated in the light of history.[38] The novel reveals that the topic of being uprooted matters more than it did in former times. 'Stories from our country of origin'[39] symbolize this unique relation of narration and identity formation. They bear witness to the intimate desire to go back to the sources of family legends and stories which stretch between the here and now and a reinvented past.

Thus, we are getting closer to a notion of integrative memory: 'It is not the suffering which prevents integration, but unacknowledged humiliation'.[40] To recover memory is to regain dignity. An example is the Italian film festival organized in Villerupt (*département* Meurthe-et-Moselle) by descendants of immigrant steel and iron workers since 1976. In the city of Villerupt, where almost half of the population is still Italian (or of Italian descent), the film festival offers a way of revealing the traces of history left behind by immigrants. Descendants of immigrants even produced a documentary about the region's immigration history, taking up the topics of mine and steel work, anti-Italian xenophobia, the search for recognition and dignity and the struggle for representation. One of the authors stated that feelings of humiliation still persist and have been transformed into 'cultural fury': 'We wanted to give history back to the deprived, our parents, who did not have the means and words to articulate it'.[41]

The individual experience of migration has thus become integrated into collective memory, which is shared by a whole group. Although the former migrant communities only have a 'residual identity',[42] the cultural specificity that persists and distinguishes them is cherished, claimed back, fervently celebrated and often also reconstructed and reinvented. This is equally true for the third generation of immigrant descendants searching for their heritage. This explains the emergence of immigrant associations, but also of more general associations dealing with cultural and historical affairs of immigration. Many organizations are regionally based, which gives them strong roots and political power on the local level to keep up their work. The local impact of immigration needs to be taken into full consideration in order to grasp and explain such processes. Foreigners, naturalized immigrants and the descendants of immigrants represent in many places a considerable demographic weight, strong enough to provide for a common feeling of identity.

A wide range of ethnic groups have carefully established social links and means of group communication. These include specialized journals that focus on cultural matters and also serve as bulletins of social action.[43] Recently Internet sites providing community information have also appeared. They facilitate quick and interactive exchanges between members of the same community. The most active associations follow a deliberate policy of passing on language as a reference point for cultural and group identity. All this marks a new era and framework for debating questions of migrant identity. It explains the current emergence of collective forms of commemorating migration history.

The community's rituals of commemoration play an important part in this context. Immigrant associations aim to maintain historical elements of group identity and to pass them onto members of the second and third generation. For instance, the Midi-Pyrénées Triveneti's Club presented an honorary medal to its nearly 100 year-old senior members who had been heroic actors in the pre-war immigration.[44] Toulouse's Italian Catholic Mission co-ordinated the writing of a booklet about this history to 'leave something' after the passing of the year 2000. The majority of immigrant associations intend to commemorate the past by saving and preserving traces and sources left behind by immigrants. However, they also try to make this history known to mainstream French society without immigrant background. Their speeches, ceremonies and symbolic acts show the will to both reassure themselves and seek recognition.

Immigrant groups' concern for their collective memory and their desire for commemoration are relatively new phenomena. It is important to remember the political implications of these processes. What is at stake here is self-recognition by the group itself as well as the more intersubjective recognition of others. While certain community commemorations tend to appear in public, it is often another one that fights to make itself visible, namely the one that is excluded from official practices of commemoration, the one that does not have an official voice. Having a militant and polemical aim, undocumented Chinese immigrants chose the French national holiday to commemorate 837 Chinese workers who died in France as a consequence of the First World War. The general public did not know anything about their existence. On 14 July 2000, the French national holiday, the activists placed flowers and banners on the victims' graves in the Noyelle-sur-Mer cemetery (*département* Somme). The banners read: 'To the Chinese workers of 1917-1920 who died for France. The Chinese workers of 1997-2000 excluded by France'.[45]

Conclusion

Generally one can support the statement that pluralism is emerging in France with regard to representing and collectively commemorating immigration (history). Could this also be taken as evidence that national history has dedicated itself to its self-transformation into a multiplicity of histories, going from a uniform point of view to one of coexisting interpretations, agreed or disagreed upon by the people who are represented? The inclusion of foreigners and immigrants in national memory serves obviously as a mechanism of fragmentation. It allows for legitimate means of partial representation and the emergence of voices from the margins. This, however, does not necessarily signal an ethnicization of the social imaginary imprinted on already existing and clearly shaped collective memories. One could also emphasize the various factors which dissolve or level differences, such as the necessity of adapting in the new society, the pressure of dominant norms on immigrant groups, the formative and normative power of French administration and bureaucracy, the desire to just forget or the refusal to single oneself out as different. Moreover, immigrant groups themselves can be very diverse and full of tensions. The only thing that can be clearly confirmed is that the revitalization of migrants' history is happening in a new context in which questions of identity and of belonging itself are in flux – for everybody. It is obvious that more is at stake than a mere questioning of historiography. Discussing immigrant incorporation leads to the re-evaluation of national history and the republican model of acculturation. Without wanting to argue that the paradigm of contemporary French history has been completely modified, one can say that the current fragmentation has not only reshaped the field of historical scholarship, but more importantly has altered the perception and self-representation of society in general.

Immigration never ceases questioning and reconstructing social memory. In today's France, the commemoration of immigration memory follows shifts in larger discussions pertaining to collective identity. One cannot say any longer that such memories are denied or hidden. However, they have opened spaces for partial, fragmented and sometimes conflicting representations, which demonstrate how difficult it is to express different dimensions of the past, as perceived by the individual, the community and the nation. However, this is after all proof that a discussion is underway. This form of collective memory is a work in progress and it manifests itself in the actions of different actors in society. These multi-dimensional perspectives on the past always express a means of belonging together in the present and facing the future together.

Notes

1 Tract du Comité italien de libération nationale et du Comité régional de la Jeunesse garibaldienne, Agen, 29 June 1944. Coll. de la BDIC (Nanterre).
2 Dewitte, 'Vercingétorix et Abd El-Kader'.
3 Weber, *La fin des terroirs.*
4 Citron, 'Mémoire nationale, mémoire plurielle'.
5 Schnapper, 'Un pays d'immigration qui s'ignore'.
6 Noiriel, 'Français et étrangers'.
7 Noiriel, *Le creuset français*, p. 24.
8 Ponty, *Polonais méconnus.*
9 Cegarra, *La mémoire confisquée.*
10 Blanc-Chaléard, 'Des logiques nationales aux logiques ethniques?'.
11 'Français d'ailleurs, peuple d'ici'.
12 Assouline and Lallaoui, *Un siècle d'immigration en France.*
13 Associations Génériques and Direction des Archives de France, *Les étrangers en France.*
14 Cf. the academic online journal: *Actes de l'histoire de l'immigration.*
15 Benguigui, *Mémoires d'immigrés.*
16 France Info, 28 June 2000, 7h40.
17 Milza, 'L'intégration des Italiens en France'.
18 *Migration: expressions de femmes.*
19 Moreover, concerning the Harkis (the Muslim Algerian population that fought on the French side during the Algerian War), the French President has recognized their fate by officially receiving representatives; however, the Harkis' demand for recognition continues. Some members of the community have entered a complaint to the Paris court for 'crimes against humanity' provoked by the French (and Algerian) governments, whom they claim are jointly responsible for their collective destiny.
20 Daeninkx, *Meurtre pour mémoire.*
21 Lallaoui, 'L'Etat doit reconnaître le crime', *Politis*, 11 October 2001.
22 Soriano, *Memorias del olvido.*
23 Fescia-Bordelais, *Colons italiens en Aquitaine dans la première moitié du XXe siècle*, pp. 135-136.

[24] El Yazami and Schwartz, 'Rapport pour la création d'un centre national'.
[25] APTIRA, *Mémoire de migrations à Trélazé.*
[26] http://www.multimania.com/passerelles.
[27] Dreano and Grizard, *Mémoire d'Argenteuil. 1918-1974.*
[28] 'Voyages, Regards croisés sur les migrations', cultural initiative in Toulouse (Haute-Garonne), 10-14 May 2000.
[29] Gervereau, Milza and Témime, *Toute la France.*
[30] 'Charbonniers de Grésigne', cultural initiative in Cordes (Tarn), 14-31 October 1999.
[31] Midi-Pyrénées, Aquitaine and Poitou-Charente regions.
[32] 'Reconnaissance'. It was an immigrant who initiated the twinning of cities.
[33] Chavanon, 'Les immigrés italiens et la mémoire familiale'.
[34] Spanghero, 'Je suis un homme de défis', *La Dépêche*, 27 May 1998.
[35] Souza, *La valise en carton.*
[36] http://www.youridjorkaeff.com.
[37] 'Midi-Pyrénées. Marc Censi prêt au compromis', *Libération*, 23 March 1998.
[38] Cagnati, *Mosé ou le lézard qui pleurait.*
[39] *Le livre du retour.*
[40] Benito, 'L'expérience migratoire à l'épreuve de la mémoire'.
[41] 'Villerupt, amore mio'.
[42] Milza, *Voyage en Ritalie* (chap. 12: 'Identité'), pp. 462-500.
[43] 'Revues de l'intégration et de l'immigration'.
[44] 'Per natale la Amicale dei Triveneti di Tolosa ha onorato i propri anziani'.
[45] 'Des "sans-papiers" chinois honorent leurs ancêtres morts pour la France', *Le Monde*, 18 July 2000.

Archival Sources

Collection de la Bibliothèque de documentation internationale contemporaine (BDIC), Nanterre:

Tract du Comité italien de libération nationale et du Comité régional de la Jeunesse garibaldienne, Agen, 29 June 1944.

References

Actes de l'histoire de l'immigration (http://barthes.ens.fr/clio).

APTIRA (Association pour la promotion des travailleurs immigrés de la région d'Anger) (ed.), *Mémoire de migrations à Trélazé*, Vauchrétien, 1996.

Associations Génériques and Direction des Archives de France (eds), *Les étrangers en France. Guide des sources d'archives publiques et privées XIXe-XXe siècles*, 3 vol., Paris, 1999.

Assouline, David and Mehdi Lallaoui (eds), *Un siècle d'immigration en France*, coll. 'Au nom de la mémoire', 3 vol., Paris, 1997.

Benguigui, Yasmina, *Mémoires d'immigrés. L'héritage maghrébin*, film documentaire, 1997.

Benito, Carolina, 'L'expérience migratoire à l'épreuve de la mémoire', in: APTIRA (ed.), *Mémoire de migrations à Trélazé*, Vauchrétien, 1996, pp. 13-31.

Birnbaum, Pierre, *'La France aux Français'. Histoire des haines nationalistes*, Paris, 1993.

Blanc-Chaléard, Marie-Claude, 'Des logiques nationales aux logiques ethniques?', *Le*

Mouvement social 188 (1999): pp. 3-16.
Breviglieri, Marc, 'L'étreinte de l'origine. Attachement, mémoire et nostalgie chez les enfants d'immigrés maghrébins', *Confluences Méditerranée* 39 (2001): pp. 34-47.
Cagnati, Inès, *Mosé ou le lézard qui pleurait*, Paris, 1979.
Cegarra, Marie, *La mémoire confisquée. Les mineurs marocains dans le Nord de la France*, Lille, 1999.
Chavanon, Olivier, 'Les immigrés italiens et la mémoire familiale', *Migrations société* 11, 62 (1999): pp. 7-32.
Citron, Suzanne, 'Mémoire nationale, mémoire plurielle', *Hommes et migrations* 1114 (1988): pp. 14-22.
Daeninkx, Didier, *Meurtre pour mémoire*, Paris, 1984.
Dewitte, Philippe, 'Vercingétorix et Abd El-Kader, une histoire plurielle de la France', *Projet* 248 (1996): pp. 25-33.
Dreano, Michel and Fabrice Grizard (eds), *Mémoire d'Argenteuil. 1918-1974. Mémoires ouvrières. Mémoires immigrées*, Mairie d'Argenteuil, coffret de 3 CD.
El Yazami, Driss and Rémy Schwartz, 'Rapport pour la création d'un centre national de l'histoire et des cultures de l'immigration', *Migrance* 19 (2001).
Fescia-Bordelais, Sylvia, *Colons italiens en Aquitaine dans la première moitié du XXe siècle*, Maison des Sciences de l'Homme d'Aquitaine, Talence, 1988.
'Français d'ailleurs, peuple d'ici', série, Paris.
Geisser, Vincent and Schérazade Kelfaoui, 'La nation d'origine réinventée. La persistance du "mythe national" chez les Français originaires du Maghreb', *Confluences Méditerranée* 39 (2001): pp. 27-35.
Gervereau, Laurent, Pierre Milza and Emile Témime (eds), *Toute la France. Histoire de l'immigration en France au XXe siècle*, Paris, 1998.
'Imaginaire colonial, figures de l'immigré', *Hommes et migrations* 1207 (1997).
'Immigration et logiques nationales', *Le Mouvement social* 188 (1999).
'Immigration, la dette à l'envers', *Hommes et migration* 1221 (1999).
'L'immigration dans l'histoire nationale', *Hommes et migrations* 1114 (1988).
Le livre du retour. Récits du pays des origines, coll. Mutations no. 173, Paris, 1997.
Lequin, Yves (ed.), *La mosaïque France. Histoire des étrangers et de l'immigration en France*, Paris, 1988.
'Mémoire des peuples', *Projet* 248 (1996).
'Mémoires en miroir. Autour d'une Méditerranée plurielle', *La Pensée de midi* 3 (2000).
'Mémoires familiales et immigration', *Informations sociales* 89 (2001).
Migration: expressions de femmes, Paris, 1992.
Milza, Pierre, 'L'intégration des Italiens en France: 'miracle' ou vertus de la longue durée?', *Pouvoirs* 47 (1987): pp. 103-113.
Milza, Pierre, *Voyage en Ritalie*, Paris, 1993.
Nicolaidis, Dimitri (ed.), *Oublier nos crimes. L'amnésie nationale, une spécificité française?*, Paris, 1994.
Noiriel, Gérard, *Le creuset français. Histoire de l'immigration, XIXe - XXe siècles*, Paris, 1988.
Noiriel, Gérard, 'Français et étrangers', in: Pierre Nora (ed.), *Les lieux de mémoire. Les Frances* , vol. 3, Paris, 1997, pp. 2433-2465.
'Per natale la Amicale dei Triveneti di Tolosa ha onorato i propri anziani', *Campana Nostra* 1-2 (1999): pp. 5-6.
'Perspectives croisées sur l'immigration', *Mots* 60 (1999): pp. 3-179.
Ponty, Janine, *Polonais méconnus. Histoire des travailleurs immigrés en France dans l'entre-deux-guerres*, Paris, 1988.
Ponty, Janine, *Les Polonais du Nord, ou la mémoire des corons*, Paris, 1995.

'Reconnaissance', *Andiamo. Journal d'information de l'Alliance franco-italienne Midi-Pyrénées/Veneto* 3 (1994), p. 8.
'Revues de l'intégration et de l'immigration', *La Revue des revues* 27, 1er sem. (2000).
Ricoeur, Paul, *La Mémoire, l'Histoire, l'Oubli*, Paris, 2000.
Rousso, Henry, *La hantise du passé*, Paris, 1998.
Schnapper, Dominique, 'Un pays d'immigration qui s'ignore', *Le Genre humain* 19 (1989): pp. 99-109.
Segalen, Martine, *Rites et rituels contemporains*, Paris, 1998.
Soriano, Antoine (ed.), *Memorias del olvido. La contribución de los Republicanos Españoles a la Resistencia y a la Liberación de Francia, 1939-1945,* Paris, 1996.
Souza, Linda de, *La valise en carton*, Paris, 1984.
Stora, Benjamin, *La gangrène et l'oubli*, Paris, 1998.
Todorov, Tzvetan, *Les abus de la mémoire*, Paris, 1995.
'Villerupt, amore mio', *Télérama*, 24 Nov. 1999, pp. 132-136.
Weber, Eugen, *La fin des terroirs*, Paris, 1976.

Index